Dambusters
The Forging of a Legend

IN MEMORY OF

'BAZ' PEARSON 1907–1997

This book is dedicated to him and to all the other unsung heroes who fought their war on the ground on the bomber stations of England.

Rained, hailed and snowed upon, blown about by icy winds and baked by the summer sun, while the aircrew got the glory, the gongs and the girls, and, all too often, the 'chop'.

Also to three special friends.

Keith Aspinall
1939–2008
'I always did what I wanted to do.'

Derek Windmill
1944–2008
'This is your Captain speaking.'

Horst Münter
1939–2008
'I told you I was dying.'

Dambusters
The Forging of a Legend

Chris Ward
Andy Lee
Andreas Wachtel

Pen & Sword
AVIATION

First published in Great Britain in 2009
and reprinted in this format in 2018 by
Pen & Sword AVIATION
An imprint of Pen & Sword Books Ltd
Yorkshire – Philadelphia

ISBN: 978 1 52672 675 9

A CIP catalogue record for this book is available from the British Library

Typeset in 10/12 Times New Roman by Concept, Huddersfield, West Yorkshire
Printed and bound in the UK by CPI UK

Pen & Sword Books Limited incorporates the imprints of Atlas, Archaeology, Aviation, Discovery, Family History, Fiction, History, Maritime, Military, Military Classics, Politics, Select, Transport, True Crime, Air World, Frontline Publishing, Leo Cooper, Remember When, Seaforth Publishing, The Praetorian Press, Wharncliffe Local History, Wharncliffe Transport, Wharncliffe True Crime and White Owl.

For a complete list of Pen & Sword titles please contact
PEN & SWORD BOOKS LIMITED
47 Church Street, Barnsley, South Yorkshire, S70 2AS, England
E-mail: enquiries@pen-and-sword.co.uk • Website: www.pen-and-sword.co.uk
Or
PEN AND SWORD BOOKS
1950 Lawrence Rd, Havertown, PA 19083, USA
E-mail: Uspen-and-sword@casematepublishers.com
Website: www.penandswordbooks.com

Contents

Forewords

By Phil Martin and Don Day, John Cockshott and Nick Knilans

On the 19th of August 1944 F/O Martin and his crew, serving with 61 'City of Lincoln' Squadron, based at Skellingthorpe just outside Lincoln, completed their tour of operations, thirty in all, with a daylight raid on La Pallice. The following day the crew was invited into the squadron commander's office to be congratulated by the CO, Wing Commander Doubleday, as the first crew to complete a tour of operations in many, many months.

He then revealed that he had that morning met with Wing Commander Tait, commanding officer of 617 Squadron, who was looking for reliable and successful crews to join his squadron. One could not volunteer for duty with 617 Squadron, an interview to volunteer was by invitation only.

Naturally, F/O Martin and his crew felt honoured to be invited, and an interview with Wing Commander Tait was arranged. F/O Martin's crew was accepted, and subsequently completed a second tour with the celebrated 'Dambusters'. This included the attack on the *Tirpitz*, (the sister ship of the *Bismarck*), several dams, a daylight, low-level raid on the Kembs Barrage, Dortmund-Ems Canal, and culminated in the dropping of the second 'Grand Slam' (22,000lb) bomb to be used operationally, scoring a direct hit on the Arnsberg Viaduct.

617 was founded initially for the famous raid on the three dams in the Ruhr Valley, but was then extended further to become an elite specialist squadron to take on missions requiring a higher degree of skill and accuracy than expected of other squadrons. The main tool of trade for the squadron was the 12,000lb 'Tallboy' bomb, which was so expensive it had to hit the target or be brought back to base. The crew, at the time of the invitation, figured they had been given some of the toughest missions of 61 Squadron, and they may as well volunteer to fly all the tough ones. It should be noted that it was expected that only one crew in three would survive one tour of operations, and only one in twelve would survive two tours.

Much has been written about the dedication and courage of bomber crews and their fearful attrition rate. Too little has been written about the squadron ground staff, who serviced aircraft and provided all the very necessary ancillary services that made the efforts of those who flew possible. To join an operational squadron was to experience an atmosphere of enthusiasm and devotion to duty of ground staff of an unparalleled magnitude. No 9 to 5 mentality here! If it took all night to do what was required, then it was done.

On many occasions F/O Martin's aircraft returned to base holed in many places by heavy anti-aircraft fire, yet, when next required for service, the aircraft had been repaired and all the equipment was in perfect working order. As the navigator once remarked, 'you could eat your dinner off the floor!' Think of the ladies doing a man's job in signals, armoury, parachute packing and many more tasks. Consider the strain imposed on those lady drivers who ferried the crews to their aircraft in dispersals to learn, all too often, that the crew they had wished 'safe journey' to in the evening had failed to return with the dawn. When F/O Martin's crew completed their tour of operations on 61 Squadron, they made a point of thanking the ground crew for the loan of their aircraft. When the crew joined 617 Squadron, they found the efforts of the ground crews and station personnel to be, if anything, more intense than any they had previously known. Not only was everyone's efficiency extremely high, but also was overlaid with a deep sense of pride in what they did.

Do not think that ground staff were immune from danger either. Whenever it could the *Luftwaffe* infiltrated the bomber stream, and many a crew happy to be circling base at the end of a mission went down under the attack of a marauding Junkers 88, who, often as not, would decide to strafe the airfield as a parting shot. One night, an attack on Coningsby, our neighbouring airfield, saw several Lancasters shot down in the circuit by a particularly large number of enemy intruders. Our own airfield was then strafed by the returning enemy aircraft. Our crews went to dispersal to find the ground churned up by the intruders, but their aircraft were scarcely damaged. A farm worker who lived in a little wooden hut behind the hedge at the rear of our dispersal point was found shot in his bed and the farmhouse torn to pieces by cannon fire. If the crews had been operating that night, one of the aircraft's ground crew, who stayed in a little tent by the dispersal ready with his torch to guide the aircraft into the space, would very likely have been killed. While the aircrew took virtually all the accolades, (and the pilots most of the decorations), the entire squadron relied on every person's dedication and efforts to be able to achieve the extraordinary success that was enjoyed by the 'Dambusters'.

That grand old man, Lord Trenchard, Marshal of the Royal Air Force, once began a speech to servicemen with the words, "Men of the Navy, Men of the Army, and Gentlemen of the Air Force". He was, you may be sure, talking not only of his pilots, but of all his Air Force's 'Gentlemen'.

Written jointly by Warrant Officer D.A. Day (Bomb Aimer) and
Flying Officer P.H. Martin DFC and bar (Pilot).

In the year of our Lord 2003, the ranks of WWII veterans are becoming thin, so there are not many of us left to pass on the message to those who follow. For this reason I welcome the publication of this definitive account of my old bomber squadron, which is the result of extensive research and the resurrection of precious memories. This book is a tribute to all who served in 617 Squadron of RAF Bomber Command during the war, especially those who gave their lives so that millions could live in peace.

Although I joined the squadron after Guy Gibson, I was fortunate enough to know him at RAF Syerston when I did my first tour with 61 Squadron. He was one of those unique characters who rise to the top in times of war and set such a fine example for all who were privileged to serve under him. The same can be said of Willie Tait, who was my commanding officer at 617 Squadron, and Leonard Cheshire, whom I met for the first time in Jamaica several years after the war, where he was attending the opening of Cheshire Homes for the Aged. Without men like Gibson, Cheshire and Tait, we might now be living under Nazi tyranny.

The co-author's grandfather, Basil Pearson, who serviced my Lancaster at Woodhall Spa during my tour of duty, would be proud of his grandson's efforts to keep alive the legacy of the Dambusters. Basil's expertise and dedication gave my crew and me the confidence and faith to do our part. We may have had some trepidation during those turbulent times, particularly as regards bad weather and enemy action, but mechanical problems were never our concern.

The message that this book sends is that while ultimately war is a no-win situation for anyone, beware any deranged dictator who tries to take away our freedom and intimidate the world. I consider it an honour to be asked to write this foreword to this memorable publication, and I wish those responsible every success.

Squadron Leader John V. Cockshott DFC, (Pilot). New York, USA

The Royal Air Force squadron 617 was a most unusual one. It was formed to carry out a special operation, the bombing of several German dams. The mission was carried out at night from 60 feet, and resulted in the breaching of two of them. For the rest of the war they were used to destroy targets from Italy to Norway.

Shortly after D-Day the squadron flew to Le Havre and Boulogne to destroy over 100 *S-Boots* menacing the invasion convoys. An Air-Chief-Marshal congratulated them by stating, 'If the Navy had done what you have done, it would have been a major naval victory'. Prime Minister Churchill also praised the squadron for their pinpoint attacks on the V-3 emplacements near Calais, which had posed a real threat to the city of London.

Decorations for courage in combat were another measure of a squadron. 617 Squadron had three pilots wearing the Victoria Cross, another was awarded four DSOs, while others had been awarded two or three. The aircrew on the squadron were well looked after by the ground crew from mechanics to WAAFs. Each aircrew put its trust and lives in the hands of the ground crews looking after its Lancaster. These mechanics of many skills worked outdoors in the dark and wet cold hours. They well deserved the heartfelt thanks from the aircrew – if they returned.

The WAAFs looked after the aircrews from the control tower to the kitchens. Some two hundred of them on each base did their duties in friendly and cheerful ways. Some drove crews out to their Lancaster prior to a mission, often giving some members affectionate farewells. Many were grief-stricken when their friends failed to return from combat.

617 Squadron averaged 140 aircrew members. The memorial to them in Woodhall Spa lists more than 200 who died in action during its time in service.

Lieutenant 'Nick' Knilans DFC (Pilot). Wisconsin, USA

Introduction

It was never my intention to write a glossy book about 617 Squadron, particularly as I still had over seventy more wartime histories to complete in my Bomber Command Squadron Profile series. I did not, though, reckon on the persistence of Andy Lee. I first met Andy on Jim Shortland's Dams trip in April 2000, when each member of the tour party was given a copy of my 617 Squadron Profile as part of the information package. Andy spent much of the coach journey to Germany poring over the book, and then kindly described it as compelling reading. He spent the remainder of the week trying to badger me into writing a full history with millions of photographs. I was flattered, but declined. I was too busy, much had already been written on the subject, and there were others better qualified. Andy persisted, and I finally agreed to write the book, on condition, that he dealt with the photographs and the begging letters. These provisos he readily accepted, and he was as good as his word. Information began to arrive from all over the world, and using my 617 Squadron Profile as the core, I set about my task, with Andy's enthusiasm for the subject driving me on.

You will notice three names on the front cover, my own as a Bomber Command historian and the author of all but one chapter, Andy's as the provider of most of the photos and author of the chapter entitled Unsung Heroes, and Andreas Wachtel's as chief researcher in Germany. The three names appear because it took three people to bring this book to fruition. I have been a 617 Squadron nut since my childhood, and a student of wartime Bomber Command since the mid eighties. I have tried as much as possible to concentrate on the events surrounding 617 Squadron personnel, and not the technical developments and political manoeuvrings to which they were generally oblivious. John Sweetman has, anyway, already covered this kind of information expertly in his book, *The Dambusters Raid.* I cannot add to or improve upon this superb work, which is a masterpiece of research, and have made no attempt to do so. I can, though, add to the detail of Operation Chastise itself and the circumstances of the losses, and I have approached each subsequent operation with the same enthusiasm if not at such great length. My overall knowledge of the squadrons of Bomber Command has enabled me to inject much background information into the story. The links between airmen whose lives came together at various points during the war, and the career paths of 617 Squadron members and those who influenced them are fascinating, and their stories are set against 617 Squadron operations and the bomber offensives in progress at the time. This is important. Many squadron histories are introspective, and this leads to a loss of perspective of the wider picture. It is also all too easy to marvel at the exploits of 617 Squadron, but to ignore the Herculean efforts of those who served in the many squadrons of the line carrying the war to Germany night after night at a terrible cost in lives. In this regard, the work of historians and authors has been made immeasurably simpler by those responsible for the Bomber Command War Diaries, namely Martin Middlebrook and Chris Everitt. Martin Middlebrook's kind permission for me to use the information from the War Diaries in my Profile series enabled me to develop a successful format, in which the life of the squadron was set against the background of Bomber Command's war. I have adopted the same format in this book. Another massive boon to historians is the *RAF Bomber Command Losses* series by Bill Chorley. These above-mentioned gentlemen are my personal heroes, and I thank them for their contribution to the recording of the RAF history of the Second World War.

Andy Lee is a music producer and manages a number of bands in Manchester. Andy's late grandfather, Basil Pearson, to whom this book is dedicated, joined 617 Squadron as ground crew in June 1943, shortly after the Dams operation. He remained with the squadron throughout the war, and worked on aircraft regularly flown by some of the original Dambusters, including Les Knight and Ken Brown. Sadly, Basil passed away just as Andy's interest in the subject was beginning to grow. Thereafter, Andy threw himself into research, and it was this that brought us together on the Dams trip in 2000. That trip was significant also for another reason. It brought Andreas Wachtel and me together face-to-face for the first time. He has become a close and valued friend to the extent that we view each other as family. He manages a children's hospital in Datteln, and is an author in his own right, specialising in the wartime history of the Dutch Frisian island of Texel, where dozens of RAF airmen lie buried in the cemetery at Den Burg. Some years ago he wrote to me to order two of my Profiles, and I replied suggesting, that it was very odd for a German to be interested in Bomber Command, and would he like to correspond with me to explain himself. It was probably the most important letter I ever wrote, and we have been visiting each other and exchanging research material ever since. He joined us for a day during the 2000 Dams tour, visiting with us the Möhne Dam and the nearby town of Neheim-Hüsten. A year later, during the 2001 Dams tour, I spent a few days with Andreas and his family, and we visited various crash sites from the Dams raid, which hadn't been examined in detail before. Over the ensuing twelve months he uncovered much new information, particularly with regard to the Dortmund-Ems Canal operation, and has found previously unpublished photographs and interviewed eyewitnesses. He has also put me in touch with his contacts in Germany, Holland and America, and this has enabled me to consider some 617 squadron operations from the German side.

This, then, is the team, which put together the original book, which forms the basis for this new updated and substantially rewritten edition. However, so many more have contributed in one way or another to both titles. It was particularly gratifying to have the support of the 617 Squadron Aircrew Association, of which Robert Owen is the official historian. Robert kindly answered all my queries and read through the original draft of each chapter, correcting errors and making suggestions. Because I chose to specify the aircraft in use for each operation by serial number, this added to the task, and required of Robert enormous concentration and attention to detail, and I thank him for his effort and commitment. I have always been aware that enthusiasts of 617 Squadron are hungry for detail, and as I, personally, view the story of Bomber Command as one primarily of people rather than aircraft, bombs and targets, I find background information on crewmembers both fascinating and vital.

The number of surviving wartime members of 617 Squadron is dwindling with each passing year. I am so grateful, therefore, to those who took the trouble to respond to Andy's letters requesting personal reminiscences. Don Cheney wrote from Canada, and his account is included. Phil Martin's son, Owen, struck up a friendship by E-Mail with Andy from Australia, and Phil kindly gave us permission to include accounts of certain operations as recorded by his bomb-aimer, Don Day. 'Nick' Knilans wrote from America to wish us well. Through Andreas I made contact with Kurt Schulze in California, a fighter pilot who flew against 617 Squadron during the final attack on the *Tirpitz*, and I am grateful to him for his contribution. Piet Meijer in Holland provided details on Les Knight's crash and much other information relating to the Dortmund-Ems Canal operation, while the late Horst Münter, an aviation archaeologist, accompanied Andreas and me to various crash sites with his metal detector and uncovered pieces of the Lancasters mentioned in this book. Hans Nauta is the acknowledged authority on the RAF attacks on the *S-Boot* pens at the Dutch port of Ijmuiden, and he generously provided photos and information. Other contributors include Heather Wareing, sister of F/L Bill Astell, who kindly sent a number of photos for inclusion, and Hartley Garshowitz, a relative of Al Garshowitz, who failed to return from the epic raid as a member of Astell's crew. Shere Lowe kindly talked to me about her father John Fraser, one of the two survivors from Hopgood's crew. By an amazing sequence of coincidences I was able to make contact with John Maltby, son of S/L David Maltby, who generously gave of his time to talk to me about his father and mother over the phone. Peter Rice, son of Geoff Rice, was also kind enough to talk to me and supply information about his father, and a brief meeting with Dutch author Theo Boiten in Amsterdam resulted in new information on Rice's loss. My thanks also go to Arthur Thorning for providing additional information on 'Dinghy' Young. I am pleased to register my grateful thanks to archivists of other squadrons, who keep alive the memory of the magnificent generation who created the history that I write about. I name them in ascending order of squadron number, and admire them all equally; Roger Audis of 9 Squadron, Henry Horscroft of 44 (Rhodesia) Squadron and the late Des Richards of 106 Squadron. Each has helped with background information on aircrew, without which the book would have been the poorer.

I am grateful also to many other people for their contributions, particularly those in Germany, who were either touched by the events of 1943 or had information to pass on. My thanks are due to the Hood family at Nordhorn, Herr Hegman at Rees, Richard and Margret Sühling at Raesfeld, the Lammers family at Marbeck, Frau Kaiser at Bergeshövede, Herr Wibbeler at Ladbergen and Frau Brönstrup at Steinbeck. A permanent memorial to the Astell crew has been erected at his crash site thanks to the efforts of Richard Sühling and the Raesfeld Heimat Verein. Thanks are also due to the Lammers family for allowing it to stand on their property. Additional photographs of the Gravenhorst area came via Frau Rumke of the local Heimat Verein, and Dr Klaus Offenberg supplied others relating to the Dortmund-Ems Canal/ Wet Triangle. There will be other contributors to whom I owe my thanks, whose names have been unintentionally omitted, and for this I apologise.

Despite the success of the original publication, which was published in April 2003 and sold out in April 2006 with a minimum of publicity, Red Kite decided against reprinting within a reasonable time. Pen & Sword books immediately expressed a desire to take me into their fold of authors, and a number of my titles have subsequently been published by them, with others waiting in the pipeline. I am delighted that Pen & Sword have taken up the challenge to reproduce Dambusters as a straight narrative, in the format I originally intended. I extend my thanks to Pen & Sword.

Naturally, everyone involved with the book hopes that it is well received, provides pleasure for those who read it, and most importantly, does justice to the people portrayed in it. Inevitably, there will be errors, no matter how strenuously one has worked to ensure none, and there will also be points of disagreement, where documents are at variance or the details of an event are open to interpretation. To deal with a subject involving hundreds of men, dozens of aircraft and a hundred operations over a two-year period more than sixty years ago, using imperfect official documents and fading memories as sources is fraught with snares even for the wary, and I concluded long ago, that there is no such thing as an indisputable historical account.

To write this book has been a privilege. It has brought me into contact with some amazing people in England, Germany and Holland, and in the case of Andy, it has led to a friendship, which, like that with Andreas, I hope will last a lifetime. I am saddened by the passing of the wartime generation, who gave so much on behalf of those who followed, but I am heartened by the way former enemies from Britain and Germany now come together as friends. Their names and their deeds pass into history but must never be forgotten, and if, with this book, we have been able in some small way to perpetuate and honour their memory, we have done something of value.

Chris Ward, Lutterworth, June 2008.

CHAPTER ONE

Enter the Leading Man

March 1943; a concept takes shape and 617 Squadron forms as the Ruhr offensive gathers pace

When 24 year-old Wing Commander Guy Penrose Gibson swept through the main gates at Scampton in the late afternoon of the 21st of March 1943, he was returning to familiar ground. It was on this station that he had undertaken and completed his first tour of operations as a member of 83 Squadron, which he had joined at the start of September 1937 when it was stationed at Turnhouse near Edinburgh. Then he had been an acting Pilot Officer, and by the time war broke out almost two years to the day later, he had dropped the word, 'acting' from his title, but remained in the lowliest of the commissioned ranks.

Gibson's operational career had begun on the first evening of the war, Sunday the 3rd of September 1939. Late on that morning the sombre voice of Prime Minister Neville Chamberlain announced over the airwaves, that Britain was once more at war with Germany, and this was less than twenty-one years after the conclusion of the so-called 'war to end all wars'. By the end of the day the last few Fairey Battle squadrons of 1 Group had joined their colleagues who had left England over the previous two days, and were now all settled on French airfields as the main component of the Advanced Air Striking Force. This left at home 2 Group, operators of the Blenheim light bomber, and 3, 4 and 5 Groups, which were equipped with Wellingtons, Whitleys and Hampdens respectively, and were looked upon as the heavy brigade. 5 Group, which considered itself to be the Command's elite, was ordered to dispatch eighteen Hampdens, including six from 83 Squadron at Scampton, to search for enemy naval units north of Wilhelmshaven. By the time the formation had negotiated difficult weather conditions to reach its destination it was already dark, and no contact was made with the enemy. Gibson landed safely from his first operational sortie, and would have to wait a further six months before he next flew in anger.

It was on the 27th of February 1940 that Gibson undertook his second operational sortie. During a short detachment by the squadron to Coastal

Command at Lossiemouth, he and his crew joined seven others in a three-hour lunchtime North Sea sweep, which almost ended in disaster when a single aircraft from the squadron inadvertently dropped bombs close to two British submarines; fortunately, no damage was done. Two days later he flew another short uneventful sweep, and that concluded his operational activity in Scotland. On the 9th of April German forces marched almost unopposed into Denmark, while others were parachuted into Norway. Unable, because of the extreme range, to support directly the British and French response at Narvik in the north, Bomber Command attacked the southern airfields acting as the gateway for German supplies of men and equipment. The Anglo-French campaign was destined from the start to be a gallant failure, but it did prompt the maiden mining or 'gardening' operations to be undertaken by Bomber Command, for which the Hampden was to prove itself eminently suitable. The shipping lanes between the north German ports and Scandinavia were in constant use, and Gibson flew his first such sortie on the night of the 11/12th, remaining airborne for more than seven hours. He took off for his second gardening operation on the evening of the 14th, and it was the early hours of the following morning before he landed at Manston in Kent after returning from northwestern waters on instruments, in poor weather. Gibson and his crew was one of three from 83 Squadron to be briefed to attack transport aircraft on Aalborg airfield in Norway during the night of the 20/21st. They took off just before midnight, but a faulty compass led Gibson astray, and they returned to Lossiemouth eight hours later without having found the target. Gibson undertook one other mining sortie on the 23/24th, before events closer to home grabbed the attention of the world.

The German '*Blitzkrieg*' advance into France and the Low Countries on the 10th of May signalled an end to the pretence and the period dubbed by the Americans the 'Phoney War'. Within days, and already too late to be effective, the Battle and Blenheim squadrons of the Advanced Air Striking Force and the Blenheims of the UK-based 2 Group were thrown into an unequal fight. They were hacked from the skies in frighteningly large numbers by marauding enemy fighters and murderous ground fire. Mid month saw the start of the strategic bombing war, when Bomber Command began to attack industrial targets east of the Rhine, particularly in the Ruhr. This gave Gibson, by then a Flying Officer, the opportunity to resume his operational career, and he threw himself into it with a will. There is little doubt that the war was to provide him with a direction and sense of purpose, and bring out in him characteristics that might otherwise have lain dormant. Certainly he revelled in his role as a bomber pilot, and soon gained a reputation for 'line-shooting' and being rather too full of himself. Within a matter of days the *Blitzkrieg* machine had swallowed up Holland, Belgium and Luxembourg, and Bomber Command was sending aircraft to mainland Germany for the first time. Gibson soon demonstrated an enthusiasm for operating, which was noticed by his colleagues, and he flew as often as possible during the summer. Having met his future wife, Eve Moore, at Coventry during the previous

December, Gibson at least had a distraction from the war, and whenever an opportunity presented itself, he would arrange to be wherever actress and dancer Eve happened to be performing at the time. His first tour ended on thirty-eight sorties with a trip to Berlin on the 23/24th of September, and he was then packed off to 14 OTU at Cottesmore.

His time in rural Rutland was brief indeed, just two weeks, part of which was spent on leave. It was at this time that he proposed to Eve and was accepted. He was soon posted to 16 OTU at Upper Heyford, but when an opportunity arose to remain on operations by undertaking a night-fighter tour, he grabbed it with both hands, and joined 29 Squadron at Digby in Lincolnshire on the 13th of November. Ten days later he and Eve were married at Penarth Anglican Church. Gibson left Bomber Command assured by his Air-Officer-Commanding, (AOC), Air Vice Marshal Sir Arthur Harris, that he could return in the fullness of time. For the next thirteen months he doggedly pursued the art of night fighting, at a time when the boffins were attempting to turn it into a science. In this they would largely succeed, but that was in the future, and although a number of shining lights, Cunningham and Braham to name but two, were emerging from among the night-fighting fraternity, Gibson was not one of them, and it was a source of frustration to him. Following his final night fighter sortie on the 15th of December 1941 his logbook showed three confirmed kills, one probable and three damaged from ninety-nine operational flights. He ached to return to bombers, and began to lobby those with influence. Harris was no longer 5 Group A-O-C, and was out of Gibson's reach at the time. His posting, therefore, to Fighter Command's 51 OTU at Cranfield as chief flying instructor seemed inevitable. However, Harris returned from America in February 1942, and within a month of his enthronement as Commander-in-Chief of Bomber Command, Gibson was out of jail and back where he belonged. Harris had suggested to AVM Slessor, the incumbent 5 Group A-O-C, that 207 Squadron would be the ideal command for Gibson, to replace W/C Fothergill, who was rarely given to operating, and, therefore, was, in Harris's eyes, not an inspiration to his men. *(A twist of fate would see Fothergill command 617 Squadron after the war).* This was not an order to Slessor, who could use his own discretion in deciding Gibson's fate, and he chose to send him instead to 106 Squadron at Coningsby, which had just traded in its Hampdens for the ill-fated Avro Manchester.

This was actually a shrewd move on the part of Slessor. 106 Squadron was already a crack unit after twelve months in the hands of the popular and well-respected W/C Bob Allen DFC*. Gibson and Allen knew each other from their Scampton days in 1940, when Allen had been a flight commander with 49 Squadron. His fine record at 106 would provide the perfect benchmark to assess Gibson's mettle as a commander. Any dip in the squadron's performance under Gibson would be noticed. In the event, he was to revel in his new responsibilities, and not only continue the excellent work of his predecessor, but build on it. Gibson was able to drag out of the Manchester a level of serviceability unsurpassed by the other squadrons, albeit at a time late in the type's operational career, when most of its debilitating tendencies had been largely suppressed. This should not detract from the fact that over the ensuing months Gibson turned 106 Squadron into the finest unit in the Group. He was an innovator, who constantly sought out new ways to increase the operational effectiveness of the squadron, and was the first to equip his aircraft with cameras to assess bombing accuracy. He began to gather around him a select band of brother officer warriors, over whom he could hold court, and this undoubtedly contributed to the spirit of the squadron. However, those excluded from his inner circle, mostly the other ranks and anyone whose face offended Gibson, could experience treatment ranging from indifference to icy coldness and even open dislike. Gibson's upbringing in India, when as a young child he had authority over the native servants, created a class gulf, which he could never shake off, and he admitted to an inability to relate to non-commissioned types, particularly those of a non-flying denomination.

The fact that 106 Squadron was given new weapons to try out on operations was an indication of Gibson's growing stature within the Group. During the four raid series against the Baltic port of Rostock in the final week of April 1942, a 5 Group element was assigned to attack the nearby Heinkel aircraft factory. The target escaped damage on the first two occasions, but then the job was given to Gibson and 106 Squadron, and the factory was hit, Gibson recording in his logbook a bombing height of 3,500 feet and good results. His style was to lead from the front, and he was generally present on the more difficult and unusual operations, such as the dusk attack on Danzig on the 11th of June, carried out by 5 Group after a long flight out in daylight. On the 25th of July he flew to Horsham-St-Faith to collect a number of dignitaries, including Sir Archibald Sinclair, the Secretary of State for Air, and delivered them to Coningsby, in his words to let them 'see a crack station'. On the 27th of August he led a force of nine 106 Squadron Lancasters to the Baltic port of Gdynia to attack the enemy's new aircraft carrier *Graf Zeppelin*, which, it was mistakenly believed, was ready to put to sea. Laid down in Kiel at the end of 1936 as the first of four proposed similar vessels with a displacement of 33,500 tons, the carrier was launched two years later, but was never completed and never commissioned. Design difficulties, internal politics and a cooling of interest by Hitler led to the cancellation of the entire programme. Two aircraft, those flown by F/Ls Whamond and Hopgood, were carrying the new 5,500lb Capital Ship bomb, just one of which could potentially sink such a vessel. Gibson's load on this occasion was a more standard six 1,000lb RDX bombs. He makes no mention of the carrier, recording in his logbook an attack on three enemy warships using the stabilized automatic bombsight (SABS). Haze prevented an accurate identification of the targets, and Gibson reports eventually bombing the *Gneisenau* on his twelfth run, but missing it by 100 yards – 'Bad luck'. If it was the *Gneisenau*, a single high explosive bomb intended for the floating dock at Kiel had already ended her sea-going career back in February. In the event, the *Graf Zeppelin* was not hit, and it survived the war only to be sunk as a target vessel in 1947.

Another 5 Group effort to the Baltic coast was directed at the Dornier aircraft factory at Wismar on the 23/24th of September, and Gibson was among those coming down to 2,000 feet in poor weather to bomb. On the 17th of October, while over eighty 5 Group Lancasters attacked the Schneider armaments works at Le Creusot, the 'Krupp' Factory of France, Gibson led a section of six aircraft in a low-level assault on the nearby transformer station at Montchanin, which supplied its electrical power. The above-mentioned John Hopgood, a close friend of Gibson, was the other 106 Squadron representative among the six, and he flew so low, that his Lancaster was damaged by fragments and debris from his own bombs. The attacks on both targets were initially believed to be accurate, but it was later discovered that only minor damage had been inflicted. Most of his operations during the remainder of the year were directed against Italy's major cities in support of Operation Torch, the Allied landings in North Africa.

Harris spent the early part of 1943 in preparation for the forthcoming assault on Germany's industrial heartland, the Ruhr, which would begin in March. In the meantime, among other operations mounted were two against Berlin on the consecutive nights of the 16th and 17th of January, and the life of the broadcaster Richard Dimbleby was entrusted to Gibson on the latter occasion. The operation was not a success, and Berlin sustained no serious damage, although this would not have been apparent to the crews at the time. Gibson recorded in his logbook, that 'the residential quarter got it!' He goes on to mention Dimbleby's broadcast on the following day, and notes that it was his own sixty-seventh bombing trip. His second bomber tour ended on twenty-nine sorties on the night of the 11/12th of March, when he flew to Stuttgart and back on 'three engines + ¼'. According to squadron records he spent most of the operation at 4,000 feet after losing power in one engine. This brought his official tally to somewhere between sixty-eight and seventy-two bomber operations, and although it has been said by some that he may not have recorded every one, the style of his logbook entries suggests otherwise. He used his logbook to record his thoughts as if it were a diary, and it demonstrates an accounting against the enemy, the zealous building of a score for personal satisfaction almost in the manner of a collector. It seems unlikely, therefore, that he would intentionally play down his part in Hitler's downfall for whatever reason. After a year at 106 Squadron his time was up anyway, no matter how many times he had operated. There was no set number of sorties for commanding officers, some flew frequently, others hardly at all, so it was not necessary for him to conceal the true figure in order to remain on operations. Indeed, as we shall see, he learned a few days later that he was guaranteed at least one more crack at the Reich, and as he generally made his logbook entries some time after the event, he had ample opportunity to fill in omissions, had there been any.

When about to join Eve in Cornwall for some well-earned leave, he was surprised to be posted instead to 5 Group HQ on the 15th, and believed, initially at least, that it was to assist in the writing of a book. It was also on this day, that Harris met with the 5 Group A-O-C, AVM Sir Ralph Cochrane, at Bomber Command HQ at High Wycombe, and told him to form a special squadron under Gibson to carry out an operation against the dams. For Gibson, the first few days of his new posting were anything but stimulating, in fact, everything to do with it was anathema to a warrior, who needed to be surrounded by the paraphernalia of war, the aircraft, the noise, the smells and the people. On the 18th he was summoned to a meeting with Cochrane at St Vincents, the imposing building set in trees on the edge of Grantham serving at the time as 5 Group HQ. Cochrane had himself been in post as A-O-C 5 Group for less than three weeks, and knew of Gibson only through Harris. Born in 1895 as the youngest son of the 1st Baron Cochrane of Cults, the Honourable Ralph Cochrane joined the Royal Navy in 1912, and transferred to the RAF in 1918. He served extensively in the Middle-East during the early twenties, for a period as a flight commander under Harris, and it was at this time that the two men forged a respect for and understanding of each other that would prove fruitful during the current conflict. Among his appointments in the thirties were spells as the first Chief of the Air Staff Royal New Zealand Air Force from the 1st of April 1937, and Air Aide-de-Camp to King George VI from September to December 1939. In October 1940 he became Director of Flying Training, a position he held until becoming A-O-C 3 Group in September 1942.

It seems, that the purpose of this initial meeting between Cochrane and Gibson was to settle just one point; was Gibson prepared to carry out one more unspecified operation? This having been established in the affirmative, Gibson was dismissed, and was recalled on the following day, when Group Captain J.N.H. Whitworth, who was known among his peers as 'Charles', joined him and Cochrane. Whitworth was the station commander at Scampton, where, Gibson soon learned, he was to form a new squadron specifically, though not exclusively, to carry out an as yet still unspecified special operation. Scampton was a pre-war station equipped to accommodate two squadrons, and as already mentioned, during Gibson's previous term here it had been occupied by 83 and 49 Squadrons. A few weeks after 83 Squadron's departure to Wyton in August 1942 as a founder member of the Pathfinder Force, 57 Squadron was drafted into 5 Group from 3 Group and installed at Scampton. However, the grass runway at Scampton was not ideal for heavy bombers with an ever-increasing payload, and 49 Squadron was moved out at the start of 1943, with a view to the laying of concrete runways later on, when a new home could be found for 57 Squadron. In the meantime, however, it was an ideal location for Gibson's Squadron X, which could occupy the vacant accommodation and launch its maiden operation.

Whitworth was the kind of officer to whom Gibson could easily relate. The two men were similar in stature, short and squat, and Whitworth possessed the cut glass English accent of the aristocracy. More important to Gibson, however, was the fact, that Whitworth had been an 'operational type' earlier in the war, flying Whitleys with 10 Squadron as a flight commander, before spending short spells in command of 78 Squadron in 1940/41 and 35 Squadron in early 1942. Gibson was frequently given to open criticism of both non-operational types and fellow fliers who were not constantly exposing themselves to danger. Of course, implicit in his criticism of other fliers' 'too safe' existence was his own contrasting dangerous life style, and this was a reverse way of drawing attention to himself, as he had in the past by line shooting and exaggerating. It was important for the success of the operation that personal relationships at senior level ran smoothly, and Whitworth's experience and understanding of Gibson's task would help matters in that regard. The meeting between Cochrane, Whitworth and Gibson established that the operation would not take place for two months, and that training should be concentrated on low-level flying.

It was on the 21st of March that instructions were issued by Bomber Command to form the new squadron, and included within them were certain principles as a guide to the selection of personnel. The majority of aircrew were to have completed one or two operational tours, and the remainder were to be specially selected. Particular attention was to be paid to the efficiency of ground officers, principal among these the armament officer. The ground crews were to be provided as far as possible from Group resources, and all were to have experience on Lancasters. Aircraft were to be provided from existing squadrons, but would be replaced later by a modified version. The squadron was to be given priority over everything else, and all endeavours were to be made to form it into an efficient unit by the earliest possible date. P/O Caple was posted in as Engineering officer, P/O Hodgson as Elect/ Engineering Officer, P/O Watson as Armaments Officer, and F/O Arthurton as Medical Officer.

On the 24th Gibson was driven to a railway station west of London, where he boarded a train for Weybridge. On arrival there he was met by Mutt Summers, a Vickers test pilot, and a man known to Gibson from years earlier. Summers drove Gibson to a country house for his first meeting with Dr Barnes Wallis, which took place in the late afternoon. Wallis was the chief structural engineer for Vickers Armstrong, a brilliant scientist and inventor, who among other achievements had designed the highly successful R100 airship, and had been a leading member of the Wellington bomber design team led by R.K. Pierson, which developed the unique geodetic, lattice-work system of aircraft construction. Now Wallis was responsible for the revolutionary weapon shortly to be delivered by Gibson and his crews against the German dams in the operation to be code-named Chastise. Gibson was still almost completely in the dark as far as the target was concerned, and Wallis lacked the official authority to enlighten him. Wallis contented himself, therefore, with a technical description of the weapon, its effects and the operational requirements for Gibson and his crews, and then showed

Gibson film of the original trials of the scaled down weapon, code-named Upkeep. Gibson returned to Scampton by the same circuitous route, having been left impressed both by Wallis the man and his inventive genius. For his part, Wallis was impressed by Gibson, and over the ensuing months a genuine friendship would develop between them. Before his trip to Weybridge, in fact, before his arrival at Scampton, Gibson, Whitworth and the Group Personnel Officer had drawn up an initial list of pilots to be posted in. Independently of the instructions outlined above concerning the forming of the squadron, Harris had intimated that the squadron should be made up of tour expired men, his 'old lags'. In the event, a number of pilots would arrive on the squadron with minimal operational experience and for some crewmembers the forthcoming operation would be their first. The initial batch of seven crews was ordered to report to Scampton on the 24th, the second seven on the 25th and the remaining seven between the 26th and 31st. By the morning of Saturday the 27th the necessary administration work to allow the postings to take place was complete, and, on paper at least, the squadron was 100% manned.

CHAPTER TWO

The Cast Assembles

From every corner of the world they come

Contrary to the belief persisting down the years, Gibson did not handpick every member of the squadron, or, indeed, even the pilots, a fact made apparent by the relative inexperience of some of those posted in. He did, however, avail himself of the best amongst those whom he knew, as in the case of his former 106 Squadron colleagues, F/Ls Hopgood and Shannon and P/O Burpee, the last mentioned one of a number of Canadians to be posted in. Hopgood was a twenty-two year old Londoner, who had passed out as a pilot at Cranwell on the 16th of February 1941. A spell at 14 OTU at Cottesmore in Rutland followed, where F/L Nettleton checked him out for his Hampden solo. Nettleton, eleven months hence, would lead the epic daylight raid by elements of 44 and 97 Squadrons against the MAN diesel works at Augsburg, and be awarded the Victoria Cross as a result. In July 1941 Hopgood was posted to 50 Squadron to begin his operational career, and flew his first sortie to Bremen on the 12th as navigator to a F/O Abbott. The fighter style single-seat cockpit of the Hampden precluded a second pilot's position, and it became standard practice for the navigator/bomb-aimer's role to be undertaken by a qualified pilot. After operating once more with F/O Abbott, Hopgood carried out eight more Hampden sorties as navigator/bomb-aimer to a P/O Smith, before being posted to 25 OTU at Finningley at the end of October. While still with 25 OTU he began converting to Manchesters at Bircotes, and it was here that he came into contact with P/O Whamond, one of the future mainstays of 106 Squadron. On the 17th of February 1942 Hopgood was signed off as a qualified Manchester pilot by W/C Lynch-Blosse, soon to be killed in action on his first sortie as commander of 44 (Rhodesia) Squadron. Hopgood was posted to Coningsby to join 106 Squadron, commanded at the time, as stated earlier, by W/C Allen. 106 Squadron was already recognised as one of 5 Group's finest units, and over the ensuing year its reputation would flourish under its new commander.

Hopgood's introduction to Manchester operations came as second pilot to Whamond for a mining sortie on the 20th of March, the day on which Gibson assumed command of the squadron. After two further operations as second pilot, he flew as captain of his own crew for the first time against

Rostock on the 23rd of April. 106 Squadron was among the last in 5 Group to take on the ill-fated Manchester, but thankfully, the type was approaching the end of its short period of service, and in May it was replaced by the Lancaster. It was Hopgood who saw Gibson safely through his conversion onto the type. Hopgood's first two Lancaster sorties were the thousand bomber raids against Cologne and Essen on the 30/31st of May and 1/2nd of June respectively. The former was an outstanding success, while the latter was an abysmal failure, but Hopgood came through both with flying colours. The remainder of his tour served to demonstrate his abilities, and it established his reputation as a first-rate pilot and captain. His press-on spirit ensured his status as a member of Gibson's inner circle, and the bond between the two men would prove to be fateful. Hopgood concluded his tour with 106 Squadron in October 1942 with a total of forty-six operations to his credit, and he was awarded the DFC on the 27th of that month. The squadron had just taken up residence at Syerston alongside the A46 in Nottinghamshire, and Hopgood's posting was to Syerston's Station HQ, where he would carry out test flights in the new Hercules-powered Mk II Lancasters, and also instruct other pilots. This was followed by periods at the Fighter Interception Unit (FIU) at Ford and 1485 Bombing Gunnery Flight at Fulbeck, where he flew half a dozen different types on various duties, and he was awarded a Bar to his DFC on the 11th of January 1943. This sojourn ended on the 29th of March, when he flew to Scampton, and officially joined the newly formed 617 Squadron under Gibson on the following day.

Hopgood picked up his new crew at Scampton, and among them was another 'faceless' Bomber Command stalwart, twenty-seven year old John Minchin, who had begun his operational career with 49 Squadron in October 1941, where he was a contemporary of future 617 Squadron personalities, Ralf Allsebrook, Barney Gumbley and navigator Keith Astbury. As a wireless operator he was the least likely member of a crew to be recognised or decorated, even though he was an integral part of it, and shared the common dangers. He completed a tour on Hampdens and Manchesters, and was on board the very last 49 Squadron operational Hampden sortie on the 23/24th of April 1942. He was also on the squadron's very first Manchester operation, which took place on the night of the 2/3rd of May. On the 28th of May he got married, but the first of the three One Thousand Bomber raids two nights later dashed any thoughts of a proper honeymoon. At the conclusion of his tour he was posted to 26 OTU, and then returned to Scampton as a founder member of 617 Squadron in early April 1943.

Shannon, an Australian, had been posted from 106 to 83 Squadron at Wyton on the 25th of March to begin Pathfinder training, and had barely had time to unpack before the call came through from Gibson. There was also a whiff of insider dealing between Gibson and W/C 'Hamish' Mahaddie to obtain Shannon's services. Mahaddie, after completing two tours with 7 Squadron, was recruited by Pathfinder chief AVM Bennett as his head-hunter, and he became known as the Pathfinder Horse Thief as he went from station to station seeking volunteers to the Pathfinder cause. The story goes, that Gibson could have Shannon as long as he kept his hands off W/C Searby. The latter, having stepped up into Gibson's shoes at 106 Squadron, was now himself a prime target for a posting to 8 Group, and, in fact, would shortly take command of the PFF's 83 Squadron. According to Mahaddie, however, in his book *Hamish, The Story of a Pathfinder*, he had not at that time heard of Searby, and had anyway been given a list of off-limits pilots by the 5 Group A-O-C, AVM Cochrane, whom he visited frequently during the course of his thievery. On this particular visit to St Vincent's at Grantham, Mahaddie apparently bumped into Gibson, who repeated the warning to 'lay off', and not knowing about the imminent formation of 617 Squadron, he assumed the incident related to 106 Squadron.

Shannon had become one of Gibson's inner circle along with Hopgood during their time together at 106 Squadron. Gibson liked to be in the company of officer class professionals, men who gladly went to war in bombers, took pride in their performance, and were not deflected from their purpose by the inherent dangers of their trade. Shannon was such a man, and one only has to read Gibson's words in his book, *Enemy Coast Ahead,* to appreciate the immense pride he felt in leading these warriors into battle. On page 1 of the first chapter, *Flight Out*, which details the journey to the Dams, he writes: 'We were flying not very high, about 100 feet, and not very far apart. I suppose to a layman it was a wonderful sight, those great powerful Lancasters in formation, flown by boys who knew their job'. On the following page he writes: 'Such is the scene. The glass house. Soft moonlight. Two silent figures, young, unbearded, new to the world, yet full of skill, full of pride in their squadron, determined to do a good job and bring the ship home'.

Shannon was just twenty years old when he joined 106 Squadron at Coningsby in June 1942, although he looked much younger. His first operation was as second pilot to S/L John Wooldridge, officer commanding B Flight, on the occasion of the third and final Thousand-Bomber Raid on the night of the 25/26th of June. Wooldridge was one of the great characters of Bomber Command, and a man who preferred to compose classical music and write plays rather than carouse his off-duty nights away with his squadron colleagues. His eventful career was to take him in 1943 to 105 Squadron, one of the Pathfinder's two 'Oboe' (a blind bombing device which allowed navigators and bomb-aimers to 'see' through the industrial haze) Mosquito units, which he would command with distinction. After the war his screenplay for *Appointment in London* became a highly successful film starring Dirk Bogarde as the commander of a Lancaster squadron, and Wooldridge also wrote the score. A number of his plays were successfully produced in London's theatre land, and he continued to write and compose classical music until his untimely death in a motor accident in the fifties. His widow, the actress Margueretta Scott, is known among other roles for her portrayal of Mrs Pomfrey in television's *All Creatures Great and Small* in the eighties. The target for Wooldridge and his young charge on this night in June 1942 was the city of Bremen in northwestern Germany, which had been a regular destination for Bomber Command almost since strategic bombing began in the summer of 1940. A total of 960 Bomber Command aircraft were dispatched, along with 102 from Coastal Command, the latter on the personal orders of Churchill, and a moderately effective operation ensued. The 5 Group effort at Bremen, amounting to 142 aircraft, was directed entirely at the city's Focke-Wulf aircraft factory, and although it was not destroyed, an assembly shop was wrecked and six other buildings were severely damaged.

Gibson had been absent from the squadron when Shannon arrived, and had not yet undertaken a Lancaster operation. His first, against Wilhelmshaven on the night of the 8/9th of July, was flown with Shannon as second pilot. Unlike many, Shannon was not overawed by Gibson's personality, and an unshakeable bond formed between the two men. Shannon's next four operations were flown as co-pilot or 'second dickey', and these included the already mentioned daylight raid by 5 Group on the distant port of Danzig on the 11th of July, when he again flew with Gibson. Shannon did not operate at all during August, and when he undertook his first sortie as captain, a gardening expedition on the 4/5th of September, it proved to be something of an anticlimax, after W/T failure forced him to return early. Another mining sortie two nights later was carried out as planned, however, and he and his crew went on to complete five more operations in September. They flew six operations in October, including 5 Group's already mentioned epic daylight attack on the Schneider armaments works at Le Creusot on the 17th, and a few days later the first rounds of the campaign against Italian cities in support of Operation Torch. Towards the end of November he was recommended for the non-immediate award of the DFC in recognition of his operational career thus far, the citation reading as follows:

> This officer has participated in twenty-six raids on enemy territory and has displayed the utmost vigour and courage in pressing home his attacks. He has attacked many of the principal German industrial targets, and apart from these, he has undertaken many raids on special objectives, such as the long-range daylight raids on Danzig, Le Creusot and Milan. His night raids have included attacks on Italy, having bombed Genoa no fewer than four times (twice obtaining pictures of the aiming points) and Turin. As a captain, he has shown the highest skill in all his sorties, and has set an example, which is attained by few but admired by all.

For whatever reason Shannon's crew, with the exception of his navigator Danny Walker, opted not to accompany him to 617 Squadron, but he would gather around him excellent replacements, including bomb-aimer Len Sumpter, a former guardsman, who was older than most, and had completed thirteen operations with 57 Squadron by the time of his posting to 617 Squadron at the start of April.

Lewis Johnstone Burpee, known as John, was born in Ottawa in March 1918, and gained a university degree before enlisting in the RCAF in December 1940. He arrived in England in late 1941, and began his first tour with 106 Squadron in October 1942. He flew his first operation as second pilot to a F/S Stan Jones on the 15th when Cologne was the target, and a week later accompanied the same crew to Genoa. He captained his own crew on an operation for the first time on the 7th of November, but was forced to abandon the trip, which was again to Genoa, when his navigator became ill. Between then and leaving 106 Squadron he flew a further twenty-six times, notching up in the process five more early returns. As far as Burpee's Dams crew is concerned, his flight engineer Guy Pegler and rear gunner Joe Brady were with him from the start of his tour, while mid-upper gunner Bill Long joined on the 9th of January, navigator Tom Jaye on the 21st, wireless operator Len Weller on the 16th of February, and bomb-aimer Jack Arthur arrived in time for their last operation, against Essen on the 12/13th of March.

The standard process for forming a new squadron began with 'beefing up' an existing squadron to three flights rather than the usual two. The third, or C Flight, would then be hived off to the other side of the station to form the nucleus of the new squadron, thus ensuring a leavening of experience, while newly qualified men from the training units were posted in to provide the bulk. The formation of 617 Squadron followed this principal in general, and it was the C Flight of fellow Scampton residents 57 Squadron, which formed the nucleus. This consisted of S/L Young, as flight commander, F/L Astell, P/O Rice, and Sgts Lancaster and Lovell. The enforced posting across the tarmac was apparently not appreciated by all those involved, and not all were destined to remain for the duration of the training programme.

Henry Melvin Young was born on the 20th of May 1915 in Belgravia, London. His father was a qualified solicitor working within the family legal business, but had joined the army during the Great War, and at the time of Henry's birth was a 2nd Lieutenant in the 4th Battalion, The Queen's Royal West Surrey Regiment. His mother, Fanny, hailed from Los Angeles, where her family was part of the social set, and she met her future husband, while he and a friend were travelling the world before settling down to careers. Both Fanny and Henry senior were talented athletes, she at tennis and he at rowing, particularly during his time at Oxford. Henry decided to remain in America to practice law, and he married Fanny in 1913. They soon moved to England, however, in time for the arrival of Henry junior, or Melvin as he was known to his family, and his sister, Angela. The Young family remained in England until 1928, when post-war austerity persuaded them to move to California. Here Melvin attended Webb School until 1928, before moving on to Kent School, Connecticut, where he met his future wife, Priscilla Rawson. In 1933 Henry senior returned to England with Melvin and his sisters, and Melvin was enrolled at Westminster school, before eventually following in Henry senior's footsteps by going up to Oxford. Once there he joined the Oxford University Rowing Club, which ultimately led to his selection at number seven in the crew for the 1938 University Boat Race, in which Oxford defeated Cambridge by two lengths.

He joined the RAF Volunteer Reserve in August 1939 as a Pilot Officer, and after training was posted on the 10th of June 1940 to 4 Group's 102 Squadron to fly Whitleys. By now a Flying Officer, here he was a colleague of P/O Leonard Cheshire, another young man who was to make a name for himself both before and after joining 617 Squadron. Young's first thirteen operations were flown as second pilot to a P/O Painter, and it was not until September, when 102 Squadron was loaned to Coastal Command for patrol duties, that he flew as crew captain for the first time. During a patrol on the 7th of October, while on detachment to Aldergrove in Northern Ireland, engine failure forced Young to ditch his Whitley in the Atlantic. He and his crew bobbed up and down in the swell for some twenty-two hours, before rescue came at the hands of HMS *St Mary* of the Royal Navy. The squadron returned to Bomber Command after a six-week tour of duty with webbed feet, and on the night of the 23/24th of November, Young found himself operating against Turin. On the way home he ran out of fuel after more than eleven hours aloft, and was forced to ditch once more, this time off the south coast of Devon. He and his crew paddled ashore in their dinghy, and as a result of this, and his previous conspicuous devotion to dinghy drill for his crew, which had twice proved well founded, 'Dinghy' became the name by which he was universally known, and the name he would carry to his untimely death.

On completion of his tour early in 1941, Young was posted to 10 OTU as an instructor, and from there to 22 OTU. His DFC was gazetted on the 9th of May, and he was promoted to Flight Lieutenant in August. In September he joined 104 Squadron, a 4 Group unit at Driffield operating the Merlin powered Wellington Mk II, and commanded by W/C Beare, whom Young knew as a flight commander from his 102 Squadron days. During October a number of squadrons sent a detachment to the Middle East to join 238 Wing of 205 Group, leaving a small home echelon to rebuild. Young's was among the fifteen crews of the 104 Squadron element departing for Malta on the 18th of October, for what was intended to be a two-month tour of duty. In the event, the move for the squadron proved to be permanent, and after something of a dispute, the overseas element retained the 104 number, while the home echelon was renumbered 158 Squadron, which, as a Halifax unit, would go on to become a mainstay of 4 Group for the remainder of the war. The detachment arrived at Luqa on the 20th of October, and Young and his crew were operating against Naples on the following night. In January 1942 the squadron moved to Kabrit in Egypt, and then on to landing grounds closer to its targets. On the 1st of June Young was promoted to Squadron Leader, and he and his crew were rested from operations. He was not immediately posted home, but took up duties at HQ 205 Group for a short period. In August he went to America, where he married Priscilla on the 10th. A Bar to his DFC was gazetted on the 18th of September recognizing fifty-one sorties, and then on the 15th of October he was sent to America for special duties. On his return to England he rejoined Bomber Command, and was posted to 57 Squadron at Scampton on the 13th of March 1943, the day after the second operation of the recently started Ruhr campaign. The next round of major operations was not destined to begin until the final week of the month, and this would have allowed Young time to settle in at his new unit, had his posting to 617 Squadron not intervened. Young's reputation as a no-nonsense, efficient organizer was known to Gibson, as was his apparent ability to sink a pint of beer faster than anyone else on earth!

Earmarked to be Young's deputy as A Flight commander at 617 Squadron, William (Bill) Astell was born in 1920 at Peover in Cheshire to an upper-class family, which, by the thirties was resident in Chapel-en-le-Frith on the edge of the Peak District of Derbyshire. His father, Godfrey, was the managing director of J & N Philips, a textile company, which he ran from its main site in Church Street, Manchester. His mother's sister was a member of the Dundas family, whose sons, and therefore Bill's cousins, John and Hugh, flew Spitfires during the Battle of Britain. John was killed, but Hugh survived to become the RAF's youngest ever Group Captain, and as Sir Hugh he became Chairman of the BET Group and Thames Television during the eighties. The Astell family's affluence enabled Bill to travel extensively overseas to broaden his education and experience, and in 1936, at the age of sixteen, he sailed to Canada to visit relatives. He also took a trip to the White Sea in a trawler. He spent the end of 1937, most of 1938 and the first half of 1939 in Germany and France, and on his return to England he joined the RAF Air Reserve, undergoing training at an airfield in nearby Staffordshire. In September 1939 he was posted to Hastings to continue his training, before being posted to Salisbury, Southern Rhodesia at the end of April 1940. He was awarded his wings in January 1941, passing out as a Pilot Officer, and he was immediately posted for duty in Malta. Before he had an opportunity to get into the war, however, he was struck down by typhoid, and was forced to spend time first in hospital and then convalescing. He finally joined 148 Squadron at Kabrit in Egypt in May 1941 and began operations as a Wellington pilot, attacking ports and landing grounds. A crash on the 30th of November left him with burns to his body, mostly his back, and cuts to his scalp and face, and although he did not consider himself to be seriously injured, he remained in hospital until February 1942. This was followed by a month's sick leave, which he spent in Kenya, before returning to duty with 148 Squadron and a new crew in March.

On the last night of May Astell took off to attack an enemy landing ground, and failed to return, triggering the obligatory telegram to his family. Five days later Astell walked in to report being attacked by an enemy fighter over the target. Apart from wounding two of his crew, the engagement left his Wellington with an unserviceable rear turret and rudder controls, and a fire in the fuselage, starboard wing and engine nacelle. He ordered his crew to bale out, and four had time to comply before they ran out of altitude. Astell pulled off a crash-landing, and he and his navigator, P/O 'Bishop' Dodds, a former cleric, emerged from the wreckage with minor burns and began walking. After a few days a British patrol was spotted, and Astell moved forward to make contact, leaving his now ailing navigator hidden. He failed to make contact on this occasion, and was unable to relocate his navigator when he went back for him. Two days later Astell was picked up by Arabs and pointed in the direction of the British lines. He spent a few days in hospital in Tobruk, before being sent home via America, arriving back in England aboard the *Queen Mary* in September. He was posted to Wigsley in Nottinghamshire, one of 5 Group's training stations, and also spent time at Hullavington and Fulbeck. Now in the rank of Flight Lieutenant he was posted to 57 Squadron at Scampton on the 25th of January 1943 to undertake a second tour, this time on Lancasters, and it was here that he acquired his new crew. Operations followed to Milan, Nuremberg, Cologne, Berlin, Hamburg and Essen, and after grabbing some sleep on return from the last mentioned on the night of the 5/6th of March he went home on leave for what turned out to be the last time during his 57 Squadron service. He returned to his squadron on the 12th, and was posted to 617 Squadron on the 25th, not knowing what lay ahead. He managed one more spell of leave sometime during the dams training period, and while visiting his father at work, he accidentally ran into one of the secretaries, knocking her over and scattering papers over the floor. Picking her up he kissed her on the cheek, and told her he would see her next leave, with the prospect of that occurring after the operation for which they were preparing. All who knew Astell, particularly those of the fairer sex, would testify to his open, friendly, charming nature, which made him immensely likeable.

Astell's crew was fairly typical of those posted in as founder members of the squadron, and it is interesting to delve a little more deeply into their individual backgrounds as representative of the squadron as a whole. Five of the crew had been together at 1654 Conversion Unit at Wigsley from October 1942 until their posting to 9 Squadron at Waddington two days before Christmas. They were navigator Floyd Wile, bomb-aimer Don Hopkinson, wireless operator Al Garshowitz and gunners Frank Garbas and Richard Bolitho. At Waddington they were teamed up with a Sgt Stephenson as their pilot, with whom they flew for the first time on Christmas Eve, carrying out circuits and landings. This association was not destined to last long, however, although Sgt Stephenson's disappearance from the scene is a little confusing. On the night of the 8/9th of January 1943 a 9 Squadron Lancaster failed to return from a raid on Duisburg, and Sgt Foote and his crew were all killed. Listed as the crew's flight engineer was Sgt M.W. Stephenson, who is assumed to be the pilot mentioned above. In 9 Squadron records, though, he is shown as a flight engineer, and not as a pilot flying as second dickey. There were seven men on board the missing Lancaster, not eight as was normal when a second pilot was being carried. However, Sgt Foote's regular flight engineer was not on the trip, and this leaves us with the conclusion, that, if these Stephensons are one and the same, he must have volunteered to act as flight engineer at short notice. Had he survived, matters might have turned out differently for his former crew.

Floyd Wile was one of three Canadians in the crew, and was born in Nova Scotia in April 1919 as the fifth of seven children. Following high school he worked on the land as a farm hand and in the lumber industry. He had shown an interest in radio during his youth, and actually studied the subject for a year at technical school. He was also keen on sporting activities, particularly skiing, skating and swimming. Before enlisting in the RCAF he joined a local army unit in Yarmouth, Nova Scotia, but resigned after a month. At 5 Initial Training School he was noted as being slow thinking, hard working, the plodder type, while at No. 8 Air Observer School he was described as average, with the comment, 'in no respect has he shown much aptitude for work.' Another report described him as a quiet lad, and backward through lack of experience in mixing. Three months later, however, his commanding officer at No. 9 Bombing and Gunnery School called him outstanding and a brilliant trainee, who was very popular and had good self-control. Despite this he passed out of No. 2 Air Navigation School with a 'not outstanding, average NCO material' tag, but was commissioned as a Pilot Officer before leaving Wigsley in December 1942.

The other Canadians in Astell's crew were Abram Garshowitz, known within his family as Albert, and Frank Garbas, who were great boyhood friends. Garshowitz was the ninth of twelve children, and was born in Hamilton Ontario in December 1920. He went to school locally, and afterwards worked in the family business selling new and used furniture. Frank Garbas was born in July 1922, ten years after his parents arrived in Canada from their native Poland. He was the fifth of nine children. Once in Canada the letter z was dropped from the family name Garbasz, while his father became Stanley rather than Stanislaus. Even so, family life revolved around Polish traditions, religion and cuisine, and Polish was the dominant language spoken at home. Frank was a gentle, quiet person, who was very close to his mother, and also, as mentioned, to Garshowitz, with whom he played semi-pro American football with the Eastwood Lions before enlisting in the RCAF, having worked briefly for Otis, the elevator manufacturers.

Donald Hopkinson was born at Royton, Oldham in Lancashire in September 1920 as a second child. Just four months later his mother died of cancer, and Donald went to live with his grandfather, and an aunt, uncle and cousin. After his father remarried, a half brother and two half sisters were added to his family. A keen cricketer Donald attended grammar school in Royton, before working in the office of the local Co-operative Society. He enlisted in the RAF in December 1941.

Richard Bolitho was born in Portrush, County Antrim in January 1920, but was brought to England early on by his parents, who kept a private hotel in Nottingham. Richard eventually moved in with his aunt, who ran a grocery shop in Kimberley, but after her death, his father sold the hotel and took over the shop. After attending school in nearby Heanor, Don worked for Ericcsons Telephones at Beeston, and enlisted in the RAF in November 1940. The final member of the crew, flight engineer John Kinnear, did not become involved with Astell and the others until they had already carried out four operations with 57 Squadron. He was born in Fife Scotland in November 1921, and grew up to be a likeable, carefree young man who was mad about flying. He worked as a mechanic until he was old enough to enlist, and this he did in 1939. He was at 1654CU at the same time as the other members of his future crew, but does not appear to have arrived at 57 Squadron until later. He flew his first operations with the crew against Hamburg on the night of the 3/4th of March 1943 and Essen two nights later.

Pilot Geoff Rice was born in Portsmouth in 1917, in the house that stands to this day to the right of the main entrance to Portsmouth Dockyard. At the time, during the First World War, the Metropolitan Police Force was responsible for dockyard security, and the house was the residence of the Chief Superintendent of the Metropolitan Police, Albert Spencer, who was Rice's maternal grandfather. However, Rice grew to manhood in the village of Burbage on the edge of Hinckley in Leicestershire. Leicestershire at the time was a county dominated by the hosiery and boot and shoe industries, and Rice's family had become related through marriage to the Bennetts who owned a hosiery factory. This enabled Rice to take up an apprenticeship as a hosiery mechanic with Bennett Bros in Hinckley, and he worked maintaining the company's knitting machines while he waited to be called up into the RAF. The young Rice's passion was cricket, and he was due for a trial with Leicestershire County Cricket Club when the war took him away, something that would always be a source of regret. It was early in 1941 when he received the call to arms, and in some ways, as was the case with many young men of the time, the war was the best thing that could have happened to him. He was packed off to Canada in August to undertake pilot training, but soon found himself in America, and was in Florida at the time of Pearl Harbour, when, he noted, the American attitudes to the war changed overnight. Having gained his wings in early 1942 he returned to the UK to complete his training. He spent the second half of 1942 at 19 OTU, before joining 57 Squadron on the 20th of February 1943. Although a naturally shy young man, Rice would be described in today's parlance as having 'attitude', and he was one of those 57 Squadron recruits to 617 Squadron who was less than happy at being uprooted from where he felt himself to be settled and content.

Throughout the war up to that time certain squadrons, like 49 and 50, had been acting almost as an academy of excellence, where many of 5 Group's future stars either graduated or at least passed through. Another route to stardom for a select few showing particular promise during the first two years of the war was through 207 Squadron. In August 1940, 207 was re-formed under the command of the former 44 Squadron flight commander, S/L

'Hettie' Hyde, to introduce the new twin engine Avro Manchester into squadron service, and it required the best of the Group's current flock of pilots. 207 Squadron spawned 97 Squadron a few months later, and the great and the good moved over from 207 to form the nucleus of this new unit. The names of those who graced these outfits is a who's who of Bomber Command's finest: Denis Balsdon, 'Penny' Beauchamp, 'Flap' Sherwood, 'Dim' Wooldridge, Reg Reynolds, along with the likes of Peter Ward-Hunt, Dave Romans and Peter Burton-Gyles. If they survived to leave 49, 50, 97 and 207 Squadrons, they permeated the Group as the experienced stratum of battle-hardened men occupying the posts of squadron and flight commanders.

In contrast to 97 and 207, 50 Squadron's commanding officers between the end of 1940 and the formation of 617 Squadron were pre-war veterans, and men of great character, Gus Walker, R.J Oxley and Bill Russell. Walker, later Sir Augustus Walker, KCB became station commander at Syerston in 1942, home at the time of 106 Squadron under Gibson. Gibson described Walker as one of the finest 'station masters' he ever served under. Despite losing his lower right arm when a Lancaster bomb load went up at Syerston, the small and pugnacious Walker was soon back in harness, moving eventually to 4 Group to continue a glittering career. Oxley used the pre-operational briefings to whip up 'Hun-hatred' amongst his charges, while Bill Russell ultimately joined 138 Squadron at Tempsford in 1944 to fly Special Operations Executive (SOE) operations, initially having to drop a rank for the privilege. He eventually regained Wing Commander status to take over the squadron, and was killed in action within a week.

It was into this rich vein of experience that some future members of 617 Squadron were posted to learn their trade, although S/L Maudslay, 617 Squadron flight commander elect, had gained much of his schooling elsewhere before joining 50 Squadron. He and the Australian, P/O Knight, were contemporaries at 50 Squadron, which had shortly before been graced by the presence of P/O Drew Wyness, whose career and untimely end at 617 Squadron lay in 1944. Shortly after Knight's arrival in October 1942, low flying expert F/L H.B 'Mick' Martin, also from Australia, completed his tour with the unit, and was packed off to 1654CU at Wigsley.

Henry Maudslay was born in Royal Leamington Spa, Warwickshire in July 1921, and four years later the family moved to the village of Sherbourne, a few miles to the southwest of Warwick. His parents were Reginald, who died in 1934, and Susan, and he had a sister, Margaret, who was eleven years his senior. The Maudslay family was connected with both the Standard Motor Company and the Maudslay Motor Company. Henry was sent to preparatory school in Gloucestershire, and attended Eton College from 1935 to 1940. Here he excelled as an athlete, both as a miler and as an oarsman, and his prowess was recognized in his election as Captain of Boats and Captain of Athletics during his final year. During this period, in 1937, the family moved to Foxhill Manor, an imposing house at Willersey in Worcestershire. Having volunteered for the RAF, he was called up in July 1940, and after beginning elementary flying training in Yorkshire and Shropshire, he was posted to Canada under the Commonwealth Air Training Plan. He returned to the UK in February 1941, and after training on Hampdens at 25 OTU, he was posted to 44 Squadron at Waddington as a Pilot Officer in May. From then until early November he flew a total of twenty-nine operations, before being detached to Boscombe Down for Lancaster training. He was also detached to Rolls-Royce at Derby from the 7th to the 10th of January 1942. He returned to 44 Squadron Conversion Flight in January as an instructor, and was promoted to Flying Officer on the 29th, the day before his DFC was gazetted. He seems to have been at Boscombe Down again from the 9th to the 15th of February in some capacity connected with the Lancaster. He carried out no further operational sorties until the first one thousand-bomber raid on Cologne on the night of the 30/31st of May. For this momentous occasion he flew the Conversion Flight's Manchester L7430, an aircraft with a reputation as a 'hack'. Two nights later he took another 'hack', Manchester L7480, to Essen for the second of the thousand-bomber raids, and completed the hat trick by operating against Bremen in the third and final of these mammoth efforts on the 25/26th of June in Lancaster R5862. In July he was posted to 1654CU at Wigsley, where 5 Group crews were converted to Lancasters, and here he came into contact with a number of future 617 Squadron recruits as they passed through his hands. He requested a return to operational duties at the earliest opportunity, and was posted to 50 Squadron at Skellingthorpe in January 1943. He completed another thirteen operations from here as a Flight Lieutenant, before moving to Scampton and 617 Squadron as a Squadron Leader and B Flight commander.

'Mick' Martin was born in New South Wales in February 1921, and joined the RAF in 1940. He qualified as a pilot in June 1941, and after further training was posted to 455 Squadron Royal Australian Air Force at Swinderby in October of that year. Flying Hampdens, Martin ultimately drew around him an all-Australian crew consisting of Jack Leggo, Tammy Simpson and Toby Foxlee. In April 1942, 455 Squadron was posted to Coastal Command, while Martin and crew moved on to 50 Squadron at Skellingthorpe to continue their bomber tour. At the time of their posting 50 Squadron had recently converted to Manchesters, but was about to take delivery of Lancasters. By the end of May Martin had passed out on Manchesters, and the squadron put up sixteen of them plus a single Lancaster for the first thousand-bomber raid on Cologne. Also flying on this operation with a P/O Atkinson was gunner F/O Bill Tytherleigh, who would team up with Maudslay at 617 Squadron. Martin reported attacking Cologne from 7,400 feet, and described it as a really good trip. He went to Essen for the second thousand-bomber raid two nights later in the same Manchester, and completed the hat trick at Bremen on the 25/26th, in what proved to be the operational swansong for the ill-fated type. Flying as navigator with a P/O Calvert on this night was F/S Taerum, who would also find his way to Scampton in March, where he would ultimately join the crew of the squadron commander.

Among the stars alongside Martin in the 50 Squadron academy at this time was flight commander S/L G.H. Everitt, who had in his crew a certain P/O Bob Hay and a Sgt Fred Spafford, both of whom were Australians who would fly to the dams as bomb-aimers, the former with Martin as squadron bombing leader, and the latter with Gibson. There was also a balding F/O Abercromby, who, on promotion to Wing Commander more than a year hence, would take over 619 Squadron, and lead an attack on the Antheor viaduct with the shattered remnant of 617 Squadron in tow on the night after the Dortmund-Ems Canal disaster. In December 1943 Abercromby would then be handed the prestigious command of the Pathfinder's 83 Squadron, only to lose his life in an exploding Lancaster on the way to Berlin in the early hours of the 2nd of January 1944. As already mentioned, Drew Wyness was a contemporary of Martin on 50 Squadron, and the two joined the rest of the squadron for a trip to Kassel on the night of the 27/28th of August. In Wyness's crew as flight engineer was Sgt John Marriott, who, like gunner Bill Tytherleigh, would eventually team up with Henry Maudslay with fatal consequences. Joining the squadron at this time as a member of S/L Moore's crew was P/O Robert Urquhart, who was also to have a seat in Maudslay's ill-fated dams Lancaster, and would, in fact, become a member of Maudslay's team at 50 Squadron in January 1943 along with rear gunner Norman Burrows. Having completed his tour with thirty-six operations to his credit, Martin was screened. He was still languishing at Wigsley when someone with influence in the formation of 617 Squadron remembered his reputation as a skilful pilot, particularly where low flying was concerned, and this was to earn him an invitation to the dance.

As Martin was preparing to leave 50 Squadron in September 1942, Sgt Les Knight arrived to start his first tour of operations. He was born in the Australian state of Victoria in 1921, and had the war not intervened, he would have become an accountant. With him came five of his eventual dams crew, only Ray Grayston, the flight engineer, being absent from the line-up, although he was already on the squadron. Knight's first operation with his new unit was against Wismar on Germany's Baltic coast on the 1/2nd of October 1942, and it was not until his tenth, against Stuttgart on the 22/23rd of November, that Grayston first flew with the crew in place of a Sgt Sunderland. It was at this time, that Hopgood's future navigator, Ken Earnshaw, started to appear in the squadron records in the crew of a Sgt Schofield, and another 617 Squadron original, gunner F/O Richard Trevor-Roper, rejoined the squadron for a second tour.

From 97 Squadron came New Zealander F/L Munro, Englishman F/L Maltby and American F/L McCarthy. Les Munro, the only Royal New Zealand Air Force pilot to join the new squadron, was born into a farming family on the North Island in 1919. He joined the RNZAF in the summer of 1941, and was undertaking training in the UK before the end of the year. It was at 1654CU at Wigsley that P/O Munro collected together a crew, which included Sgt Frank Appleby as flight engineer. Appleby flew training sorties in Manchesters with Maudslay as well as Munro during October 1942, and had the month's summary in his logbook signed by the Officer-Commanding D Flight, S/L Paape DFC, who, on his return to operations as a flight commander with 467 Squadron RAAF, was destined to be shot down and killed over the Ruhr at the start of April 1943. By December 1942 Munro was a Flying Officer, and having fully converted to the Lancaster, he and his crew were posted to 97 Squadron at Woodhall Spa on the 7th. The remainder of the year was spent working up to operational readiness, and it was not until the night of the 2/3rd of January that Munro and his crew carried out their first operation, a mining sortie to the Gironde Estuary. A second mining sortie followed in northern waters six nights later, before they undertook their first bombing operation on the 11/12th. This was one of seven small-scale raids against Essen between the 3/4th and 13/14th of January as part of the Oboe trials programme, and involved Mosquitos of 109 Squadron and Lancasters from 1 and 5 Groups. After another trip to Essen, the crew took part in the earlier-mentioned disappointing attacks on Berlin on the consecutive nights of the 16/17th and 17/18th, and raided Düsseldorf and Hamburg during the final week of January, bringing the month's tally to eight operations. A further eight operations were completed in February, including trips to Turin and Milan in Italy, and Cologne, each twice, and Wilhelmshaven and Nuremberg. When Munro flew to St Nazaire on the last night of the month it was as a Flight Lieutenant, and he began the month of March with a return to Berlin on the 1/2nd and Hamburg on the 3/4th. Two nights later the Ruhr offensive began at Essen, but Munro and crew sat this one out, and remained off the order of battle until the 11/12th, when they, like many of the future 617 Squadron recruits, went to Stuttgart. The crew's final operation with 97 Squadron was flown against St Nazaire on the 22/23rd, and they were posted to Scampton to join 617 Squadron on the 25th.

Born in Brooklyn, New York in 1919, big, blond-haired Joe McCarthy enlisted in the RCAF before America became involved in the war. He qualified as a pilot on the 24th of September 1941 in Canada, and arrived in England in January 1942 to continue his training. A period at 14 OTU ended in August, and a posting followed to 97 Squadron Conversion Flight on the 6th of September. 97 Squadron was stationed at Woodhall Spa, while its Conversion Flight was just a few miles away at Coningsby, home until the end of the month of 106 Squadron, and it is likely, that McCarthy came to the attention of Gibson during this brief period. His first few flights were on Manchesters, but a S/L Stenner introduced him to the Lancaster on the 9th of September. The names of Sgts Radcliffe and Batson as members of his regular crew appear in his logbook for the first time on the 11th of September, and Sgt Eaton is mentioned on the 14th. McCarthy's training schedule is signed on the 1st of October by S/L 'Darkie' Hallows, who had been a member of the 97 Squadron element for the epic Augsburg raid mentioned earlier. Contact during their training with veterans such as Hallows and

Nettleton, not to mention the scores of other tour expired 'bomber boys', must have influenced for the better those preparing to follow in their footsteps. McCarthy's first operation with 97 Squadron was against Krefeld on the 2/3rd of October, when he flew as second pilot to a F/O Kier with four of his own crew on board. His first operation as captain came just three nights later against Aachen, but as he never specified the individual members of his crew, it is not clear when his entire dams team came together. Certainly by the 4th of February 1943 only the navigator, F/S McLean, was missing from his crew list, but he was also a member of 97 Squadron, currently flying with a F/L Tew. McCarthy's tour with 97 Squadron continued through the winter of 1942, during which he crossed the Alps to Italy on a number of occasions. His tour ended on the night of the 22/23rd of March 1943, when the French port of St Nazaire was the target, and this brought his total, according to his logbook, to thirty operations plus three early returns. He was signed off by his flight commander, S/L Ken Burns, another of the Command's outstanding characters. Within a month of McCarthy's departure to 617 Squadron, 97 Squadron would be posted to the Pathfinders, where Burns was to become one of the 'Master Bomber' fraternity, a select group of highly experienced and talented men given the responsibility of controlling operations from the air like a ringmaster in a circus. The role model for this as yet untested procedure would be Gibson during the forthcoming attack on the dams. On the last night of August during a heavy raid on Berlin, Burns, by then a Wing Commander, would be blown out of his Lancaster as one of five survivors of his crew, and lose a hand in the process. After repatriation he would continue his flying career with a false hand. Back, though, to McCarthy, and before the month was out he was at Scampton and undertaking his first training flight with 617 Squadron.

David Maltby was born in 1920. His family came from Margate in Kent, and his father was a headmaster. Maltby junior was educated at Marlborough College, and is remembered as a shy and modest young man, who displayed a determination and steadfastness of purpose. These were attributes, which would stand him in good stead, and along with his natural generosity, would make him a popular colleague and an inspiration to those around him. He trained as a mining engineer, partly because the air underground was considered beneficial for his asthma, but his career was interrupted by the onset of war. He enlisted on the 4th of September 1939, keeping his asthma a secret, but had a frustrating wait until the following year before his call-up came. He was married in May 1942 in the church at Wickhambreux in north Kent, where his in-laws were fruit growers. By coincidence his wife's sister owned a house in Woodhall Spa, where he and his wife lived while he served his tour with 97 Squadron. He had just returned to 97 Squadron for a second tour when his posting to 617 Squadron came about.

49 Squadron supplied the services of Sgts Townsend and Anderson. Townsend was born in Gloucestershire in January 1921, and was educated at Monmouth School, where he became head boy and captained the rugby

football team. It had always been his intention to join the Indian Army, but his application was deferred initially because of over-subscription. He was eventually called up to join the Royal Artillery on his twentieth birthday, but he found life less satisfying than expected, and volunteered to transfer to the RAF for pilot training. His new life began on the 14th of May 1941, and during the course of the next thirteen months he progressed through various training units, overcoming a tendency towards airsickness in the process. His training was completed at 16 OTU at Upper Heyford, from where he took part in his first operational sorties, the Thousand Bomber Raids on Cologne and Essen. He was posted to 49 Squadron at Scampton on the 12th of June 1942, and spent his first few months on the Conversion Flight learning to fly Manchesters and Lancasters. He began operations with the squadron in September, and by the time he joined 617 Squadron, his tally stood at twenty-seven. In contrast to Townsend, who was about to finish his tour, Anderson had only just started, having arrived from 1654 Conversion Unit (CU) on the 23rd of February. His posting to 617 Squadron was received on the 24th of March, and one has to question his selection, when so many more experienced candidates were available. He remained at 49 Squadron until early April to get a few operations under his belt, and his first two were flown as second pilot to Sgt Barney Gumbley, who would himself join 617 Squadron later in the war and lose his life shortly before the end. They attacked Nuremberg on the 25/26th of February and Cologne twenty-four hours later. Anderson and his crew operated together for the first time against Essen on the 12/13th of March, and returned on three engines. They went to St Nazaire on the 22/23rd, Duisburg on the 26/27th and Berlin on the 27/28th. Two nights later they were bound for Berlin again, but were forced to turn back after the air speed indicator failed.

F/L Barlow, an Australian from Melbourne, was a graduate of the Commonwealth Air Training Plan, and began a tour with 61 Squadron in the autumn of 1942. At almost 32 years of age he was one of a number of more senior pilots to be posted to 617 Squadron. Having brought a badly damaged Lancaster home on a number of occasions, 'Norm' Barlow had become regarded as a press-on type. At least two of his own crew, flight engineer, Sgt Sam Whillis, and bomb-aimer, Sgt Alan Gillespie, came to Scampton with him, and the other members of his dams crew were also recruited from 61 Squadron. His wireless operator, F/O Williams, was another of the 30+ brigade, and was actually in his thirty-fifth year, having been born in Queensland, Australia in 1909. He hoped to be retained by 61 Squadron as a non-flying signals officer at the conclusion of his tour, now just two trips away, and there is a suggestion that he and other members of this crew were 'sold' on the move to 617 Squadron, on the basis of doing just one more operation rather than two.

Two crews were posted in from 44 (Rhodesia) Squadron, those of F/L H.S. Wilson and F/S Ken Brown. Harold Wilson, in his late twenties, was another who was a little older than the average member of aircrew being posted in. In the rank of Pilot Officer he arrived at Waddington from 1654 CU with all but one of his future 617 Squadron crew three days before Christmas 1942. Air gunner Sgt Payne was posted in from 1660 CU to join them on the 1st of January 1943. Wilson's first operation was as second pilot to a F/O Walker on the 8th of January 1943, when Duisburg was the target for 1 and 5 Group Lancasters as part of the Oboe trials programme. He flew as crew captain for the first time against Cologne on the night of the 2/3rd of February, and forty-eight hours later carried a bomb bay full of 4lb incendiaries to Turin. A trip to Lorient was followed by a raid on Wilhelmshaven on the 11/12th, during which, two enemy night fighters were evaded through the excellent work of both gunners. Other operations in February took Wilson and his crew to Bremen, Nuremberg, Cologne and St Nazaire, although Sgt Payne was substituted for the last three of these, possibly through illness. The destination for the crew on the 1/2nd of March was Berlin, and then came the opening salvo of the Ruhr campaign at Essen on the night of the 5/6th, to be followed by Munich on the 9/10th and the second Essen raid on the 12/13th. This, Wilson's final operation with 44 Squadron, almost ended in a collision with a Ju88, but good co-operation between pilot and mid-upper gunner saved the day. This brought Wilson's operations tally to thirteen, by which time he was a Flying Officer. He and his crew were among the first to be posted to 617 Squadron, on the 24th, and he probably arrived at Scampton as an acting Flight Lieutenant.

Ken Brown was born in Saskatchewan, Canada, in August 1920, and joined the RCAF in 1941. He arrived in England in May 1942, where his training continued at various conversion units, culminating in a spell at 1654 CU at Wigsley. He was posted with his crew to 44 (Rhodesia) Squadron at Waddington on the 5th of February 1943, and operated for the first time on the night of the 11/12th, when flying to Wilhelmshaven as second pilot to a S/L Whitehead. Two nights later he went to Lorient as 'second dickey' to a F/S Raymond, and then waited an entire month before operating for the first time as crew captain. On the 9/10th of March he took part in a moderately effective attack on Munich, which was followed on the 11/12th by the many times already mentioned operation to Stuttgart, Gibson's last with 106 Squadron. Like Gibson's, Brown's Lancaster also suffered technical problems on this night, when his port-inner engine failed and his starboard outer overheated, forcing him to return early after jettisoning his bomb load. On his next sortie, to St Nazaire on the 22/23rd, he was let down by the starboard-inner engine, and again returned early having dumped his bombs in the sea. On the 26/27th he completed a trip to Duisburg as part of the ongoing Ruhr offensive, and went to the 'Big City', Berlin, on the following night, before being posted to 617 Squadron on the 29th.

P/O Byers, also a Canadian, came from 467 Squadron, RAAF, and was yet another mature man, having attained 32 years of age. He was already 30 when he joined the RCAF, and was probably close to the upper age limit for new recruits. He arrived at 467 Squadron from 1654 Conversion Unit on the

5th of February 1943, along with two of his dams crew, flight engineer Sgt Taylor, and wireless operator Sgt Wilkinson. While at 1654 CU he flew on four occasions with 'Mick' Martin, who was instructing there at the time. It seems, that Byers filled the remaining crew positions with spare bods who had been at 467 Squadron since November 1942. By the time of Byer's posting to 617 Squadron he had managed to get four operations under his belt, including a mining sortie, a trip to Stuttgart with an unserviceable rear turret, and a raid on St Nazaire.

P/O Warner Ottley was born in Battersea, London in 1923, and was educated at Hurstpierpoint College on the south coast. At the time of his service with Bomber Command he was resident in Letchworth in Hertfordshire, although his parents lived at Herne Bay in Kent. Coincidentally, his rear gunner, Sgt Fred Tees, also lived in Letchworth. Despite being one of the youngest pilots to join 617 Squadron, he had completed a full tour of operations with 207 Squadron, and the citation for his DFC, which was gazetted posthumously in June 1945, confirms that he was a press-on type, referring to an attack on Wilhelmshaven, when he made three runs across the target to ensure accuracy, and a gardening (mining) sortie, during which his aircraft was damaged by flak ships. Ottley is said to have applied for a posting to the Pathfinder Force on completion of his tour with 207 Squadron, but with no vacancy existing, he then approached Gibson personally. It is inconceivable, however, that no room could be found in the Pathfinder Force for such an experienced pilot. Shannon had just been posted to Wyton for PFF training, and as has already been stated, W/C 'Hamish' Mahaddie was employed full time specifically to recruit crews on an on-going basis to compensate for the almost nightly attrition. Ottley's reputation as a 'press-on type' would have had Mahaddie beating a path to his door, so we are forced to conclude that his application to join 8 Group was either a myth, or, perhaps, it coincided with a personal approach to Gibson, who got in with the first offer.

As already established, three members of Gibson's crew, Taerum, Spafford and Trevor-Roper, arrived via the 50 Squadron academy and 1654 CU, while his wireless operator, Bob Hutchison, was well known to Gibson from his 106 days. His flight engineer, Sgt John Pulford, who was posted in in early April, and about whom Gibson made only belittling comments, had served previously with 97 Squadron. Front gunner, George Deering, whom Gibson described in *Enemy Coast Ahead* as green, had actually completed a first tour, and Operation Chastise would be his thirty-sixth sortie. His previous operations had been undertaken on Wellingtons with 1 Group's 103 Squadron, which he joined from 21 OTU on the 16th of August 1941. After screening he went to 22 OTU, on the 11th of May 1942, and took part in one or more of the thousand bomber raids.

It will be noted, that of the established 5 Group units, 9 Squadron was the only one from whose ranks pilots were not drawn, but Sgt Hill, who would fly to the dams as Maltby's front gunner was posted in from there on the 7th of May. Operation Chastise would be Hill's twenty-third operation.

These, then, were some of the men who became founder members of the most famous squadron in RAF history. It is not possible in this chapter to detail every one, but all were brave young men, and each was someone's son, husband, father or brother. All would survive the period leading to the operation, an achievement in itself, but not all would see the training through to the end. Of those who did, not all would take part in the historic operation, and of those who went all the way, many would not come back. Among those who did return were many who would not live to see the peace for which they had fought so bravely.

Chapter Three

Harris the Impresario

Because of the nature of 617 Squadron's wartime career, in which it acted almost exclusively as an independent unit, and in view of the outstanding success it achieved, it is all too easy to lose sight of what was going on around it. Its reputation for excellence was legitimately earned, but it was never part of the nightly grind, which was the lot of the other heavy squadrons. It was only because of the existence of these, hammering away night after night in the various campaigns, that 617 Squadron could retain its independence, and be guaranteed the very best in crews, most of whom had been tempered in the heat of battle with these squadrons of the line. It is right, therefore, to put 617 Squadron within the context of the Command as a whole, and to see the wider picture of contemporary events, while also tracing the development of the bomber offensive under the direction of Air Chief Marshall Sir Arthur Harris.

While the formation and progress towards operational readiness of 617 Squadron had been taking place, the other heavy squadrons of Bomber Command were embroiled in the Ruhr offensive. A number of 617 Squadron's crews had actually participated in the first two rounds of this, on the 5/6th and 12/13th of March, both of which were directed with great success at Essen. This was the first offensive for which the Command was genuinely equipped and prepared, and it would signal the end for the hitherto elusive towns and cities of the region, which had always managed to hide beneath an ever-present cloak of industrial haze. Harris had been trying to deliver a decisive blow against Essen in particular, ever since taking up the reins of Bomber Command over twelve months earlier. Thus far, however, almost every attempt had resulted in bombs being sprayed liberally around the region, and never once had he achieved anything like the concentration necessary to destroy an urban target. He had arrived at the helm of Bomber Command on the 22nd of February 1942 to find it at its lowest ebb since the war began. Just six months earlier the Butt Report had sent shock waves reverberating around the corridors of Whitehall, when it revealed for the first time the inadequacies of the bomber offensive thus far. Rather than bringing Germany to its knees as the propagandists suggested, Bomber Command had wasted most of its effort, and had managed to get only one bomb in ten within five miles of the intended targets. In return it had lost hundreds of aircraft and the cream of its pre-war airmen, and ever since, powerful voices had been calling for its dissolution and the redistribution of its aircraft to other causes, principally the *U-Boot* war in the Atlantic and to reverse recent setbacks in the Middle East. Since November 1941 the Command had existed under a cloud, and had been allowed to carry out only limited operations while its future was being considered at the highest level.

Harris's first task was to save the Command from the vultures. He did now at least have in his armoury the Area Bombing Directive, which had been issued by the Air Ministry eight days before his enthronement, and although he was not, as many people mistakenly believe, the architect of the policy, he was among its fiercest advocates. Area bombing had, of course, been engaged in from the beginning of strategic bombing shortly after German forces had rolled through the Ardennes and into France, Luxembourg, Holland and Belgium. Publicly, of course, the Command had only ever attacked military and war production targets within urban areas. Now there would be no pretence, and Harris could pursue his quest to win the war by bombing alone. He took up his post as C-in-C with firm ideas already in place about how to achieve this, and gradually, over the remainder of 1942, he oversaw the development of tactics and technology, which would lead him to the Ruhr and beyond. This had culminated in an unprecedented series of highly effective operations during a two-week period in September 1942, and if any period in the Command's evolution to effectiveness could be identified as the turning point, then, perhaps, this had been it.

Harris had realized from the start, that to deal effectively with an urban target, it was necessary to overwhelm the defences. From the outset, he dispensed with his predecessor's system of small-scale raids on multiple targets, and introduced the bomber stream, which pushed the maximum number of aircraft across an aiming point in the shortest possible time. He also knew that built-up areas are most efficiently destroyed by fire rather than blast, and the bomb loads carried by his aircraft soon reflected this thinking. Major successes against Lübeck at the end of March 1942, and Rostock a month later, were outstanding examples of fire-raising and city busting, and were a foretaste of the devastation inflicted on Cologne by Operation Millennium at the end of May. Although the two subsequent Thousand Bomber Raids were disappointing in comparison, Harris had made his point, and the basis of all future operations had been established. The advent of the Pathfinder Force in August added a new dimension, and the pioneering work with the Mosquito-borne Oboe blind bombing device carried out by one of its founder units, 109 Squadron, during the remainder of the year, was to prove absolutely critical in the current campaign. It was this technological breakthrough, which allowed navigators and bomb-aimers to pinpoint Essen and Duisburg, and all the other cities and towns in Germany's heartland, which were so vitally important to its capacity to wage war. With Oboe up his sleeve, and a predominantly four-engine, genuinely heavy bomber force at his disposal, Harris could now embark with abandon on his quest to dismantle Germany and win the war by bombing alone.

As already mentioned, the Ruhr campaign began on the night of the 5/6th of March, and participating in this operation, but later with 617 Squadron, were the crews of the then F/O Wilson, Sgt Townsend, F/L Knight, F/L Astell, F/L Barlow and F/S Burpee. Also on the order of battle were other future 617 Squadron stalwarts, F/L Allsebrook, Sgt Gumbley, P/O Cockshott, F/L Youseman and F/L Suggitt. It is sad to relate, and indicative of the casualty rate within Bomber Command that of the eleven pilots mentioned above only Townsend and Cockshott were to survive the remaining two years of war. The raid on this night destroyed over 3,000 houses, and damaged fifty-three buildings within the giant Krupp complex, and when the operation was repeated a week later, a 30 per cent greater degree of damage was inflicted on the buildings of this munitions-producing giant. On the 26/27th equipment failure among a large proportion of the Oboe Mosquito element led to a disappointing raid on Duisburg, and this city would continue to lead a comparatively charmed life until only days before 617 Squadron went to war for the first time.

April proved to be the least rewarding month of the Ruhr period, largely because of the number of operations directed at targets outside of the region, and beyond the range of Oboe. It began promisingly enough, though, with another successful tilt at Essen on the 3/4th, when over six hundred buildings were destroyed. Duisburg again escaped serious damage on the 8/9th and 9/10th, before operations to other regions of Germany resulted in a failure at Frankfurt on the 10/11th, and only modest success at Stuttgart on the 14/15th. An attempt to bomb the Skoda armaments works at Pilsen in Czechoslovakia on the 16/17th was a dismal failure for the loss of thirty-six Lancasters and Halifaxes, and a diversionary operation against Mannheim on the same night cost a further eighteen Wellingtons, Stirlings and Halifaxes. This brought the night's total to a new record casualty figure of fifty-four aircraft. A massive area in the centre of Stettin was devastated on the 20/21st, and then a moderately effective attack was delivered on Duisburg on the 26/27th. The month closed at Essen on the night of the 30th, and although this was a useful raid, it fell short of the success of the earlier efforts. A record non-one thousand force of 596 aircraft took off for Dortmund to open May's account on the 4/5th, and those reaching the target destroyed over 1,200 buildings. Duisburg finally succumbed to an outstandingly accurate and concentrated attack on the 12/13th, when almost 1,600 buildings were reduced to rubble, and 60,000 tons of shipping was sunk or seriously damaged in the inland port. Bochum suffered a moderately damaging assault on the following night, before a nine-day lull in main force operations allowed the crews a welcome rest. It was during this period, that 617 Squadron was to earn itself a place in aviation history, with its famous feat of arms against some of Germany's principal dams.

CHAPTER FOUR

Rehearsals

Training for the performance, while trials of the props continue back stage

Such, then, were the events forming the backcloth to 617 Squadron's conception and early life. These operations were providing the headlines in the newspapers read daily by the squadron members. They would be thinking about the participation of their colleagues recently left behind. They would hear familiar names among the ranks of the missing as news filtered through from other stations, and they would talk in the messes with 57 Squadron aircrew about the previous night's operation. For the newly arrived 617 Squadron recruits, however, the next six weeks were to bring no operations, and this would be a source of intrigue to the 57 Squadron boys, and an excuse to engage in good-natured sniping at their 'armchair' neighbours. An intense programme of concentrated training was about to begin in standard Lancasters borrowed for the occasion. Some of the crews posted in to Scampton brought a Lancaster with them to make up an initial complement of ten on loan pending the delivery of the modified variant some weeks hence. Allocated to A Flight were; W4921, which arrived from 106 Squadron on the 26th of March, eventually to be coded AJ-C, W4929, which was also taken on charge on the 26th from 61 Squadron as AJ-J, W4940 AJ-B from 57 Squadron on the 27th, ED756 AJ-H from 49 Squadron on the 30th and ED763 AJ-D from 467 Squadron on the 2nd of April. B Flight received W4926 as AJ-Z from 97 Squadron, LM309 as AJ-X from 9 Squadron, ED329 as AJ-T from 207 Squadron, ED437 as AJ-N from 50 Squadron and ED735 as AJ-R from 44 Squadron, all on the 27th. ED437 was recoded to AJ-V eight days later. It will be noted, that each Squadron donated one aircraft, and it seems, that for a few days at least, they were flown with their old codes.

On the evening of the 26th Gibson and Whitworth walked into the officers' bar to mingle for the first time with those pilots and other aircrew officers that had thus far assembled, although by no means the entire complement had yet done so. There is no question, that the gathering of such a high proportion of officers in a new squadron was unusual, and inevitably gave rise to much speculation. Equally inevitable were the questions from those present about what lay ahead. Gibson fielded the requests for information by claiming to know less than they, but added that a briefing on the morrow would reveal something of the squadron's purpose. The passage dealing with the informal gathering in the mess in *Enemy Coast Ahead* further reveals Gibson's pride in being a 'Bomber Boy'. He describes,

> ... a babbling of conversation and the hum of shop being happily exchanged, of old faces, old names, targets, bases and of bombs. This was the conversation that only fliers can talk, and by that I don't mean movie fliers. These were real living chaps who had all done their stuff. By their eyes you could see that. But they were ready for more. These were the aces of Bomber Command.

At the first official briefing on the following morning Gibson stood before his charges and revealed to them what little he could, the gist of which, according to *Enemy Coast Ahead*, was as follows.

They had all been wondering what this was all about, and he couldn't tell them. He could say, however, that they were here to do a special job, and they had been brought together as a crack squadron to carry out a raid on Germany, which, he'd been told, would have startling results. Some said it might even shorten the war. What the target was he couldn't tell them, nor could he tell them where it was. All he could tell them was, that they would have to practice low flying day and night until they could do it with their eyes shut. If he told them to fly to a tree in the middle of England, he would expect them to be able to do it. If he told them to fly through a hangar, they would have to do it, even though their wingtips might hit each side. Discipline and secrecy were absolutely vital, and it was obvious, that they were going to be talked about. It was very unusual to have such a crack crowd of boys in one squadron, and there was bound to be a lot of rumour, he'd heard some already. It was up to them to stop these rumours, to say nothing! When they went into pubs at night, they had to keep their mouths shut! When boys from other squadrons asked them what they were doing, they were just to tell them to mind their own business, because of all things in this game security was the greatest factor. If we can surprise the enemy everything will be fine, but if they're ready for us ... He allowed the men to come to their own conclusions on that question.

Then it was Whitworth's turn to address the gathering, and he did so in a way that Gibson found impressive. Whitworth alluded to the feature film *In Which We Serve*, citing the scene in which Noel Coward as the ship's captain asks the assembled crew what makes a good ship. A seaman calls out, 'A happy ship, Sir'. Whitworth said, that he wanted to create a happy ship situation at Scampton. He invoked the frequently used Bomber Command verb to bind, and promised the men, that if they didn't bind him, he wouldn't bind them.

It was on the 27th that Gibson received a memorandum from G/C Satterly, the Senior Air Staff Officer at 5 Group HQ, Grantham. The document outlined the training programme for the squadron, and mentioned that a number of lightly defended targets were to be attacked, necessitating low-level navigation in moonlight, giving visibility of about one mile over enemy territory. The final approach to the target would be at 100 feet at about 240 mph. Crews were to be trained to meet the following requirements by the 10th of May.

(1) Accurate navigation under moonlight/simulated moonlight conditions at a height which would give best immunity from fighter attack.
(2) A final approach to the target at a height of 100 feet and approx. 240 mph. 'It will be convenient to practice this over water.'
(3) Bomb release to be carried out visually at an estimated range gauged either by a landmark on a nearby shore, or by timing a run from a given landmark.

An accuracy of plus or minus 40 yards was required. It was suggested, that the training requirements could best be met by routes laid over an area south-east of the Wash extending to the north Midlands or the mountainous region of North Wales, with training for the final approach taking place over one of the many reservoirs in these areas. A list of nine lakes was appended including some nearer to Scampton for use when weather conditions prevented a trip to the more distant ones. Among these bodies of water were Lakes Bala and Vyrnwy in Wales, and reservoirs at Frewston and Goathwaite near Bradford, another to the west of Darlington, and three in Leicestershire at Cropston, Thornton and Shepshed (Blackbrook). None of those used for the final dress rehearsals was mentioned on this list. The memorandum went on to say, that the routes should be planned to avoid passing near any point defended by light anti-aircraft guns, and when training by day, the pilot and bomb-aimer should wear dark goggles with the correct lenses to simulate moonlight conditions. A safety pilot should be carried, who would mark the actual track flown, to provide assessment of the standard of navigation achieved.

Although training for the forthcoming operation was formally to begin on the 31st, the first squadron flight occurred on that very afternoon of the 27th, when Astell took off at 15.30 in W4940 to carry out a two-hour photographic survey of lakes. As far as 617 Squadron personnel were concerned, this flight was undertaken at the behest of AVM Cochrane to work out cross-country routes for the OTUs, and 617 was the only squadron available with time on its hands to carry out the job. At 11.30 on the following morning Astell and his crew undertook another trip in the same aircraft with the same purpose, only this time at high level, but cloud rendered the exercise ineffective. Gibson took Young and Hopgood for a trip to Derwent Reservoir late that afternoon in W4940 to assess the problems of estimating height over water.

During daylight it proved to be relatively simple, but at dusk, when the horizon became indistinct, they almost hit the surface of the lake. On the 29th, Astell flew a cross-country of around two hours duration, and Gibson met with Cochrane to have the targets revealed to him at last. He was shown painstakingly prepared models of the Möhne, Eder and Sorpe reservoirs and dams, and was cautioned to keep the information to himself.

The Möhne reservoir lies twenty-five miles east of Dortmund, in a beautiful hilly region a few miles beyond the industrial Ruhr and south of the small town of Soest. The huge dam, at the time the largest in Europe, took four years to construct and was completed in 1913. It stands at the northwestern corner of the reservoir, a gentle arc of concrete and masonry stretching 850 yards across the valley, with its twenty-five-foot wide crest and roadway standing 120 feet above the bedrock to which the structure is anchored. At its base the dam is more than 100 feet thick, and after each year's spring rains its gravity and form alone hold in check around 140 million tons of water. Although never seriously considered by the German authorities to be a potential target, the dam face was protected by two substantial torpedo nets that were suspended from wooden booms and reached the lakebed. A matter of days before the war broke out a Ruhr city official had written to the authorities raising the matter of protection for the dams in the event of attack from the air, and he had at first been politely humoured. After about three years of correspondence, however, and a number of testy responses to the constant nagging, a few 20mm flak pieces were sent to the Möhne in the hope that that would put an end to the matter. In contrast, no one believed the Eder dam required a defence. It lies in equally beautiful but more rugged terrain some sixty miles to the south-east of the Möhne, and is enfolded in high hills providing natural protection. The Eder was completed in 1914, and although only half the span of the Möhne, it stands 25 feet higher, with a 20 foot wide crest and 119 foot base. The Eder reservoir was the largest in Germany and at its fullest contains 200,000,000 tons of water. The Sorpe reservoir is situated nine miles to the south-west of the Möhne and has perhaps the most picturesque setting of all. Its dam offered an altogether different set of problems to the men preparing a plan of attack. The Sorpe is not a masonry structure but a giant earthen rampart with a triangular cross section supporting a concrete core. It took eight years to build and was completed in 1935. It is 700 yards in length, stands a massive 200 feet high with a narrow roadway forming its crest, and holds back around 70,000,000 tons of water.

Thus far, apart from Gibson, only Astell and crew had flown any kind of sortie, but most of the others got into the air before the month ended, flying a mixture of high and low level cross-country routes. As the full complement of aircraft had not yet arrived, and while ground crews swarmed over those that had, McCarthy and Townsend took advantage of the only lull in the training programme to grab some leave for themselves and their crews.

The main concerns for the forthcoming operation involved navigation and the accurate delivery of the weapon from a predetermined height. Low-level navigation at night was a major problem, and Gibson made this the first priority of the training schedule. Initially, the minimum height for training flights was set at 150 feet, and ten standard routes were laid out, although, in time, three would be used to simulate the actual flight to the targets. Over the ensuing weeks the crews were to plough these increasingly familiar furrows. The second phase of training would address the need to fly across relatively calm water at a height of 150 feet, for which there would be no help from cockpit instruments. The problems of sighting and establishing a correct bomb release height were eventually solved through simple expedients. The Dann sight, a wooden hand-held triangular device boasting two nails to represent the towers on the dams and a peephole would provide the bomb-aimers with a precise point of release, although some bomb-aimers elected to use an alternative and more stable system of sighting, employing chinagraph marks on their clear vision panels instead of the nails, and a triangulation of string attached to nuts either side of the Perspex nose.

To gauge height a calibrated spotlight altimeter was fitted, a First World War system resurrected in 1941 for use by Coastal Command. It consisted of converging spotlight beams, but it had proved to be ineffective over the sea because of the choppiness of the surface. Benjamin Lockspeiser of the Ministry of Aircraft Production recalled the trials, and suggested the system might work on the calmer waters of a lake. It required the installation of a standard Aldis lamp in the redundant camera position under the bomb-aimer's compartment, angled downwards and outwards to leave a circle of light on the surface of the water ahead of the starboard wing leading edge. A second lamp fitted in the ventral gun fairing was angled downwards and forwards to create a second circle of light, which at the prescribed height touched the first to form a figure of eight at right angles to the fuselage. Assuming the aircraft had to descend to achieve the release height, the front spot would appear to remain still, while the rear one moved backwards from a position diagonally ahead to the right until the two pools of light came together. In the unlikely event that the aircraft had to climb to gain the correct release height, the rear spot would appear to move forward diagonally to the right until coming together with the front one. On the 4th of April Maudslay took W4926 to Farnborough to have the spotlights fitted. He returned to Scampton on the 8th, and demonstrated the system to other members of the squadron. Other standard Lancasters, W4921, W4940 and ED756 were fitted with spotlights at Scampton by the squadron's own electricians.

From the outset training was comprehensive, and frequently required half or more of the squadron to take to the air each day. The first week of April saw crews flying trips of between two and five hours, which often involved dropping a number of practice bombs, some by the pilot using his release handle in the cockpit, and the rest by the bomb-aimer. A total of 665 practice bombs were dropped between the 2nd and the 8th, Rice producing A Flight's best result with an average error of 36 yards, while Knight managed 32 for B Flight. The average error for the squadron was 50.5 yards. As a late arrival on the squadron Ottley flew only one five-hour exercise during the period, and dropped twelve practice bombs with an average error of 57 yards. It was at this time that Lovell's crew was deemed to be below the required standard and was sent back to 57 Squadron. Their performance was by no means the worst in the squadron, but Lovell had spent some of his spell at 617 Squadron in sickbay, and this might have been taken into consideration. P/O Divall and crew were posted in from 57 Squadron on the 10th as replacements. Midway through the second week of April suitable moon conditions allowed night flying to begin. The weather generally was good and this enabled flying to take place on each day between the 9th and 15th. Bombing accuracy was gradually improving, and by mid month the average error in yards hovered between the high 30s and low 40s. It was at this time that pilots relinquished the role of releasing bombs in favour of their bomb-aimers, most of whom had decided for themselves which sighting method to adopt. The best performance was achieved by F/S Clifford, the bomb-aimer in F/S Lancaster's crew, who managed an amazing average error of just 4 yards with six bombs. Despite this, Gibson considered the navigator to be suspect, and Lancaster was given the choice of replacing him or leaving the squadron. The close-knit nature of a bomber crew persuaded him to choose the latter option, and they undertook the short journey back across the tarmac to their former unit on the 17th. By the end of the third week of April the gunners had loosed off some 42,000 rounds of .303 ammunition over the sea, and it had been decided in the interests of comfort that the smaller of a crew's gunners should occupy the front turret. It was further decided to equip the turret with stirrups to prevent his feet from dangling into the bomb-aimer's compartment and distracting him.

Typical of the training schedule for the period was that followed by Shannon, who flew route 1 in W4929 on the 6th of April. This involved a trip from Base to Sudbury – Langham, then to a point over the North Sea at 53°30′N–02°00′E – Flamborough Head near Bridlington on the Yorkshire coast – Ripon – a lake at 53°23′N–00°46′E, where a bombing run was carried out, and thence to Didcot – Wainfleet and back to Scampton. The round trip lasted five hours, as did route 2, which Shannon undertook on the 8th, also in W4940. This led from Scampton to Stafford – Llanwddyn – Lake Vyrnwy – Caldy Isle – Porthleven – Wells – Halstead – Potter – Heigham – Wainfleet and back to Scampton. Route 3, which Shannon flew in W4929 on the 11th, encompassed Scampton – Shrewsbury – Bromyard – Haslemere – Malmsbury – Wainfleet, thence to a point over the North Sea at 54°40′–00°00′ – Thirsk – Base, and this was completed in four hours twenty-five minutes.

Also on the 11th Young and Rice flew to the Empire Central Flying School at Hullavington in ED763 to have the simulated night-flying system installed. Known as the day/night flying system it consisted of blue Perspex panels fitted inside the glasshouse, which in combination with amber goggles worn by the pilot gave the impression of a moonlit night. The system, which was not yet in service use, had been checked out by Young on the 31st of March, and endorsed by Gibson after he examined samples brought back by Young to Scampton. Three other standard aircraft, W4929, ED735 and ED756, subsequently had the system installed, as eventually did ED934, one of the Type 464 Provisioning Lancasters specially modified for the operation. Shannon's schedule continued on the 13th, when route 1 was flown at low level in formation. The 14th was a busy day requiring of Shannon and his crew a night flying test (NFT), a fighter affiliation exercise, beam flying and a low-level night cross-country on route 1. There was no more flying for Shannon then until the 19th, when he and his crew undertook a low-level night cross-country via route 2 again in W4929. On the 21st Shannon got his hands on ED763, one of the Lancasters fitted with the day/night system, and took it on a cross-country trip over route 2. On the 24th and 25th the crew undertook low-level practice bombing at Wainfleet in a standard Lancaster, while on the 27th spotlight altimeter runs were made over the wash in W4940 with Ottley and Byers on board along with some of the former's crew.

Gibson had made as one of his first tasks the removal of the Bomber Command appointed adjutant, F/L Pain, who was posted to 18 OTU during week ending Friday 2nd of April. Gibson apparently decided very quickly that Pain was unsuitable, it is believed because he was too old, and in his place on the 24th of March, probably the day Pain actually departed the post, he brought in acting F/L Humphries from Syerston, whom he knew from his 106 Squadron days. Humphries was a bespectacled 28 year old, who had wanted to fly, but had failed to meet the physical requirements. To compensate for the disappointment he set out to become the best adjutant he could be, and his excellent relationship with Gibson demonstrated his success in achieving that goal.

Delivery of the modified Type 464 Provisioning Lancasters began on the 8th of April, when the first prototype, ED765/G, left the Avro factory at Woodford, Manchester bound for the Royal Aircraft Establishment at Farnborough, where it would remain until July. The external appearance of the normally aesthetically pleasing Lancaster had been radically altered by the removal of the bomb doors and the addition of a fairing at each end of the bomb bay. A spring-loaded V shaped calliper arm extending downwards on each side of the fuselage held the mine in position, and allowed it to be rotated backwards by means of a belt drive attached to a hydraulic motor mounted on the fuselage floor. A further modification was the removal of the mid-upper turret and fairing to save weight. The second prototype, ED817/G, left the factory on the 16th, and went to Manston on the 20th, from where it would carry out drop testing off the beach at Reculver. It eventually arrived at Scampton on the 30th to be coded AJ-C. ED825/G, the 3rd prototype, departed the factory on the 17th, and was at Boscombe Down by the 22nd. Its delivery to Scampton as AJ-T would not take place until the very afternoon of Operation Chastise. The original intention had been to deliver the modified aircraft from the factory to Farnborough for acceptance trials by Vickers, who had manufactured the additional parts, and to whom the Type 464 Provisioning designation belonged. The initial batch of production aircraft seems to have followed this route, until time overtook the process and aircraft were delivered directly to Scampton. ED864/G left the factory on the 18th and arrived at Scampton on the 22nd to become AJ-B. It was followed by ED865/G and ED887/G, AJ-S and AJ-A respectively, which were flown out of Woodford in the hands of Avro test pilots on the 19th, and touched down at Scampton on the 22nd. The 21st saw three aircraft leave the factory, two of them, ED886/G and ED909/G, going directly to Scampton, where they were given the codes AJ-O and AJ-P respectively, while ED906, AJ-J, stopped off elsewhere and only reached Scampton on the 23rd. It was the 25th before the next pair arrived, ED910/G, which would share the AJ-C code with ED817/G, and ED915/G, AJ-Q. ED921/G came in on the 27th as AJ-W, and the following day saw the arrival of ED918/G and ED925/G as AJ-F and AJ-M. ED924/G, AJ-Y was delivered on the 29th, ED929/G, AJ-L, and ED932/G, AJ-G on the 30th, while ED912/G, ED927/G and ED934/G were taken on charge on the 1st of May as AJ-N, AJ-E and AJ-K respectively. ED933/G and ED936/G became resident on the 2nd as AJ-X and AJ-H, and ED937/G, AJ-Z, arrived two days later to make up a full complement of twenty-one aircraft. On the Avro daily movement sheets the destination of these aircraft was shown as a question mark.

More problematic than any of the issues being resolved at Scampton was the weapon itself, which came to be known as the 'bouncing bomb', but was, in fact, a revolving depth charge with an ability to skip. Testing of a smaller version of Upkeep had been in progress since December 1942, but development of the full-sized weapon did not begin in earnest until the nod was given for the operation to take place. Trials began on the 13th of April, at which time even the shape of the casing was still in doubt. Originally encased in a wooden spherical skin with flattened poles, it proved unable to withstand the impact with water, even when the release height was reduced from 150 to a dangerously low 60 feet. Nevertheless, on occasions, even as the wooden outer skin disintegrated in a mass of spray and splinters, the oil drum-shaped bomb, 59⅞ inches long and 50 inches in diameter, retained the capacity to travel horizontally across the surface of the water. A backspin of 500 revolutions per minute was designed both to assist the mine's ability to bounce, and to help it maintain contact with the dam wall as it sank to its hydrostatically controlled detonation depth of 30 feet. On the 24th of April Gibson flew down to Weybridge to meet with Wallis to discuss various topics, one of which was the release height. Wallis informed Gibson, that the optimum release height was 60 feet at a speed of 232 mph and some 475 yards from the target. Gibson's reaction is not recorded, but one can imagine his thoughts as he considered the fact, that this represented only 9 feet more than the distance from the centre line of a Lancaster's fuselage to the wingtip.

During further trials on the 28th of April, Highballs were dropped from 50 feet at a speed of 258 mph also with a backspin of 500 rpm. This was the smaller version of the weapon, which was being developed alongside for use against capital ships, and which traversed the surface in giant skips as if weightless. It was actually official footage of Highball that appeared in the famous Dambusters movie starring Richard Todd. Six bounces were achieved on this occasion and a distance of 2,000 feet. A single Upkeep was dropped at Reculver on the following day, and its success confirmed in Wallis's mind the final configuration of the weapon, which weighed in at 9,250lb, of which 6,600lb was Torpex underwater explosive compound.

Two days after Gibson's meeting with Wallis, crews were instructed to conduct spotlight flying from the new height of 60 feet, although, until all of the Lancasters' spotlights had been adjusted, some continued to train at 150 feet. Between the 23rd and 29th of April twenty-seven operational exercises were carried out, amounting to 186 attacks, half of which were considered to be successful. By month's end more than 1,800 practice bombs had been delivered from a variety of heights, and eighteen modified Lancasters were on charge. The posting in and out of personnel was still in progress even at this late stage, and three gunners, two navigators and a flight engineer departed the squadron on the 25th. On the 29th navigator F/O Ken Earnshaw, a Canadian, and gunner Sgt Brian Jagger arrived from 50 Squadron, the former having flown in the same crew as Gibson's rear gunner Trevor-Roper. He would be drafted into Hopgood's crew, while Jagger would find himself at the pointy end of Shannon's Lancaster.

With the intense training programme in full swing accidents were inevitable, and crews regularly came back with aircraft adorned by foliage stuffed in radiators and wrapped round tail wheels, while a number experienced more serious incidents. Barlow almost came to grief on the 9th of April when a bird strike and a collision with a tree left him with an unserviceable starboard-inner engine and damage to the Perspex nose. It would be a further nine days before the Lancaster was fit to fly again. Naturally, to a collection of high-spirited young men who would normally be hauled before the squadron commander for low flying, the opportunity to beat up the countryside at zero feet with official blessing was manna from heaven, and they indulged themselves with a will. However, such was the frequency of incidents, that Gibson instituted a squadron fund, into which those guilty of damaging their aircraft were obliged to pay a fine. Throughout this training period Gibson's time had largely been taken up with meetings and planning, and he had left the supervision of the training to his very able flight commanders. He flew when he could, however, and his logbook entries together with those of Taerum and Hutchison, his navigator and wireless operator respectively, give an insight into his schedule. He flew locally for an hour on the 1st of April, and then on the 4th he took W4940 for a short trip, described by Taerum as 'local – Base – Sheffield area,' and by Hutchison as 'a low level X-country'. Sheffield area refers to Derwent Reservoir, a short distance to the west of the city, and Gibson confirms 'a lake near Sheffield' as the destination for this flight. Gibson's log does not mention the flight to Derwent on the 28th of March with Hopgood and Young, which almost resulted in a watery end. It has been suggested, that the flight recorded by Gibson in his logbook on the 4th was the one during which the incident took place, but the problem with this is the timing. With BST in force it is broad daylight in early April until after 19.00 hours. With double BST, as during the war, this is extended by a further hour, while the flight recorded by Gibson, Taerum and Hutchison would have ended by around 19.00, and would not have allowed for a run across the reservoir in twilight. In addition, neither Hopgood nor Young note any flight with Gibson in their logbooks during the entire training period.

On the following day Gibson flew a cross-country to Scotland, which lasted a little over four hours. Hutchison, as the squadron signals leader, flew as a passenger with 'Dinghy' Young at lunchtime on the 9th in ED756 to carry out a R/T range test, and then rejoined Gibson and crew for a low-level cross-country exercise to Derwent and Uppingham Reservoirs later in the afternoon in ED329. On the 13th Gibson took the squadron bombing leader, Bob Hay of Martin's crew, for a trip to Manston to watch dropping trials in the company of Wallis and others. The occasion was something of a disappointment as all the trials ended in failure after the casings broke on impact with the sea. Undaunted, Wallis went back to the drawing board, while Gibson and Hay returned to Scampton. They borrowed a single engine Magister from the Manston-resident 137 Squadron, a Whirlwind unit, and had to force-land in a field following engine failure over Margate. (After Operation Chastise Gibson received a telegram from 137 Squadron's commanding officer. It read, 'Many congratulations on your success. The squadron has a new Maggie ready for pranging!') On the 15th Gibson flew to Fairoaks in an Oxford, where he met up with the Vickers test pilot Maurice 'Shorty' Longbottom for a thirty-minute trip to Weybridge in a Mosquito. The 16th was devoted to a five hour cross-country to his native Cornwall, during which, dummy attacks were carried out on lakes, while similar attacks were simulated over many reservoirs by night on the 20th. When Gibson wasn't flying on the 11th, Taerum teamed up with Martin to act as his bomb-aimer for a night cross-country on route 1 in LM309, while on the 12th he reverted to navigator, again for Martin, on a daylight cross-country over route 3 in ED735. He flew with Martin again on the 15th, when they took W4926 to the reservoirs at Colchester and Uppingham and the bombing range at Wainfleet. On the 21st Gibson flew a one hour sortie in ED763 to check out the synthetic night flying equipment, and repeated the exercise on the 25th with a trip of five hours and forty minutes, culminating in dummy attacks on Welsh dams.

The question of good clear communications was another problem dogging the training. It was essential, that air-to-air communication was good, as Gibson would be directing attacks over the target in plain language. He would also have to maintain contact with HQ at Grantham by W/T, so that the reserve wave of aircraft could be assigned to their targets. It was decided to dispense with the standard TR1154/55 set, which consisted of two separate units, and employ the TR1196 transceiver, a more powerful and smaller single unit. Trials showed it to be effective at up to forty miles at 2,600 feet, but its performance was generally below par, especially at night, when interference was encountered from Morse code. Despite adjustments, a test flight by Young on the 4th of May confirmed the need to find an alternative. The squadron contacted the Royal Aircraft Establishment about the problem, and F/L Bone, a specialist in their radio department, suggested the installation of TR1143 VHF sets, the equipment normally fitted in fighter aircraft. A team under his supervision travelled to Scampton to install a set in one of the Lancasters. At the end of the first week of May an air-test was flown by Maudslay, and after some small adjustments, which were tested by Young on the 9th and Hopgood on the 10th, the problem was deemed to be solved. Several sets were also installed in the crew room, so that training could continue on the ground.

The arrival of May brought a greater intensity of flying for Gibson, and although all of his sorties were of short duration, they were frequent. He flew on each of the first eight days of the month, although the flight on the 1st was a trip to Manston with Young to attend dropping trials at Reculver. On the 2nd he undertook a low-level reconnaissance flight at midday, and a bombing exercise that night, although he did not record the latter in his logbook. Gibson delivered ten practice bombs in special attacks on the 3rd, went to Manston on the 4th, Grantham on the 5th, followed by a special night attack, and carried out spotlight flying at 60 feet on the evening of the 6th. On the 11th he dropped an Upkeep from 60 feet, and achieved what he described in his logbook as a 'good run of 600 yards.' By this time the strain of the past six weeks was beginning to tell on Gibson, and a painful carbuncle formed on his face close to his nose. This made it uncomfortable for him to wear his oxygen mask, which would be clipped in place throughout the attack phase of the operation as it contained his microphone. On seeking advice from the senior medical advisor at Scampton, Dr Weddle, he was told to rest. Gibson found this amusing in view of what lay ahead, and laughed, much to the bemusement of the doctor, who, of course, was unaware of the impending operation.

A number of squadron crews conducted trial drops just short of the beach at Reculver in North Kent between the 11th and the 14th of May using either the ruins of an old fort as an aiming point or dummy markers, and the weapon performed sufficiently well in their hands for the operation to be considered feasible. To say that Upkeep 'bounced', was sometimes overstating the case somewhat, and in no way did its performance mirror that of Highball. Each trial drop of an Upkeep demonstrated a lack of consistency in its performance, sometimes producing a healthy first bounce, and at other times a reluctant parting of company with the surface of the water in a way that can only be described as laboured. However, it worked sufficiently well for the requirements of Operation Chastise. On the 13th a live Upkeep was dropped into the sea five miles off Broadstairs in Kent by a Lancaster flying south-west to north-east, and this successful trial, which culminated in a massive explosion and a plume of water over 700 feet high, was recorded for posterity by a camera on North Foreland, and by another in a second Lancaster. Munro had Townsend on board when he dropped his Upkeep from below 60 feet, and the spray from the impact with the sea damaged ED921; fortunately it was repairable. ED933 was more severely damaged, though, after Maudslay dropped his Upkeep from even lower. The plume of water and shingle thrown up by the impact tore at the Lancaster, and pieces could be seen to fall away. The Lancaster was nursed back to Scampton, and such was the damage, that repairs should have been undertaken either at the Avro factory or a maintenance unit. Unfortunately, there was insufficient time, and it was decided to attempt the job at Scampton. ED906 was returned to Avro for repairs to its bomb bay fairing on this day, but it was back at Scampton on the 14th.

May was also relatively busy for the rest of the squadron's airmen as the operation drew ever nearer, and Shannon's schedule was typical. He carried out spotlight altimeter runs on the 3rd with Ken Brown and members of his crew on board Lancaster W4940. From now on Shannon would carry out most of the remaining training in his own ED929 'L for Leather', although he used ED756 for spotlight altimeter runs on the 5th with Divall and some of his crew, and ED763 on the 6th for simulated night flying. Then it was back to ED929 for hydraulic tests on the 7th under the supervision of a Rolls-Royce expert. Shannon remained on the ground for the next three days but took to the air twice on the 11th, first for a low-level cross-country culminating in dummy attacks from 60 feet, and then for a low-level cross-country flight in formation. On the following day he dropped his first Upkeep at Reculver with Barlow as a passenger, and on the 13th carried out runs over the Uppingham (Eyebrook) and Colchester (Abberton) reservoirs during the course of a cross-country exercise. The day ended with a tactical exercise, in which four bombs were dropped during spotlight altimeter runs. On the 14th he flew to Manston and back in ED763 for an unspecified reason, but as Manston usually meant Reculver, it was almost certainly to do with the dropping of an Upkeep, although not by him, as ED763 was not a modified Lancaster.

Astell wrote home for the last time on the 14th, and although tension must have been growing at Scampton, he took pains to keep any hint of it from his family. He enclosed a copy of his will, joking that the Air Force takes on some funny ideas in telling all squadron members to make one. He closed by saying, 'There is no news at all from here. Lovely weather and a very quiet life'. Astell's will was witnessed by Henry Maudslay and 'Norm' Barlow, and fate would decree, that the lives of these three men and their crews would end within a few miles of each other in the flatlands of rural Germany between the Ruhr and the Dutch frontier a few days hence. That night a four-hour dress rehearsal was carried out by all crews in the formations to be adopted for the operation itself, although the crews themselves would remain unaware of the significance until final briefing on the day of the operation. Nine crews in three formations of three navigated a special route to Eyebrook and thence to Abberton to simulate the sequence for the Möhne and Eder. At each body of water they carried out a simulated attack from 60 feet at 232 mph under the direction of Gibson by R/T. Shannon was in Byers's eventual dams Lancaster, ED934, and specifies only a run at 60 feet on Uppingham Lake. Meanwhile, the six crews who were to be assigned to the Sorpe carried out a simulated attack at the Derwent, and the remainder, who were to form the mobile reserve, practised over the Wash. None of them at this stage would have been aware of the significance of dams. Gibson took Whitworth with him in ED932, and was able to note in his logbook that the exercise was 'completely successful.'

There would be little flying on the 15th as all aircraft underwent maintenance checks and some Upkeeps were loaded. Wallis was flown from Brooklands to Scampton by Mutt Summers in a white-painted Wellington on the afternoon of the 15th. At an informal briefing at Whitworth's residence in the evening, Gibson and Wallis revealed the targets to Young and Maudslay, and, perhaps as a last minute decision, to Hopgood, as Gibson's deputy at the Möhne, and Bob Hay, the squadron bombing leader. It was after the meeting had concluded, that Whitworth took Gibson aside and told him that his black semi-Labrador, Nigger, had been killed by a car outside the main guardroom on the A15. Contrary to the impression given in the feature film, *The Dambusters*, the driver did stop after the accident. The body of the animal was carried into the guardroom and formally identified by 'Chiefy' Powell. The passing of Nigger, an animal with something of an evil reputation, while a bitter blow to Gibson, was not a source of sadness to all. Gibson arranged with 'Chiefy' Powell to have him interred outside his office on the night of the operation at around the time he expected to be 'going in' over Germany.

CHAPTER FIVE

Opening Night Act One

The attack on the Möhne Dam and the first attempt on the Sorpe

Volumes have already been written about Operation Chastise, and my favourites are, *The Dambusters Raid* by John Sweetman, which is a masterpiece of research as well as being immensely readable, Paul Brickhill's *The Dambusters*, is a classic of wartime literature with a riveting narrative made even more remarkable by the lack of information available to the author at the time, and of course, Gibson's own account in *Enemy Coast Ahead*. This account will pay particular attention to timings, as it is easy to overlook the fact that this was a complex three-phase operation, spanning 8 hours and 47 minutes, with action occurring simultaneously at widely dispersed locations. It also attempts to settle finally the circumstances of the losses, by examining the testimony of eyewitnesses on both sides, and presenting arguments to help readers decide for themselves what actually happened where accounts are contradictory or at variance.

Wallis rose late for breakfast at Scampton on Sunday 16th May as the bustle of a busy operational bomber station went on around him. There was no luncheon break for 617 Squadron as many of the participants in the forthcoming night's activities were required to attend various meetings. In the early afternoon Gibson and Wallis briefed the pilots and navigators, while W/C Dunn attended to the wireless operators who would be communicating important messages by W/T (Morse code). Bomb-aimers and gunners were also involved, joining their pilots and navigators at various times, studying the models of the targets, and going away to draw them, before coming back to check on their accuracy. This process occupied around five hours, during which time Wallis and Mutt Summers communed with the ground crews and moved from aircraft to aircraft carrying out inspections. Then, at 18.00 hours, came the full briefing to the entire squadron behind locked and guarded doors, when Gibson outlined the operational details, Wallis repeated his explanation of the bomb's workings and effects, and Cochrane delivered a pep talk.

The final order of battle was governed to an extent by the availability of only twenty Lancasters after defeat was finally admitted during the 16th on the attempt to return ED933 to a state of serviceability. In the event, after the failure of another aircraft at start-up, this would leave two crews without the means to fulfil the hard work put in during training, but we are told that illness would have prevented Wilson and Divall and their crews from taking part anyway. The remaining nineteen crews were assigned to specific waves, with orders to attack primary and perhaps secondary targets as dictated by the unfolding events. Wave 1 consisted of three sections of three aircraft, which were to take off at ten-minute intervals and fly at low level on a south-easterly course across the North Sea to reach the enemy coast at the Scheldt Estuary between the islands of Schouwen and Walcheren. They were then to head for Roosendal in Holland's southwestern corner before continuing more or less in an easterly direction to thread their way between the night-fighter airfields at Gilze-Rijen and Eindhoven before adopting an almost due-easterly course towards the German frontier. Just a short distance beyond the frontier lay the towns and cities of the Ruhr Valley, starting with Duisburg on the Rhine's eastern bank. Already embroiled in a battle for survival with Bomber Command, these industrial centres were alert and protected by hundreds of lethal anti-aircraft guns, which had already cost the lives of countless bomber crewmen, and would claim even more in the remaining weeks of the campaign. The Lancasters were to turn to the north-east to skirt this region on its northern side, and continue past Hamm at its eastern end before turning sharply to the south to attack the first objective, the Möhne Dam, target X. Those with Upkeep still attached after the destruction of target X were to proceed eastwards to the Eder, target Y, and thence to the Sorpe, target Z.

Through the absence of Wilson the second wave now consisted of five aircraft, which would actually take off first at one-minute intervals, and fly independently of each other to the Sorpe Dam, target Z. They were to adopt an easterly track across the North Sea, and were timed to make landfall at the Dutch coast simultaneously with wave one, but at a point more than a hundred miles further north in order to create a diversion and split any enemy response. This, though, in no way suggests, that the Sorpe was intended as a diversionary target. They were to make their approach via the Dutch Frisian islands, making sure to pass over the more lightly defended Vlieland rather than Texel further south, which, with its marine flak units, had become one of the main guard posts to welcome British and American bombers to the European mainland, and to offer them a fond farewell on their way back out. They were then to follow a south-easterly course across the Ijsselmeer and Holland until meeting up with the wave 1 route just inside Germany. As in the case of the first wave, should any Upkeeps remain after the destruction of the primary objective, 'last resort' targets were to be attacked.

The third wave, also now consisting of five aircraft in the absence of Divall, was to remain at Scampton until after midnight. This would allow for its recall if all of the objectives had been destroyed by the first two waves. They were to approach the enemy coast along the same southerly track taken by wave 1, and then act as a mobile reserve to be assigned as required according to the status of the operation at the time of their arrival in enemy air space. If all had gone well before them, they were likely to be directed to the 'last resort' targets, D, the Lister, E, the Ennepe and F, the Diemel. Although termed last resort, this was only in comparison with the primary targets, and each was important in its own right. If destroyed in concert with other dams, the devastation and disruption in the Ruhr region would be immeasurably increased.

It is interesting to speculate on how crews were selected for each wave; was it, for example, based on rank, experience or performance during training? The first thing we notice is that all three NCO pilots were assigned to the third wave. Was this to do with Gibson's difficulty in accepting them as being of equal value, or was it purely their comparative lack of experience or, perhaps that they were the least effective in practice bombing. Both Townsend and Brown would prove themselves to be first-rate pilots during the operation, and surely this would have become apparent during training. Certainly, the first wave pilots were all officers and the most experienced, and one has to say, members of Gibson's inner circle, or at least on the fringe. In the event it would be the wave 3 crews who faced the most testing time, arriving over enemy territory after the defences had been stirred up by the first two waves.

There were many code words for the appropriate crewmembers to memorise, but three vital ones as far as this account is concerned. 'Goner' followed by two digits and a letter would signify release of Upkeep and its manner and position of detonation; 'Nigger', in honour of Gibson's recently departed dog, would mean that the Möhne Dam had been breached, divert to the Eder, while 'Dinghy' would convey a similar message with regard to the Eder, divert to the Sorpe.

Order of Battle

Wave 1

	ED932 G	ED925 M	ED909 P
Pilot	W/C G.P. Gibson	F/L J.V. Hopgood	F/L H.B. Martin (A)
Flight engineer	Sgt J. Pulford	Sgt C Brennan	P/O I. Whittaker
Navigator	P/O H.T. Taerum (C)	F/O K. Earnshaw (C)	F/L J.F. Leggo (A)
Wireless op.	F/L R.E.G. Hutchison	Sgt J.W. Minchin	F/O L. Chambers (NZ)
Bomb-aimer	P/O F.M. Spafford (A)	F/S J.W. Fraser (C)	F/L R.C. Hay (A)
Front Gunner	F/S G.A. Deering (C)	P/O G.H.F.G. Gregory	P/O T.B. Foxlee (A)
Rear gunner	F/L R.D. Trevor-Roper	P/O A.F. Burcher (A)	F/S T.D. Simpson (A)

	ED887 A	ED906 J	ED929 L
Pilot	S/L H.M. Young	F/L D.J.H. Maltby	F/L D.J. Shannon (A)
Flight engineer	Sgt D.T Horsfall	Sgt W. Hatton	Sgt R.J. Henderson
Navigator	F/S C.W. Roberts	Sgt V. Nicholson	F/O D.R. Walker (C)
Wireless op.	Sgt L.W. Nichols	Sgt A.J.B. Stone	F/O B. Goodale
Bomb-aimer	F/O V.S. MacCausland (C)	P/O J. Fort	F/S L.J. Sumpter
Front Gunner	Sgt G. Yeo	Sgt V. Hill	Sgt B. Jagger
Rear gunner	Sgt W. Ibbotson	Sgt H.T. Simmonds	F/O J. Buckley

	ED937 Z	ED864 B	ED912 N
Pilot	S/L H.E. Maudslay	F/L W. Astell	P/O L.G. Knight (A)
Flight engineer	Sgt J Marriott	Sgt J. Kinnear	Sgt R.E. Grayston
Navigator	F/O R.A. Urquhart (C)	P/O F.A. Wile (C)	F/O H.S. Hobday
Wireless op.	W/O A.P. Cottam	W/O A.A. Garshowitz (C)	F/S R.G.T. Kellow (A)
Bomb-aimer	P/O M.J.D. Fuller	F/O D Hopkinson	F/O E.C. Johnson
Front Gunner	F/O W.J. Tytherleigh	F/S F.A. Garbas (C)	Sgt F.E. Sutherland (C)
Rear gunner	Sgt N.R. Burrows	Sgt R. Bolitho	Sgt H.E. O'Brien (C)

Wave 2

	ED927 E	ED921 W	ED934 K
Pilot	F/L R.N.G. Barlow (A)	F/L J.L. Munro (NZ)	P/O V.W. Byers (C)
Flight engineer	P/O S.L. Whillis	Sgt F.E. Appleby	Sgt A.J. Taylor
Navigator	F/O P.S. Burgess	F/O F.G. Rumbles	F/O J.H. Warner
Wireless op.	F/O C.R. Williams (A)	W/O P.E. Pigeon	Sgt J. Wilkinson
Bomb-aimer	P/O A Gillespie	Sgt J.H. Clay	P/O A.N. Whitaker
Front Gunner	F/O H.S. Glinz (C)	Sgt W. Howarth	Sgt C. McA. Jarvie
Rear gunner	Sgt J.R.G. Liddell	F/S H.A. Weeks (C)	F/S J. McDowell (C)

	ED936 H	ED825 T
Pilot	P/O G. Rice	F/L J.C. McCarthy (USA)
Flight engineer	Sgt E.C. Smith	Sgt W.G Radcliffe
Navigator	F/O R. MacFarlane	F/S D.A. MacLean (C)
Wireless op.	W/O C.B. Gowrie (C)	F/S L. Eaton
Bomb-aimer	W/O J.W. Thrasher (C)	Sgt G.L. Johnson
Front Gunner	Sgt T.W. Maynard	Sgt R. Batson
Rear gunner	Sgt S. Burns	F/O D Rodger (USA)

Wave 3

	ED910 C	ED865 S	ED918 F
Pilot	P/O W.H.T. Ottley	P/O L.J. Burpee (C)	F/S K.W. Brown (C)
Flight engineer	Sgt R. Marsden	Sgt G. Pegler	Sgt H.B. Feneron
Navigator	F/O J.K. Barrett	Sgt T. Jaye	Sgt D.P. Heal
Wireless op.	Sgt J. Guterman	P/O L.G. Weller	Sgt H.J. Hewstone
Bomb-aimer	F/S T.B. Johnston	F/S J.L. Arthur (C)	Sgt S. Oancia (C)
Front Gunner	Sgt H.J. Strange	Sgt W.C.A. Long	Sgt D. Allatson
Rear gunner	Sgt F. Tees	W/O J.G. Brady (C)	F/S G.S. MacDonald (C)

	ED886 O	ED924 Y
Pilot	F/S W.C. Townsend	F/S C.T. Anderson
Flight engineer	gt D.J.D. Powell	Sgt R.C. Paterson
Navigator	P/O C.L. Howard (A)	Sgt J.P. Nugent
Wireless op.	F/S G.A. Chalmers	Sgt W.D. Bickle
Bomb-aimer	Sgt C.E. Franklin	Sgt G.J. Green
Front Gunner	Sgt D.E. Webb	Sgt E. Ewan
Rear gunner	Sgt R. Wilkinson	Sgt A.W. Buck

Supper in both the officers' and sergeants' messes had been a little tense, but then it generally was before an operation. At least you had a genuine egg on your plate, and there would be another to greet you on your return, if, in fact, you did return. Had they just consumed their last ever egg? There was apparently the usual exchange between Gibson and Young about claiming the other's egg if one of them failed to make it home. For some reason a few participants in the forthcoming operation couldn't convince themselves that they were going to return. Townsend was one, but despite an eventful trip, he would come back and survive the war. Hopgood was another, it is said, who confessed to a profound feeling that he was not destined to survive, and his premonition would come true. Wallis dined with the officers, but seemed distracted throughout.

After supper there was often time to kill, particularly during summer months when dusk arrived late over the bomber counties of eastern England. It didn't do to announce oneself over enemy territory until the cloak of darkness offered a measure of protection, so take-off was generally late in the evening. In the meantime one had to deal with the spare time and not use it to dwell on what lay ahead. Some returned to their rooms to tidy up or perhaps write the letter that would be opened and read only if they didn't come back. Others took a bath and a shave or tried to catnap. It would be fine once they were in the aircraft, it always was. That was when the relentless training came into its own and took over, occupying the mind with the countless details that had to be attended to. There was also a responsibility to your crewmates to do your job well and not let them down, and this helped temporarily at least to push thoughts of mortality into a tiny corner of the brain to be released at a later time. Every man dealt with the question of death in his own way. Some seemed genuinely unconcerned and breezed through their tour of operations without a care. The rest knew that such men were going to survive, and they always did. Others, though, carried their fears around with them where ever they went. The strain was etched on their faces; they were nervy, fidgety, they slept badly, their nights constantly interrupted by vivid dreams of falling, burning, crashing and dying. They would wake in a sweat and carry the lead weight of fear in the pit of their stomach for the remainder of the day until falling exhausted into another fitful sleep. And yet they went on, day after day, night after night, operation after operation, until their time came. They simply disappeared from the scene, their faces no longer visible at meal-times or at briefing, their names missing from the order of battle pinned to the notice board, and far too soon their features would fade from the memory. These were the really brave men, those who pushed themselves to carry on and on, when every fibre of their being screamed at them to stop and each moment was a torture to which only the end of a tour, capture or death could bring relief.

There was something incongruous about the scene facing the 133 young men who were about to create their own page in history on this quintessentially English evening in mid May. They drifted outside at around 20.00 hours and stood or sat in little groups on the lawn in front of the squadron hangar, some in deck chairs, others on the grass itself, a few even played cricket, and while it might have appeared that their attention was firmly fixed on the book, the conversation, the game, the here and now, their eyes and their thoughts were being drawn across the flat expanse of the airfield to what lay ahead. Away to the left the towering spires of Lincoln Cathedral shimmered faintly in the heat haze on the skyline some four miles south of the airfield, a reassuring and familiar landmark to all 5 Group crews, and one that would be sought out by those returning a few hours hence. Above them a blue, cloudless sky betokened a peace and tranquillity, which had in truth, been too long absent. The air clung tenaciously to the warmth generated by the sun earlier in the day, reluctant to surrender it to the approaching night, and yet knowing it must. Now that the activity of the day had largely subsided and given way to a relative calm, one could imagine sanity had returned to the world. That was, of course, part of the cruel joke that was life in Bomber Command. Uniquely of all the fighting services its combatants spent their days in the safety of the English countryside, and yet, within hours could be at 20,000 feet over Berlin, totally engulfed in the potential to die suddenly and horribly. For those involved in tonight's performance this was the lull before the storm. Even so, just at this precise moment, in this infinitesimally tiny segment of time, and if one closed one's eyes, it was possible to forget that all-out war had been raging for the best part of four years. Now just the occasional bang of a tool on metal, a shout from within the hangar, the rumble of a jeep's motor, the low babble of conversation, a peel of nervous laughter and the raucous call of a crow were the scene's only audible accompaniments. Soon, though, they would give way to a new and terrible noise that would smash this false impression of peace and normality. This was the sound of war, when aero engines came to life and set the air vibrating. Sometimes, when 57 Squadron was putting up a maximum effort for the Ruhr, Scampton resounded to the clamour of eighty engines or even more, all turning at once. It began quite gently, like an orchestra tuning up, as first one and then another and another ran each of its four engines individually from idle to maximum revolutions to test the magnetos. The slamming cacophony would crescendo to a peak of discomfort before falling off to a uniform loud rumble until the order to taxi to take-off positions sent the decibels rising again.

When Gibson came among the gathering and called an end to the waiting and the time killing, each man scooped up his parachute pack and made his way to one of the assorted lorries and buses waiting to take them to the aircraft at the dispersals out on the field. Soon a snake of transports was jerking away from the concrete apron in front of the hangar and beginning its journey across the bumpy grass. The back doors were left open and allowed to swing to and fro with the motion, providing the occupants with a lingering look back at the hangers and billet blocks that represented home and safety. In the distance the Lancasters squatted silently; dark, brooding, menacing shapes at rest, and yet alert. Even when dormant their profile bespoke their deadly purpose. Like mighty predators these devourers of cities crouched, their snouts sniffing the air for the telltale scent of prey, ready in an instant to launch themselves. All they awaited was the arrival of the crews to breathe life into them, to make them come alive with an awesome, ear-splitting roar. Like dragons the engines would soon belch fire as they struggled to catch, and then suddenly the propellers would spin, slowly at first, smoothly, freely, then faster and faster, driving the beasts' hot breath behind them. From that moment the airfield would literally tremble as dozens of Rolls-Royce Merlin engines competed for attention, communicating with onlookers through their feet as well as through their ears.

The lorries separated as they approached the dispersals and made for their respective destinations, each carrying one or more crews. At every stop seven men tumbled out and began the pre-flight rituals that some believed kept them alive. Many airmen were prone to superstition, slavishly clinging to any belief that might help them stay ahead of the odds. It was common practice to urinate on the tail wheel, or board the aircraft in a particular order, wear a certain item of clothing, perhaps carry something as a lucky mascot. The trucks moved on, leaving the crew alone, isolated, looking up at the monster that would be their home for the next six or seven hours. The pilot and flight engineer began their tour of inspection, checking tyres, looking for oil and glycol leaks, making sure the pitot head cover had been removed. Some crew members were getting their first view of the huge cylindrical bomb suspended beneath the modified belly of the Lancaster, and had certainly seen nothing like it before. Astell's wireless operator, Albert Garshowitz, had chalked something on the Upkeep suspended under AJ-B. It read, 'Never has so much been expected of so few'. He was another, it is said, that carried with him a premonition of death. Finally, satisfied that all was well, the pilot took the form 700 from the groundcrew chief and signed it to signify acceptance of the aircraft in airworthy condition. As far as the groundcrew were concerned, they were just loaning out their precious aircraft to the aircrew, sometimes against their better judgement.

In those last few moments before climbing on board, each man was an island, keeping private from the others his innermost thoughts and fears. They would have mixed emotions. On the one hand they were glad that the waiting was finally over, but on the other, the experienced ones in particular had almost forgotten what it was like to operate after almost two months off the order of battle. When you operated regularly, say twice a week, you got used to it; living with the prospect of death was part of life's routine. Now it was hard to be going back, and they knew, that although the others weren't showing it, they too were experiencing the same misgivings. Men like Hopgood, Maudslay and Astell at least knew what to expect. There were some crewmembers, though, who were flying tonight on their very first operation. How must they be feeling? Although quietly confident in the ability of themselves and their crews, the experienced captains would not have deluded themselves about the extreme difficulty of the job ahead. At least it wasn't the suicide operation some had predicted. Nevertheless, butterflies the size of chickens would continue to perform complex aerobatics in their stomachs right up to the moment when they mounted the five-rung ladder at the right-hand rear of the fuselage just ahead of the tail plane, and ducked into the dark and cramped confines of the bomber. In the meantime it was this damned waiting that got to you; that time between briefing and climbing aboard, when there was not quite enough to occupy your mind fully, and anxiety began to gnaw away at whatever confidence and resolve had been built up since the last op. They just wanted to get on with it. It would be all right once they were seated in the 'office' going through the pre-flight checks. Then they would be at work. Inspections complete, they looked at their watches for the thousandth time since supper, and then, finally, with a last lingering glance at the scene around them they filed up the ladders and were swallowed up by their Lancasters, some never to feel England beneath their feet again. Cochrane was driven out to G-George as Gibson and crew were about to board. He congratulated Gibson on a job well done and wished him and his crew good luck.

And so it was, that at 21.28, the duty officer flashed the green Aldis lamp from the control caravan to set the first of the specially modified Lancasters of the second wave, ED927 AJ-E, on its way from the southern end of the grass runway. At the controls was F/L Barlow, who was bound by the northern route via the Frisian island of Vlieland for the Sorpe Dam, and timed to arrive at the enemy coast at the same time as the south-routed first wave. It was still broad daylight, for which double summertime was responsible, and darkness would not be complete until some time after 23.00. Despite the fact that all but a select few of the station's personnel were not supposed to know that this was the real thing rather than a training flight, there had been a 'feeling' around the airfield all day. There was an unspoken knowing, a tacit understanding that the boys were going to war tonight, and the supper-time eggs had been one of a number of dead give-aways. That was why small knots of well-wishers had gathered at various vantage points, WAAFs and other non-flying personnel, who, from their perspective as among the safest serving men and women, regularly expressed solidarity with their at-extreme-risk colleagues by taking the trouble to see them off. Fingers waggled and sentiments of good luck were mouthed; there was no point in trying to be heard over the slam of engines even if they were just idling. Among the onlookers on this night were Wallis and Cochrane. For Wallis this was the culmination of years of dogged work, not only in developing his theory, but also of selling his ideas to those in authority. With the others he followed AJ-E's progress across his line of sight, and watched, probably fingers crossed, as Barlow heaved the heavily laden bomber over the northern perimeter fence, before banking it to starboard to pick up his track to the east coast. He was followed at 21.29 by Munro in ED921 AJ-W, Byers in ED934 AJ-K at 21.30 and Rice in ED936 AJ-H at 21.31. It would take them twenty-five minutes to reach the coast, and a further sixty-two minutes to cross the North Sea.

At 21.39 Gibson began his take off in ED932 AJ-G, with Hopgood to his right in ED925 AJ-M and Martin to his left in ED909 AJ-P, and they were followed at 21.47 by Young in ED887 AJ-A, Maltby in ED906 AJ-J and Shannon in ED929 AJ-L. Last away of the Möhne/Eder contingent were Maudslay in ED937 AJ-Z, Astell in ED864 AJ-B and Knight in ED912 AJ-N at 21.59. These nine crews had further to travel to their point of exit at the English coast at Southwold than those of wave 2. It was ten minutes after taking off that they set course for the south-east, and according to the log of Viv Nicholson, who was one of those going into battle for the very first time and was now seated in his small curtained-off compartment in ED906, it was 22.38 when Young, Maltby and Shannon began the sea crossing.

McCarthy, whose departure from Scampton should have preceded that of Barlow, finally got away at 22.01 in the spare aircraft AJ-T, his own beloved ED915 AJ-Q 'Queenie' having sprung a glycol leak during start up. The spare aircraft, ED825, had been flown over from Boscombe Down only that afternoon, and there had not been time to fit the VHF equipment or the altimeter spot lamps. There was also a problem with the number three engine, which, under normal circumstances would have persuaded Commander Bergel of 9 Ferry Pilots Pool (9FPP), who had delivered the aircraft, to declare it unserviceable. Fortunately, the lack of equipment would not be of critical importance at the Sorpe, and, as events were to prove, the engine abnormality was inconsequential. Of more immediate concern to McCarthy was the absence of the compass deviation card. Each compass had its own small inaccuracy, and the card told the pilot by how much to compensate. Without it the pinpoint navigation absolutely vital to this operation would be impossible. The account of McCarthy's mad dash to the instrument section in a semi-commandeered vehicle to locate the errant card has passed into folklore along with the story of his parachute billowing open after he scooped it up by the D-ring. As he cursed and vowed to go without a chute because they would be flying too low for one to be of use anyway, someone managed to push a replacement pack through the open window of the truck as it sped back towards AJ-T's dispersal, and the crew got away without further incident to play its part in Operation Chastise. The final five crews now had a nervous wait of more than two hours on the ground at Scampton, and they would not reach enemy territory until after 01.30, by which time a clearer picture of unfolding events would determine where they were needed. Having seen the first two waves off, Wallis and Cochrane departed for 5 Group HQ at Grantham, where they would meet up with Harris, who was on his way from High Wycombe. They would spend the ensuing few hours in the operations room under extreme tension as messages were passed to and fro via W/T, and a picture developed of the fortunes of the nineteen Lancasters and crews.

Gibson, Hopgood and Martin watched Southwold slide by beneath them in the fading light, and then pushed the Lancasters' noses down until they were racing towards the enemy coast at a bare 50 feet. So low were they that the prop wash flicked the tops off the wave crests and produced mini wakes. We know little about what was said, but Gibson gave us an insight in his narrative in *Enemy Coast Ahead*. It was warm in the cockpit, and flying a fully laden Lancaster at low level was physically demanding. There would be no respite for the pilots on this trip, no opportunity to engage George, the automatic pilot. The slightest hiccup at such low level could send them crashing headlong into the sea or into the ground. Turbulence was more noticeable also at low level, and so strong arms and hands were required on the control yoke for the full duration of the operation. Consequently, Gibson was flying in shirtsleeves under his Mae West, and he called for Hutchison to turn off the heating as he began to perspire. We also know of a conversation by Aldis lamp between the aircraft of Hopgood and Martin, the gist of which concerned drinking themselves into a state of oblivion when they got home. There would have been communication between Gibson and Taerum concerning compass bearings and turning points, and Gibson would have given permission for the gunners to test their .303 Brownings once over the water, Richard Trevor-Roper in the rear and George Deering up front. Taerum would also have asked Trevor-Roper to release a flame float to check how much the wind was causing them to drift off track. Bob Hutchison the wireless operator suffered from airsickness, and in all probability he quietly threw up in his RAF issue spew bag without complaint or fuss, and then got on with his job.

They would be over the sea for a little more than an hour, and as the dusk drew towards night the line on the horizon where sea and sky merged became increasingly difficult to identify. In the nose of G George bomb-aimer 'Spam' Spafford lay prone in his compartment, he, best of all on board, experienced the impression of speed as the darkening surface of the North Sea rolled underneath his clear vision panel in a blur. He and the other bomb-aimers had an important job on this night even before the targets were reached. They would support the navigators, who, cloistered in their compartment at the rear of the flight deck, had only a small window out onto the world, and could not themselves identify pinpoints. 'Terry' Taerum would give Spafford pinpoints to look out for, rivers, lakes, railway lines, and Spafford would report on what he was seeing and trace the route himself on a roller or folded map. He also had to be aware of ground obstacles like radar masts, chimneys, church spires, electricity pylons and cables and shout a warning to Gibson in good time to allow his pilot to take the necessary evasive action. They were fairly relaxed while over the water, but they could not indefinitely put off that dread moment when they would sweep across the enemy shoreline and enter the lion's den.

As the second wave approached the Dutch Frisians shortly before 23.00, Byers climbed to establish his position and clear the rising ground ahead. There was tension on board. With only four operations behind them, and the last of those more than six weeks ago, they were still learning the ropes, gradually acquiring the skills that might just see them survive their first tour of operations. They were aware that they were still in the dangerous phase for freshman crews. It seemed to be the case, that if you survived your first five sorties, the odds shifted in your favour, and there was a good chance of making it through at least to the mid twenties. Then the odds turned against you again to make the final few operations a trial of nerve. It was tragic how many crews failed to return from their twenty-ninth or thirtieth trip. With only one in three crews getting to celebrate the magic thirty, the odds were stacked against you from the start. But, just to wave off that occasional crew through the main gates on their way to six months screening at some OTU or HCU, was a victory in itself. If one crew could make it to the end, then there was a glimmer of hope for all the others.

As far as tonight was concerned, crossing the enemy coast over the Dutch Frisians was a new experience for Byers. To the old hands, of course, and under normal circumstances, it didn't much matter where you entered Fortress Europe, the reception was generally the same. When coming this way on a main force operation you knew precisely where you were and what to expect. On a clear night like tonight you could look down from 15,000 feet and more at the dark shapes that were Texel and Vlieland, and watch the peremptory tracer begin its seemingly slow ascent. You felt you could dodge it if you had to, but safe within the bomber stream you were relatively unconcerned about ground fire. It would be different over the target, naturally, but the immediate concerns were night fighters and collisions. Anyway, nine times out of ten you couldn't even see the ground because of cloud. Not so tonight! It was uncomfortable to be so close to the earth over enemy territory. Lying prone in K-King's nose bomb-aimer Arthur Whitaker felt the floor press against his legs and torso as the Lancaster rose suddenly. Now he had a better impression of the profile of the land they were about to pass over, and with the benefit of the moonlight that was now coming into play, he could pick out the white splash of surf on the shoreline and even the relief of the terrain. What he saw, however, was not what he had expected to see. There were two islands, and AJ-K was passing over the northern end of one of them. That could only mean Texel! They must be starboard of track! In no time at all it seemed the ground fell away again and gave way to a further expanse of dark water, and as the island slipped behind, tension slackened enough to allow the seven occupants of ED934 to relax a little. They could count on a few more minutes of uneventful flight over water before the long, low profile of mainland Holland raised their heart rates once more ...

Keen eyes in other nearby Lancasters saw Byers away to starboard climbing over the northern tip of Texel, clearly south of the planned track, which should have taken him over Vlieland. They watched as the flak followed him and a single shell found him at about 450 feet. They held their breath as AJ-K caught fire and traced a graceful, burning arc, which terminated in the Waddenzee beyond the island and about eighteen miles west of Harlingen at 22.57. There were no survivors, and only the body of rear gunner McDowell would eventually be recovered from the sea after being found off Harlingen in June. Local fishermen would claim the bomb went off on the seabed some six weeks later. Byers and his crew were desperately unlucky to be brought down in this way, as they were the victims of a single speculative shot fired from behind more in hope than in expectation. The members of the flak crew would have been more than a little surprised by their success when the shell tore the Lancaster apart and brought it down immediately. In his account John Sweetman states, that 1 and 3/Marine Artillery 201 and 3/808 units were officially credited with bringing down AJ-K. Certainly, the time of 22.57 stated in the report is consistent, as is the reference actually to shooting down rather than simply engaging an aircraft. The inconsistency is in the fact that a Spitfire is cited as the victim, but perhaps we must put this down to poor aircraft recognition, or that it was further than realised from the battery, and higher, and therefore appeared to be a smaller type. As a postscript the same unit reported firing at an unidentified enemy aircraft at 01.58, which was about the time that Joe McCarthy was in the vicinity on his way home.

Vlieland was more heavily defended than was believed by the British, and 3/Marine Flak 246, situated at its most westerly point, and therefore close to Texel, reported firing at a Lancaster that night at 22.59. Almost certainly, this unit was responsible for the enforced early return of another Chastise crew. At almost the same moment as Byers crashed, Munro's aircraft was fired on and hit over Vlieland. In addition to a large hole in the fuselage the Lancaster sustained terminal damage to the transmitter, the intercom and the master compass. The loss of the intercom meant that the various crew-members would not be able to communicate with each other and co-ordinate their roles during the vital moments of the attack, and they would also be unable to announce their presence to other aircraft. Bitterly disappointed, and after a crew conference conducted with pencil and paper, Munro abandoned the sortie and turned for home. Meanwhile, Rice had crossed Vlieland, and was approaching the Afsluitdijk just after 23.00, when he momentarily lost the horizon in the half-light conditions and struck the sea, tearing off the Upkeep weapon. The bomb impacted the tail wheel in passing, and forced it upwards into the fuselage, where it wrecked the Elsan toilet. Fortunately, no one was using it at the time! Mercifully the engines were undamaged, and Rice managed to haul the Lancaster off the water, although not before the buckled bomb bay fabrication had scooped up vast quantities of water. This instantly found its way into the rear turret as the aircraft climbed, much to the discomfort of the occupant, Sgt Sandy Burns. At 23.06 Rice, like Munro, was forced to abandon his sortie and turn for home.

The status of the operation at this point was less secure than might have been expected, and certainly less than would have been hoped for by the planners. Of the original five participants of wave 2 only Barlow and McCarthy were pressing on towards the Sorpe Dam. Barlow was past the Afsluitdijk and over the Ijsselmeer, while McCarthy was still over the North Sea, but making up time. He would reach Vlieland at 23.13, having cut his deficit from thirty-three minutes to twenty-one. Rice and Munro were now clear of the Frisians in their damaged aircraft and well on their way home. Meanwhile, the leading element of wave 1, consisting of Gibson, Hopgood and Martin, had made landfall at the Scheldt Estuary without incident. However, the fact that they were over the island of Walcheren, rather than the stretch of water separating it from Schouwen, came like a splash of cold water in Gibson's face. It meant they were south of the planned track, and needed to sort out the navigation without delay. Gibson would later admit that they were fortunate to get away with the low pass over Walcheren, which was bristling with sufficient weaponry to bring down the entire squadron, let alone him. Gibson reminded navigator Taerum of the need for accurate navigation as they climbed briefly to establish position, and then hit the deck again to push on for the next pinpoint at Roosendaal. At the same moment Young, Maltby and Shannon were approaching landfall, which they would make at 23.12, almost certainly a fraction north of Gibson's track, while Maudslay, Astell and Knight were still over the North Sea ten minutes behind. There is no question that the wind was having an influence on the progress of the operation. The log at the airfield at De Kooy, further up the Dutch coast near Den Helder, recorded the average wind speed and direction for the 16/17th of May as four metres per second from the NNW. The main problem, however, was not the effect of the stronger-than-forecast wind, but rather the difficulty of navigating, of identifying ground features at such low level to confirm the accuracy or otherwise of the track being followed. What is clear is that the operation was already beginning to fall behind schedule. This was all still academic as far as the reserve force was concerned, which remained on the ground at Scampton awaiting orders.

As far as we know Barlow made his pinpoint at Stavoren on the north-eastern shore of the Isselmeer, and reached Harderwijk near its southern extremity without incident before pressing on towards the Rhine at Rees. This was the point on the map where the first and second wave routes came together, north-west of the cauldron that was the Ruhr, or in the black humour of the day, 'Happy Valley'. For Barlow this meant turning to port to adopt an easterly heading, which would take him beyond the Ruhr Valley to the next turning point north-east of Hamm some seventy miles away. At 23.50, having just passed over the Dutch/German frontier, AJ-E crashed onto farmland east of Rees. This typical Rhineland terrain is a continuation of the flatlands of Holland, and the lie of the land contains no natural surprises to catch low flying aircraft. Today, more than sixty-five years on, tall trees reach skyward in lines and small concentrations form wooded areas and copses bordering the crop fields and meadows. They would perhaps have been less lofty in 1943 as Barlow approached them, and would have been moderately easy to see in moonlight. It was something else that brought him down, though, in fact, it was the greatest hazard to face ultra-low flyers. High-tension cables, strung like spiders' webs across the countryside, were supported by tall steel pylons at regular intervals, and racing towards them 50 feet up at over two hundred miles an hour was always going to be a little like Russian Roulette. It is debatable whether they would have shown up against the backcloth of night sky and dark earth merging on the horizon. Perhaps the only chance of catching a glimpse in time would be the glint of moonlight on metalwork, and certainly, to meet the cables or pylons head-on at the last moment would offer no chance of avoiding them. The droop of the cables at the midpoint between the pylons left dangerously little ground clearance, and in order to fly beneath them, it would be necessary to line the aircraft up a mile beforehand and pray. It would be impossible to change the pitch of a heavy aircraft at the last moment to get underneath without nosing into the ground. On the other hand, the spread of the cables from top to bottom at any point amounted to a catch net, and meeting them at mid point would allow only a marginally better chance of missing them topside. In essence, you were either at the right height to avoid them or you weren't. It is known, that these obstacles were a cause for concern for the crews, once they learned they were to operate at ultra low level, and they were identified at briefing as a hazard.

Barlow had approached his turning point near Rees from the north-northwest, and it is likely, that he had just adopted the easterly course. This being the case, he would have encountered the high-tension cables at roughly 8 o'clock to 2 o'clock across his path. Ahead of them lay a few small trees and a meadow, used at the time for grazing cattle. Hedges are few in this region, and today, as then, the right hand edge of the meadow is bordered by one of the typical single-track tarmac roads criss-crossing the region linking the farms, and this extends along the bottom end of the field to the left, while to the right it winds away to a collection of farmhouses. There is some unconfirmed evidence that Barlow may have been attempting to avoid searchlights as his Lancaster struck the top of a pylon, but there would have been little benefit to the Germans of placing a battery in the area. Deprived of its flying speed, and who knows what parts of its control surfaces, AJ-E impacted the meadow and slithered to a halt in the bottom right-hand corner, where it was consumed by fire. Beyond the far end of the meadow is another of shallow proportions, perhaps little more than the length of a cricket pitch, and then a small pond. One local farmer describes the nose of AJ-E crossing the road and resting against the fence on the edge of the pond, but another claims the entire body of the aircraft remained in the first field. Although the latter farmer, Herr Hegmann, was born in 1943 and knew of the downed bomber from his father, he had remarkably never heard of the RAF attack on the dams. It seems, that no one actually witnessed the crash, but a large explosion was heard, which brought people out of their cellars to gather at the scene. The onlookers found the Lancaster a blazing wreck, and all the crew were apparently burned beyond recognition. Some fifty metres away the Upkeep weapon remained intact to fall into enemy hands. The local Bürgermeister, believing the bomb to be a petrol tank, had himself photographed standing on top of it. Someone apparently apprised him later of the true nature of the giant cylinder. The bomb was defused and removed initially to Kalkum near Düsseldorf, and eventually to Rechlin, the German equivalent of Farnborough. Within ten days drawings were produced by German engineers, describing the device as a revolving depth charge, with accurate descriptions of the mechanisms and release gear along with the modifications to the Lancaster.

Meanwhile, Gibson had again found himself south of track, this time by about six miles, and was heading towards Duisburg, the industrial giant perched on the Rhine on the Ruhr's western edge. The city had been attacked at the end of March, three times in April, and had been severely battered just four nights earlier in Bomber Command's most successful raid upon it of the war to date. Its hundreds of heavy and light flak batteries would be attended by excessively twitchy and trigger-happy crews, who would make it a very unhealthy place for Gibson and Co to present themselves at around 100 feet. Gibson reacted instantly to the news of their false position, and pulled the Lancaster round to the north to follow the Rhine to the correct turning point at Rees. Taerum had apparently misread his figures. This violent change of direction caught Hopgood and Martin by surprise, and not for the first time during the outward flight, they temporarily lost contact with their leader. Gibson's trio encountered unanticipated flak at a number of points along the route, with particular concentrations in the Buchholt–Borken area, north-west of Dorsten, and again near the lakes at Dülmen. Searchlights held the Lancasters, bathing them in a blinding glare until tracer from the rear turrets popped them out or sent the gunners scattering. Even so, the last of these inflicted damage to Hopgood's Lancaster, possibly knocking out an engine, while a number of the crew sustained injuries. It seems that a shell exploded somewhere on or near the flight deck, and it is likely that the front gunner, P/O Gregory, was mortally wounded at this point, as he failed to respond to intercom enquiries. The wireless operator, Sgt Minchin, certainly sustained a severe leg wound, which left the limb almost severed, and P/O Burcher in the rear turret took some flak splinters. Conversations at the front of the aircraft overheard by Burcher in his turret suggested that Hopgood had sustained a serious facial injury, which flight engineer Brennan attended to as best he could. In numerous accounts over the years it has been asserted that this incident took place while AJ-M was still an hour away from the target. In fact, the entire journey from the English coast to the Möhne Lake took only around an hour and three quarters, and at least half of that was taken up by the sea crossing. It was actually shortly after being hit that they reached the final turning point near Ahlen, and pointed their noses to the south on a direct heading to the Möhnesee. A short distance to the rear Young, Maltby and Shannon shadowed the leading element, seemingly without undue alarm, although Young persisted in flying higher than necessary, up to around 500 feet, and this did give cause for concern on board AJ-J and L for Leather.

Many miles to the west, at 00.09 Ottley took off from Scampton in ED910 AJ-C as the first of the final wave of Operation Chastise. As Burpee followed in ED865 AJ-S at 0011, Gibson was transmitting a flak warning to base at 51′48″N and 07′12″E, which Group rebroadcast at full power a minute later. Burpee was followed into the air by Brown in ED918 AJ-F at 00.12, and by Townsend in ED886 AJ-O at 00.14. At 00.15 a number of incidents took place. Anderson completed the final take-off of the operation in ED924 AJ-Y, Gibson, Hopgood and Martin arrived at the Möhne Lake, McCarthy reached his target area around the Sorpe, and Astell and his crew perished.

No one knows why Astell failed to make a course change with Maudslay and Knight, possibly at Rees. It seems there had been little difficulty in maintaining contact thus far, and perhaps Astell was following the navigation of his leader and simply lost sight of him for a brief moment, causing him to fall behind. Alternatively, navigator Wile and bomb-aimer Hopkinson might have been unsure of their position and delayed the turn until they could confirm a pinpoint. Whatever the reason, AJ-B had fallen at least a mile and probably more behind Maudslay and Knight as they covered the ground between Rees and the little town of Marbeck. According to the testimony of a local farmer, Herr Tücking, he was awoken by the noise of low-flying aircraft, which almost removed his roof. Such low flying was entirely beyond the experience of people in this community, and for this reason Herr Tücking ran downstairs in his nightclothes to take a look. On going outside he observed another aircraft strike an electricity pylon a few hundred yards away to his right, bringing down the top section along with two cables. A young maidservant in the Thesing household, whose farmhouse lies to this day between those of Herr Tücking and Herr Lammers, was outside at the time with old Herr Thesing near to midnight. She observed the low-flying four-engine aircraft, which she quite reasonably assumed to be German, as RAF heavy aircraft were not accustomed to flying low over Germany at that stage of the war. The first one flew across the Tücking house away to her left, to be followed one or two minutes later by a second one from the same direction, but a little closer. She confirms, that Astell's Lancaster followed behind the others by a minute or more and was heading straight for the Thesing house, from her standpoint, therefore, to the right of the path flown by the two earlier aircraft. Perhaps that was what made the difference between life and death, maybe just a hundred metres or so of airspace that put an electricity pylon directly in Astell's path. The bomber was instantly engulfed in flames as it somehow staggered over the roof of the Thesing house, before crashing in flames in the meadow beyond and behind the Lammers house, where it exploded in a kaleidoscope of igniting tracer ammunition.

Herr Tücking then described watching from his vantage-point behind a wall, as a fire-red ball separated from the disintegrating aircraft and rolled another 150 metres, before detonating deafeningly and violently some ninety seconds or so later. This created a crater deep enough to bury a house, blew out windows and doors and stripped tiles from the roofs of the three neighbouring farmhouses. Miraculously, though, it left unscathed a wayside shrine to St Joseph, which stood behind the Lammers farmhouse on the edge of the field, just fifty metres from where the Lancaster crashed. It was half an hour before onlookers could approach the scene, where close to the aircraft wreckage they found the charred remains of one of the crew in 'a stooping position, propped up on his hands'. The bodies were gathered and laid out in the corner of the next field by the single-track road adjoining the farm buildings, and the state of the remains is confirmed by a handwritten document produced at the time by the Marbeck–Raesfeld authorities, probably, in fact, by the local policeman, in which only Astell, Kinnear and Wile are positively identified. Three of the others are described as unidentified English airmen and a fourth as an unidentified Canadian airman. A list of personal items found at the crash site included money, a ring, a cigarette case, an engraved wristwatch, a lighter and a bunch of keys. Once on the scene the local police cordoned off the crash site to keep the inquisitive away, and no report of the incident appeared in the local press. Nevertheless, Raesfeld resident Ignatz Böckenhoff managed to record the tragic scene in three photographs. The bodies were interred in the local cemetery at Borken later on the 17th, and remained there until their exhumation and transfer to the Commonwealth War Graves Cemetery at Reichswald on the 5th of February 1947.

Astell's Lancaster was reputedly observed by a member of Knight's crew to pass through a cross fire of tracer from the ground and catch fire before crashing onto the farmland, presumably having fallen victim to the flak position near Dorsten. However, Richard Sühling, an engineering consultant and local historian and curator of the little museum at nearby Raesfeld, maintains that no flak batteries were positioned close to the crash site at the time. There was a searchlight on the edge of Raesfeld, and it was the nearest to the scene of Astell's demise, but it was not activated until after the aircraft had passed. It would, anyway, not have been able to illuminate such a low-flying aircraft. The flak positions near Dorsten reported by Gibson were presumably installed to protect the town, but could only be brought to bear against very low flying aircraft if they were almost overhead. An aircraft at 50 feet is past in a flash, and line of sight might well be obscured by trees, or even buildings. Most tellingly, the eyewitnesses on the ground were agreed that AJ-B was not on fire before the impact with the pylon. The conclusion, therefore, must be, that the destruction of AJ-B was caused solely by that collision. What, then, could account for the testimony of Knight's crew, that AJ-B was hit by flak? The likelihood is that the impact with the pylon created a giant flash and sparks, which might easily be mistaken for tracer ammunition. It must be understood, that Knight's aircraft was already a few miles ahead of the incident, and was drawing away from the scene at over two hundred miles an hour. In those adrenalin-packed seconds it would have been easy to misinterpret the source of bright dots of light in a quickly receding image, which at such a low altitude, must have fallen out of sight behind trees almost immediately, leaving only a reflection in the sky. One has to say that the distance between the Lancasters of Knight and Astell at the time of the incident would not have allowed for anything more than an impression upon which to hang an interpretation, and flak would be the first and most obvious to spring to mind.

Assuming a minimum of deviation following the impact with the pylon, it is possible to estimate Astell's heading as being a little north-east of due east, with Marbeck a short distance ahead. On crossing a copse or small wood he was immediately confronted by a line of high-tension cables stretching across his path at 10 o'clock to 4 o'clock. On the same heading within 100 yards was a line of trees, and behind them the farmhouse belonging to Herr Thesing. Having hit the pylon, and now on fire, AJ-B ballooned diagonally over the roof with little to spare, and dropped into a meadow perhaps 200 yards beyond. From the initial impact with the pylon to the crash there can have elapsed no more than five or six seconds, and it was probably more like four. It has been suggested, that Astell may have jettisoned the bomb before impact, using the quick release handle available to him, and this may, indeed, be the case. The only question is, would he have had the presence of mind in those four to five seconds to make that decision and act upon it? The sudden impact with the pylon must almost certainly have frozen rational thought for a second or two. Did Astell see the pylon fleetingly first, or was it a sudden bang, a jolt, followed by a 'What the hell ...!'. The shock, the pounding heart ... already he was over the Thesing house. Did it register in the remaining few seconds before impact with the ground that the aircraft was finished? Did he have time even to consider an attempt to control the coming to earth? To stand on the spot where he and his crew died and look towards the pylon only confirms the lack of time for rational thought, and we will never know conclusively how the bomb became separated from the aircraft. The probability is that it was loosened by the impact with the pylon, and either fell off a microsecond before contact with the ground, or in the act of impacting the ground. All eyewitnesses are in agreement, though, that the Upkeep was on fire as it rolled across the meadow.

If one stands on the crash site looking back along Astell's line of approach, one sees four farmhouses in an arc across the flight path. On the far left is the Tücking residence, to its right that belonging to the Bösing family, then Herr Thesing's and finally on the right the Lammers homestead. It was behind the Lammers house that the statue of St Joseph stood, and the present day Frau Lammers is the daughter of the Herr Tücking who witnessed these terrible events. The statue now stands in a new position in front of the house. It is indeed a miracle, that it remained unscathed in such close proximity to the crash and bomb detonation. Frau Lammers' brother is the present day representative of the Tücking family farming this picturesque land.

By the time that Gibson was ready to begin his attack, the second trio had arrived on the scene, and gathered at the eastern end of the reservoir to wait for their turn in the proceedings. Gibson called all the aircraft of the first wave, and established that only Astell was unaccounted for. After imparting final instructions to the other pilots, Gibson broke from his left-hand circuit of the lake at its eastern end somewhere near the Körbecker bridge and made his way towards the Heversberg, the wooded hill directly opposite the black line of the dam wall sitting low and seemingly immovable a mile distant across the dark water. At 00.28 AJ-G crested the treetops and dropped towards the lake's surface, the Upkeep already spinning at the required 500 r.p.m., and creating a ripple of vibration through the structure of the aircraft. Taerum had taken up his station on the right side of the flight deck behind Pulford, and like the pilot and flight engineer he was nothing more than a silhouette in the dark confines of the glasshouse, which was illuminated only by pale moonlight and the weak bulbs in the control panel instruments. He peered down through the blister in the side of the canopy from where the two pools of light cast by the spots in the nose and rear bomb bay were clearly visible. It was Taerum's task to talk Gibson down to the bomb release height of 60 feet, at which point the two circles of light would have moved together to touch in a figure of eight ahead of the starboard leading edge, and there were just fourteen seconds available to make this happen. Gibson's eyes were fixed on the centre of the dam wall as he called on Taerum and Spafford to do their stuff while straining to catch their instructions above the blare of the engines. When Gibson spoke to Taerum, Spafford, Hutchison and Trevor-Roper it was 'Terry' 'Spam', 'Hutch' and 'Trev', but it was always 'Pulford' when he addressed his flight engineer, a man he unkindly described in the initial draft of *Enemy Coast Ahead* as being incapable of independent thought. 'Down ...

down ... down.' The Canadian navigator's voice was an assured monotone in Gibson's headphones as he watched the foremost circle cast by the rear spotlight move from ahead of the aircraft back towards the constant point of light from the front spot just forward of the leading edge. They had done this many times before during training, and it was now that the value of that hard work kicked in. Gibson concentrated on his line as Pulford manipulated the throttles to keep the Lancaster at the required speed. 'Steadyyyy ... steadyyyy ... steadyyyy,' Taerum's voice was almost hypnotic. Lying prone in the nose Spafford was becoming excited at the clarity of the scene in front of him, announcing that he could see everything. Then the defences sprang into life alerted by the appearance of lights approaching low over the water, and angry, red and green projectiles flew into the faces of the attackers from the roofs of the sluice towers. They reflected in the water, giving the impression that twice as many guns were firing at them as in reality were. Suddenly there was a deafening clatter from the front turret as George Deering opened up with his two guns, returning the enemy fire with a stream of 100% tracer aimed at its source. This added to the general vibration and filled the cockpit with the acrid smell of cordite. These were the sights, the sounds, the smells and the sensations of war that made the moment so gut-wrenchingly terrifying and the retelling of it so compellingly exciting. Gibson called tersely to Pulford to leave the throttles and be prepared to pull him out of his seat if he were hit. At that moment, staring certain death in the face, Gibson came close to losing his nerve before steeling himself and becoming resigned to his fate. Anticipating the fatal shell, he committed himself to the bombing run and had control now only over his role in the event. At this point he couldn't even see the target as the front turret blocked his view. Time seemed to stand still, and afterwards memory of his run would be a confused kaleidoscope of images. Of Gibson's crew only wireless operator Hutchison and rear gunner Trevor-Roper were unoccupied during the bombing run, but their time would come as AJ-G rocketed over the dam a bare couple of seconds after releasing the weapon. Then Hutchison would fire a red Very cartridge to signal to the others that the first attack was completed, and Trevor-Roper would have his chance at the receding dam's defenders with his four Browning .303s.

The German gunners had been spending another boring night on the dam, some on duty on the gun platforms atop the two sluice towers, and others in the accommodation beneath. A posting to this idyllic backwater meant a life of general inactivity and minimal excitement. It was not unusual to hear the sound of enemy aircraft high above, but they were always bound elsewhere in the Reich, and on a clear night might have been using the lake as a navigation pinpoint. The first indication of the approach of aircraft on this night was the sound of engines from the north in the direction of Soest. The flak crews automatically assumed that the lake was again about to be navigated upon, and they opened up as soon as the first Lancasters came within range just to discourage the interlopers from taking liberties and getting too close. Even as Gibson's Lancaster came at them low over the water with the spotlights clearly visible, it still didn't register that the dam was the target. Nevertheless, they fired with a will and watched the tracer bridge the rapidly decreasing gap between themselves and the black monster bearing down on them at speed from out of the shadow of the Heversberg. Only when the bomb fell away and exploded beneath the water did it become clear that the attack was indeed meant for the dam.

The dozen or so seconds of the bombing run had expanded into minutes by the time Spafford's strident 'bomb gone!' broke the spell. Gibson hauled back on the control yoke to get some clearance as they shot between the angry towers, and heaved the Lancaster over the ridge of hills bordering the left side of the compensating basin. Liberated from the weight of the bomb, AJ-G was once more agile and made easy work of the climb. This was when the flak position at Günne on the far right corner of the compensating basin came into play, and it managed a few squirts at Gibson before he was out of range. Gibson wheeled round, anxious to see the results of his effort, and within seconds a yellow flash beneath the water signalled the Upkeep's detonation. A giant column of water reached skywards for many hundreds of feet, and remained as if fixed for a moment or two before falling back to the lake to leave only a mist of spray hanging in the air. The shock of the explosion sent sheets of water cascading over the dam's parapet, and at first it appeared to onlookers that the wall was collapsing, but as the agitation calmed the dam stared back at them, defiant and solid, still holding back the 134,000,000 ton contents of the reservoir. Some commentators, and the epic film of 1954, suggest that Gibson's mine scored a direct hit in the centre of the dam wall before exploding, and the squadron's Operations Record Book describes an accurate attack. In fact, as Gibson's transmission to base at 00.37, GONER 68A shows, the weapon fell short by 5–50 yards, and eyewitness testimony from those on the dam suggests that it veered to the left, and detonated close to the southern sluice tower.

At 00.33, Maudslay and Knight arrived at the lake, just in time to catch Hopgood's bombing run. Only those on board M-Mother knew of the damage and injuries inflicted by the earlier flak, and there was no hint of a problem in Hopgood's voice as he calmly announced over the VHF channel that he was going in to attack. Now that the defenders knew the direction from which he would come, and had the spotlights as a reference point, they were ready. They fired for all they were worth and watched the stream of shells fly into the face of the onrushing Lancaster, which was hit several times. Both port engines sustained damage, one of them erupting in flames, as did the starboard wing when a fierce fire developed in a petrol tank and began to consume the metalwork around it. One can only imagine the scene at the front of the aircraft in those few critical moments before the bomb fell away. Hopgood's face wound would have been unattended as both his hands grasped the control yoke and Brennan juggled with the throttles and flaps. Ken Earnshaw would have been calling the height, while George Gregory was probably slumped lifeless against the Perspex side of his turret. He was past caring, but all of the others would have been aware of the hopelessness of their predicament with a burning wing and engine, and knew that in the unlikely event of their survival, they absolutely would not be going home tonight. P/O Fraser, the bomb aimer, was probably distracted by the commotion coming from behind and above him, and knew of the severity of the situation. When he let the bomb go, he knew that he had done so too late for an effective attack. The mine skipped over the crest of the dam, demolishing the power station at the base of the airside when it detonated on impact. The blast threw the dam's gunners to the floor, while the swirling dust took their breath away for a few seconds.

As Hopgood struggled for height, probably now with only two good engines, Burcher was furiously hand-cranking his turret to the fore and aft position to give himself access to his parachute stowed in the fuselage. He had watched with alarm as the tongues of flame danced past his position on each side, and guessed the end was near. The hydraulic power for his turret came from the port outer engine, so clearly, that engine had either failed, or the pipework from it had been damaged. Once in the body of the Lancaster, and in the flickering light streaming through the side windows from the burgeoning fire outside, Burcher encountered the wireless operator, Sgt John Minchin, white-faced with pain and shock, crawling down the steeply inclining fuselage towards the rear in search of his own parachute, and dragging his shattered leg. How he had negotiated the main spar will never be known, but it must have required a Herculean effort of will. Before attending to his own survival Burcher assisted his wounded colleague to the rear door, and having clipped on his parachute, pushed him through, holding on to the D-ring as he went. Sadly, Minchin's chute did not have time to fully deploy, and his body was discovered later on the Haarhöhe, the high ground bordering the western edge of the valley to the north of the dam. His death came just eleven days short of his first wedding anniversary.

Up front in the nose of AJ-M, John Fraser had by this time opened the escape hatch in the floor of his compartment, and noted with alarm the close proximity of the treetops. He unpacked his parachute inside the aircraft, and kneeling behind the hole in the floor in the prescribed manner, fed the canopy into the slipstream as he rolled forward. He was snatched into the night sky, and sensed as much as saw the tail wheel flash past his face. He was conscious of swinging wildly as he floated the short distance to earth, and in those few seconds before he met the ground, AJ-M was rent by an explosion, which tore off a wing. The shattered and burning remains of the Lancaster plunged around 500 feet to the ground with Hopgood, Brennan, Earnshaw and Gregory still aboard. It disintegrated almost totally on impact in a meadow near the village of Ostönnen, 6km in a straight line beyond the dam, and the tail plane was the only recognisable part of the still smouldering wreckage available for inspection by the German military later in the day.

Rear gunner Burcher's survival was entirely arbitrary. His instinct, after Minchin's departure, was to plug into the intercom to tell Hopgood he was going, so that his skipper would not remain with the aircraft a second longer than necessary. Like Fraser, Burcher understood that his only chance of survival lay in disgorging the contents of his parachute pack, and bundling the silk and rigging under his arm. He heard Hopgood scream, 'For Christ's sake get out of here!' and then memory ceased until he came to on the ground in considerable pain. As he stood on the threshold of the open door, the explosion occurred, flinging him outwards. His back was struck a damaging blow by the tail plane, but the parachute canopy, while not deploying fully, filled with sufficient air to cushion his fall to earth. Burcher was unable to walk, and he endured hours of extreme discomfort until he was found and taken into captivity. His initial treatment by the enemy was anything but gentle in view of the severity of his back injury, but like Fraser, he would survive as a prisoner of war. We will return later to pick up John Fraser's story.

At 00.38, Martin began his run across the Möhne Lake towards the dam that now had a pall of black smoke from the shattered power station as a backdrop. The gunners had picked themselves up, and despite the choking dust still hanging in the air, made ready to face the next onslaught. The mood inside the circling Lancasters was now sombre. 'Hoppy' and the boys were gone, and the gunners on the dam would be buoyed up by their success and confident of their ability to deal with whatever the 'Tommys' could throw at them. This was when Gibson's leadership qualities came to the fore. He knew he had to distract the gunners or risk the operation failing. As Martin bore down on the dam Gibson made a pass at right angles above it to draw off the fire. It seemed to have the desired effect and Martin reached the point of release unscathed. Bob Hay called 'bomb gone!', and P-Popsie shot between the towers before hauling off to port, at which moment two shells struck the starboard wing and lodged in a petrol tank. Fortunately, the tank was empty and the damage would not compromise the safe return of the crew. As they looked back at their work, Martin and his crew were disappointed to see that the bomb had veered dramatically off course, and exploded in the mud flats on the left-hand bank. The gunners on the southern sluice tower, already drenched from the detonation of Gibson's bomb, were treated to another soaking, and it was probably at this point that the gun was thrown from its mount. It also became necessary at this time to change the red-hot barrels on the battery perched on the northern tower.

Away from this cauldron of fierce activity, the five aircraft of the third wave were still over England and making their way to the coast. Meanwhile, a little south of the Möhnesee Joe McCarthy was having problems with his approach at the Sorpe, and was making repeated runs across the dam until his bomb aimer was satisfied. The problem was in part a church in the village of Langscheid, high up on the northern bank of the reservoir almost in line with the target, which interfered with McCarthy's preferred approach.

There was also mist rising up from the lake and obscuring important ground detail until they were almost upon it. Lying on his stomach in the nose of T-Tommy Sgt George 'Johnny' Johnson seemed oblivious to the growing impatience of his crewmates as he called 'dummy run' time after time as if it were just another training sortie. He had come all the way to Germany at extreme personal risk to place his very expensive bomb in exactly the right place, and he was not going to let it go until he was completely satisfied. The Sorpe required a different form of attack, because its construction differed markedly from that of the Möhne and Eder. As described earlier, rather than being a vertical wall of masonry, its cross-section was triangular, with gently sloping earthen banks either side of a concrete core. It provided little vertical masonry for the mine to slam into to arrest its forward progress as in the case of a traditional gravity dam, and the high water level would have ensured the mine's passage straight over the top. It also lacked towers to use as a reference. The attacks on the Sorpe had to be carried out along the length of the dam, rather than at right angles to it, from as low a height and speed as possible, and without revolving the mine. The weapon was to be released as close to the centre point as could be determined, so that it would roll down the stone-clad face on the reservoir side of the dam to the required depth. As the residents of Langscheid were having their sleep disturbed by McCarthy and crew, at the same time over Lincolnshire Rice and Munro were on final approach to Scampton, each unaware of the other's presence, a situation that was about to set hearts pounding. As far as the big picture was concerned, of the original nineteen Lancasters four had already been lost, and two others had been knocked out of the operation for, as yet, no profit.

Rice, minus tail wheel and hydraulics, and having circled for about twenty minutes while some unfortunate crew members pumped the wheels down, was about to land, when Munro, without the means to communicate, cut in front and lobbed down. As Rice was completing another circuit, Young was making his attack at the Möhne, with Gibson and Martin flying above and ahead on either side to attract the attention of the defenders. At about the same time, McCarthy's bomb aimer, Sgt Johnson, was finally preparing to release his weapon at the Sorpe, on what would be the tenth run. At 00.46, to the immense relief of his six fellow occupants of AJ-T, Johnson pressed the bomb release 'tit' and delivered his precious Upkeep, according to the ORB, from a perilously low 30 feet and at a speed of 170 mph. Seconds later the hamlet of Langscheid was rocked by a huge explosion that rattled every window and broke a few. McCarthy and crew flew back over the dam to examine the fruits of their labour, and were encouraged to notice some crumbling of the crest and roadway, but could not report a breach. At 00.47, Rice finally put down at Scampton, and in the absence of a tail wheel, the Lancaster sustained further damage, this time to the bottom of the fins.

Back at the Möhne Young had carried out a copybook attack, the first so far. The defenders and their equipment were tiring and were now able to offer only a token level of opposition. Young's Upkeep had struck the face of the dam right at its centre, and sunk to the required depth before exploding with the now familiar column of water and major agitation of the surface. When the scene had calmed, the dam was still there, apparently undamaged, and now half of the bombs of the first wave, intended for use against both the Möhne and the Eder, had been used. Gibson called up David Maltby and ordered him into the attack at 00.49. As he sped towards the dam, he became aware that something was happening to the dam, its upper profile was no longer smooth, and there were signs of debris on the top. The Möhne dam was beginning to break, and a breach was forming before his very eyes. He was about to abandon his run when the bomb aimer, P/O Fort, released the Upkeep, which bounced four times, and impacted the dam in precisely the prescribed manner, before sinking and exploding. The already fatally wounded structure could no longer cope with the enormous weight of water heaving against its fractured masonry, and a large section simply toppled over, releasing a torrent of floodwater, which tore at the edges of the breach, widening it before cascading down the valley to engulf villages in its path and the small town of Neheim-Hüsten. It also swept away wooden barrack buildings containing hundreds of eastern European female forced workers. Most of them perished, and these would represent a large proportion of what ultimately became the highest death toll to date from a Bomber Command operation of 1,249 people. At 00.50, Group received 'Goner 78A' from A-Apple, a full thirteen minutes after Gibson's coded message. Knowing the planned sequence of bombing, those at Group must have wondered about Hopgood, Martin and Maltby, but then, at 00.53 came Martin's 'Goner 58A'. Two minutes later, Maltby's wireless operator, Sgt Stone, sent 'Goner 78A', at which point those waiting at Grantham must have been close to despair. At last, at 00.56, Gibson was able to transmit the long awaited 'Nigger' signal to Group, announcing the destruction of the Möhne Dam. Group asked for confirmation a minute later, and duly received it. There would be no further exchanges between Group and Chastise aircraft for forty-eight minutes. Martin and Maltby turned for home, while Gibson, with Young as deputy, Shannon, Maudslay and Knight headed eastwards to the Eder.

CHAPTER SIX

Opening Night Act Two

The Eder and Sorpe dams

Despite being undefended, the Eder presented a more challenging proposition because of the hilly terrain surrounding it. Whereas at the Möhne, the crews had about fourteen seconds in which to adjust track, height and speed before the point of release, the approach at the Eder allowed only half that time. On arrival at the Eder reservoir, difficulty in locating the position of the dam threw the operation further behind schedule, and it was necessary for Gibson to fire off a Very cartridge to attract Shannon from the defunct Rehbach dam on the other side of the headland. With the minutes ticking away towards 01.30, Gibson called in Shannon to make his attack. The approach took him along a valley to a cutting in the ring of hills surrounding the lake on its northern side. The Germans had thoughtfully provided a navigation point in the imposing form of Waldeck Castle, perched right on the edge of the shoulder of cliff that formed the left side of the gap from Shannon's perspective. The ground then fell away in a sheer drop of many hundreds of feet to the surface of the reservoir. This was the challenge facing Shannon and the others who still had an Upkeep to deliver. To attain the required bombing height of 60 feet it was necessary to shed altitude at a stomach-churning rate, while aiming for a spit of land reaching out into the lake directly opposite and running parallel with the dam wall. The descent had to be accomplished through the skilful use of throttles and flaps, and be under sufficient control to allow an immediate forty-five degree turn to port over the spit to find the line, height and speed ready for the bomb release. After a number of unsuccessful attempts by Shannon to establish an accurate approach, Maudslay was invited to try, but experienced similar problems. At 01.30, as the third wave crews were just making landfall at the enemy coast, Shannon was called in again, and made two more dummy runs, angling his approach to bypass the spit of land designated as the starting point for the straight and level run. It was this that had been largely responsible for the difficulties, but now, on the third run, F/S Len Sumpter in the nose of AJ-L was able to release the mine. The time was 01.39, and the drop was accurate, although because of the angle of approach, the mine struck the dam wall well to the right of centre, possibly even at the right-hand extremity of the structure.

Despite the fact that no damage was apparent, Shannon was convinced that a small breach had occurred. Eventually, at 02.06, he signalled 5 Group HQ accordingly with the code 'Goner 79B'. Maudslay attacked at about 01.45, with AJ-Z, according to eyewitnesses, displaying signs of damage to the underside in the form of something sticking out. In *Enemy Coast Ahead*, Gibson comments on a curious incident as Maudslay approached Waldeck Castle in preparation for his bombing run. He describes the Lancaster pulling away suddenly as if something was wrong, but quickly resuming its course and carrying out its attack. A possible explanation for the sudden deviation and apparent damage is that AJ-Z was confronted by treetops, and pulled away to avoid them. Perhaps the Lancaster actually made contact with trees or some other object on the ground, and either the bomb release mechanism was damaged in some way, or the bomb was knocked out of alignment between the retaining arms, thus altering the profile of the underside as seen by those watching. Alternatively, a piece of branch may have become jammed in some way around the bomb with the same result. It is also possible, that none of this happened, and that AJ-Z was simply travelling too fast at the moment of release. Whatever the truth, the mine, it seems, struck the parapet of the dam without having made contact with the water, although even this is uncertain, and detonated on impact. At that moment AJ-Z was illuminated, and was clearly seen to be above and just beyond the point of explosion. Maudslay responded faintly to the later of two R/T enquiries from Gibson immediately afterwards, but then nothing more was heard by the crews, although a coded message of 'Goner 28B' was received from Maudslay by Group at 01.57 confirming his attack, and the fact that he was still alive.

Knight carried the first wave's last hope slung under AJ-N, and following one dummy run and much advice from Shannon, he delivered a perfect attack at 01.52, on a heading fifteen degrees to the left of Shannon's. As he did so, Hutchison, in Gibson's aircraft, twice vainly called Astell by W/T. Knight's bomb punched a hole through the wall at the point of detonation below the waterline a little to the right of centre, releasing a horizontal jet of water. The masonry above the hole collapsed, creating a V-shaped fissure, which was narrower than that at the Möhne, but deeper. At 01.53, as the awestruck onlookers watched the torrent of water crashing down the valley, Maltby cleared the Dutch coast via the Helder peninsula, and gained the safety of the North Sea with Martin only minutes behind. At 01.54 the codeword 'Dinghy' crossed the ether from Gibson's aircraft to be received joyously at HQ Grantham, and within a minute, HQ had requested and received confirmation. At 02.00 Goner 710B was transmitted to Group by AJ-N, and thus, the three messages informing Grantham that Shannon, Maudslay and Knight had carried out their attacks arrived at Grantham only after the confirmation had already been received, that the Eder had been breached.

The method of attack by both Shannon and Knight, i.e., not precisely at right angles to the wall, raises an interesting question. In order to release the Upkeep at the optimum distance from the dam wall it was necessary to employ a system of triangulation based on the measurement between the two towers, whether utilising the Dann sight or the string and chinagraph marks on the clear vision panel. This would not be possible to achieve in the kind of angled approach demanded of Shannon and Knight, once the original plan had been abandoned as impractical. Ray Grayston remembers Knight's attack as being at right angles, which is not quite borne out by the evidence, but perhaps Knight was able to apply a degree or two of yaw at the right moment to bring the nose round sufficiently for Johnson, the bomb-aimer, to get an accurate fix. Exactly how it was done we will never know, but it was a remarkable feat of airmanship involving Knight at the control yoke and pedals and Grayston on the throttles and flaps.

As these events were unfolding, the third wave aircraft were picking their way across Holland, and were approaching the narrow gap between the enemy night-fighter airfields at Gilze-Rijen and Eindhoven to its south-east. Burpee flew into a pocket of flak and took what evasive action he could at such low level. Whether or not he instantly realised he had stumbled into the defence zone of Gilze-Rijen airfield we will never know, but when the dread reality dawned on him, Gibson's warning at briefing must have rung in his ears. The commanding officer's imperative had come after Hopgood raised the matter of flak at Hüls during a recent operation that had nearly spelled his end. Gibson agreed to take the course a little further north, but referring to Gilze-Rijen and Eindhoven he had added, 'the gap isn't too wide. Watch it you navigators!' Burpee pushed the nose of AJ-S even lower as he desperately sought cover, but now he was over a wooded section of the airfield itself. The branches reached up clawing and grabbing at the Lancaster, catching hold of it, snagging it, robbing it of flying speed until dragging it down to a violent impact on a piece of open ground. Earthbound eyewitnesses and those in the air all described the detonation of the Upkeep as resembling a rising sun that lit up the landscape like day.

What befell Burpee and his crew at 02.00, at the precise moment, that Knight's wireless operator, Bob Kellow, was tapping out his message of success at the Eder, was supposedly witnessed by Herbert Scholl, a Ju88 wireless operator serving with E/NJG/2. The letter E stands for Ergänzung, which was a unit attached to the main squadron to provide finishing training for new crews in an operational environment. The following report is translated from the publication Jäger Blatt Nr XXIV February 1974, and also appears in the book Wasserkrieg by Helmut Euler minus a line or two. Few of the events on this night are clear-cut, and Herr Scholl's testimony contains discrepancies, the first of which relates to the time. The German time would rarely harmonize with British double summer time, but the difference would have been one hour or two at the most, with German time ahead of British. As the occasion was recalled by the eyewitness many years later, the time must be considered to be a rough estimate. Secondly, he describes the airfield as completely dark with no moon, on a night that we know to have been moonlit. This is hard to explain, as skies over England and Germany, west and east of Gilze-Rijen were clear. Thirdly, the aircraft is misidentified as a Halifax, but such mistakes were commonplace. A photograph of the tail section taken on the following morning apparently shows the wreckage to be that of a Lancaster. In the final analysis, only one four engine RAF bomber crashed onto Gilze-Rijen aerodrome on the night of the 16/17th of May 1943, and that was the one containing Burpee and crew. There is, of course, the possibility, that Herr Scholl is describing an event at some other airfield on a different date, which has become confused in his memory, but this seems unlikely.

The shooting down of a Halifax by a searchlight at night on the aerodrome at Gilze-Rijen, Holland.

It was 22.30 hours on Sunday, the 16th of May 1943, on the aerodrome at Gilze-Rijen, when the place was crossed for the first time by a low-flying English four-engine aircraft. The crews of the E/NJG/2, who were on standby, were standing in front of their barracks, looking out for the bomber, which according to its sound, was getting lower and lower as it stooged around in the vicinity. It was assumed that the bomber's crew was searching for a specific objective on the airfield or nearby. The place was completely dark, and not even the moon was shining as the bomber approached the airfield a second time. It came from the west, as a searchlight, which had been built on a tower between the command post and repair hangar, directed its beam onto the bomber. The bomber was already very low, and the searchlight beam caught it almost horizontally as it approached, presumably blinding the pilot, because it was pushed even lower into trees, through which it tore a great swathe, before crashing onto an empty military vehicle garage belonging to the airfield flak section. It burned immediately. Seconds later there was an ear-splitting explosion caused by an air mine. The crash site was about a hundred metres west of the repair hangar, between it and the command post. The shock wave was so strong, that it engulfed the E/NJG/2 crews, who were standing on the far side, about six to seven hundred metres away. On the following morning, one could recognise, that it was a Halifax, which presumably had a Dutch crew on board. The aircraft was totally destroyed, only the rear turret and tail plane remaining almost unscathed, this part having been torn off on impact at its joint with the main fuselage section. The crew were dead, the rear gunner showing no signs of injury outwardly, and very scantily dressed in lace-up shoes, with worn-through soles, and thin, unpressed uniform trousers. It would have been bad, had the bomber flown on for another one or two hundred metres, because it would literally have rammed the searchlight tower. Why the flak did not open fire is not known. In any event, the successful kill by a searchlight has a certain rarity value.

Perhaps this final sentence in Herr Scholl's testimony provides a clue to the veracity or otherwise of the account. At a time when hundreds of enemy aircraft were falling victim to flak and fighters, the above offers a more unusual and dramatic alternative.

A Dutch eyewitness to the events on that night recorded much activity in the general vicinity of the airfield at Gilze-Rijen. Although he could not see the airfield itself, he describes many RAF fighter-bombers buzzing the area, which were obviously part of the intruder operations designed to help Chastise by keeping enemy night fighters on the ground. A lot of flak was thrown up both from the airfield and from flak installations up to a few miles distant, particularly in the Tilburg area, and he believed that the Lancaster was hit by flak and was on fire before crashing onto the airfield. A member of Ken Brown's crew also witnessed the end of AJ-S from a position about ten miles behind and to starboard, and is very clear in his opinion, that the Lancaster was hit by flak from the airfield and was well on fire before impacting the ground. One can only say, that every witness would probably have a different recollection, even immediately after the event. There is no question, that having faced attack by intruders, the flak gunners at Gilze-Rijen would have been alert and fired-up, as would those in the general area. As Burpee's arrival over the airfield occurred some time after the earlier events, one might ask whether the gunners would have advertised their position by firing, when not directly under attack? I suspect that they would, and, initially, I found Herr Scholl's account to be less convincing. That left me with two accounts of Burpee's end so different, that they could not be reconciled. However, a recent discussion between Andreas and an historian associated with the museum sited on the Royal Dutch Air Force station at Gilze-Rijen today, seems to confirm the truth of both accounts. It seems certain that Burpee's Lancaster was hit by flak before reaching Gilze-Rijen, and that the pilot was then blinded by the searchlight as he stumbled across the airfield. In a vain attempt to escape the glare, he ploughed through treetops, lost control of an already doomed aircraft and crashed, causing extensive damage to buildings and installations in the process as the Upkeep detonated. A German report on the consequences of the crash described the main flak accommodation, the transport, kitchen, administrative and ablutions blocks as severely damaged, with slight to heavy damage to the buildings of the technical section. Total damage was estimated at around 1,500,000 Dutch Gilders. The difficulty in establishing an accurate and undisputed sequence of events is not confined to AJ-S, and as we are about to discover, the accounts of Maudslay's final moments are not entirely clear-cut.

The confirmation of the destruction of the Eder Dam set off a flurry of communications between Group and the attacking force. At 02.10 Group enquired of Gibson how many aircraft of the first wave were available for target C, the Sorpe. At 02.11 Gibson replied, that there was none. Some minutes later Group called up the third wave crews, receiving a response from Townsend in AJ-O at 02.21. At 02.22 Townsend was given the code word 'Gilbert', directing him to attack the last resort target assigned to him, which was the Ennepe Dam, and Brown in AJ-F announced himself ready to receive his orders. They were encapsulated in the code word 'Dinghy', which confirmed the destruction of the Eder and pointed him towards the Sorpe. At 02.25 Group repeated its message to Townsend, and a minute later called up Anderson in AJ-Y. Anderson confirmed receipt of his signal at 02.28, as Group was in the process of contacting Ottley in AJ-C. Ottley acknowledged receiving the code word 'Gilbert' at 02.31, and this series of signals ended with two from Group to the now dead Burpee at 02.32 and 02.33.

At 02.35, while Gibson, Young, Shannon and Knight were making their way westwards across Germany, Gibson noted an aircraft to port falling in flames near Hamm. Ottley, through an error in navigation, had turned south too early, and had come within range of the defences concentrated around an area just west of Hamm's northern suburbs. Hamm was a major railway centre, well known to Bomber Command, and a town which had already been stirred up by McCarthy, who had darted backwards and forwards over the marshalling yards at 50 feet, while trying to find his way home over an hour earlier. McCarthy survived, Ottley did not. Ottley was in the act of informing his crew of the change of target from the Lister to the Sorpe, but the words were still on his lips as the Lancaster was suddenly bathed in the glare of searchlights predominantly from the port side, and was rocked by a direct hit from a flak shell. The flak battery was on the Kötterberg, south of Ottley's position, and close to an aircraft listening station manned by part-time local traders and tradesmen including an innkeeper, a master hair-dresser, a farmer, a roof tiler, a tailor and a couple of grocers. The Lancaster did not fall instantly, but it was immediately clear to Ottley that AJ-C was lost. As it flew eastwards across the village of Bockum-Hövel Ottley was heard by rear gunner, Freddie Tees, to say, "I'm sorry boys, we've had it". Having flown over the village the aircraft briefly adopted a north-northeasterly course until a fuel tank exploded. One German eyewitness from the listening station described the tail section breaking away and falling two hundred metres from the rest of the aircraft. As the Lancaster hit the ground in a field on the edge of a wooded area called the Ostbusch, no more than a mile from the village, the Upkeep exploded, creating a large crater and spreading the wreckage around.

There were no survivors in the main part of the aircraft, but miraculously, Sgt Tees, the rear gunner, was still alive, although he sustained flash burns to his hands and face. In a dazed and shocked state he eventually extricated himself from his turret, and wandered along a narrow path through the trees.

As he emerged into the open at the edge of the wood, he was confronted by two teenaged members of the Hitler Youth, one of whom had seen the explosion from his bedroom window a couple of miles away. He remained to apprehend Tees, who offered no resistance, while the other ran to a nearby house to raise the alarm. Tees was eventually handed over to a policeman, and was held in the farmhouse of Herr and Frau Blix and their daughter, a few hundred yards east of the crash site, where he remained in a state of shock until the military arrived to collect him. He was to spend a considerable time in hospital before being moved to a PoW camp. Meanwhile, at the crash site, there was apparently no effort by German soldiers to remove what remained of the bodies from the flames, and one eyewitness account describes an airman impaled upon a branch. The local people who witnessed the event are convinced that Ottley purposely kept the Lancaster airborne to avoid civilian casualties in the village, and he is considered a hero. While this is a touching story, it has to be said, that self preservation and the welfare of his crew demanded that Ottley put the aircraft down in as controlled a fashion as possible, and this required open ground. Sadly, he ran out of time.

One minute after Ottley's crew met its end, Maudslay's did likewise. At 02.36, having limped westwards from the Eder, AJ-Z was brought down by the flak defences at the frontier town of Emmerich, nestling on the eastern bank of the Rhine right on the border with Holland. It is inconceivable that Maudslay had intended to cross the Rhine at Emmerich, a town with oil storage facilities, and, therefore, a town defended. It is likely that navigational problems had brought AJ-Z to this point, and that at such low level it was upon the blacked out town before the crew had time to react. Almost immediately the flak found AJ-Z, and it crashed north-east of the town into a meadow bounded now on its northern side by a motorway, and within touching distance of Holland. This time there were no survivors. There have been persistent rumours, that a number of Maudslay's crew, up to five, survived the impact, and were subsequently murdered by local police or civilians before the military arrived on the scene. It is fitting to bring all of the available evidence together to attempt to put an end to this speculation. There were four flak batteries with a total of twelve guns within range of AJ-Z as it approached Emmerich from the direction of the Ruhr. Members of two different batteries, Herr Doerwald and Herr Feldmann, later recorded their impressions of the final moments of AJ-Z. The following is a translation of their testimony.

> I belonged to Home Flak. Our position, equipped with three 2cm anti-aircraft guns, was situated near the industrial harbour in front of the River Rhine lock. Earlier in the evening aircraft had flown in the direction of the Möhne Dam and returned without load (bomb). At about 3 o'clock in the morning one single Lancaster came in flying very low. The aircraft was fired upon, and fire broke out. It came down near Klein Netterden. The crash took place in a meadow east of the Industria

> Brickworks along the Osterholt Road. I was a gun layer, and I received a medal for shooting down the plane. Afterwards, we heard that officers of high rank were on board the plane. The whole crew, about seven or eight men, were killed.
>
> Reported by Johannes Doerwald.

> The aircraft returned from the Ruhr in the early morning. It was fired upon first by the anti-aircraft battery in the keep. Along the Nierenbergerstrasse and near the harbour there were 2cm anti-aircraft positions of the Home Flak. Each battery had three guns. The plane turned away, and the rear gunner fired at the battery near the lock. Then all twelve guns were shooting at the plane, and the engines caught fire. Then it crashed and exploded. People said there were seven crewmembers on board. Our battery was situated on the harbour breakwater. With our fire we shaved the poplars standing on the harbour. The aircraft was flying at such low level, that we had to aim the guns at a very low angle.
>
> Reported by Feldmann.

In May 2003 Andreas and I sat with Herr Doerwald over a drink in Emmerich, where he has lived for his entire life. We had earlier visited the town's museum, and spoken to a curator, who described Maudslay's Lancaster actually flying over the town before being forced away by the ground fire. This seems to harmonise with the report by Herr Feldmann quoted above. However, the account given to me in person by Herr Doerwald is sufficiently at odds with that of Herr Feldmann to be almost a different incident. According to Herr Doerwald, who was sixteen years old at the time, his battery engaged Maudslay's Lancaster as it approached them at a range of about a kilometre. The battery was situated on the south-eastern edge of the town with the Rhein at the gunners' backs, and Maudslay was approaching at very low level from the east. Herr Doerwald is convinced that a shell struck the cockpit area, killing the pilot instantly. His conviction is based on the fact that the aircraft flipped over immediately and went straight into the ground. He further attested, that there was no fire before the impact. This final detail, however, contradicts his own testimony recorded above, which claims that fire broke out before the Lancaster came to earth. It should also be said, that the effective destructive range of 2cm flak is only around 500 to 700 metres, considerably less than the 1,000 metres at which Herr Doerwald claims to have engaged AJ-Z. Herr Doerwald related the events in a very matter-of-fact manner with no embellishments for effect, and his story bore the ring of truth. He is a respected member of the local community, and served for many years as the town's deputy mayor. It is impossible to reconcile such different accounts, but I favour those recorded immediately after the event, before time, repetition and failing memory had opportunity to corrupt them. In the final analysis it is the reader who must decide which to believe.

The telling features of both reports are, that the aircraft was very low, precluding any chance of survival by parachute, and that it crashed and exploded. It is believed that only Maudslay and rear gunner Burrows were positively identified, while those in the main body of the Lancaster were beyond recognition, and three of them were initially interred in a single grave. The crash took place in countryside some distance outside of the town, and it would have taken some time for local civilians to reach the location, even had they wished to do so at that unearthly hour. Clive Richards of the Air Historical Branch kindly perused for me the files containing the casualty reports, and was able to confirm, that any rumour of foul play regarding the Maudslay crew was without foundation, and that no evidence has ever been uncovered relating to war crimes committed against crews involved in Operation Chastise. An American investigator is known to have confused the Maudslay incident with that of S/L Wyness, which occurred during the attack on the Kembs barrage in October 1944. This is dealt with at the appropriate point in the narrative.

As disaster was befalling Maudslay and his crew, Brown and Anderson were pressing on towards their objective, the Sorpe, while Townsend headed for the Ennepe, the progress of all three made increasingly difficult by ground mist forming in the valleys. The defences had been stirred up by the earlier waves, and all three of these late-comers had been subjected to ground fire, Townsend, particularly, having experienced a torrid time, during which he was forced to demonstrate his not inconsiderable skills as a pilot. As the time drew towards 03.00, Gibson, Young, Shannon and Knight were approaching or crossing the Dutch coast, although not in sight of each other, and at slightly different points. The plan allowed for the first wave aircraft to exit Fortress Europe via the known gap in the defences between Egmond and the *Elefant* radar antenna system a little to the south. This array consisted of three towers, the northernmost of which was a receiver standing thirty to forty metres high and called *Kleine* Heidelberg, or Little Heidelberg. A kilometre to the south stood the *Grosse Elefant*, or Big Elephant, a massive wooden construction of one hundred metres in height, with the fifty metre-high *Kleine Elefant*, or Little Elephant, a further kilometre along the headland. Stout wooden posts or *Paals* mark the beach at 250 metre intervals, the kilometre posts bearing consecutive identification numbers. The perfect route took the Lancasters between *Paals* 41 and 42, ideally 200 yards to the right of *Kleine* Heidelberg. Gibson climbed briefly to 300 feet to establish a fix on the towers, and then stuck the nose down to gather speed for the final dash to the Atlantic Wall and freedom. The Lancaster was travelling faster than at any time that night, around 260 m.p.h., as it screamed over the shoreline within feet of the dunes. Shannon had already passed this way just a few minutes earlier, and Knight followed in Gibson's wake so low, that his tail wheel almost impacted a concrete structure nestling in the sand and course grass, and invisible to all on board but the rear gunner. He alone knew how close they had come to losing the wheel, if nothing else.

At 02.55 A-Apple was racing for the coast, which lay just a few miles and even less minutes away. The seven occupants were experiencing the mixed emotions of excitement and anxiety, excitement at the prospect of making the North Sea and safety after a successful operation, and anxiety at still being over hostile territory with the chance that something even now could go awry to rob them of their prize at the last moment. Shannon would later talk of the euphoria on board L-Leather as they made the sea crossing relieved of all tension and eagerly anticipating the party that would break out as soon as debriefing was over. There would have been no chatter on board A-Apple; that would come once they had gained the safety of the North Sea. Young was an old hand and kept a disciplined ship, and anyway, everyone's attention at the sharp end of the Lancaster was fixed on the horizon dead ahead. Eyes were straining to pick out the three radar towers, to the right of which lay the gateway to England's east coast. The four Merlins were thrumming loudly and reassuringly, and in a little over an hour they would be on final approach to Scampton with the prospect of a hearty breakfast and as much beer as they could sink. They knew that tonight had been special, and that they had played an important role in something unique and spectacular. The memory of the torrent of water spewing out of the breached Möhne Dam was fresh in their minds, as was the maelstrom at the Eder snaking and tearing its way down the valley towards Kassel. No crews had witnessed anything like it before, and they had been mesmerised by the sight as they circled a few hundred feet above, trying to take in the enormity of their triumph. It had almost been difficult for them to drag themselves away from the Möhne to head for the Eder, and then to leave the unfolding scene at the Eder to go home. It was Gibson, conscious of the approach of daylight, who had reminded them of the need to curtail their sightseeing, point their noses towards the west and hit the deck.

Young couldn't see the radar towers, just the rise of the dunes in the distance, and he decided to climb a little to get his bearings. He eased the yoke back just a tad and the Lancaster rose effortlessly like the thoroughbred that it was, particularly when relieved of its bomb load and most of its fuel. Now Vance MacCausland, the Canadian bomb-aimer, could make out the dark line of the North Sea, and before it the irregular shapes of the rooftops of a small coastal town nestling beneath the high dunes. Suddenly they were in the thick of accurate light flak. It whipped up at them from out of the darkness without warning and followed them scoring hits. Within seconds A-Apple was out of range but had been wounded, and as the occupants took stock of their situation, their hearts hammering in their chests, another battery ahead of them opened up, squirting a stream of hot metal into their faces. Fresh strikes on the Lancaster decided the issue once and for all, and Young maintained control for the time it took to breast the dunes. AJ-A came to rest on a sand bar off the beach near Castricum aan Zee opposite Paal 47, with its nose pointing towards the north. This suggests that Young made a starboard turn to run parallel with the beach in an attempt to pull off a ditching or crash-landing. Clearly the impact was too violent for the crew to survive.

A-Apple had been south of the preferred crossing point by around ten kilometres, and Young's decision to climb made him an easy target for two batteries belonging to the Ijmuiden flak defence zone, the northern extremity of which was at Wijk aan Zee, the little sea-side resort close to *Paal* 52. 7/816 Marine Flak battery reported firing upon a Halifax at 02.57, and battery 6/816 reported shooting it down at 02.59. As we have already seen, mistaking a Lancaster for a Halifax was not an unusual occurrence. It was later on the 17th that the body of Sgt Roberts, the navigator, was washed ashore, while the sea gave up the others at various points along the Dutch coast between the 27th and 30th. As AJ-A went into the sea, Joe McCarthy was only twenty minutes away from Scampton, and it was at this point that wireless operator Eaton tapped out the message 'Goner 79C', signifying, that the Upkeep had exploded in contact with the Sorpe Dam and caused a small breach.

Meanwhile, Anderson, forced off track by searchlights, unable to establish his position after searching for forty minutes, and now behind schedule with an unserviceable rear turret, was considering his options. As Maltby touched down at Scampton at 03.11, the first back from Operation Chastise, Anderson was abandoning his sortie, and returning on a reciprocal course. At the same time Brown was following in McCarthy's footsteps at the Sorpe, trying to find his line in the mist. On one run he emerged from the mist on the dry side of the dam, and after negotiating the hill at the far end found his flying speed dropping off so dramatically that he had to pull off a stall turn to regain it. Finally, on his fourth attempt at 03.14, and having dropped flares to mark his path, Brown's bomb aimer, Sgt Oancia, released his Upkeep two thirds of the way along the length of the dam. It was an accurate drop from 60 feet, and further crumbling of the crest resulted, but again there was no breach. Five minutes later, at 03.19, Martin landed at Scampton, followed at 03.23 by McCarthy with a burst tyre, courtesy of a brief but spirited encounter with a flak train on the outward flight. Gibson, Shannon and Knight were now well into their crossing of the North Sea, Brown and Anderson were still deep in Germany, and Townsend had arrived in the vicinity of the Ennepe. He was experiencing difficulty, first in identifying the target, and then in establishing a line of approach, and he was also aware of a marked vibration when the weapon was rotated. At 03.37, the bomb aimer in AJ-O, Sgt Franklin, released the final Upkeep of Operation Chastise, and the pattern of rings in the water following the explosion showed that it had fallen short, leaving the dam intact. In recent years it has been suggested that Townsend attacked the Bever dam rather than the Ennepe, and evidence has been produced to support that view. However, German author Helmut Euler, whose fascination with Operation Chastise has led to exhaustive research and a number of books on the subject, is convinced that Townsend did indeed attack the Ennepe, and can also provide supporting evidence. His argument is that a Mosquito carried out an Upkeep-style bombing run on the Bever, which, if so, would have been a remarkable coincidence in time and place. Perhaps the strongest evidence to support Townsend being at the Bever is the compass heading used for the bombing run and the position of the moon as stated at debriefing. Whichever is the case, Townsend's flight was an epic, which did not end with the release of his mine. He was now alone over Germany, a good thirty minutes behind Brown, with the sky to his rear lightening perceptibly. As the Lancaster raced across Germany at treetop height at 04.11, wireless operator Chalmers tapped out 'Goner 58E'. AJ-O would ultimately cross the flat plain of Holland in broad daylight and somehow get away with it.

At 04.06, Shannon landed at Scampton, followed by Gibson at 04.15, five minutes before Knight, and at about the same time that Anderson and Brown were crossing the Dutch coast, having picked their way across Holland in the twilight of dawn. Anderson landed at 05.30 with his bomb still aboard, and Brown touched down three minutes later. At 06.15, Townsend also landed, bringing Operation Chastise to a close. At a cost of eight Lancasters, and fifty-six men missing, all but three of them dead, two dams had been breached, and one had been damaged superficially. Harris, Wallis and Cochrane had by this time arrived back at Scampton to gain intelligence from the crews at first hand, and they set about interviewing individual crewmembers. Wallis was genuinely and visibly shocked to learn of the enormous casualties resulting from the operation inspired by his genius, and thereafter, he would always carry with him a misplaced sense of guilt. Gibson tried to console him with the assertion that the men would have gone anyway, even had they known they wouldn't return, and their loss was just an inevitable consequence of war. As Gibson walked off to attend to fifty-six casualty letters, he knew he had failed to convince Wallis.

Now let us return to Hopgood's bomb-aimer, John Fraser, who was coming to terms with his predicament as a hunted man in a hostile country. Fraser was a native of Nanaimo in British Columbia, and as a woodsman, was entirely capable of surviving on the ground and living off the land. He also had the advantage of being trained as a navigator before becoming a bomb-aimer, and this would enable him to use the stars to guide him across Germany at night. He was no novice in military terms either, and would have been regarded in Bomber Command circles as an old hand having already completed a tour of operations with 50 Squadron. At the end of April, with training for Operation Chastise in full swing, Gibson had allowed Fraser a 24 hour pass to marry his fiancée Doris. The ceremony took place on the 29th at Skellingthorpe, where Fraser had been stationed while with 50 Squadron. Little did they know that this brief interlude would be their only time together for the next two years. Fraser's survival was remarkable in two ways, firstly that he left the burning Lancaster literally a matter of seconds before it was torn apart, and secondly, that he did so at what he estimated was around three hundred feet. The narrowness of the margin between his life and death could be measured in the few hundred yards that lay between him and the

Sgt Don Buntaine was Ken Brown's regular mid-upper gunner. He trained for Operation *Chastise,* but missed out on the night through illness.

Sgt Harry Hewstone, wireless operator in Ken Brown's crew.

F/Sgt Ken Brown, one of many Canadian participants in Operation *Chastise*.

F/Sgt Grant MacDonald, Brown's rear gunner, was another Canadian.

King George IV and Queen Elizabeth visited Scampton on Thursday 27th of May. Here Queen Elizabeth is introduced to P/O Lance Howard RAAF, navigator to Townsend.

P/O Warner Ottley and some of his crew pictured while serving with 207 Squadron probably at Langar.

Officers pose in front of the officers mess at Scampton post Operation *Chastise*.

American Nick Knilans posing with his crew at Woodhall Spa, where they spent their entire operational careers with 619 and 617 Squadrons.

S/L Cockshott and crew at Woodhall Spa with their Lancaster PD238 KC-H.

S/L David Maltby and crew at Blida in North Africa after bombing installations at San Polo D'enza 15/16.7 43. Behind them stands EE130 AJ-A, the Lancaster in which S/L Allsebrook and crew would lose their lives while canal-busting in September.

Australians Mick Martin and Bob Hay at Scampton. Hay was 617 Squadron's bombing leader.

W/C Gibson on the terrace at the rear of the Petwood Hotel at Woodhall Spa, home to officers serving on the nearby bomber station. To Gibson's left is the portly figure of G/C "Tiny" Evans-Evans, station commander at Coningsby, who would lose his life in a Lancaster in February 1945.

Ken Brown with air and ground crews at Woodhall Spa January 1944.

As above.

W/C Gibson in thoughtful mood post 617 Squadron.

Guy and Eve Gibson flanked by 617 Squadron officers in London after the investiture on 22.6.43.

Official last picture of Gibson as a member of 617 Squadron taken on 2.8.43. He stands next to his successor, W/C George Holden, in front of his air and ground crews and his Dams aircraft ED932.

The same group with the exception of Holden, who is taking the photograph with a private camera.

P/O Burpee and five of his crew during their service with 106 Squadron at Syerston. Burpee is 4th from the left.

Another shot of Burpee and crew.

F/O Weeden and crew in front of ED825, AJ-E, which had flown to the dams in the hands of Joe McCarthy and crew as AJ-T. This Lancaster was lost over France with the Weeden crew on the night of 10/11.12.43 while engaged in an S.O.E. operation.

W/O Joe Brady,
Burpee's rear gunner.

Don Cheney's Dark Victor, KC-V.

A close-up of Dark Victor's motif.

The 12,000lb light case Blockbuster seen at Coningsby on a 57 Squadron trolley. The weapon was employed for the first time at the Dortmund-Ems Canal 15/16.9.43.

Phil Martin in his office with the St George and Dragon motif beneath his open cockpit panel.

Another Australian Martin, this one Phil, with his crew at Woodhall Spa in 1944.

Phil Martin and crew pose on the sturdy port wing of their Lancaster.

Another shot of Phil Martin and crew, who came to 617 Squadron from 61 Squadron.

Left foreground W/C Cheshire, 617 Squadron's commanding officer, shakes hands with General Spaatz of the USAAF. On Cheshire's left shoulder is G/C Philpott, Woodhall Spa's station commander. AVM Cochrane stands between Cheshire and Spaatz, with Colonel Jimmy Doolittle behind his superior. The date is 31.3.44. During the previous night Bomber Command had suffered its greatest defeat of the war, losing 95 aircraft during a raid on Nuremberg.

Gibson's dams Lancaster ED932, during the summer of 1943.

smouldering remains of AJ-M. Fraser hid his parachute in a culvert, and managed to remain unnoticed by the throng of German military personnel who had gathered to survey the shattered dam and the crash site. Having slipped through the cordon, he made his way towards the west, living off turnips and anything else he could forage from the land as he had learned to do before leaving his native Canada. During the next ten days or so he rested during the day and picked his way by night towards the west, almost retracing the route he had flown to the Möhne reservoir. He came upon few road signs to inform him of his precise location, but he could judge his progress by the shape of the terrain. When his journey began it was hilly and undulating, but by the time he had skirted the towns to the north of the Ruhr, he found himself in the flat pastureland that defines the Rhine region and the Netherlands. Now he was close to where Astell, Barlow and Maudslay and their crews had met their end. When he reached the Wesel area on the east bank of the Rhine, he was thirty miles from the Dutch frontier, and had walked around one hundred miles across fields, through woods and along railway tracks. It was here that his gallant evasion came to an end when he was apprehended by a policeman.

The issue of revealing information to the enemy under interrogation is a sensitive one, and it would be appropriate to consider the fate that awaited freshly captured airmen at a time in their lives when they were probably at their lowest ebb, alone amidst a hated and hostile enemy. Most found themselves at the interrogation centre at Oberursel near Frankfurt, where they would be placed in solitary confinement to increase their sense of loneliness, isolation and uncertainty until they acclimatised to their situation. They were generally invited to complete what purported to be a Red Cross questionnaire, so that their relatives could be informed as soon as possible that they were safe and well. Some of the questions were designed to elicit information, but it was also a subtle way of introducing the captive to the idea of giving up small pieces of seemingly unimportant detail. As they became accustomed to answering their interrogators, so it got easier to give more away. The Germans had a dossier on most Bomber Command squadrons, and many captives were astounded at the wealth of detail contained therein, including the names of commanding officers and flight commanders. Such information could only come from captured airmen, but in truth, very few possessed anything that was likely to be of use to the enemy. As Operation Chastise was 617 Squadron's maiden outing, the Germans would have been particularly keen to glean whatever they could from Fraser, but only Gibson, Young and Maudslay might have been in possession of anything useful, and none of these fell into enemy hands. Fraser held out for seven days in solitary, and his interrogation report reveals that he refused to give away anything that he considered might be of use. What he did say about the Dam sight, which was nothing more technical than wood and nails, and the task performed by each crewmember during the attack, was totally insignificant, and could easily have been worked out by the Germans themselves. He did make it clear to his captors, however, that he was proud of his part in the operation, and after that he was packed off to the first of four PoW camps, including Stalag Luft III of Great Escape fame, that would be his home for the next two years.

Let us now consider the operation with the benefit of hindsight, and assess its degree of success against that hoped for by those responsible for its conception and planning. Wallis had said that a single bomb accurately placed against the dam wall at the prescribed depth would, in conjuction with the weight of water, have the capacity to create a breach. For the operation to be considered completely successful, all six dams on the revised target list would have had to be destroyed. A seventh, the Henne, was removed from this list late on. All but the Sorpe were gravity dams, that is, they were masonry structures, and thereby susceptible to the method of attack formulated during training. The Sorpe was an earthen rampart with a concrete core, and Wallis had expressed doubts about Upkeep's effectiveness against it. That apart, as the operation began, nineteen bombs were available to pit against these six targets, allowing for three to be used against each, with one left over. On the face of it, if Wallis's calculations were correct and the best case scenario was enacted, complete success was possible, theoretically with some Upkeeps left over to return to store. Of course, in time of war, it is almost without precedent for matters to proceed exactly as planned, and Bomber Command had learned some hard lessons in the past.

Nine aircraft set out for the Möhne, and those, if any, with an Upkeep still on board after its destruction were to go on to the Eder and then to the Sorpe. Of those nine bombs, the first fell short, the second flew over the top, the third exploded in the mud banks of the southern shore, and only the fourth was delivered in precisely the manner required. This Upkeep, dropped by Young, fulfilled Wallis's prediction by actually causing the masonry to crumble, and there is little doubt, that the weight of water pressing against the fracture would have rolled the wall over in time. The fifth bomb was delivered by Maltby also with great accuracy, and if one is prepared to be pedantic, it could be said, that it was unnecessary and wasted. However, at low level over Germany with the flames from Hopgood's funeral pyre visible in the distance, time pressing on towards dawn and the Eder Dam still to be located and attacked, such considerations were out of place. The orders were to attack target X until it was clearly breached, before moving on to target Y, the Eder. It was only after Maltby's attack, that that particular criterion was satisfied. There certainly was no time to loiter in the target area to see what might happen if sufficient time was allowed. The sixth Upkeep was delivered at the Eder by Shannon, and it did explode more or less in contact with the wall, albeit well right of centre. We cannot say it was delivered precisely in the prescribed manner because of that fact, and we will never know the extent of the damage it caused. The seventh bomb detonated against the parapet causing only superficial damage, while the eighth never reached the target at all, having gone down with Astell on the way in. Knight delivered the ninth perfectly, which brought about a catastrophic failure of the wall. Thus, of wave 1's nine Upkeeps, only 1 in 3 had been used effectively.

What, then, of wave 2? If we continue the ordinal sequence and ignore the chronological order of events Barlow was carrying the tenth bomb, which did not reach its target, the Sorpe. The same applies to the eleventh, which was returned to Scampton by Munro. The twelfth ended up on the seabed between the Frisians and the mainland coast of Holland, as did the thirteenth soon afterwards when Rice bounced off the water. The fourteenth found its way to the Sorpe, and was dropped accurately by McCarthy and crew. Thus, after the expenditure of fourteen Upkeeps, four attacks can be described as effective, and two of the primary targets had been destroyed. Now to wave 3 and bomb number fifteen, which was lost with Ottley, while number sixteen caused massive devastation to Gilze-Rijen airfield, but failed to reach its intended target. The seventeenth added to the superficial damage at the Sorpe in the hands of Brown and crew, in what can be counted as the fifth effective delivery. The eighteenth was launched against the Bever or Ennepe Dam, but fell ineffectively short, and Anderson brought the nineteenth and last Upkeep home. The bald statistics of the operation are, that in round figures, 26 per cent of the available Upkeeps were delivered in the prescribed manner, and each was effective. 42 per cent of the available Upkeeps failed to arrive at their designated targets, and a further 31 per cent were delivered inaccurately. This last point is not a slight against the crews, but rather an indication of the range of variables beyond the control of the crews, which could affect the outcome. Based on the success of those dropped exactly as Wallis had intended, and bearing in mind, that the Sorpe's construction made it impregnable, the destruction of the five gravity dams was a realistic possibility if one ignores the incredibly difficult and demanding operational requirements. Almost every operation mounted by Bomber Command suffered from early returns, failure by some to locate the target, losses to enemy defences, hang-ups and inaccurate bombing, and most were far less intricate than Operation Chastise. All things considered, the attack on the dams has to be seen as a remarkable and successful undertaking, the high cost in lives serving only to demonstrate the degree of difficulty demanded of the participants. The loss of eight out of nineteen Lancasters represented 42 per cent of those dispatched, and while this was by no means a record, such a casualty figure involving a single squadron represented a body blow for the survivors to cope with. Back in 1940, 82 Squadron twice lost eleven out of twelve Blenheims within the space of about three months. 617 Squadron's second operation over Germany four months hence would result in an even greater percentage loss rate than that incurred at the dams.

From the moment that the news was released to the press and the BBC on the morning of the 17th, 617 Squadron became famous, and Operation Chastise the most celebrated feat of arms in aviation history. Maltby was granted the acting rank of Squadron Leader on the 18th, and the first replacement crew, that of F/L Allsebrook, arrived on the 20th from 49 Squadron.

This was the destination for Anderson and his crew officially on the 2nd of June, returning from whence they had come in April, although it seems, that they probably departed 617 Squadron earlier. They did so under a cloud, their position at 617 Squadron having been made untenable in the light of the performances of Brown and Townsend under similar circumstances. Gibson's self-confessed inability to relate to other ranks made him less sympathetic to Anderson as an NCO than he might have been to an officer. Certainly, Gibson was understanding of Rice's mishap with his bomb, possibly because of almost having come to grief himself in a similar way during the early days of training. For his part, Rice admitted to pilot error, and was never able to forgive himself. Any suggestion that Anderson acted in a cowardly manner is misplaced and unjust. It was not the action of a coward to return with his weapon and admit failure, when he could have jettisoned it over a body of water, and concocted an irrefutable excuse to explain it, or claimed to have attacked his assigned objective, but without success. We will never know precisely what was said, and Anderson and his crew took their side of the story to the grave. They returned to operations with 49 Squadron at Krefeld on the 21/22nd of June, and completed a further thirteen, some of them incident packed. Rear gunner Arthur Buck was lucky to survive a near miss by flak, which shattered his turret Perspex during a trip to Cologne on the 8/9th of July, and they landed short of fuel at Upper Heyford on return from Turin on the morning of the 13th. On the opening night of the Battle of Hamburg, on the 24/25th, when 'Window' (the tinfoil-backed strips of paper designed to blind the enemy night fighter, searchlight and gun-laying radar, by swamping it with false returns) was being employed for the first time, it blacked out the mid-upper turret. Their luck finally deserted them during an operation to Mannheim on the 23/24th of September, when they were shot down near Offenbach. It was the 27th trip of their tour. They now rest side by side in the peaceful surroundings of the Rheinberg Cemetery, a few yards from Hopgood and four of his crew.

Gibson was awarded the Victoria Cross, and thirty-three other participants in the operation also received decorations, including Townsend and Brown, who were awarded the much-prized Conspicuous Gallantry Medal. The recommendation for Martin's DSO written by Whitworth on the 20th read:

> This officer flew as No. 3 in the leading formation detailed to attack the Möhne Dam. On the way in he showed outstanding skill as pilot by keeping formation with the leader during the most difficult circumstances. When he reached the target flak was heavier than expected, and the aircraft, which attacked before him was shot down. Despite this F/L Martin attacked with great accuracy, and although his aircraft was badly damaged by flak and difficult to control, he flew successfully back to base. F/L Martin has displayed on all his 36 sorties the highest devotion to duty, and has a reputation, which, though admired by all, is

attained by few. I strongly recommend the immediate award to him of the Distinguished Service Order.

In recommending awards to Shannon, Danny Walker and Sumpter Whitworth stated:

> F/L Shannon was captain, Flying Officer Walker, navigator and Flight Sergeant Sumpter air bomber of the Lancaster detailed to attack the Eder Dam. With great skill and determination they succeeded in dropping their mine in exactly the right position. This was due to the excellent spirit and understanding in the crew. By their efforts they ensured the final breaching of this dam. Flight Lieutenant Shannon and Flying Officer Walker have flown together on many operations, and at all times they have displayed courage of a high order. I strongly recommend that the excellent work of this crew be recognised by the immediate award of the Distinguished Service Order to Flight Lieutenant Shannon and of the first Bar to the DFC to Flying Officer Walker, and of the Distinguished Flying Medal to Flight Sergeant Sumpter.

The other awards consisted of the DSO to Maltby, McCarthy, Martin and Knight, a Bar to the DFC for Hutchison, Leggo and Hay, a DFC to Chambers, Howard, Deering, Taerum, Spafford, Trevor-Roper, Fort, Hobday, Johnson (of Knight's crew) and Buckley, a Bar to the DFM for Franklin, and the DFM to Simpson, Heal, MacLean, Oancia, Johnson, (McCarthy's crew), Chalmers, Nicholson, Wilkinson, Pulford and Webb. Despite Gibson's low opinion of Pulford, Whitworth's citation read as follows:

> This NCO flew as flight engineer in Wing Commander Gibson's aircraft, which led the attack on the Mohne Dam. Throughout the sortie he displayed courage and devotion to duty of a high order and he was of great assistance to the pilot on many occasions. I strongly recommend that his good work on the occasion of this outstanding raid be recognised by the immediate award of the Distinguished Flying Medal.

Trevor-Roper's part in the operation was described by Whitworth in the following manner:

> This officer flew as rear gunner in the leading Lancaster which attacked the Möhne Dam. During the run in, his aircraft was subjected to stiff opposition from flak defences situated along the top of the Dam. By using his rear guns with great skill, even though bullets were passing through the rear structure of the aircraft just behind him, he succeeded not only in deterring the aim of the defences, but later in drawing the fire away from other aircraft which were actually making their bombing

> runs. As gunnery leader, Flight Lieutenant Trevor-Roper has set a magnificent example which is an inspiration to all the other gunners in the squadron.

Avro's daily movement sheet records ED915 as being received at the factory on the 19th for repairs to a damaged rudder incurred during a landing, and that it was returned to Scampton on the following day. The first replacement aircraft, two standard Lancasters, left the Avro factory for Scampton on the 26th in the form of EE130 and EE131, and after acceptance checks were taken on charge on the 2nd of June. For the first time since its formation, 617 Squadron was specified on the Avro daily movement sheet as the recipient. Further replacement Lancasters DV155 and DV156 arrived on the 29th, and EE144 and EE145 followed on the 31st, each to be taken on charge within a matter of days. During the course of Thursday the 27th of May the King and Queen visited a number of RAF stations, beginning at North Coates before moving on to Binbrook. At 13.00 hours the royal party arrived at Scampton and proceeded to the Officers' Mess for lunch. The seating plan had G/C Whitworth seated at the centre, flanked on his right by the King and on his left by the Queen. AVM Cochrane sat on the King's right, while to the Queen's left sat G/C Leonard Slee, who had recently completed a tour as 49 Squadron's commanding officer, and in August would move on to lead the Pathfinder's 139 Squadron. Gibson sat opposite the King, W/C Hopcroft of 57 Squadron opposite the Queen, and between them, facing Whitworth, was Wallis. After lunch the party moved outside to the tarmac, where an inspection of the aircrew from 617 and 57 Squadrons began at 14.05. This was followed by an inspection of one aircraft from each squadron complete with air and ground crew, before adjourning to the No. 2 hangar crew room, where the models of the dams were on display along with a collection of reconnaissance photographs. Gibson gave a full description of Operation Chastise assisted by the participating crew captains. Wallis was on hand as the royal couple inspected a modified Lancaster with Upkeep, and then the inspection moved on to other sections. At 15.30 the royal party departed Scampton and headed to their final appointment of the day at Digby.

Chapter Seven

Fresh Blood and a New Leading Man

Rebuilding. 1943 June to August. The Ruhr campaign ends. Hamburg, Italy and Peenemünde

While the congratulations and celebrations had been going on at Scampton, and the world was devouring the press and radio coverage, the unsung element of the Command was continuing the assault on Hitler's war-materials-producing Ruhr region. Having sent a record force to Dortmund early in the month of May, Harris despatched a new record force of 826 aircraft to the same destination on the 23/24th, and completely destroyed almost two thousand buildings. A number of important war industry factories were also hit, resulting in loss of output, but the defenders fought back to bring down thirty-eight bombers, the highest casualty figure at a Ruhr target during the campaign to date. Over seven hundred aircraft raided Düsseldorf on the 25/26th, but this operation failed in the face of complete cloud cover, which hampered the Pathfinders' attempts to provide concentrated marking. Almost five hundred buildings were destroyed at Essen on the 27/28th, and this was followed by one of the most awesomely destructive raids of the entire offensive. The town of Barmen is one half of the twin towns known jointly as Wuppertal, which nestles in a valley to the east of Düsseldorf. It was attacked by almost 700 aircraft on the 29/30th, and was left with over 80 per cent of its built-up area destroyed. A little short of 4,000 houses were reduced to ruins, and five of the town's six largest factories were gutted, along with over 200 other industrial premises. The death toll exceeded 3,000 people, and this was a new record for the war. The defenders again had their say, however, and thirty-three bombers failed to return home.

There were no major operations during the first ten nights of June, and squadrons were able to use this time to rest and replenish. An expansion programme had been under way during the spring and early summer, which resulted in a C Flight being added to many squadrons, while a number of completely new ones were formed from scratch. 617 Squadron's rebuilding had started with the arrival of Ralf Allsebrook and crew a few days after Operation Chastise, and continued with the acquisition of Lancasters EE146,

EE147, EE148, EE149 and EE150 on the 1st of June. There were, of course, still thirteen Type 464 Lancasters on charge, and these would be retained, while Upkeep was being considered for further operations. Some of the trials were intended to ascertain its effectiveness on land, and for this purpose ED915 and ED932 were flown to Farnborough, where the rotation mechanism was reversed to allow for forward spin to be imparted to the weapon in an attempt to increase range. The second prototype, ED817, which had spent its time as a trials aircraft at Manston, was taken on 617 Squadron charge as AJ-C on the 30th of May, and it would be joined by the first prototype, ED765, as AJ-M in early July.

Allsebrook came to the squadron as something of a veteran, having begun his operational career with 49 Squadron at Scampton back in the Hampden days. On the night of the 14/15th of February 1942, his crew had been one of ninety-eight dispatched to Mannheim for an area attack on the city, the first such indiscriminate raid to be officially sanctioned since the issuing of the controversial area bombing directive by the Air Ministry earlier that very day. At least part of the return journey was undertaken on one engine, and this failed as the south coast of England hove into sight. A successful ditching was carried out, and the crew took to their dinghy, which was spotted by a Beaufighter crew returning from a patrol. They were soon picked up by a coastguard launch, but three of them had by then suffered frostbite in the freezing conditions. As a Flying Officer, Allsebrook was awarded a DFC in April 1942, just as the trusty Hampden was being replaced by the unpopular Manchester. He returned to 49 Squadron for a second tour at the end of January 1943 as a Flight Lieutenant, and operated against Hamburg on the 3/4th of February, when he experienced an engine fire over the target. Two trips to Lorient in mid month sandwiched one to Milan, and the month ended with operations against Cologne and St Nazaire. By the end of the first week of March Allsebrook and his crew had added to their tally with sorties to Berlin, Hamburg and Essen, and then they operated against Nuremberg, Munich and Stuttgart during the course of the following six nights. The pace slackened somewhat for them in April and May before their posting to 617 Squadron.

After their arrival, and like the rest of their new colleagues at 617 Squadron, Allsebrook and crew carried out no flying until, in their case, the evening of the 29th of May, and probably spent some of the intervening period on leave. Both flight commanders had been lost during Operation Chastise, and Allsebrook and the newly promoted Squadron Leader David Maltby filled the vacancies. The Allsebrook crew took part in a two-hour formation flying exercise in ED437, and repeated it in Gibson's ED932 on the following afternoon, before carrying out a short air-test in EE131 on the 31st. After an uneventful first week of June, which saw the crew fly a low-level bombing exercise on the 1st, the pace picked up from the 7th, and almost every day thereafter up to and including the 1st of July they were in the air carrying out some kind of training. Initially, this mostly took the form of low-level cross-countries in daylight culminating in bombing, but then a night exercise on the 9th in ED932 using the spotlights presaged a combination of day and night cross-countries, although not in type 464 Lancasters again for this crew at least.

Shannon's schedule was again typical of squadron activities for the period. He took ED932 to Farnborough on the 2nd of June with an inert Upkeep weighing 7,000lb, compared with the 9,000lb weight of the weapon used against the dams, and spent the 3rd learning how to fly a Horsa glider. He departed Farnborough on the 4th with the Upkeep to carry out a tactical trial, and was back in his own L for Leather, ED929, on the 5th for a low-level cross-country and bombing exercise with his future wife, Section Officer Ann Fowler, on board. It was similar fare on the 6th in ED825, while Wainfleet was the venue for low-level bombing on the 7th. On the 8th he delivered four bombs at Wainfleet from 2,000 feet using the Mk XIV bombsight in a standard Lancaster, before reverting to ED932 on the 9th for formation flying and a tactical trial undertaken at Salisbury Plain with a 7,000lb Upkeep. On the 14th Shannon was again in ED932 for low-level bombing and spotlight altimeter runs, and this was followed up next day by dummy runs on the Derwent and Ladybower reservoirs near Sheffield in the same aircraft, and after dark spotlight altimeter tests in ED933. During the last week of June bombing levels were raised to medium and then high level. Shannon was at Wainfleet on the 25th and 26th to deliver six bombs from 2,000 feet on the former and four from 4,000 feet on the latter. He made three flights on the 27th in EE130 and EE131, dropping eight bombs from 20,000 feet and a further eight from 15,000 feet at dusk. Training also required him to cross the Irish Sea on the 29th in a flight also taking in various points on the Scottish coast and north-west England.

Incidents during June included EE145 skidding on the wet grass in the hands of Munro on return from a training flight at 17.30 on the 6th, which caused the undercarriage to collapse, but all the occupants emerged unscathed. While training over the North Sea on the 10th Joe McCarthy spotted a dinghy in the swell below, and obtained a couple of fixes, which were passed on to the rescue services. As a result the occupants were pulled to safety on the following day, and their commanding officer phoned the station to offer his thanks. As far as the main force was concerned, it was not until the night of the 11/12th that the heavy squadrons returned to the fray, when Düsseldorf was the target for over 700 aircraft, and despite an errant Oboe marker, which attracted a proportion of the bombs, massive damage was inflicted on the city. Almost 9,000 fires were recorded in an area measuring 8km by 5km, and nearly 1,300 people lost their lives. This was another night of heavy losses, though, which cost the Command 38 aircraft. A further 24 were missing from Bochum on the 12/13th, after an operation inflicting severe damage on the city's central districts. Oberhausen wilted under an all Lancaster assault on the 14/15th, before a moderately effective raid fell on Cologne two nights later.

5 Group had always believed itself to be the elite Group, and had an almost independent air about it, which would become something of a reality in 1944 as a result of events within 617 Squadron. The Group, or one or more of its squadrons, had operated famously and independently of the main force on a number of occasions in the past, most notably those mentioned earlier against the MAN factory at Augsburg in April 1942, Danzig in July, the Schneider armaments works at Le Creusot in October, and, of course, the recent Dams raid. Now, on the 20/21st of June, 60 of its Lancasters were sent to attack the old Zeppelin factory at Friedrichshafen, deep in southern Germany, wherein lay the manufacturing base of the Würzburg radar sets, which were being used by the enemy night-fighter force to intercept Bomber Command aircraft. The two phase operation was led by W/C Slee of 49 Squadron, who was forced to hand over to W/C Gomm of 467 Squadron, when his Lancaster lost an engine while outbound. The second phase crews adopted a 5 Group inspired 'time and distance' method of bombing, which was designed to negate the effects of smoke concealing the aiming point, and 10 per cent of the bombs hit the relatively small target, causing extensive damage. Other nearby factories were also afflicted, and the force then flew on to airfields in North Africa, in what was the first shuttle operation of the war.

A hectic round of four major operations in the space of five nights began for the main force at Krefeld on the 21/22nd. This was an outstandingly concentrated raid, which created a massive area of fire, and destroyed over 5,500 houses, while killing 1,000 people. A massive 44 aircraft failed to return, however, and this was a new record for the Ruhr campaign. The investiture for the Dams heroes was held at Buckingham Palace on the 22nd, and in a departure from normal practice on such occasions, Gibson was honoured by being first in line, and accepted the ultimate award from the hand of Her Majesty Queen Elizabeth in the absence of King George VI. That night it was the turn of Mülheim to reel under a devastating blow, which accounted for over 1,100 houses, and damaged scores of public buildings. The loss of 35 aircraft was another high price to pay, and 'Happy Valley's' reputation was by now set for all time. After a night's rest, the Elberfeld half of Wuppertal went the way of its twin Barmen a month earlier, and suffered the destruction of over 90 per cent of its built-up area, amounting to 3,000 houses destroyed, with a further 2,500 and 53 industrial premises seriously damaged. This operation cost the Command 34 aircraft, and a further 30 were missing following a failed attempt to visit similar damage on the important oil town of Gelsenkirchen on the 25/26th. In an echo of the past, bombs were sprayed all over the Ruhr, and few if any, fell on the intended target.

June ended with the first of three cataclysmic raids on Cologne, which spanned the turn of the month. Mounted on the 28/29th, the almost 600 strong force destroyed over 6,300 buildings, and killed 4,300 people. A further 2,200 houses were reduced to rubble on the 3/4th of July, and an all Lancaster force completed the carnage on the 8/9th, when almost 2,400 houses and apartment blocks were levelled. When the smoke had cleared and the dust settled the city authorities were able to establish that these three raids had destroyed 11,000 buildings, killed 5,500 people, and rendered a further 350,000 homeless. The combined cost to the Command had been 62 aircraft, which, at an average of twenty-one per operation, compared more than favourably with recent experiences. Another failure took place at Gelsenkirchen on the 9/10th, and although two more operations to the region would be undertaken at the end of the month, the Ruhr offensive had now effectively run its course. Harris could look back over the past five months with genuine satisfaction at the performance of his squadrons, but would derive his greatest pleasure from the success of Oboe, which had proved to be crucial to the outcome.

617 Squadron was not involved in any of the above operations as it continued to rebuild and train for further special operations. F/L Kellaway and his crew were posted in from 3 Group's 149 Squadron on the 30th of June and they were joined on the 2nd of July by two men from 4 Group, S/L George Holden late of 102 Squadron and P/O 'Bunny' Clayton from 51 Squadron. In April Squadron Leader Holden had completed six months as an acting Wing Commander in command of 102 Squadron, 'Dinghy' Young's old unit. On the 1st of July he flew to Scampton in an Anson, and was officially post to the station on the following day as commanding officer elect and senior flight commander. It would be a further month before Gibson departed the squadron, and Holden needed time to learn the ways of the Lancaster, a type unfamiliar to him and to all others whose careers had been spent in 4 Group.

Why was Holden, a 4 Group man to the core, selected to replace the charismatic Gibson, now the most celebrated squadron commander in the entire service? His selection actually began a trend of appointing 4 Group men to the position, Cheshire, Tait and Fauquier, men who would carry the squadron through to the end of the bombing war in late April 1945. If Harris, and one might reasonably assume some involvement on his part, was prepared to look outside of 5 Group for Gibson's successor, why did he sanction the appointment of Holden from among the wealth of qualified existing squadron commanders available? It has to be said, that there was something of the Gibson character in Holden. His career to this point had been distinguished, and he had been involved in some unusual and spectacular operations. He had also rubbed shoulders with some of the Command's finest young bloods, many of whom were gathered within the squadrons of 4 Group, and were themselves seen as shining lights. Not all had survived to the summer of 1943, and of those who had, whose operational careers had begun in 1940, Holden was unquestionably among the brightest prospects. If 'Dinghy' Young had survived, he a 4 Group contemporary of Holden and Cheshire, or perhaps even Henry Maudslay from the 'class of 41', then they would also undoubtedly have been in the frame, but they were gone, and Cheshire had progressed to the rank of Group Captain, which generally speaking at that time, precluded him from the command of a squadron. This latter restriction was in the process of being revised, however, as Pathfinder squadrons were now being led by Group Captains, with Wing Commanders filling the roll of flight commander.

Holden began basic training, presumably part time as a reservist, in May 1937. On the 1st of September 1939, the day German forces began their assault on Poland, he joined 9 FTS at Hullavington, moved on to Benson between January and early May 1940, and thence to 10 OTU at Abingdon, where he learned to fly Whitleys. This was the type operated by 4 Group until the advent of the Halifax, and it would be the spring of 1942 before it was finally withdrawn from operational service with the Command. He passed out as a first pilot, day only, with an average rating on the 18th of September, and immediately joined 78 Squadron at Dishforth. Here he began working up to operational status, and undertook his first sortie as second pilot to a F/L Pattison in a raid on Antwerp on the night of the 26/27th of September. His second sortie was flown to Amsterdam with his flight commander, S/L Wildey, who would eventually take command of 10 Squadron, and lose his life in action in October 1942, the same month in which Holden would gain his first command. Finally, on the 11th of November, Holden was signed out as a fully qualified Whitley captain by the newly appointed commanding officer, W/C 'Charles' Whitworth, now base commander of Scampton. Two nights later he undertook his first operation as crew captain, his eighth sortie in all, but like many others operating in poor weather conditions that night, he was forced to abandon his sortie and return home. He put matters right on the 15/16th, however, when participating in an unusually effective raid on Hamburg.

Late in 1940 Churchill pressed for the formation of a paratroop unit, as the forerunner of an airborne force for use in a future invasion of Europe. Plans were put in hand to carry out a special operation under the codename Colossus, with the purpose of ascertaining the viability of such an undertaking. Volunteers were brought together as X-Troop No. 11 SAS Battalion for an attack on an aqueduct over the River Tragino in Italy to be launched from Malta. Two aircraft were to carry out a diversionary bombing attack on marshalling yards at nearby Foggia, while six others delivered the parachutists into position. 51 and 78 Squadrons were each selected to provide four aircraft and crews under the command of W/C James Tait, who had recently begun a short spell as commanding officer of the former. Among the pilots from 78 Squadron was P/O Holden, who flew with Tait on a container-dropping test as part of the run-up on the 2nd of February. On completion of their task the surviving commandos were to gather at a point on the coast for evacuation by submarine. The force departed for Malta on the night of the 7/8th of February, and carried out the operation on the 10/11th. In the event, not all the commandos were dropped within range of their target, and if this was not unfortunate enough, one of the diversionary Whitleys had to be abandoned in the area selected for the ground force's withdrawal, thus alerting the local defenders. Some damage was inflicted upon the aqueduct, but all the soldiers were captured on their way to the rendezvous, and they were joined soon afterwards by the Whitley crew.

This operation was Holden's twentieth, and his last with 78 Squadron, which he left with an above average rating to join 35 Squadron at Linton-on-Ouse. 35 Squadron had been re-formed at Boscombe Down in November 1940 to introduce the Halifax into operational service, and was attracting the leading bomber pilots in 4 Group. Holden arrived on the 25th of February 1941, and met up again with Tait, who had now reverted to Squadron Leader rank and was a flight commander under the portly personage of the squadron commander, W/C R.W.P. Collings, another of the Command's great characters. The Halifax suffered many teething problems, and the demand for modifications ensured only a trickle of new aircraft from the factories. As a result, following its operational baptism in March, the type operated only intermittently and in very small numbers for some time. Holden flew his first Halifax sortie against Duisburg on the 11/12th of June, and over the ensuing five weeks managed ten more. A major assault on the German cruisers *Scharnhorst*, *Gneisenau* and *Prinz Eugen* at Brest, the first two-named having been in residence there since the end of March, was planned for the 24th of July. The operation was to be undertaken in daylight by Halifaxes accompanied by 1 and 3 Group Wellingtons, and under extensive diversionary activity and a heavy fighter escort. It was discovered at the eleventh hour, however, that the *Scharnhorst* had slipped away to La Pallice, some 200 miles further south, and it was decided to send the Halifax element after her, while the remainder of the original plan went ahead at Brest. Fifteen Halifaxes from 35 and 76 Squadrons duly attacked the *Scharnhorst*, causing extensive damage, but lost five of their number in the process, and all the surviving aircraft sustained damage to some degree. Holden was forced to bring his bombs home after flak shot away the electrical release gear. One of his crew was killed, while two others were wounded, one seriously. Holden's flight commander at the time was S/L Jimmy Marks, one of the brightest stars in Bomber Command, and an officer who would gain command of 35 Squadron in 1942, only to then lose his life in action shortly after taking it into the Pathfinder Force as one of the founder units.

Holden concluded his tour on a total of thirty-two operations, and was posted to the Heavy Conversion Flight at Linton-on-Ouse on the 18th of August. Here he remained until December, when he was detached to Upavon, before progressing to Marston Moor, Leeming and Pocklington progressively in the role of instructor. At Pocklington, and now in the rank of Squadron Leader, he was put in charge of the Conversion Flight of 405 Squadron, a Canadian unit commanded by W/C Johnny Fauquier. While there, Holden flew on the second thousand bomber raid against Essen on the 1/2nd of June 1942, and the third and final one on Bremen on the 25/26th, his thirty-third and thirty-fourth sorties. In July he was posted to 158 Squadron's Conversion Flight at East Moor, where he remained until the 25th of October. In the early hours of the previous day, 102 Squadron's commanding officer,

W/C Bintley, had been killed in a freak accident on the runway at Holme-on-Spalding-Moor on return from Genoa, when another Halifax had crushed his cockpit on landing. Holden was posted in as his replacement on the 25th, and began a successful period of command, during which he operated a further eleven times, bringing his tally to forty-five. He was rested again on the 20th of April 1943, and thereafter seemed to kick his heels somewhat until the call came through from 617 Squadron. Although on the face of it straight out of the Gibson mould, Holden did not have his predecessor's leadership qualities and presence. He cut an unimposing figure, was given to acts of arrogance, and was not at all popular. On the 4th of July, two days after his arrival at Scampton, he was taken up by Martin in EE148 for a local familiarization trip, and the two paired up again on the following two days. On the 7th Holden flew with Gibson's Dams crew, and although he names the individual officers in his logbook, there is a Gibsonesque omission of Pulford's name, or for that matter, any other NCO flight engineer.

617 Squadron's two-month period of operational inactivity came to an end on the 15th of July, when twelve crews were briefed for targets in Italy, a country now teetering on the brink of capitulation. The 617 Squadron elements were to be accompanied by twelve other aircraft from the Group for an operation undertaken as part of a campaign to dislocate enemy transport facilities, specifically the railway system. Two targets were to be attacked, at Aquata Scrivia and San Polo d'Enza, both of them electrical transformer and switching stations. Assigned to the former were S/L Holden in 57 Squadron's EE931, with Gibson's full former crew including Pulford, F/L Allsebrook in ED999, a Lancaster borrowed from 49 Squadron, F/L Wilson in EE197, P/O Brown in EE185, P/O Townsend in DV178, and P/O Clayton in JA703, which was on loan from 44 Squadron. S/L Maltby headed the second element in EE130, along with F/L Martin in EE144, F/L McCarthy in EE148, F/L Munro in EE150, P/O Divall in EE146, and P/O Rice in W5008, which was another one borrowed from 57 Squadron. Two other targets, at Bologna and Reggio Emilia, were to be attacked simultaneously by other squadrons, while a 4 and 8 Group raid at Montbeliard would provide a diversion. The 617 Squadron crews were all airborne shortly before 22.30 hours, and it was more than five hours later that the attacks were carried out from between 800 and 1,600 feet. The poor visibility over the target was apparently made worse by glare and smoke, after Townsend bombed marshalling yards before Holden's arrival, causing an ammunition train to erupt in spectacular fashion. Despite this, Holden and Allsebrook both claimed direct hits among the pylons of the transformer station, and then, along with Clayton, they machine-gunned the target before flying on to land at Blida in North Africa. A number of crews reported seeing fires and blue flashes at both targets, but the full extent of the damage inflicted could not be accurately assessed in the conditions, and the consensus was, that flares would have been of benefit. Post raid reconnaissance revealed hits on nearby railway tracks at Aquata Scrivia, and craters within the perimeter of the transformer station, with

the roof of one transformer building damaged. At San Paulo damage was inflicted upon buildings containing high frequency equipment, and possibly a transformer, while adjacent railway track was hit and a pylon brought down.

The crews remained at Blida until between 21.05 and 21.30 on the evening of the 24th, when they all took off to return home, briefed to bomb the docks and harbour installations at Leghorn on the way. This required a north-northeasterly course from North Africa across the Mediterranean to the island of Corsica, from where a time and distance run was undertaken to the target on Italy's western coast. It took over three hours to reach the objective, and the bombing times were spread between Divall at 00.21 and Allsebrook at 01.02. Allsebrook was the last to arrive after his starboard outer propeller sheared away, but it didn't prevent him from continuing on to bomb. Martin's bombing time in the ORB is given as 00.02, which seems to be out of synchrony with the others, and is almost certainly recorded in GMT. If adjusted by one hour it would read 01.02, the same as that of Allsebrook. It is wholly consistent with the spirit of the squadron that Martin, as a senior captain, would remain with Allsebrook as an escort at least as far as the target, while the other crews pressed on. Evidence of this comes with Martin's bombing height of 9,500 feet, 500 feet higher than that recorded by Allsebrook, while the other crews made their attacks from between 16,000 and 18,000 feet. Allsebrook afterwards made the point himself, that he could not maintain height on three engines with a bomb load, and it reflects great credit on him, that he did not jettison his twelve 500 pounders and ninety 4lb incendiaries immediately and head for home. The return flight from Italy took more than four hours for everyone, but even longer for Allsebrook, who, without a bomb load, did not need shepherding and came home alone to touch down last, a full forty-five minutes after the one before him. Rice, Townsend and Clayton brought back a few 500 pounders each after they suffered hang-ups. It had proved difficult to assess the outcome of the raid, but a number of crews identified direct hits on oil storage tanks from the red flames and thick smoke. Holden thought the bombing to be scattered, and once again he did not mention Pulford when listing his crew, and one wonders if some incident had soured Holden's attitude, or did he, indeed, share Gibson's poor opinion of the 'great unwashed', otherwise known as non-commissioned officers? Whatever the case, the result of the inharmonious relations between them would see Pulford survive his commanding officer by four months.

It was on this night that Harris launched the first round of Operation Gomorrah, a short, sharp series of attacks on Hamburg, designed to send shock waves resounding around the Reich. Bomber Command had gone to Hamburg during the final week of July in each year of the war to date, and this tradition would be continued in 1944. Having been spared by the weather from hosting the first one thousand-bomber raid in history more than a year earlier, Hamburg suited Harris's criteria now in a number of respects. As Germany's Second City, its political status was undeniable, as was its importance as a centre of war production, particularly with regard to *U-Boot* construction. It was also accessible to the Command without the need to traverse large tracts of hostile territory, and its location near a coastline would both aid navigation, and allow the aircraft to approach and retreat during the few hours of total darkness afforded by mid summer. Finally, lying beyond the range of Oboe, Hamburg boasted the wide River Elbe to provide a strong H2s signature for the navigators flying high above.

A force of almost 800 aircraft took off, carrying for the first time thousands of bundles of Window. This device had actually been available for twelve months, but the War Cabinet had vetoed its use, lest the enemy copy it. The enemy, as it happened, already had its own version known as Düppel, and this had also been withheld for the same reason. The effects of Window were made apparent by the few combats taking place during the outward flight, and although a number of aircraft were shot down at this stage, they were invariably off course, and outside of the protection of the bomber stream. Once in the target area, it was noted that the usually efficient co-ordination between the searchlight and flak batteries was absent, and defence from the ground was at best random. The Pathfinder marking was slightly misplaced, and a pronounced creep-back developed, which cut a swathe of destruction from the city centre, northwestwards along the line of approach, and out into open country, where a proportion of the bombing was wasted. Fifteen hundred people died under the bombs, and the destruction inflicted represented an encouraging start to the campaign. Perhaps of greater significance was the loss of just twelve aircraft, a clear sign of the efficacy of Window. On the following night, Harris switched his force to Essen, to take advantage of the body blow dealt to the enemy's defensive system by Window, and this was another outstandingly accurate attack, which destroyed almost 3,000 houses, and inflicted the greatest damage of the war on the Krupp complex.

F/L Youseman was posted to 617 Squadron from 214 Squadron, a 3 Group Stirling unit, on the 26th, and a number of his former colleagues followed to make up his crew. Gibson went to London on temporary duty on the following day, and W/C Holden assumed command in his absence. That night, almost 800 aircraft took off to return to Hamburg, and what followed their arrival over Germany's Second City was both unprecedented and unforeseeable, and was the result of a conspiracy of circumstances. A period of unusually hot and dry weather had left tinderbox conditions within the city, and the initial spark to ignite it came with the Pathfinder markers. These fell two miles to the east of the intended city centre aiming point, but with great concentration into the densely populated working class residential districts of Hamm, Hammerbrook and Borgfeld. The main force followed up with unaccustomed accuracy and scarcely any creep-back, and deposited much of its 2,300 tons of bombs into this relatively compact area. The individual fires joined together to form one giant conflagration, which sucked in oxygen at hurricane speed from surrounding areas to feed its voracious appetite. Such was the force of this meteorological event, that trees were uprooted and flung bodily into the flames, along with debris and people, and temperatures at its seat exceeded 1,000 degrees Celsius. The inferno only subsided when all the combustible material had been consumed, by which time there was no one within the firestorm area to rescue. Forty thousand people perished on this one night alone, and on the following morning the first of an eventual exodus of 1,200,000 people began to file out of the city.

On the 29th nine 617 Squadron crews were briefed for a special leaflet drop over four cities in northern Italy. Assigned to Milan were S/L Maltby in EE146, F/L Kellaway in JA894, P/O Divall in W4822 and F/L McCarthy in EE148. Bologna was the destination for F/L Shannon in ED763, Turin for P/O Rice in ED805 and F/O Knight in JA703, and Genoa for W/C Holden in EE150 and F/L Munro in W4358. Holden borrowed F/S Webb from Townsend's crew as a replacement gunner for Trevor-Roper, while a Sgt Hill occupied the flight engineer's position, possibly because he was about to be commissioned in a little over a week. They took off around 23.00 hours, and reached their respective target areas between four and five hours later to deliver their fourteen SBCs (small bomb canisters) from between 5,000 and 13,000 feet. McCarthy was unable to locate Bologna, and dropped his 'Nickels' (propaganda leaflets) over Milan instead, after which he and the others flew on to Blida without incident. While this was in progress, over 700 aircraft were returning to Hamburg to deliver the third raid of the series on this tortured city. The marking was again misplaced, and this time a creep-back developed partly across the already devastated firestorm area, before hitting other residential districts to the north. Further massive damage was inflicted, but in a sign that the *Luftwaffe* was beginning to recover from the chaos caused by Window, the losses on this night amounted to twenty-eight aircraft. On the following night a force of only moderate proportions decimated Remscheid in the operation that brought down the final curtain on the Ruhr campaign.

Seven of the 617 Squadron shuttle crews took off from Blida for the return journey to Scampton at around 08.00 hours on the 31st, stopping off at a forward landing ground at Ras-el-Ma on the way. They departed from there at 21.30 that evening for what was approximately an eight-hour flight. McCarthy and Munro remained in North Africa while repairs were carried out on their aircraft, the former arriving home on the 5th, and the latter on the 8th. Meanwhile, a scratch crew was drawn together on the 2nd to carry out a five-hour search for a lifeboat over the North Sea. The pilot of the 57 Squadron Lancaster was S/L Crocker, an American flight commander with 57, and the rest of the crew was made up of Ken Brown, with Sumpter, Henderson and Jagger of Shannon's crew and Hill of Maltby's. The lifeboat was not spotted, but Danish fishing boats were. The popular Malcolm Crocker would take command of 49 Squadron in May 1944 and be lost on the disastrous 5 Group raid on the oil refinery at Wesseling on the night of the 21/22nd of June.

The end of the Gibson era had come on the 3rd, when he was officially posted from the squadron to join the Prime Minister's party on a trip to Canada, where he would conduct a lecture tour. W/C Holden was confirmed as his successor, and on the 2nd, Gibson's final day on the squadron, Gibson, his dams crew and Holden enjoyed a 1 hour 25 minute farewell cross-country flight together in ED933. In the meantime, plans were being drawn up to seal off the Ruhr by destroying the main railway viaducts and draining the canal system linking the region with other parts of Germany. The intention was to employ the newly developed 12,000lb light case blockbuster against the canal embankments and Upkeep against the viaducts, and training began on the 4th, when six aircraft were flown to Ashley Walk bombing range to drop live Upkeeps against screens 200 feet long. One bomb failed to release, but the remaining five achieved an average of 1,100 yards before detonation. On the following day a similar trial was carried out at Ashley Walk, using a concrete structure 70 feet long by 12 feet high as the objective. This time the results of the first five deliveries were inconsistent. The aircraft came in in line astern with Kellaway at the back in ED765. As he turned in he caught the slipstream of the previous Lancaster, which caused him to lose control. As Kellaway fought to regain equilibrium he was faced by high-tension cables, which he attempted to fly under. In tightening his turn to port his wingtip touched the ground and the aircraft crashed, remarkably without fatalities, although Kellaway sustained a broken leg and his bomb-aimer, F/S Harris, serious injuries, which required a lengthy stay in hospital and ended his operational career. It seems, that the Upkeep acted as a substitute undercarriage, enabling the Lancaster to roll for some distance, and this resulted in only minor injuries to the other crewmembers. ED765 was extensively damaged by fire, however, and was eventually struck off charge on the 14th. In the face of the disappointing second trial it was decided not to employ Upkeep against the viaducts, but an operation against the Dortmund-Ems Canal with 12,000 pounders remained in prospect.

Training for the period was a mixture of high and low-level exercises and formation flying, and a further Upkeep trial was carried out on the 12th. On the 13th Holden took the now Air Commodore 'Charles' Whitworth for a cross-country flight, and the 17th saw the arrival at Scampton of S/L Richardson, an armaments expert, whose devotion to the science of ordnance and bomb-aiming would soon see him christened 'Talking Bomb'. Having completed the series against Hamburg on the 2/3rd, an operation ruined by adverse weather during the outward flight, it was now the turn of the main force to follow in 617 Squadron's footsteps and traverse the Alps to Italy. This was to be the final fling against the country's major cities to consolidate its imminent capitulation. 1, 5 and 8 Groups opened proceedings on the 7/8th at Genoa, Milan and Turin, and the same two cities jointly or individually hosted further raids on the 12/13th, 14/15th, 15/16th and 16/17th. Earlier, the southern German cities of Mannheim and Nuremberg had been targeted to good effect on consecutive nights on the 9th and 10th.

Since the start of hostilities, intelligence had filtered through concerning German research into rocket technology. Gradually, by means of the interception and decoding of signals, and then through photographic reconnaissance, it became clear that the centre of this activity was Peenemünde, on the island of Usedom on the Baltic coast. Churchill's chief scientific adviser, Professor Lindemann, or Lord Cherwell, as he became, steadfastly refused to give credence to such weapons, and even remained unmoved when confronted with a photograph of a V-2 at Peenemünde taken by a PRU Mosquito as recently as June. It took the combined urgings of Duncan Sandys and the brilliant scientist, Dr R.V. Jones, to convince Churchill of the urgency of the threat, and at last, an operation was ordered for the first available opportunity. This arose on the night of the 17/18th of August, for which a complex plan was prepared.

The overall operation was to be controlled by a Master of Ceremonies in the manner of Gibson at the Dams, and the officer selected for this vital role was G/C Searby of 83 Squadron, who had been posted to the Pathfinders only a few months after stepping into Gibson's shoes at 106 Squadron. His first Deputy was to be W/C Johnny Fauquier of 405 Squadron RCAF, a future commanding officer of 617 Squadron. Three aiming points were to be attacked, the workers' housing estate, the factory and the experimental site, each assigned to a specific wave of bombers, respectively 3 and 4 Groups, 1 Group and 5 and 6 Groups, with the Pathfinders responsible for shifting the point of aim accordingly. 597 aircraft were made available, the numbers somewhat depleted by the late arrival at their stations of a proportion of the Stirling force, which had been diverted on return from Italy the night before, and could not be made ready in time. A spoof operation by Mosquitos of 139 Squadron was laid on at Berlin to draw off the night fighters, and this was led by the former 49 Squadron commanding officer, G/C Slee. The operation began inauspiciously, when the initial markers intended for the housing estate fell more than a mile beyond, and onto the forced workers camp at Trassenheide. These inevitably attracted a proportion of the bombs, and the friendly foreign nationals, who were trapped inside their wooden barracks, sustained heavy casualties. Once rectified, the operation proceeded more or less according to plan, but when the night fighters belatedly arrived from Berlin, they took a heavy toll of bombers, both in the skies over Peenemünde and on the route home towards Denmark. There were predominantly 5 and 6 Group aircraft in the target area at the time, and twenty-nine of the forty missing aircraft belonged to them. While not totally successful, the operation caused sufficient damage to set the development programme of the V-2 back by a number of weeks, and to send the production of secret weapons underground.

Harris had long believed that Berlin, as the seat and the symbol of Nazi power, held the key to ultimate victory. Having personally witnessed the carnage of trench warfare twenty-five years earlier, he believed that he could avoid a repeat, save Allied lives and win the war by bombing alone. The destruction of Berlin, in his opinion, would bring this about by destroying the morale of the civilian population, who would, according to the theory, lobby their leaders to sue for peace. Harris embarked on the opening phase of his campaign against the Capital on the night of the 23/24th, for which over 700 aircraft were despatched. Despite the markers falling onto the southern outskirts of the city, the raid developed into the most damaging yet on Berlin, with over 2,600 buildings destroyed or seriously damaged. Residential districts were those hardest hit, but industry also sustained damage, and more than 800 people lost their lives. The flak and night fighter defences were extremely spirited, however, and a new record of fifty-six aircraft failed to return home.

F/L D.J. Wilson was posted to 617 Squadron from 1660CU on the 27th. D.J. Wilson is not to be confused with F/L H.S. Wilson, who had trained for Operation Chastise but missed out, and was still active within the squadron. A raid by the main force on Nuremberg that night resulted in most of the bombing finding open country, and this demonstrated that operations beyond the range of Oboe were still something of a lottery. Later on the 28th, 57 Squadron moved out of Scampton, and took up residence at East Kirkby. On the 30th, 617 Squadron also departed the station with which it will always be synonymous, and moved to Coningsby, after which, Scampton became non-operational while concrete runways were laid. That night the twin towns of Mönchengladbach and Rheydt were subjected to a ferocious attack by over 600 aircraft, which destroyed a total of 2,300 buildings. Twenty-four hours later 600 aircraft returned to Berlin, where the Pathfinders again failed to mark the centre of the city. The target indicators fell well to the south, and most of the bombing undershot by up to thirty miles, a disappointment compounded by the loss of forty-seven aircraft.

An all Lancaster heavy force conducted the final raid against the 'Big City' in the current phase on the 3/4th of September. The attack again suffered from undershooting, but a number of residential districts were hit, and some war industry factories in the Siemensstadt area suffered loss of production. Later on the 4th three Mosquitos each from 605 and 418 Squadrons arrived at Coningsby with their crews for co-operation with 617 Squadron. They were led by S/L Gibb of 605 Squadron, who, a year hence, would attain command of 239 Squadron, one of the Serrate Mosquito units of 100 Group which would become the scourge of enemy night-fighters.

The opening salvoes of the Berlin offensive had been only partially effective and very expensive, but some compensation was gained on the 5/6th, when the twin cities of Mannheim and Ludwigshafen were the objectives for 600 aircraft of the main force. The marking was accurately placed in the eastern half of Mannheim, so that the creep-back along the line of approach would spread westwards across the city and over the Rhine into Ludwigshafen. Catastrophic damage was caused at the former, while almost 2,000 fires in the latter contributed to the destruction of over a thousand houses. Later that day 617 Squadron began training in co-operation with the Mosquitos in preparation for an operation later in the month. Shannon was in ED918, and carried one of the 605 Squadron navigators, F/S Tredwen, as a passenger. On the 9th S/L Gibb's navigator, P/O Mills, joined the Shannon crew along with F/O Franklin of 418 Squadron, and then later in the day, after unspecified modifications were carried out, S/L Gibb himself replaced Franklin. The accent throughout this period was on low-level cross-country and bombing exercises. Almost 400 aircraft of the main force and Pathfinders carried out an inconclusive attack on Munich on the 6/7th, and this was followed by a period of minor operations and stand-down. On the 11th two original members of the squadron, Jack Leggo and Len Chambers, both of Martin's crew, were posted to 13 ITW for a pilot's course, and they were replaced by F/L Stott, posted in from 1654CU on the 14th, and F/O Curtis as navigator and wireless operator respectively.

Chapter Eight

Black Thursday

The Dortmund-Ems canal

On the 14th of September, eight crews were briefed for an attack that night on the Dortmund-Ems Canal, a target with a strong 5 Group association since 1940. The first attempts to disrupt this very important component of the German communications system took place in June of that year, just before the fall of France. The point chosen for these early attacks by Hampdens was near Ladbergen, where twin aqueducts, one old and the other newer, carried the waterway over the River Glane, just west of the town. The vulnerability of these raised sections made them the favoured target, along with one on the nearby Mittelland Canal at the point where it crossed the Ibbenbürener Aa River. The rivers passed beneath the canals through large concrete tunnels known in German as a '*Durchlass*', literally let-through or underpass. The latter is mentioned as a target for twenty-one 5 Group Hampdens on the night of the 20/21st of August 1940, and while the precise location of the intended aiming point is not known, it is likely to have been this point near Gravenhorst, north of Ladbergen, and just a mile and a half east of the point where the Mittelland and Dortmund-Ems Canals meet in a triangular basin known as '*Das Nasse Dreieck*', the 'Wet Triangle' at Bergeshövede. Later in the war, from November 1944, a greater emphasis would be placed upon attacking this area in tandem with the continuing assault on the Dortmund-Ems. It was on the night of the 12/13th of August 1940 that the then S/L Learoyd of 49 Squadron earned a Victoria Cross for pressing home his attack against the older of the two Dortmund-Ems Canal aqueducts in the face of furious ground fire. The defences on this night had been strongly reinforced after a successful attack by 61 and 144 Squadrons from Hemswell had left the newer branch damaged and drained at the end of July. This was to be a Scampton show involving six aircraft from 49 Squadron and five from Gibson's 83 Squadron, and although he trained for the occasion, he was on leave celebrating his twenty-second birthday when it took place.

The section of the waterway chosen for the 617 Squadron attack, according to a Bomber Command Summary of Operations sheet, was at Greven, a small town to the south-west of Ladbergen. However, as Greven lies a few kilometres west of the canal, it was probably named as the last major pin-point before the canal itself. A very short flying time beyond Greven in a northeasterly direction is the point where the Dortmund-Ems Canal, running north–south, crosses the River Glane, and this is, in fact, the same twin aqueduct section referred to in the past simply as Ladbergen. However, the intention of the attack was given as specifically to breach the canal banks, rather than destroy the aqueducts. The carrying of the Dortmund-Ems and Mittelland Canals over the Glane and the Aa required the respective waterways to be raised above the natural level of the surrounding terrain. The embankments built to contain them were, as already stated, inevitably vulnerable to air attack and ideal for targeting with the new 12,000lb light case bomb, which was being employed operationally for the first time. (This is not to be confused with the 12,000lb Barnes Wallis-designed Tallboy deep penetration weapon introduced by the squadron in June 1944.) Nine gunners had been posted in on the 10th from 44, 49, 50 and 106 Squadrons and 1660CU for this low level operation, so that all three gun turrets could be occupied throughout. Remarkably, despite having been in existence for six months, this would be only the second operation for 617 Squadron over Germany.

The aircraft all got away without incident, but at 00.40 hours, while they were still over the North Sea, a recall signal was sent, following a report from a weather Mosquito of poor conditions in the target area. During the process of turning his heavily laden Lancaster back towards England at 00.45, Maltby appears to have lost control of JA981, and the aircraft cartwheeled into the sea eight miles north-east of Cromer with the loss of all on board. The accident card for this incident states, that the aircraft was lost when it hit the sea,

> ... after some obscure explosion and a fire had occurred in the aircraft. It is possible that the pilot partially lost control in a turn ... explosion may have been caused by bouncing on the water ... none of the equipment is likely to have exploded in the air.

It also makes the point, that the large bomb doors fitted to accommodate the 12,000 pounder affected the aircraft's stability when lowered. The question is, had the bomb doors been lowered? Was Maltby in the process of jettisoning part of, or his entire bomb load? All aircraft were carrying incendiaries on this night in addition to a 12,000 pounder each, and at least one aircraft is known to have jettisoned its incendiaries after the recall, while all seem to have landed with their blockbuster still on board. It is unlikely that Maltby was attempting to jettison his 12,000 pounder, a weapon not yet officially cleared for service use, and one too valuable to be dumped in any other than an emergency situation. (Knight would experience such circumstances twenty-four hours later.) An alternative scenario is that Maltby was in collision with a 139 Squadron Mosquito, which disappeared without trace that night during an operation to Berlin. Had F/L Colledge and his navigator completed their operation as briefed, departing Wyton at 19.36, they could easily have been in the same general airspace as Maltby on their way home at the time of the incident. This would account for the explosion. In the final analysis, whether it was a jettisoning accident brought about by the loss of trim as the bomb doors were lowered, slipstream turbulence or collision with a Mosquito will never be known. Shannon circled the spot for over two hours directing the air-sea rescue operation, but no one could be saved. Later that day F/L Humphries delivered the tragic news to Mrs Maltby, whose son John was just six weeks old. David Maltby's body was recovered during the course of the 15th, but the others were lost forever in the murky depths of the North Sea.

On the following night the operation was rescheduled, with Martin taking the place of Maltby. Crew captains and aircraft were; W/C Holden in EE144, F/L Knight in JB144, F/L H. Wilson in JA848, F/L Martin in EE150 as one section, and F/L Allsebrook in EE130, F/L Shannon in EE146, P/O Divall in JA874 and P/O Rice in EE131 as the other. They took off either side of midnight to approach the target by different routes, and were followed away some thirty minutes later by the Mosquito element of S/L Gibb/P/O Mills, F/O Mitchie/F/S Tredwen, P/O Woods/Sgt Johnson of 605 Squadron, and F/L Lisson/F/O Franklin, F/O Scherf/F/O Brown and F/O Rowlands/Sgt Medhurst of 418 Squadron. The route to the target for Holden's formation was almost identical to that of the second wave for Operation Chastise in its initial stages. After taking off they were to adopt a course slightly south of east across the North Sea to Vlieland, some 218 miles and seventy-eight minutes flying time from Coningsby, and then turn onto a south-easterly heading to take them over the Waddenzee and the Ijsselmeer to Stavoren. From here the course deviated from the Chastise route by passing over the Ketelmeer, a small body of water branching inland from the eastern shore of the Ijsselmeer a little to the north of Elburg, and then turning east until reaching the village of Gramsbergen. Here, the formation was to swing to starboard to take up a south-easterly course again, which took it across the frontier into Germany, thereafter proceeding past Nordhorn and continuing on to Wettringen just west of the target, where the intention was to rendezvous with Allsebrook's formation. Allsebrook's route crossed the Dutch coast at a point roughly a third of the way between Den Helder and Egmond, and reached the western shore of the Ijsselmeer near Hoorn. The route then converged on Holden's to cross the eastern shore of the Ijsselmeer at Elburg, remaining thereafter on a more or less parallel course a few miles to the south until just beyond Den Ham, from where it headed directly for Wettringen and the rendezvous. The Lancasters dropped down to 50 feet over the sea, but climbed to 2,000 feet to get their bearings as they crossed the Dutch coast before immediately returning to rooftop height. To provide a diary of Holden's section's journey to the target we can use the timings of Knight's crew as gleaned by Dutch researcher Piet Meijer, who is an authority on the events surrounding Knight's flight on this night.

Having left Coningsby within a few minutes of each other around midnight and formed up, the four Lancasters reached Vlieland at 01.15, giving an average cruising speed of around 170 mph. Eleven minutes and thirty-one miles later they arrived at the pinpoint at Stavoren and headed for the Ketelmeer twenty-eight miles and ten minutes further on. The pinpoint at the village of Gramsbergen was reached at 01.48 after a further thirty-five miles, leaving forty miles and fourteen minutes flying time to the rendezvous point at Wettringen. They crossed the Dutch/German frontier with the section of four intact, presumably having navigated accurately up to this point in good weather conditions. It was during this leg that W/C Holden led his formation directly across the small town of Nordhorn some twenty miles and seven minutes further on from Gramsbergen. In their path close to the town centre lay a white church and steeple, which, rather than skirting, Holden chose to climb over at around 300 feet. Tracer was observed to emanate from the ground from the starboard flank, and EE144 was hit in the starboard inner fuel tank, causing an instant fierce fire to erupt. According to Bob Kellow, as recorded in his superb personal account, *Paths to Freedom*, the accompanying three aircraft followed Holden's lead in climbing over the church, while Piet Meijer's understanding, based on his personal discussions with the individual crewmen, is that they remained low. Kellow claimed that the tracer came from the churchyard, but it seems unlikely that a churchyard would be selected as the location for a gun battery, as the church itself would inevitably restrict the field of fire. Piet Meijer asserts that the flak position was on a tower on top of a textiles factory, and its general location is confirmed by local eyewitnesses. According to Kellow and Martin, Holden's Lancaster trailed a long ribbon of flame until the tank blew up, causing the aircraft to veer sharply to the left, roll and dive straight down, narrowly missing Knight and Wilson as they broke outwards and upwards to avoid a collision and the anticipated explosion of the 12,000 pounder. Kellow goes on to say, that the aircraft impacted the ground at a steep angle close to the church.

This account demonstrates the difficulty of interpreting events in the white heat of battle, and we must compare Kellow's testimony with that of the German family who suffered their own tragedy as a result of these events. Herr and Frau Hood live in a bungalow within a farmyard on the Hesepeweg in the Altendorf district of Nordhorn, and this has been Herr Hood's home for his entire life. Their son and daughter-in-law now occupy the farmhouse itself, which, at the time of these events, had just been rebuilt after being destroyed by a stray bomb in 1942. Herr Hood was six years old in September 1943, and vividly remembers how his world was shattered both literally and metaphorically. What follows is the sequence of events as told to him by his father.

> Aircraft were heard approaching approximately from the north-west towards the farm, which lies about half a mile south-east of the town. A burst of tracer travelled from left to right from a factory roof on the

south-eastern outskirts of Nordhorn, and was seen to hit one of the aircraft, which immediately began to burn fiercely. It continued on its way above the farmhouse, but as it did so the port wing dropped, and the aircraft turned back on itself before plunging into the ground nose first within feet of the farmyard and its buildings. As the wreckage burned, Herr and Frau Hood led their six children into the cellar beneath the farmhouse, planning to spend the night there. After a few minutes, though, the parents decided to venture back up into the house to fetch additional night clothing for the children, and Frau Hood was about to re-enter the cellar from a doorway in the centre of the house when the 12,000 pounder went up about fifteen minutes after the crash. The bombs in use on this night contained a delay fuse timed to detonate between 26 and 90 seconds after release, but in the case of a crash with the bomb still attached, if the arming wires remained intact, the weapon would technically be safe until 'cooked' in any ensuing fire. It is not difficult to imagine the effect of a 12,000lb light case blast bomb, when we know of the devastation caused in urban areas by its smaller cousin, the 4,000lb cookie. The effect on the Hood homestead was catastrophic, and it left every building in the farmyard flattened and on fire, the house and outbuildings, and a line of substantial oak trees. A small section of the house wall was all that remained upright, and standing against it in a state of shock was Herr Hood senior. Of his wife there was initially no trace, but eventually, what little remained of her was found amongst the rubble. Perishing in the Lancaster with Holden were Taerum, Spafford, Hutchison and Deering of Gibson's Dams crew, Powell of Townsend's Dam's crew, and F/O Pringle, mid-upper gunner to F/L D.J. Wilson, who was not flying on this night, and P/O Meikle, the rear gunner. All were initially interred in the Neuer Friedhof cemetery at Lingen, although, it is believed that only Holden and Deering were positively identified. After the war their remains were taken to the Reichswald Commonwealth War Graves cemetery.

On a night of heavy casualties for 617 Squadron, Frau Hood was the only German fatality arising from the operation. Property damage in Nordhorn, however, was massive, and few houses within a 2,000-metre radius managed to retain their windows. In a letter to the Weser–Ems building authorities dated 17th September 1943, the local building inspector described 5–600 cases of damage thus far established, these ranging from severe to slight, and noted a serious shortage of roof tiles available with which to make repair. Nevertheless he had set the work in progress, and engaged craftsmen to carry it out.

Martin now assumed the lead of the formation, with Knight to starboard and Wilson to port, while Allsebrook took over the direction of the operation as a whole. Heavy fog had been encountered at the German frontier, which Martin described as coming down like a wall, and it persisted all the way to the target area. Martin's formation turned earlier than intended, before reaching Wettringen, when the flare path of an airfield was spotted directly ahead. Martin assessed the visibility at this stage as 500 yards. Had they continued on to the proposed rendezvous with Allsebrook's section at Wettringen, they would then have been eighteen miles and six minutes flying time from the target, which would have lain on an east–south-easterly course. However, this deviation from the planned route took the three Lancasters into the defences of the town of Rheine, which they twice tried to break through, but were forced to pull away and orbit. Finally, Martin led his section round the town on its northern side, thus putting them about ten miles to the north of the target. It was shortly afterwards that Martin lost visual contact with Knight, and became convinced that his friend and fellow countryman had been brought down by the flak from Rheine. The weather was continuing to deteriorate, forcing the crews to stumble around blindly to find a reference on the ground, and Martin guessed that they had probably crossed their pinpoints without knowing.

The conditions were now directly responsible for the sad loss of a veteran Dams pilot as he and his crew tried to fix their position. To facilitate orientation and target identification, assuming favourable visibility, the plan had allowed for one or more crews to drop white flashing beacons at three specific datum points, and another a few miles away as a decoy, while incendiaries were carried as a back-up. The beacons appear to have been inconspicuous, and it seems that incendiaries were also employed. As Les Knight approached the target from the west, having seemingly established its whereabouts, he turned to port to begin flying a box circuit, or one-minute square, as briefed, while awaiting further instructions from Allsebrook. The square required Knight to fly north for one minute, then east, south and west for an equal time, theoretically to arrive back at his starting point. There was apparently some concern about getting too close to the aircraft in front, presumably that containing Martin and crew, which had either been observed visually or at least perceived by its tell-tale slipstream, and Knight decided to lengthen the first and third sides of the square. At the end of the first circuit the canal was not where it was supposed to be, suggesting that they had lost their bearings slightly. During the course of the second orbit, Knight's crew heard Allsebrook direct two other crews, it is believed those of Wilson and Divall, to carry out their attacks. According to an account written by Piet Meijer, 'Obie' O'Brien then watched from his vantage point in Knight's rear turret as Wilson's Lancaster sustained flak hits at about this time and crashed in flames next to the canal, and he reported this to the rest of the crew over the intercom. This provides us with a picture of the three Lancasters of Martin's section following in each other's wake, with Martin in the lead, Knight next and Wilson bringing up the rear, although Martin was clearly not aware of Knight's close proximity.

Knight was about to embark on a third orbit, when, according to flight engineer Ray Grayston, someone called, 'you're too high!' Apparently Knight instinctively pushed the nose down, and almost immediately the Lancaster was rocked by an impact of some sort. After the crewmembers had regained their composure, 'Doc' Sutherland reported from the mid-upper turret that he had seen trees emerge through the swirling mist atop high ground, but had not been able to shout a warning in time. Another member of the crew also believed he had glimpsed one of the beacons or an incendiary at the same moment. Grayston reported rising temperatures on both port engines, which had branches and foliage stuffed in their radiators and soon began to smoke. Knight ordered them to be shut down, and apparently attempted to contact Allsebrook, as the raid controller, for permission to jettison the bomb. As a new weapon, it was undesirable to allow it to fall intact into enemy hands. However, to jettison it live meant exposing Knight and his crew to the risk of destruction in the ensuing blast wave. The safe height in the case of the much smaller 4,000lb cookie was 4,000 feet, and clearly, substantially more height would be required for a bomb three times more powerful. There was absolutely no possibility of Knight dragging his wounded Lancaster to a safe altitude, and so he followed protocol by seeking permission from higher authority to let it go unfused, knowing that the enemy would recover it. In the event, Knight was unable to raise Allsebrook, and turned instead to Martin, his section leader. It has always been assumed, that Knight failed to contact Allsebrook, because Allsebrook and his crew were already dead by this time, and one of the challenges of recording the events of this night is to establish their sequence and timing, particularly with regard to Allsebrook's fate. Let us, therefore, return to Martin's post-raid account to attempt to unravel part of the mystery surrounding the time of Allsebrook's loss. Martin states, that five to ten minutes after clearing Rheine, Knight called him up to report that he had lost two engines, and could he have permission to jettison his bomb? Martin replied, 'OK, jettison. Good Luck.' Martin does not say he heard Knight try to call up Allsebrook first, but does assert, that he heard Allsebrook add his own good luck wishes to Knight, proving that Allsebrook was still alive at this time. The question is, if Knight attempted to contact Allsebrook for permission to jettison his bomb, why did he fail to raise his raid leader, when the latter's radio was clearly working? Also, if it was protocol to seek Allsebrook's permission to carry out an attack, as has already been established in the cases of Wilson and Divall, why did Knight seek Martin's approval to dump his bomb if Allsebrook was still alive? We will clearly never know, and it is an interesting rather than important point. We will return later to Knight and his crew, and pick up the story again after his request to jettison the bomb.

As already mentioned, the destruction of F/L Wilson's Lancaster had been witnessed by Knight's rear gunner. Wilson and crew were squadron founder members, and among the first crews to be posted in to 617 Squadron, but they had missed Operation Chastise through a lack of serviceable aircraft and possibly illness. They were all killed when they fell victim to light flak in the manner described above by O'Brien. Two German sources, a local resident and a book detailing the history of Ladbergen, reveal the circumstances of his loss and, in so doing, confirm O'Brien's account. On page 213 of the latter, entitled *Land und Lüe, Beiträge zur Heimatgeschichte* by Heinrich Stork (Land and lore, contributions to local history), we find the following insight:

> For the protection of the Canal a 3.7cm flak battery was established at the start of the war, and between March 1943 and June 1944 it was strengthened by a trained Ladbergen home defence unit (consisting of Hitler youth). On 16.9.43 the aqueduct again became the target for an English special squadron ... Although the flak was forbidden to open fire on this day, because of operations over England by *Luftwaffe* aircraft from (nearby) Handorf, when a fourth approach was made on the aqueduct from such a low level that the aircraft's national markings were identifiable, the battery commander gave the order to fire. After several direct hits the aircraft crashed close to the Canal with the 5 ton special bomb on board, and exploded.

Herr Wibbeler was a twenty-one year old soldier at the time, at home on leave from the east, and he confirmed this account in a hand-written note sent to Andreas Wachtel. It translates as follows:

> The aircraft, well illuminated [by two converging searchlights], flew at low level over our farmhouse. It came down about 300 metres further on. My father and I went to within about 80 metres of the aircraft, which was ablaze. The flames were a couple of metres high and the ammunition was exploding. About fifteen minutes elapsed between the crash and the explosion. The alleged cries for help [as mentioned in Alan Cooper's book, *From the Dams to the Tirpitz*] emanated from my anxious mother, and not from the crew. Herr Wibbeler confirmed this account in person to the author as we stood on the crash site in May 2002.

These two accounts, and a November 1944 target photograph contributed by Herr Wibbeler, upon which he kindly marked the following three reference points, a line of trees clipped by the Lancaster, his house, and the crash site, enable us to piece together the events of the loss of JA898 KC-X, and the precise location. Wilson had clearly identified the target area, and his was one of the Lancasters passing over the aiming point on a north to south heading. One can imagine the frustration of the battery commander as each of these four passes was made over or close to his position, providing him with ample opportunity to anticipate the line of approach, and it was Wilson's misfortune to be the one that finally tempted him, the only adult member of the unit, to disobey orders and open fire, for which he would later be reprimanded. Searchlight beams suddenly sprang into life ensnaring the

Lancaster, which was hit several times and immediately caught fire. It then clipped a line of trees forming a right angle with the eastern bank of the canal at the southern end of the twin aqueduct section, and about 100 metres after the point at which they merged into a single channel. Continuing in the same direction it passed over the Wibbeler homestead a few hundred metres further on, having to climb to clear the roof, before crashing a field's width from the canal with the bomb still on board. Just like Holden's bomb, it took around fifteen minutes cooking time before it eventually exploded. A row of houses on the far side of the narrow lane bordering the field sustained heavy damage to roofs and windows from the bomb blast, and one house, according to Herr Wibbeler, actually burned down completely. With Holden and Wilson gone, and Knight out of the picture, Martin was now the sole survivor of the first formation, and we will leave him temporarily as he searches for the aiming point.

Let us now focus on Allsebrook's section, which somehow found itself in the region of the Mittelland Canal. Quite how they came to be so far north of where they should have been is not immediately apparent, and in order accurately to interpret the course of events on this night, it is important to understand the geographical situation, and how it might have appeared to those of Allsebrook's section as they glimpsed the ground briefly and intermittently while searching for their target. The Mittelland Canal approaches the region from the east, although by no means in a straight line, and curves sharply towards the south as it enters the target area. It doglegs to the west immediately north of Gravenhorst, where it crosses the River Aa, before feeding into the Wet Triangle almost on a due south heading. The Dortmund-Ems Canal, on the other hand, approaches from the south, heading almost due north, before veering north-north-west, and then curving onto a westerly heading to feed into the Wet Triangle. It leaves the Triangle at its most westerly point, and continues in that general direction. It is possible, that any of these waterways could be mistaken for the intended target near Ladbergen, although the compass heading available to the pilot and navigator should have been sufficient to prevent such a misinterpretation. Certainly, though, the latticework of rivers, canals and water junctions in such a small area would have made identification of a precise aiming point from low level in darkness an absolute nightmare even in favourable conditions, let alone in those faced by the crews on this night. What seems to be the case, particularly in view of German timings, is that Allsebrook's section arrived in the target area in advance of Martin's, partly because his planned course was more direct than Martin's, and because it would have been made even more direct if they, like Martin, turned earlier than briefed towards the east. A plausible scenario is, that in the prevailing conditions, Allsebrook decided to straighten his track and pass north of Rheine, putting his section ahead of schedule, possibly having also spotted the airfield flare path close to his briefed route. The defences would have been alerted to the presence of enemy aircraft, but might not have opened up because of the *Luftwaffe* operations already described. However, on hearing the approach of Martin's section, the defenders then decided to try their luck, and in negotiating his passage round the town, Martin delayed the arrival of his formation in the target area, putting them behind schedule, and increasing the gap between himself and Allsebrook. This is an important fact in establishing a sequence of events to correlate with the German timing of the start of the raid and the loss of Allsebrook. Meanwhile, Allsebrook's new course would have brought him directly over the intersection of the Dortmund-Ems and Mittelland Canals and the nearby River Aa, and he began his search for the target in this area.

We do not know the precise sequence of events, only that Allsebrook and his crew met their end at the point where the Dortmund-Ems and Mittelland Canals join at Bergeshövede in the body of water already referred to as *Das Nasse Dreieck*, the Wet Triangle. As the meeting point for two major waterways it acted then, like today, as a passing zone and a harbour for the canal traffic. During the war it contained typical port installations, like cranes for the loading and unloading of stores, equipment and provisions and there were also storage facilities for coal. The basin is bordered on its north-eastern quadrant by a chain of hills bisected by the Mittelland Canal. A light flak emplacement and searchlight had been installed in a field beyond the north-facing side of the hill known as the Huckberg on the canal's western bank, and the platoon leader was the late husband of Frau Erika Kaiser, who still lives in the same house on the quayside at Bergeshövede, and who was an eyewitness to the recovery of Allsebrook's Lancaster. There was also a flak tower in Bergeshövede itself, right on the edge of the Wet Triangle. Frau Kaiser was told, that the bomber had been caught by three searchlights, was on fire, and had lost part of a wing to anti-aircraft fire from one or perhaps both of the above-mentioned positions. Immediately thereafter, and apparently in trying to make an emergency landing, it clipped the roof of the end house on the quayside at the south-facing foot of the Huckberg, before colliding with a crane, which toppled over into the water. The Lancaster then flipped onto its back and plunged inverted into the harbour basin. An eyewitness described the burning wreckage slowly rising and falling until finally settling on the bottom, blocking the lock gates. A report written later on the 16th to the head of the Tecklenburg local authority and marked as only for official service use states the following:

> Further to the telephone report of earlier today, I now confirm the details on the official proforma. The aircraft was shot down shortly before 4 o'clock, and landed by the small lock in the Dortmund-Ems Canal. More precise information cannot yet be established as the aircraft is lying completely in the water and only two wheels are visible.

The wreckage was recovered and loaded onto barges on the following day, and, according to some reports, Allsebrook was found strapped in his seat, his hands firmly grasping the control column. However, an article written in 1999 for the local magazine celebrating a hundred years of the Dortmund-Ems Canal states that onlookers were horrified to discover that some members of the crew had been decapitated by the collision with the crane. Another report written on the day of the crash suggests that seven bodies were recovered intact, and that, of the eighth, a leg, ears and pieces of a skull were found floating on the surface of the water. It is quite possible that body parts were recovered from the water, particularly if the cockpit itself came into contact with the crane. The crane was later dragged out of the basin, found to be undamaged, and was put back on its rails and returned to use. A different report has most of the crew as unidentifiable. A more reliable source, though, is the graves register for this crew, which shows five members identified and buried individually, while the flight engineer and rear and mid-upper gunners were initially interred in a joint grave.

What is not in question is the fact that the bomb was not on board the Lancaster at the time of the crash. Precisely what happened to it, though, is less certain. It is possible that Allsebrook intended to drop his bomb on the *Durchlass*, or underpass, carrying the Ibbenbürener Aa River under the Mittelland Canal at Gravenhorst. The Aa is a smallish river, which, in the conditions, might easily have been mistaken for the aqueduct section of the Dortmund-Ems Canal as it crossed the River Glane between Greven and Ladbergen. On the other hand, and this is equally possible, he jettisoned the 12,000 pounder after being snared by the searchlights and hit by flak. Between November 1944 and February 1945 a number of 5 Group raids on the Mittelland Canal left the Gravenhorst locality in a state of total devastation. The course of the Canal has been altered since the war, but part of the original waterway still exists, and can be traced to the point where it crossed the Aa in 1943. It is north-east of Bergeshövede, and assuming from the events of the final few seconds of Allsebrook's life, that he did, indeed, carry out his attack on a north-east/south-west heading, he would have been instantly in range of the flak battery in the field ahead and to his right. Almost as rapidly he would pass between the hills on either side of the Mittelland Canal, with the Huckberg to his right, exactly at the point where it enters the Wet Triangle, and thus be out of sight of the flak position. In his book, *Beyond the Dams to the Tirpitz*, Alan Cooper states that Allsebrook called Martin to tell him to hold on a minute, 'until I get out of this', possibly referring to the flak or perhaps the low-lying mist. Later still he is said to have reported, that he was returning to base, but this is unconfirmed. The squadron ORB records Allsebrook as carrying out an attack, and this presumably came from other crews during debriefing.

An RAF reconnaissance photograph taken a year later in preparation for the above-mentioned 5 Group campaign against the Gravenhorst section of the Mittelland Canal, reveals a large bomb crater and two smaller ones within 100 yards of the eastern bank and quite close to the Aa Durchlass. I initially believed this to be evidence of Allsebrook's bomb, but the fact that local people had no recollection of a monster explosion made me think again. It is not possible that such a detonation would go unnoticed, as there would have been extensive property damage in Gravenhorst. I was fortunate to meet Herr Walter Luth, one of Germany's foremost bomb disposal experts, who has defused many Allied bombs. It was his professional opinion, that the crater in the photograph was not consistent with the detonation of a 12,000lb light case bomb. However, he alluded to another photo he had seen of an apparent excavation site on one of the canal's banks, which would have been consistent with the unearthing of an unexploded high capacity bomb. He then provided me with a detailed drawing of the very bomb employed by 617 Squadron against the canals on this night. The drawing was made by a German draughtsman shortly after the events here described. Similar in style to the sketch of the Dams bomb produced by the Germans within ten days of that attack, this one of the 12,000 pounder contains the lettering stencilled on the casing, including the date 9/43. The weapon is accurately described, along with its fusing mechanism, and is categorized as 'For use at low level against canals, first used 16.9.43'. As this ordnance was not employed again until November against the Antheor Viaduct in southern France, and thereafter during December and January against flying bomb sites also in France, it seems likely that the Germans acquired an intact example from the Dortmund-Ems Canal operation. In fact, Allsebrook's was almost certainly one of two examples of the weapon recovered by the Germans on this night. As far as Allsebrook's final moments are concerned, there are two possible scenarios. Firstly, that he jettisoned his bomb in a vain attempt to remain airborne, letting it go 'safe' in case it detonated on impact and engulfed the low flying, already damaged Lancaster in its massive shock wave. Secondly, that he did carry out an attack on the banks of the Mittelland Canal, but the bomb failed to detonate. Of course, both offerings are conjecture, and we will never know the truth.

Now let us return to Knight immediately after he had dutifully obtained permission from Martin to jettison his bomb. All Knight could manage on two good engines was a paltry 1,200 feet, and the aircraft leapt as the massive bulk of the 12,000 pounder fell away. According to Martin, three or four minutes elapsed between Knight's request to jettison his bomb and his announcement, 'I have successfully jettisoned, and am endeavouring to return to base.' Martin heard other pilots wish Knight good luck, and even fellow Australian, F/O Charlie Scherf, chipped in, while flying high above in his 418 Squadron Mosquito. Now, as the temperature of the starboard-inner engine began to climb, and they headed west towards the Dutch frontier, Knight ordered everything removable to be thrown out to save weight. He was struggling to keep the aircraft flying straight and level, partly because of the uneven pull of the engines, and partly because of the severe damage to the control surfaces and cables. He called on rear gunner, 'Obie' O'Brien, to take up a position in the bomb-aimer's compartment and pull on the starboard rudder pedal to help to ease the pressure on his leg. O'Brien succeeded in doing so, and the Lancaster's nose swung to the right, but it was an intolerable strain also on O'Brien, and he couldn't maintain the pressure for long. One of the port engines was restarted, and seemed to be working, but it soon failed and had to be shut down again. KC-N was now losing height, and as there was no chance of getting home, Knight gave the order to bale out. Someone clipped Knight's chute on as he sat calmly at the controls, and one by one the crew said farewell over the intercom before dropping into the night sky for the very short journey to earth. Such was the pressure required on the yoke and pedals to keep the aircraft upright, that Knight would have known he could not leave his seat, and that his only chance of survival lay in putting the aircraft down under some semblance of control.

During the bale-out procedure, KC-N's path had described a gentle anti-clockwise curve from a south-westerly starting point, and Hobday, Kellow and Johnson left the aircraft as it headed almost due south. By the time that Sutherland and Woollard jumped clear, KC-N was pointing back towards Germany, and was just south-west of the little town of Den Ham. In the few remaining moments left to him, Knight brought the Lancaster over the western edge of the town in what was now a tightening turn to port, and was actually heading a little north of due west as the aircraft, by this time almost totally unfit for flight, clipped trees on the edge of a meadow. This ended all hopes of a controlled forced-landing, and deprived suddenly of its flying speed, the Lancaster plunged nose first into the ground, where the wreckage immediately caught fire. It was 02.46. A mile or two to the north-west the navigator, Bob Kellow, heard the boom of KC-N's end, while he was reeling in the cords of his parachute. The Lancaster had actually come full circle, and was pointing directly at where Kellow was standing as it disintegrated and took Knight's young life. The body of the gallant and highly popular Les Knight was found by local civilians still at the controls, and in defiance of the German authorities they honoured him in a manner befitting his gallantry with a funeral at 18.00 hours that same day.

P/O Divall, who, along with his crew had been the last of the original pre-dams recruits to join the squadron, and who, like Wilson, had missed the dams operation through a lack of serviceable aircraft or illness, was in JA874, and this Lancaster likewise became a victim of the light flak, which was so lethal to low flying heavy bombers. Just as Allsebrook and possibly Rice had done, he was searching an area some distance away to the north of Ladbergen around the Mittelland Canal. Frau Anneliese Brönstrup was ten years old at the time, and lived as she still does in a farmhouse at Steinbeck near the little town of Recke, and right on the north bank of the Canal closest to the point where Divall and his crew perished. She is the only surviving coherent witness to the events, which she heard from the cellar rather than saw, but she was allowed to view one of the bodies on the following morning. This is her story.

An aircraft flew backwards and forwards at low level between Achmer in the east and Bergeshövede in the south-west searching for its target. At each location it ran into flak and eventually made a final approach towards the farmhouse on fire from the general direction of the west. It was on the southern or far side of the canal, and all the following action took place over a perfectly straight stretch of the waterway of perhaps half a mile between the Kälberberg and Bad Bridges. The aircraft dropped its bomb almost immediately on passing the former, and the weapon landed either in the water or on the towpath. Within seconds of releasing the bomb the aircraft also came down a few hundred yards further along the bank almost opposite Frau Brönstrup's farmhouse, and was rent by a violent explosion, which flattened the trees lining the canal and flung the rear turret over onto the northern bank with its occupant still inside. The rest of the wreckage was in the water and on the southern bank. When the bomb went up seconds later, its blast also shattered the trees lining the canal, and sent vast quantities of water cascading over the adjacent field, while also causing a collapse of the bank into the water. On the following morning the body of the rear gunner was laid out in the field close to the farmhouse, and apart from a bruise on his forehead, he showed no external sign of injury.

Now we have to interpret these events to piece together the final moments of the crew. Frau Brönstrup speaks of hearing *an* aircraft flying backwards and forwards searching for its target. I believe she probably heard a number of Lancasters, perhaps those of Allsebrook, Divall and Rice, all members of the south-routed and lost second formation. Based on timings examined in detail later in this chapter one can estimate, that aircraft were in the vicinity of the Mittelland Canal and within earshot of Steinbeck for up to roughly twenty-five minutes, culminating in Divall's crash, and this might not have allowed time for a single aircraft to cover the distance repeatedly between Achmer and wherever in search of its aiming point. She might well have heard the drone of Allsebrook's engines, but he flew off to the south-west and was brought down almost immediately some distance away as we have already seen. She may have briefly heard the sound of Shannon's engines, if he were indeed there, before he realised his error and headed south, where he found the correct target area relatively quickly thereafter. We do not know where Rice was at the time, but he probably passed fairly close to Steinbeck at some point. She certainly heard Divall's Lancaster as it flew on fire at very low level towards the farmhouse from the west, appearing to follow the course of the canal. The bomb was dropped on the canal, where we assume it exploded within 26 to 90 seconds.

There is, of course, the question as to whether or not the bomb was delivered, or simply jettisoned live in a last desperate effort to keep the aircraft airborne or in preparation for a forced landing. It must have been apparent to the crew that the Lancaster was finished, and at such low level there was clearly no prospect of them baling out. If the intention had been to jettison the bomb, however, there were plenty of opportunities to do so before the point was reached where it actually fell. There had likewise been many open fields in which to put the Lancaster down under some kind of control.

I believe, therefore, that Divall followed the course of the Mittelland Canal, probably at treetop height, and at the point when it became clear to him that the end was at hand, he sought permission from Allsebrook to drop his bomb, and aimed it at the bank as a last resort target. Almost immediately after releasing the weapon the Lancaster crashed further along the southern bank with a violent explosion, killing all on board and flinging the rear turret onto the northern bank to within a few yards of the farmhouse, close to the Bad Bridge. The occupant of the turret was Sgt Daniel Allatson, who had accompanied Brown to the Sorpe Dam in May as a replacement for Brown's own front gunner, who was ill at the time. Divall and his three gunners were the only members of the crew to be positively identified, and all were initially laid to rest in the evangelical cemetery at nearby Bramsche at 16.00 hours on the 18th. The German burial report states that the remains of Divall and two of his unidentified colleagues were interred in one grave, and the other two unidentified men shared another, while the three gunners were given individual graves. After the war their remains were moved to the Commonwealth War Graves Cemetery at Reichswald.

Martin, now, as already stated, the lone survivor of the first section, eventually came upon the Ladbergen stretch of the canal, after initially looking for it ten miles to the north somewhere near the Wet Triangle. Having found it, though, he then experienced the same problems as the others in picking out the aiming point in the conditions. Having declared their position when accounting for Wilson, it was now open season for the flak gunners, and they squirted at Martin every time he came within range, and then gave the same treatment to Shannon when he turned up, he having begun his search some three to four miles to the north. Shannon found that he could only pick up the canal when directly over it at a height of not more than 150 feet, and he eventually released his bomb from that altitude at 02.36. It exploded on the towpath on the eastern bank, and failed to create any breach. Some time after Shannon turned for home, Martin called up Rice and told him to abandon his search and return to base, while he continued on alone. It was around forty minutes after Shannon's attack that Martin managed to get a reasonably clear run, after stumbling into searchlights and flak during earlier attempts. In order to make a bombing run Martin needed to meet the canal at the kind of wide angle, which would allow him to turn immediately onto it. The problem was, that, like Shannon, he could only catch a glimpse of the water when directly above it, and that was too late for him to make the turn and keep the canal in sight. Finally, he managed to pick it up in such a way as to be able to embark on a timed circuit, which, if judged to perfection, would bring him round exactly onto the track he had been searching for all along. His skill and determination were rewarded as the canal emerged from the mist beneath him and stretched ahead straight and wide, inviting bomb-aimer Bob Hay to press the 'tit'. After a tense moment or two, while the line was adjusted slightly, the 12,000 pounder was dropped from 200 feet, and was seen to explode in the water, apparently without causing damage.

Tragically, either Martin's or Shannon's bomb detonated close to a barge carrying ore, killing the Dutch husband and wife crew of Abel and Meetje Stuut from Groningen, who were both just twenty-two years old.

On his way home, according to the ORB, Rice jettisoned his bomb safe in the Waddenzee between the Dutch coast and Terschelling, although in his logbook he cites the Zuider Zee, now known as the Ijsselmeer, as the location. He arrived back at 05.22, having logged a flight of five hours twenty minutes, and Martin touched down a couple of minutes later, reporting the visibility as clearing only once he reached the Zuider Zee. Shannon had been first home, arriving some forty-five minutes before Rice. The Mosquito crews reported reaching the target area shortly before 02.00 hours, and confirmed the poor state of the visibility. F/O Mitchie recorded fairly intense flak, while P/O Woods and F/L Lisson each commented on the searchlight activity as little or not troublesome. For their part, F/Os Scherf and Rowlands each reported being fired upon by flak around the town of Rheine. Only S/L Gibb reported attacking flak positions, and these were around the twin aqueduct section near Ladbergen.

It has proved very difficult to establish a sequence of events during this operation because of the difference in the clocks in Britain, Germany and Holland, and contradictory timings recorded by some RAF participants weeks later. The references available to us come from the ORB, crew statements, German documents and Piet Meijer, each using a different clock. In 1943 double BST, or GMT + 2, ended in Britain on the 15th of August, when the clock reverted to BST or GMT + 1. We know the Lancasters left Coningsby around midnight, and that the Mosquitos' arrival in the target area shortly before 02.00 hours was intended to coincide with that of the heavy brigade. However, on return to the UK some weeks later, members of Knights crew reported their departure time from Coningsby as being around 23.00 hours, using GMT, and we must, therefore, add one hour to all timings given by this crew in statements. Nordhorn is only ten to fifteen minutes flying time from Ladbergen, and according to Piet Meijer's timetable of Knight's journey to the target we can fairly accurately place Holden's crash as taking place at 01.55. In Bomber Command Losses Volume 4 Bill Chorley places Knight's crash at 03.46, which is local Dutch time, and is one hour ahead of GMT + 1 and one hour behind German time. In British time, GMT + 1, Knight's crash would have been at 02.46, and this is confirmed by Bob Kellow's reminiscence, that he began his walk to freedom at 02.20 GMT, which, as we have already decided, should be moved forward by one hour to 03.20 GMT + 1. Confused? I was! We have, therefore, two definitive times to help us, those of Holden's crash and of Knight's, and by working with these we can arrive at a fairly accurate timetable for the others. We can assume that Knight knew his operation was over the moment he lost two engines, and would have pointed his Lancaster towards the west even as he was seeking permission to jettison his bomb. With only two good engines he would have managed around 135 mph, and as he would have been constantly correcting the Lancaster's tendency to deviate from a straight line it would have taken roughly thirty-one minutes to cover the fifty-seven miles to Den Ham. Counting back from 02.46 gives us a time of 02.15 when he hit the trees. At that moment he was about to begin a third orbit, having just completed his second, during which Wilson was seen to crash. This places Wilson's crash at 02.12 or thereabouts. Allsebrook was alive at 02.15, when Knight asked to be allowed to jettison his bomb, and had already given permission for Wilson and Divall to make their attacks. Wilson's crash site within yards of the canal and in sight of the aiming point shows him to have been on his bombing run when the end came, and we know that Divall crashed within seconds of dropping his bomb, which must also have been at around 02.15. There is no further mention of Allesbrook in post raid reports after wishing Knight good luck at 02.15, and were he still alive for any length of time after that, it is reasonable to assume, that as raid controller, he would have been heard. Therefore, we must conclude that he himself crashed almost immediately, sometime between 02.15 and 02.20.

The German authorities recorded the time of Allsebrook's crash as being shortly before 04.00, and that of Divall as 04.15, which confirms German time as one hour ahead of Dutch time and two ahead of GMT + 1. The German timings are consistent with each other, and this adds weight to the belief that Allsebrook's section's arrival in what they thought was the target area preceded that of Martin's for the reasons already offered. The timings from German sources adjusted to harmonize with GMT + 1 state, that the air raid alarm lasted from 01.00 until 03.45, and that the attack began at 01.40. If this were the case, and both sections arrived at the same time, it would put Holden's crash at around 01.30, which is not possible within the timings thus far established. However, if, as the timings suggest, Allsebrook's section arrived earlier than briefed in the target area by whatever means, it would account for the German assessment of 01.40 as the starting time for the attack. The one flaw in this reasoning is, as mentioned above, that the initial German report puts Allsebrook's crash at shortly before 04.00, or 02.00 GMT + 1, and we know for the reasons already outlined, that he was still alive at around 02.15. However, the German record of Divall's crash places it at 04.15 or 02.15 GMT + 1, which is in agreement with the timings suggested above. It should be understood, of course, that the German official who placed Allsebrook's crash at around 02.00 would have been given that information as an approximation by locals, and his telephone report to higher authorities and the written confirmation were made within hours of the event. It is quite likely, that an amended time appears on a later document. I believe, therefore, that Allsebrook crashed at around 02.20, after searching for up to forty minutes for the aiming point.

There is now one final mystery to address. A question posed by a Dutch enthusiast some years ago was; did 617 Squadron attack the wrong canal? This arises not out of the bombing of the Mittelland by Divall, but out of the dropping of a large bomb near Denekamp, a small Dutch town south-west of Nordhorn, and like Nordhorn just a stone's throw from the Dutch/German frontier. The Almelo–Nordhorn Canal passes through the centre of Nordhorn, exiting the town at its southern extremity, before arcing towards the west and passing the northern rim of Denekamp. At 04.08 local time, or 03.08 GMT + 1 on the 16th of September 1943 a huge bomb, described by residents as an earthquake bomb, exploded in the vicinity of the canal causing serious damage to seven houses and varying degrees of damage to 113 others within a one mile radius. Six people were injured, although none fatally. There is no doubt whatsoever, that this bomb came from a 617 Squadron aircraft, as the only other operation in progress on this night was against a Dunlop Rubber factory in central France. Not only is it highly unlikely that any of the more than 300 aircraft involved would have strayed over eastern Holland, none of the participants was carrying a 12,000 pounder. The Dutch enthusiast, Jos Knippers, is convinced that the bomb in question was that jettisoned by Knight, but as it was recovered intact by the Germans, clearly that cannot be the case. Although we cannot be absolutely certain whether or not Allsebrook's bomb exploded, there is no possibility of him being in the vicinity of Denekamp at any time during the operation, and he and his crew were long dead by the time the Denekamp bomb went off.

All of the above means that we can account with a reasonable degree of certainty for seven of the eight bombs departing Coningsby on that night, and the only one for which we cannot is that of Geoff Rice. He reported having jettisoned it 'safe' either in the Waddenzee near the Frisian island of Terschelling if we accept the ORB entry, or in the Zuider Zee if we use his logbook. The Waddenzee lies between the Dutch Frisians and the mainland, while the Zuider Zee, now known as the Ijsselmeer, is situated inside the Afsluitdijk. That said, to some crews they were one and the same. Rice searched for eighty minutes before being sent home by Martin, and he could, therefore, have been within the general vicinity of Denekamp at the time in question. One is compelled to ask why Rice would hang on to his bomb as he flew home across Holland, only to jettison it when he reached the comparative safety of the North Sea. Knowing his bomb would fall into enemy hands, Knight had sought permission to jettison it in safe condition. Rice would not need permission if his bomb were either dropped live onto land or safe into the sea, where it could not be recovered. In the final analysis the Denekamp incident is yet another mystery of war, and we will never know for certain to whom the bomb belonged.

These grievous losses to the squadron were sustained without the compensation of a successful operation. Initial photographic reconnaissance suggested a slight interruption of rail traffic resulting from a near miss, but this was scant consolation for such a heavy loss of life. In view of the squadron's later record of success, it is useful to examine the reasons for this failure. Holden was lost only a few minutes flying time from the target, and his demise can be attributed to bad luck more than anything else. That said, experience should have told him to stay low and skirt the town, but he was, of course, inexperienced in leading low-level formations. In his mind, the likelihood of being hit in a fuel tank by non-predicted flak in the few seconds it took to cross Nordhorn was no doubt small indeed. However, the expert advice available to him would have recommended staying on the deck and altering course to avoid obstacles. Responsibility for the operation was then immediately thrust upon Allsebrook just as the conditions were deteriorating. Perhaps, in view of these conditions, Allsebrook should have abandoned the operation there and then, but it would have required a very brave decision on his part after the previous night's failure to complete and the subsequent loss of the popular Maltby and crew. Allsebrook was a brave man, and he decided to adopt the 'fortune favours the brave' approach to the operation. Later in the war, when the squadron was carrying even more expensive bombs, it would become common practice to abandon an operation repeatedly if the conditions were questionable. It seems certain, that Allsebrook's section was lost, and north of the intended aiming point. The likelihood is, that they caught glimpses of a waterway in a region centred upon the Wet Triangle, and circled this area. The location of both his and Divall's crash sites is not consistent with them having found the briefed target area south of Ladbergen. Stooging around at low level for an extended period provided the flak gunners with ample opportunity to draw a bead on their quarry, and Allsebrook, Wilson and Divall all met their end in this way. The operation was further confirmation to Harris, that low-level operations in heavy bombers were too expensive, and it would be more than twelve months before 617 Squadron attempted anything like this again.

Meanwhile, back in Holland, seven members of Knight's crew were coming to terms with their predicament. Flight engineer Ray Grayston and rear gunner 'Obie' O'Brien fell into enemy hands, and during Grayston's interrogation he was questioned about the bomb recovered by his captors. He also received a visit from a triumphant *Luftwaffe* officer, presumably attached to a flak battery, who claimed to have shot down AJ-N, and Grayston took great delight in informing him that he was mistaken. The remaining five men ultimately evaded capture, Kellow beginning his journey to freedom at 02.20 GMT or 03.20 GMT + 1 on the morning of the 16th, having hidden all trace of his arrival in northern Holland. He knew from the escape and evasion lectures, that he must head in a south-westerly direction and make for Belgium, and thence to France and Spain. The fact that he achieved this some six weeks later is testimony to the patience and selfless courage of dozens of ordinary people, who sheltered him, fed him, clothed him, schooled him and generally befriended him during his foot-slogging, bicycle, tram and train odyssey through four countries. Unknown to him, his crewmates were only a day or so behind, travelling by an entirely different route, and helped by other magnificent people.

Hobday and Sutherland began their journeys home independently, but met up on the 17th while in Dutch hands, and were then fed through the escape network. The following is taken from their statements on return to the UK.

> We left Coningsby at 23.00 hours (GMT) on 15 Sep 43 in a Lancaster bomber for a low-level bombing attack on the Dortmund-Ems Canal. The weather turned very misty, and whilst circling the target waiting our turn to go in to drop our bombs, we lost our bearings slightly. We were all looking for landmarks, when, in avoiding a hill, we crashed through the tops of some trees. The two port engines were badly damaged and knocked out completely. The pilot called up the leader and got permission to jettison the bomb loads and make for base. After we dropped the bomb, the starboard engines began to get very hot. The aircraft was difficult to manoeuvre, as the tail plane also seemed to have been damaged. Base was wirelessed, and the pilot ordered us to bale out. The time was then about 02.15 hours. [16th Sep.]

Hobday and Sutherland then gave separate accounts, Hobday first.

> Before I baled out I saw all the crew with the exception of the pilot bale out. I came down in the midst of some trees. My parachute was caught on some branches, so I left it and started walking south until I came to a canal. I then walked east until I crossed the canal, when I again proceeded south to Hellendoorn. I circled one village, but walked through Hellendoorn. A woman passed me on a bicycle about 09.00 hrs. I then cut off my rank stripes and badges. Shortly afterwards I met some schoolboys who asked me if I was English. They gave me some apples. They told me two RAF had passed through earlier. One was P/O Kellow by the description. A man then came along after I had said I was English. He made a rendezvous with me in a small wood nearby for 12.00 hrs. I rested in the wood until he appeared punctually, bringing me some civilian clothes. He directed me to Raalte, and told me he would meet me there. I met him again in Raalte at 14.30 hrs. He got on the telephone to some people and made some arrangements. Afterwards he gave me a card, which indicated that I was deaf and dumb. He then bought me a railway ticket for Baarn, gave me directions, and put me on a train, which left at 16.10 hrs. I had to change trains twice. The second change at Amersfoort, where I arrived at 19.30 hrs, was a bit complicated. I got rather mixed up in the stations and got on the wrong train at first. The station also seemed to be full of Germans. My train left at 19.58 hrs, and arrived at Baarn at 20.10 hrs. I was met there and taken to a public park by a man. Shortly afterwards another man arrived and interrogated me as to my identity and that of my companions in the aircraft. We then cycled to a wood north of Lage Vuursche, arriving there about 22.00 hrs. I was taken to a shack, where I met about ten Dutchmen, including two Dutch Army officers and a Jewish lad of about 16 years of age. The

remainder of the Dutchmen were hiding from conscription to labour camps. On the afternoon of 17 Sep I was told that another RAF evader was coming. This turned out to be Sgt Sutherland.

Sutherland wrote:

I baled out and came down in a paddock. I gathered up my parachute and hid it in a ditch. I then started walking west. After crossing a canal I turned south and walked until daybreak. I found some trees and rested there until 19.00 hrs. [16 Sep]. Shortly after I started out again a woman came up on a bicycle near a farmhouse. I was taken into the farmhouse and given some food. After dark I set out again and came to another house a quarter of a mile further on. I knocked on the door and asked for help. The man said he thought he would be able to help, and took me to another house. The owner of the house spoke a little English and gave me a civilian jacket. I then went back and spent the night at the farmhouse. At 07.00 hrs next day [17 Sep] I set out again and met the son (aged about 18) of the house I had visited the previous night. He said he would definitely help, and took me to an attic in his house. About 15.00 hrs two men arrived with civilian clothes. At about 15.30 hrs the youth and I walked to a railway station, where he bought a ticket for me. We both travelled to Baarn, changing once, and arrived there at 21.00 hrs. The youth handed me over to a man, who took me to a public park. There I was interrogated as to my identity and that of my companions in the aircraft. We then cycled to a shack in a wood, where I met F/O Hobday.

Among the options offered to Kellow on his return was the chance to go back to Australia, and this, ultimately, was the decision he took. He departed the UK on the 12th of February 1944, and headed home via the USA and Canada.

CHAPTER NINE

Stagehands, The Unsung Heroes Who Served Behind The Scenes

'The Merlin Man' by Andy Lee

LAC Basil 'BAZ' Pearson 870794, 617 Squadron A Flight & R&I Section 1943–1945

Some of my earliest recollections as a young boy are of visiting my grandparents in Wetherby in Yorkshire in the early 1970s. I was around the age of four or five when my father started buying and making Airfix kits for me. Lightnings, Harriers and Red Arrows Gnats were great, but my favourites were the Lancaster, Spitfire and Hurricane. My grandfather [Basil Pearson] would tell me stories of the days when he serviced Merlin engines on Lancasters in the war. This made a life-long impression on me. The most amazing story he told was of the Dambusters. I was given all the details of the special 'spinning bomb' that had to be dropped from 60 feet at night and blew up the German Dams. He would show me details with two wooden scale model Lancasters he made at Scampton and Woodhall Spa. They were perfect six-inch miniature 'Lancs' with canopies and gun turrets made out of small pieces of perspex from the smashed canopies of 617 Squadron aircraft.

Shortly after this my father made me a Revell 'Dambuster' Lancaster with a bouncing bomb. My grandfather's stories then became more detailed, and as I got older I started asking more questions. In his hallway was a 4 feet long framed photograph of all the Squadron personnel taken in front of a Lancaster. I was later to learn this was taken on the 9th of July 1943. Basil would pick me up, and show me where he was in the picture, in the middle, three rows back from and behind W/C Guy Gibson. He would pick out the pilots he worked for and show me where they were. Brown, Shannon, Maltby,

Gibson, Martin, Rice and Allsebrook all became names I knew, and each time I visited he would ask me to point out who was sitting where. On the day the picture was taken he was servicing the aircraft used in the background, ED763 AJ-D, a standard Lancaster. This aircraft was one of the original ten borrowed Lancasters used to form the Squadron. It did not take part in the Dams Raid itself, but was used for practising low-level flying for the raid. ED763 was kept on even after the Type 464 Provisioning Lancasters were delivered. As the 464s were so secret, ED763 was used in the Squadron picture. (Careful examination shows the engines do not have flash suppressors fitted.) Basil helped move the aircraft into position behind the semi-circle of chairs set up for the photograph. This was *his* plane, one of the first aircraft he worked on when he arrived at Scampton on the 24th of June 1943. He regularly serviced the Merlin engines on it, and practically the whole of A Flight flew this aircraft at some point during the period 1943 to 1945. Ken Brown and Ralph Allsebrook both flew it regularly throughout June to August 1943. In the year 2000 Ken wrote to me explaining how Basil worked on his aircraft for eight months from June 1943 to February 1944, when he was sometimes using three aircraft. It became a problem to know which one might be used next and which had to be kept serviceable from day to day. These were ED918 AJ-F, a Type 464 aircraft, and ED763 AJ-D and DV394 KC-M, both standard Lancasters fitted with SABS.

As I reached the age of ten I began to stay with my grandparents in the summer holidays, and that was when I really appreciated what my grandfather did with 617 Squadron. He would show me his textbooks, all meticulously written out by hand, detailing all aspects of engine maintenance, aircraft marshalling and day-to-day inspection routines. He started to show me photos he took of W/C Cheshire's Lancaster at Woodhall Spa in 1944, and to recount the 'other stories' of 617. He would say, that everyone knew of the Dams Raid because of the huge amount of press at the time and the 50s movie, but very few people really knew the work 617 Squadron did after this and up to the end of the war. This included the 12,000lb 'Factory Buster' raids on French aero-engine plants, the Tallboy raids on V-Weapons sites and *U-boot* pens, along with the other 'Dams Raids' against the Urft Dam and the Kembs barrage, the sinking of the *Tirpitz*, and finally, the Grand Slam raids on the viaducts in the closing months of the war. These stories fascinated me, especially those detailing his work with W/C Cheshire for whom he had the greatest admiration, 'Cheshire was a great man,' he would say, 'to service his aircraft was an honour.' From February to June 1944 he regularly serviced the engines on Cheshire's Lancaster DV390 KC-N. This was during and after the time when Cheshire and 'Mick' Martin had so successfully pioneered the low-level marking technique. Basil would be asked personally by Cheshire to work on his aircraft, to look at specific areas he wanted checking. Basil, at thirty-seven by this time, was older than most of the other fitters, and because of this was maybe considered more reliable by Cheshire. Even in his seventies and eighties Basil's car engine looked immaculate, like a highly polished showroom custom engine. He produced a very high standard of work even all these years later in his retirement. The values, honour and integrity that were so important then, stayed with him for the rest of his life.

So, during my stays he would gradually tell me more and more about life with 617 Squadron, like his time at Thorpe Camp at Woodhall Spa, where he was constantly awoken by woodpeckers in the trees nearby. It drove him mad! The time at Woodhall Spa was the most productive for 617 Squadron, which was being used as a precision 'sniper' unit for high priority targets. Ground crews regularly turned aircraft around in record times for urgent missions, all the time maintaining a very high standard of work on the aircraft.

All 617 Squadron personnel took great pride in the sinking of the *Tirpitz*, and the work done by the ground crews for the three missions to sink her was amazing. The refitting of Merlin Type 24s to all aircraft involved in the second *Tirpitz* attack on the 29th of October 1944 was a massive feat. Basil was pulling Merlin Type 24s out of new aircraft delivered to other squadrons and replacing them with 'old' 617 Squadron Merlin Type 22s. Some pilots from these squadrons, who did not know what was going on, were non too pleased to be getting second hand engines in their 'new planes'. Basil said this was a mammoth job, but they all got down to it and successfully completed the task. He always said, that the American Packard Merlins with the Stromberg carburettors were great engines, and each engine came with a wonderfully made tool kit. He and his workmates took this opportunity to make sure that they each had a new kit for their efforts! When he first joined 617 Squadron he even made his own tools when things were in short supply, and also used his own motorbike tool kit at times. This was where his love of engines started. Basil and my grandmother Kathie loved motorbikes, and in the years before the war Basil would like nothing more than to work on his Ariel 500cc motorbike. He would regularly take the entire bike to pieces and lay it all out on a ground sheet in the garden. Kathie would be horrified to see the whole thing in bits! He would clean and polish the parts and tweak the engine to get every spare hp out of it. It was this knowledge and love of engines that eventually led him to 617 Squadron. In the lounge there was always a photo of him in his leathers with helmet and goggles, and I'm sure he was a bit of a 'speed demon' on that bike at the time. I would ask him why he did not have any more photos of 617 Squadron from this period, unaware that the ones he did have were unofficial and would have got him into trouble. During research for this book I have discovered, that most former members of 617 Squadron have amazing previously unseen photos in their albums, all taken unofficially and all a unique glimpse of the time we are writing about.

Each time I saw my grandfather he would tell me a little more. Like many of his colleagues, he would not say too much, as 617 Squadron was so unique and the technology so cutting-edge at the time, they were all told not to talk about it. This attitude carried on for many years after the war ... it was still secret ... even to family. When I got into my teens the stories became longer and more detailed, and he would quite happily talk to me all Sunday afternoon about Merlin engines, and how they tuned them on a daily basis to get every last drop of power out of them. I'm sure they would eat, sleep and drink Merlin engines while they were there. Some nights at Woodhall Spa, particularly if it was a difficult mission, he would sleep by the dispersal point in his great coat on the ground waiting for his crew to come home. It was very tense, wondering whether his crew would get home safely, and would his engines be reliable. How had the mission gone, had it been a success? All ground crews went through the same emotions each night. One of the most distressing jobs was removing injured or dead crewmembers. I know he did this on more than one occasion, but he never could talk about it, as it was too distressing. To this day my grandmother still says what an awful job it was, cleaning up after people you knew and worked with. As Basil was older than some of the young lads working with him, he just got on with this job, feeling that they were too young to have to do it. Many of the younger fitters, who were typically eighteen to twenty year-olds, came to him for advice and looked up to him. He was the 'old man', Dad, in their eyes.

Some of his fondest memories were of W/C Cheshire, who would have a cup of tea under the wing of his plane, and talk with the ground crew after each mission to discuss any maintenance issues and chat generally if the mission was a success. This closeness and willingness to spend time with his ground crews was one of Cheshire's great qualities. For Basil, as for any ground crew member, the loss of a crew he worked with was a particularly difficult thing to deal with. Basil's first taste of this was the Dortmund-Ems Canal raid on the night of the 14/15th of September 1943. That night S/L David Maltby was lost on the way home after the mission was aborted. Maltby had been made A Flight commander after the Dams Raid, and at the time of his death was the most senior pilot for whom Basil worked. This was because Gibson did not fly at all during June 1943, and very little in July and he left the Squadron in August for a tour of the USA. The next night, September the 15th, Basil was once again working on the aircraft of Allsebrook and Divall. (Thankfully, Ken Brown did not take part in that mission.) The full story of these tragic losses is covered in the previous chapter. Basil was deeply affected by losing his two crews that night. He had worked with them both extensively since June. He did not like to talk about this much as it saddened him. The research into their losses has been of immense personal interest to me, as Allsebrook was one of the faces etched in my memory from being a young child. Basil would point him out in the Squadron picture on his wall, Allsebrook sat in the middle of the group next to the then F/L Maltby and F/L Hutchison, directly below my Grandfather. Slowly we have uncovered the full details of this historic raid. Very little has been written about it, and the loss of entire crews has been almost dismissively summed up as 'shot down or lost in fog'. For me this operation is equally as important as the epic Dams Raid. It involved a brand new special weapon, untried in combat, and demanded low-level flying all the way there and back. It consisted of two formations crossing the coast simultaneously at different locations intending to meet up prior to the run-in to the target, and it was led by a new commanding officer briefed to use the 'Master Bomber' technique, perfected so well in the Dams Raid. The similarities with the Dams Raid are all there, but this one went tragically wrong.

For Basil it was a personal disaster, that his two crews failed to return, and for a long time very little information existed to tell us what actually happened. It is only now, after my grandfather's death in 1997, that a true picture of this mission has been uncovered. If I had had this information then, I'm sure I would have drawn more stories from him. With such heavy losses over the two nights, this was one of the blackest periods for the Squadron. The men on the ground were very sad to have lost so many great aircrews on this mission. All this happened just when 617 Squadron was regrouping and retraining with a new commanding officer, after the very heavy losses resulting from the Dams Raid. Basil suffered other sad losses in 1943. Geoff Rice was another A Flight pilot who was lost with his crew in December 1943, after Ted Youseman and his crew had gone missing in November. However, the end of 1943 brought a change and new tactics.

In January 1944, 617 Squadron moved from Coningsby to Woodhall Spa, just down the road. Here Basil was stationed in Nissen Hut 46 on site 3, which was also home to the infamous woodpeckers, as remembered by other ground crew. Coningsby and Scampton were both 'brick-built' pre-war airfields, and were 'not bad' compared to Woodhall Spa, a hastily built wartime airfield of the prefab variety. On his rare days off Basil would cycle, walk or beg a lift, whatever was necessary, to get to Grimsby for 24 hours leave to see my grandmother and my mother Beryl, who was then five years old. Sometimes he would just turn up and stay for a few hours then return to Woodhall Spa. My grandmother still recounts the tale of the occasion when Basil came home on leave, and my mother, who had grown up with him always being away, said, 'He's a nice Daddy, but he doesn't live here!' They had moved from Hull to Grimsby so that Basil could get to see them more often, as Hull was just too far to get there and back in a day. All the family were worried, because Grimsby was constantly under German air attack, and there was an anti-aircraft gun in the field just in front of grandmother's house in St Michael's Avenue. It was their nightly routine to go into the Anderson shelter. Basil had tried to put some home comforts into it as my grandmother and mother spent each night in there.

One morning, after the AA gun had been installed, my grandmother was talking with a neighbour, when a German Me109 flew down her street at very low level looking for it. They both dived to the ground as the neighbour shouted, 'Look its got a Swastika on the side!' On another occasion a V-1 flew straight overhead belching flame from its ramjet engine. No one knew what it was, and only the next day did they find out it was a deadly

'Doodlebug'. Little did my grandmother know of the efforts 617 Squadron were making to hit the mobile launchers responsible for sending these terror weapons.

My grandfather's military career had begun in 1939. With the prospect of war looming over Europe, Basil joined the Auxiliary Air force so he would be posted locally. He enlisted as an Aircraftman Second Class (AC2) in the RAF on the 6th of March 1939 as a member of 942 Barrage Balloon Squadron, which formed part of the defence of the Humber Estuary. His forthcoming Service Trade would be ACH/Bln Op. (Aircraft Hand/Balloon Operator). He went through training after work and during weekends. He was working at the time in Hull at Horne Brothers Gentleman's Outfitters on Jameson Street. Many balloon workers came from a civilian background in upholstery, seamstressing and tailoring.

Basil joined up for four years, and was 31 at the time. On August the 24th 1939 he got his formal full time call-up papers through the post. He was required to report to 942 BB Sqn at Sutton, Hull, no later than 09.00 hours. The morning post was very reliable, and approximately 300 local Auxiliary Air Force men also received their call up that day, all with the same instruction to report by 09.00 hours. Basil only had a few hours to pack everything up, not knowing how long he would be gone. He had time to pose for some photographs in his uniform before he went, and these are some of the best pictures taken of him. Gran took them with his Zeiss Ikon medium format camera. The mobilisation of these personnel enabled the Auxiliary Air Force to bring forty-four balloon squadrons into immediate use at the outbreak of war. After the initial induction he qualified as a fabric worker on the 4th of November 1939. He had been trained in the maintenance and repair of balloons, doping, stitching, attachment of cable anchors to the fabric etc. By December the 31st he had been upgraded to balloon rigger, still a Group 3 trade.

On the 1st of June 1940 he was promoted to Aircraftman First Class (AC1). He was re-categorised on the 6th of September 1940 as AC1 Balloon Operator, a more skilled role requiring training in the flying of the balloons. Two months later he was transferred to 944 BB Squadron as an AC1 Balloon Operator. Life as a balloon operator was more dangerous, as Basil found out when he was dragged into the air by the ankle as a balloon was being flown. He managed to shake free of the cable at North Wall, on Grimsby docks, but ended up on crutches for a while afterwards.

During 1940 and 1941 attacks by the *Luftwaffe* on Hull kept the balloon units in this area very busy. Hull was a prime target identified by Hitler in his Directive No. 9 of the 29th of November 1939. As a coal port it was constantly attacked. There were very heavy attacks on Hull in the spring of 1941, on the nights of the 7/8th and 8/9th of May in particular, when 450 people were killed and some 30,000 others, 10 per cent of the city's population, were made homeless. Grimsby docks also came under heavy attack. On the 1st of March 1941 Basil was reclassified as Leading Aircraftman (LAC) following a trade test board in February. In the spring he was admitted to RAF Hospital Rauceby, near Sleaford in Lincolnshire. We still do not know exactly why he was taken in, only that he was in intensive care for a while with massive respiratory problems. Grandmother was told he could die at any time, and she should get to the hospital as soon as possible. He underwent an emergency operation. Even after the war his medical records were not released to his GP. We can only assume that he inhaled or otherwise came into contact with some poisonous substance, perhaps dope fumes, or that an accident occurred at the docks involving poison gas, which was hushed up. He was discharged on the 12th of May. While he recovered he was put on signals and radio operations, light duties at which he could sit down. Basil returned to 944 BB Sqn and was rated 'very good character' in his annual appraisal on the 31st of December 1941. He was posted back to 942 BB Sqn on the 18th of April 1942. His first Good Conduct Badge was awarded on the 24th of August 1942. This was awarded after three years of main service, whether or not an airman applied for it. The award was presented by an officer of not below the rank of Wing Commander. During the two years prior to the award,

> The airman must not have incurred any entry on his service sheet except any award of confinement to camp not exceeding ten days, or stoppage of smoking on board ship, and he must have conducted himself with sobriety, activity and attention. During this period his conduct in the opinion of his commanding officer must have been uninterruptedly very good. (King's Regulations.)

In 1943 the increased demand for aircrew had meant a number of ground crew volunteering to remuster as aircrew. The knock-on effect was a shortage of ground crew. This is probably what led to Basil being posted to No. 3 School of Technical Training at Squires Gate in Blackpool on the 28th of January 1943, for instruction as an engine mechanic. My grandmother and mother moved with Basil to Blackpool, and lived in the front room of a Wing Commander's digs on the sea front, now called the Golden Mile. Basil was back in his element, engines again! His love of all things mechanical, especially engines, made this the natural course for him. Blackpool provided a much easier life style for grandmother after the constant nightly ritual of the air raid shelter in Grimsby. Basil attended classes every day and took notes in his books on all aspects of aero engines, radial and in-line, how they worked, how to maintain them, superchargers and even details on aircraft marshalling and refuelling. My grandmother would watch him hold drill on the sea front on a Saturday morning.

Basil completed this course on the 16th of June 1943, and was regraded Aircraftman Second Class (AC2) Flight Mechanic Engines. Largely because of his meticulous work and attention to detail he was posted to 617 Squadron on the 24th of June 1943 at RAF Scampton. This is where my story started. He had joined the RAF's most elite squadron and was servicing aircraft on

A Flight. As already mentioned, S/L Maltby was A Flight Commander at this time and Basil was immediately put to work for pilots who had returned from the Dams Raid. The Squadron had received massive worldwide publicity for the raid and many had just returned from Buckingham Palace where they received their awards for this mission. W/C Gibson was awarded the VC and was the most highly decorated pilot in the RAF. Basil was very aware he was working with a special group of men. Gibson in particular was a national hero at this time. 617 Squadron was experimenting with dropping Upkeep on land, and two Type 464 Lancasters were modified to allow forward spin to be imparted to the bomb in an attempt to achieve extended range. At the end of May ED915 and ED932 were sent to RAE Farnborough for these modifications.

On the 2nd of July Basil serviced ED906, the aircraft being used by Gibson for a training flight. ED906 was Maltby's Dams aircraft, but Gibson flew it on a low-level cross-country to Cornwall. ED932 was checked out on an air test on the 4th of July at 15.05 on its return from RAE Farnborough, and went back up again at 15.25 for a tactical exercise. This was one of the few times, that Gibson flew ED932 after the Dams Raid. ED932 was used by nearly every pilot on A Flight, and was not the sole preserve of W/C Gibson. It was treated as just another plane, and Basil regularly looked over its Merlins, especially for Maltby, Allsebrook, Rice, Divall and Ken Brown, whom he started working with more and more around this time. On the 9th of July W/C Gibson flew with Les Knight in Lancaster 'R'. Knight's logbook states, 'W/Cdr Gibson and 4 crew – West Malling, land and return'. This was Gibson's return to his old Fighter Command base for a party, and it is not mentioned in his own logbook. Gibson's last significant Upkeep flight took place on the 17th of July, again with Les Knight in ED765 AJ-M. This time the logbook entry read, 'W/Cdr Gibson, Self + Crew. To Southend: Test Drop of one Upkeep, land and return'. This was in the Reculver area where all the dams testing had been done in May 1943. This was most likely a live drop of Upkeep in the sea, and is significantly his last drop of this unique weapon. Gibson made seven other flights in AJ-M mainly flying to Grantham, Northolt, Fairwood, Woodhall Spa and finally to the Isle of Man for a party.

S/L G.W Holden was posted to 617 Squadron, and on the 4th of July he started a four-day rapid Lancaster conversion course, with S/L Martin showing him the ropes. Holden was a Halifax man and these were his first flights in a Lancaster. By the 7th of July he was working with Gibson's crew, which he had inherited, and they embarked on a series of high-level, cross-country, night, low-level and formation flights, all to get the new commanding officer up to speed in time for an operation to Aquata Scrivia on the 15th of July. The new CO was flying in ED932 and ED933, which had now been repaired and returned to squadron use. During this period Basil checked out the new CO's plane along with the old CO, who was still on the base.

Standard Lancaster ED763 was still Basil's main aircraft, and he worked on this extensively from June to December 1943. 617 Squadron was training new crews to use Upkeep in anger again. June to August saw a lot of training flights, and the remaining Type 464 Provisioning Lancasters were in heavy use day after day. The Type 464 Lancaster most worked on by Basil was ED918 AJ-F, in which Ken Brown was very busy flying many low-level practice exercises throughout July and August. On the 30th of August Ken flew ED918 from Scampton to Coningsby, then returned to Scampton to ferry ED763 along with his ground crew with full kit bags to Coningsby. Ken Brown wrote to me in the year 2000 and enclosed a page from his logbook with Basil's name listed as a passenger on this ferry flight. It was a twenty-minute hop with Sgt John Pulford from W/C Gibson's Dams crew acting as the flight engineer. Pulford had flown the 24th of June mission to Leghorn with Brown, as Basil Feneron, this crew's usual flight engineer, was in hospital in North Africa.

It was sometimes necessary to press Type 464 Lancasters into service after they were modified to carry the 12,000 pounder and other more conventional bombs. ED912, ED932, ED825, ED886 and ED906 were all used operationally during this period having also had SABS installed, but ED886 AJ-O and ED825 AJ-E were both lost over France on a secret SOE mission on the 10th of December. The Dams Lancasters were being used less and less by then, and examples of the type were involved in only one mission in January 1944. Gradually, during November and December, new standard Lancasters in the DV serial range had come onto the Squadron, like DV394 KC-M, which was taken over by Ken Brown. These were the first Lancasters to have the new paddle blade design of propeller to give a better speed and range. As a note, Basil was always adamant, that ED932, Gibson's Dams aircraft now coded AJ-V, did not carry Tallboys later on in 1944 as has been written in other books, because it never underwent the necessary modifications to carry the weapon. During this period of intense activity at Coningsby in the last quarter of 1943, when W/C Leonard Cheshire arrived as the new commanding officer, Basil was promoted to Aircraftman First Class (AC1) FME on the 1st of November.

The 7th of January 1944 brought a move to Woodhall Spa, and during my research I was lucky enough to be given a copy of a picture of Basil along with Ken Brown's air and ground crew at Woodhall Spa. They are standing in front of DV394 KC-M, possibly at dispersal point No. 9 on the eastern corner, diagonally opposite the main technical site. This was a group photo of the 'lads' all together at their new base. Jan and Connie van den Driesschen had this picture in their collection. I met up with them in May 2000 at the Petwood Hotel, when Jan very kindly lent me his photo collection. On looking through the unique photos I was amazed to find one of Basil at work with his colleagues in 617 Squadron. This was the picture I had prayed I would find one day, as he was naturally never in any of the pictures he had taken. None of my family, especially my grandmother, had ever seen this picture, and Jan was sure there were more in the sequence. Alex Bateman had a newspaper cutting from the 1970s containing a second picture taken on this day. I wrote a letter to Mrs Feneron, the widow of flight engineer Basil Feneron, and she very kindly lent me the original to copy. The shot is of the same group, probably taken a few minutes after Jan's photo. For me, these are the two most significant pictures that I have uncovered during the research for this book. Alex then came back to me with another shot taken on the same day of Ken Brown and his aircrew by the side of DV394.

During January and February 1944 Basil continued to work with Ken Brown and KC-M. They took part in the historic attack on the Gnome Rhone aero engine factory at Limoges on the 8th of February, when W/C Cheshire used his low-level marking technique for the first time. After Ken left the Squadron Basil started to service the aircraft of A Flight Commander S/L Dave Shannon and W/C Cheshire. He also worked for Bunny Clayton and 'Mac' Hamilton, who has been of immense help with his book. The factory-busting period saw 617 Squadron start to come into its element, attacking precision high-value targets. Many new crews arrived around this time, and the ground crews became very busy as missions became much more regular. Towards the end of June W/C Cheshire and S/L Shannon were regularly flying Mosquitos, so Basil turned his attention to servicing the aircraft of A Flight pilots F/O 'Mac' Hamilton, F/L Leonard Hadland and F/L Kit Howard, who had adopted ED763 AJ-D, and flew it on twenty or so missions. AJ-D was recoded AJ-Z and acquired nose art in the form of a lion, with the name 'Honor' painted on it.

On the 1st of June 1944 Basil was promoted to Leading Aircraftsman (LAC) FME. When W/C Cheshire left the Squadron along with S/L Shannon, Basil formed relationships with his new crews. In August S/L J.V. Cockshott arrived on A Flight, and he flew his first mission as 'second dickie' to Kit Howard in ED763 on the 5th of August against Brest. F/L T.C. Iveson arrived around this time too. Basil struck up a good relationship with Cockshott that lasted right through to March 1945 and the arrival of the Grand Slam Lancasters. Very early on Cockshott took on a new Lancaster, PD238 KC-H, and he flew this extensively until he was assigned PD114 YZ-B.

The latter part of 1944 brought major successes and also some sad losses. Kit Howard went down on the very dangerous low-level daylight raid on the Kembs Barrage. This was one of the most daring raids undertaken by 617 Squadron, as the target was very heavily defended, much more so than the dams in 1943. In researching this book I contacted Owen Martin, F/O Phil Martin's son in Australia. Owen has been very helpful with photographs and information regarding his father and this raid. One of Phil's closest friends on the Squadron was Kit Howard. Kit was flying Phil's assigned aircraft on that mission, 'Q' Queenie, which had armour-plated engines, and an inert fuel system, to which standard only a few aircraft had been modified. Kit's loss was a great blow to the squadron and to his friends. He had become one of the most experienced and likable pilots on the squadron.

In late February 1945 the new B1 Special Lancasters started to arrive to carry the Grand Slam. Basil was particularly fond of these aircraft, with their stripped down armament and up-rated engines. Basil was still working principally with S/L J.V. Cockshott, who was now flying PD114 YZ-B, and F/L Bob Horsley, who had PB997 YZ-E. Horsley also took over Cockshott's standard Lancaster, PD238 KC-H, for Tallboy raids. This period at the end of the war saw some very accurate bombing by 617 Squadron on viaducts and railway bridges to cripple the rail network, and this all contributed to the rapid end to six years of hostilities. Basil went on a 'cook's tour' on the 15th of May 1945 to fly over key 617 targets. The route took them over the Frisian Islands, Heligoland, Hamburg, Brunswick, Hanover, Bielefeld, the Dortmund-Ems Canal, the Möhne Dam, Cologne, the Ruhr Valley, Wesel, Ijmuiden and back to Woodhall Spa. These trips were to show ground staff the effect of all their hard work over the past two years. The view was one of utter devastation, especially at Hamburg and Cologne. The craters left by Grand Slams and Tallboys were still visible as a reminder of 617 Squadron's contribution to ending the war.

Basil moved to Waddington on the 17th of June in preparation for Tiger Force, the deployment of 617 Squadron to the Far East to help end the war against Japan. From there he moved to 102 Personnel Dispatch Centre on the 20th of August to be 'demobbed', almost six years to the day since his call-up. This relatively fast demobilisation most likely resulted from his comparatively advanced age, and the fact that he had originally signed up for only four years of service. After six years of war and living apart Basil, my grandmother and mother were all together again. They moved to Wetherby in Yorkshire, where Basil started his own gentleman's outfitters, which he and my grandmother ran happily until their retirement in the early 1970s. As mentioned earlier, it was here that I, as a small grandson, first gained the passion that has led me to this book with Chris and Andreas.

Basil passed away on the 19th of July 1997 after fighting cancer. I realised during his illness, that I should have done more to find those he worked with while in 617 Squadron. Basil was a very humble, modest man, and was under the impression, that not many former 617 Squadron crews were still around. He was a lifetime member of the Bomber Command Association, and he proudly wore his Association tie each day. I felt I should have started this book ten years ago, when he could have helped me with all my questions. I have had to piece together my recollections from years of conversations with him, and write letters to many people who worked with him. He would have been very shocked to realise, that so many of the pilots he worked for still remembered him, particularly Ken Brown and John Cockshott. He would also probably be very surprised, that I had found them and made contact with them.

I would like to thank Ken Brown, Grant McDonald, John Cockshott, Bob Horsley, Nick Knilans, 'Mac' Hamilton, Don Cheney, Jean Feneron, Ted Wass, Tony Iveson, Phil Martin, Don Day, Owen Martin, Dennis Oldman, Colin Cole, Jan and Connie van den Driesschen, Tom Wilkinson, Tom Hocker and Albert Sansom. My thanks go also to Robert Owen for receiving my many letters and phone calls, and for helping me to decipher Basil's service record and work out all the correct dates; to Alex Bateman also for hours of phone calls and dozens of letters over the years to help in my quest to uncover details about Basil and his 617 Squadron career; to Chris and Andreas for many hours of research and their field trips to crash sites to find out what really happened; to Jim Shortland for helping me embark on my research and for pointing me in the right direction; to my parents Beryl and Harry for starting the interest when I was young, and most of all to my grandmother, Kathie, for giving me access to all Basil's photographs and service records kept by her since his call-up. Thank you.

CHAPTER TEN

A Man For All Seasons

Rebuilding again, Cheshire arrives, Berlin, the winter campaign

The first two operations over Germany had cost 617 Squadron fourteen crews, including the accidental loss of Maltby, and the squadron took on the reputation of a suicide unit. 'Mick' Martin was promoted to acting Squadron Leader and given temporary command of the squadron on the morning following the Dortmund-Ems Canal disaster, and was anxious to rectify the previous night's failure by going back immediately that night. In the light of such extreme losses, however, it was deemed inadvisable to attack such a well-defended target so soon. The youthful G/C Sam Patch, the station commander at Coningsby, spent time with Martin, helping him to make some sense of the night's tragic events, but doubted that Cochrane would sanction another go at the Canal straight away. Nevertheless, on the principle of getting straight back onto the horse after falling off, it was decided that the remnant should operate that night, but join an element from 619 Squadron to try to knock out the Antheor Viaduct in Southern France. The operation was led by the already mentioned commanding officer of 619 Squadron, W/C Abercromby, and involved six crews from each Squadron. The 617 Squadron element consisted of F/L Munro in EE150, F/L Youseman in ED763, P/O Clayton in EE131, F/L Wilson in JB139, F/L McCarthy in ED735 and P/O Brown in EE146. With the exception of McCarthy and Youseman, who were carrying seven 1,000lb bombs, the Lancasters were loaded with one 4,000 pounder and three 1,000 pounders each. Having taken off either side of 20.00 hours it took over five hours to reach the target area close to the Franco-Italian frontier. EE131 suffered from severe icing, and P/O Clayton was forced to jettison his bombs and return home. Visibility in the target area was good, and the 617 Squadron crews released their bombs from 300 to 350 feet between about 01.10 and 01.35, but no results were observed, and the tired crews eventually got back home between 05.56 and 07.30. It transpired from post raid reconnaissance that no direct hits had been scored, and of three large craters seen, one was a mere 15 feet from the viaduct, which sustained slight damage to one of its piers. Unfortunately, near misses were not good enough at this type of target. Successive failures and the heavy losses recently sustained no doubt saw the squadron's confidence beginning to ebb.

David Maltby was laid to rest on the 18th in a private plot in the village churchyard at Wickhambreaux, where he had married. The ceremony was to be attended by F/O Howard of Townsend's crew as the squadron representative, but he arrived late, after the church service had finished. Rebuilding began with volunteers interviewed by Martin, and meanwhile, the squadron got on with the business of training. F/L Kearns arrived from 11 OTU on the 20th, the day on which the surviving gunners posted in for the Dortmund-Ems Canal operation returned to their parent units. Martin was granted the acting rank of Squadron Leader on the following day, by which time he had lost the services of Townsend and three of his crew, Howard, Webb and Wilkinson, who were all declared tour expired on the 17th and were sent on leave. Two more crews arrived on the 28th, those of P/O Weeden from 207 Squadron, and P/O Stout from 9 Squadron, while 49 Squadron contributed W/O Bull on the day after, and F/L O'Shaughnessy joined from 619 Squadron on the 30th. In view of the squadron's future record of low losses, which would be in stark contrast to its past, it was a remarkable fact, that of the four pilots mentioned above, three would be killed and the fourth become a PoW. Geoff Stout joined 9 Squadron as a sergeant pilot in April, while 617 Squadron was training for the dams, and the Ruhr campaign was taking something of a back seat in favour of more distant targets. On the night of the 14/15th he flew to Stuttgart as 'second dickey' to a F/L Hobbs, and operated as crew captain for the first time when Stettin was the target on the 20/21st. Later he went to Duisburg, Dortmund, Düsseldorf twice, Essen, Wuppertal, Oberhausen, Cologne and Gelsenkirchen, as well as Pilsen, and then took part in three of the four Hamburg raids. Operations followed in August to Mannheim and Milan, Peenemünde and Berlin, while September brought trips to Mannheim twice more, sandwiching an early return from Hanover. His final operation with 9 Squadron was, in fact, the one against Mannheim on the 23/24th, which is mentioned in the following paragraph in connection with another crew, and this appears to be his first sortie as a commissioned officer. He undertook a total of twenty-three operations with 9 Squadron, including two early returns. 'Chuffy' Bull began his operational career with the devastating raid on Wuppertal-Elberfeld on the 24/25th of June, and was a regular on the 49 Squadron order of battle until his final sortie, also the one against Mannheim mentioned below.

Elsewhere, the main force had by this time returned to full activity, after forces from predominantly 3, 4 and 6 Groups had conducted a number of operations against French targets in mid month. A series of four raids on Hanover, spread over the following four weeks, began on the 22/23rd, but despite the commitment of over 700 aircraft, stronger than forecast winds badly affected the bombing, and it is likely that most of the effort fell into open country to the south. Mannheim rarely escaped lightly, however, and 600 aircraft carried out an accurate attack on its northern half on the 23/24th, before the later stages of the bombing spilled across the Rhine into the northern districts of Ludwigshafen. Thirty-two aircraft failed to return, and among them was the 49 Squadron Lancaster containing the recently commissioned P/O Anderson and crew, who had been dismissed from 617 Squadron by Gibson following their failure to complete their assigned task during Operation Chastise. They were all killed. The second Hanover operation was mounted on the 27/28th, and this cost thirty-eight aircraft for little or no return, after most of the bombs again found open country, although this time to the north of the city. The final operation of the month took place on the 29/30th against Bochum, which, together with its surrounding communities, suffered the destruction of over 500 houses.

Having returned from leave, Townsend and two of his crew were posted to 1668CU at Balderton on the 2nd of October to take up instructional duties, an occupation considered by many to be more hazardous than operations. Townsend's promotion to Flying Officer had just come through, and he left the squadron with a DFM gazetted on the 14th of May, and a highly prized CGM gazetted two weeks later. After only a month at Balderton, Townsend would be posted to 29 OTU at Bruntingthorpe in Leicestershire, and thence to 85 OTU at Husbands Bosworth in the same county, ultimately completing his wartime service in India with South-East Asia Command.

P/O Piggin and his crew were posted in from 57 Squadron on the 3rd, and were posted back on the 13th, while in between, P/O Willsher and his crew arrived from 61 Squadron on the 5th. The main force Lancaster crews in particular experienced a busy time at the start of the month, finding themselves involved in six operations during the first eight nights. It began on the 1/2nd at Hagen, where Oboe again proved its worth, and the 1 and 5 Group main force exploited the accurate skymarking in the face of complete cloud cover. The same two Groups raided Munich on the following night, but the 5 Group time and distance method led to much of its bombing falling short of the target, while a good proportion of the 1 Group effort hit southern and south-eastern districts. The Halifaxes joined in on the 3/4th and contributed to a partially successful attack on Kassel, where one eastern suburb was consumed by fire, and two aircraft factories were among many buildings damaged in the city's western half. Frankfurt followed on the 4/5th, and this suffered severe damage from the city centre eastwards, where large areas of fire were created, and the docks were also reported to be a sea of flames. After a two-night rest the southern city of Stuttgart hosted an all Lancaster raid by over 300 aircraft drawn from 1, 3, 5, 6 and 8 Groups. This was the occasion on which 101 Squadron's ABC Lancasters operated in numbers in their Radio Countermeasures role for the first time. Only four aircraft were lost, suggesting, that for the time being at least, the Command had stolen a march on the enemy with this device, and the operation itself was moderately successful.

The third raid on Hanover was mounted on the 8/9th, and for the first time at this target the operation proceeded according to plan. The Pathfinders marked the centre of the city, and the main force followed up with accurate and concentrated bombing with only a relatively short creep-back. The result was that most parts of the city sustained severe damage, and almost 4,000 buildings were completely destroyed, while a further 30,000 were damaged to some extent. Later on the 9th 'Chuffy' Bull hit trees while low flying, but landed safely with no crew casualties. The middle of the month brought minor operations, and a welcome rest for the main force crews. This was ended by the final attack on Hanover on the 18/19th, which developed into the third failure of the four operations, and cost eighteen of the all Lancaster force. The first major raid of the war on Leipzig followed on the 20/21st, and was attended by appalling weather conditions, which rendered the operation ineffective. The final raid of the month brought a return to Kassel on the 22/23rd, and on this occasion, everything went according to plan. A firestorm developed, which contributed to the destruction of over 4,300 apartment blocks, while a further 6,700 were damaged. This amounted to over 53,000 separate dwelling units, or 63 per cent of the city's accommodation, and at least 6,000 people lost their lives.

617 Squadron, meanwhile, conducted no operations during the month, and continued its rebuilding process. Three more pilots were installed by the end of the month, the first of whom was P/O Ross from 1 Group's 103 Squadron on the 16th. S/L Suggitt came in from 6 Group's 428 Squadron officially on the 26th, having been the commanding officer of that unit for the six weeks immediately prior to his posting, and he would take on the role of B Flight commander. It seems, though, that he actually arrived a few days after the date recorded, and was immediately packed off on a conversion course, which would keep him from the squadron until the 10th of November. P/O Gingles arrived from 432 Squadron, another 6 Group unit, on the 31st, while F/O Stout and crew were posted out to 619 Squadron on the 21st after a short stay. They would return to 617 Squadron on the 10th of January 1944. Nicky Ross was already a veteran when he arrived at Coningsby, having completed forty-nine sorties as a NCO pilot. His operational career began at 40 Squadron, a 3 Group Wellington unit at Wyton and Alconbury, where he spent the first seven months of 1941. From then until March 1943 he was a fixture on training units, but then resumed his operational career at Elsham Wolds with 103 Squadron of 1 Group on the 26th, just as 617 Squadron was forming and the Ruhr offensive was getting into full swing. His last operation from Elsham Wolds was against Krefeld on the night of the 21/22nd of June, and then on the 28th he and his crew took a Lancaster up to Prestwick as a staging point before crossing the Atlantic to Canada and America. He returned to 103 Squadron on the 5th of October, but took part in no operations before his posting to 617 Squadron, where he flew his first

practice sortie in Mickey Martin's Dams Lancaster ED909 on the 30th. For almost the next two months he remained off the order of battle waiting to register his fiftieth sortie. As far as training for the squadron in general was concerned it was now almost exclusively high level. Shannon's bomb-aimer, Len Sumpter, recorded sixteen flights during October, of which, those on the 2nd, 14th, 16th and 19th were low-level, while nine were high-level and on the 8th he flew as a passenger with Bunny Clayton on a trip to Farnborough and back.

November would bring the resumption of the Berlin offensive for the main force, and the next operations for 617 Squadron under a new leader. First, however, over 500 aircraft of the main force were sent to Düsseldorf on the 3/4th, and they inflicted extensive damage on housing and industry. Training continued for the 617 Squadron crews, nine of which were involved in bulls-eye (cross-country) exercises on the 5th. The stabilized automatic bombsight, or SABS, had been installed in the squadron's Lancasters, and intensive high-level training had been taking place for some time under the watchful eye of S/L Richardson, the bombing expert. 'Chuffy' Bull was involved in another incident on the 10th, when flying in ED909, which this time suffered an engine fire, but he again landed safely.

The Cheshire era also began on that day, although it appears that he did not actually arrive on station until after the squadron got back from North Africa, following another crack at the Antheor Viaduct on the 11/12th. Eleven crews were detailed for the operation, which was led by S/L Martin in DV246. The others involved were; F/L Shannon in EE146, F/L Munro in EE150, F/L Kearns in ED912, F/L Wilson in ED932, Gibson's Dams aircraft, F/L Youseman in ED735, F/L O'Shaughnessy in ED825, F/O Rice in EE131, F/O Brown in ED763, F/O Clayton in ED906 and W/O Bull in ED886. Shannon lost an engine on take-off, and was forced to abandon his sortie without even getting airborne, but the remainder got away safely around 18.30 and headed for southern France. Each was carrying a 12,000lb light case bomb, as used at the Dortmund-Ems Canal in September, and although this might be viewed as three cookies bolted together, it was, in fact, an entirely new weapon with a wider girth than the 4,000 pounder. Martin bombed from 5,800 feet at an indicated air speed of 160 m.p.h., and saw his effort fall onto a railway line to the left of the target. Munro's bombsight began to play up, and he attempted to bomb in formation with others. After two dummy runs he watched the bombs miss the target by half a mile to the north-east. He also noted in his post raid report that the rest of the force was told they were bombing the wrong bay. Kearns missed by 60 yards from 8,000 feet, while Wilson managed a 30-yard miss at the western end from the same altitude, after making his first run over the wrong bay. In the event, it was later discovered that six crews had bombed the wrong bridge, at nearby Agay, and had caused considerable damage. The four that got it right by attacking the Antheor Viaduct caused only slight damage to the railway track. At least no casualties were sustained, and the crews flew on to Blida.

The Americans were also doing their best to get the viaduct, using smaller bombs by day, but they were meeting with similar difficulties. On the 15th, the shuttle crews flew from Blida to Rabat, and on the 18th they came home. F/L Youseman failed to arrive, and he and his crew were lost without trace in the Bay of Biscay in ED735. F/L Kellaway, now recovered from the injuries sustained in the training accident at the Ashley Walk bombing range in August, had been posted to 630 Squadron at East Kirkby on the 15th.

W/C Cheshire had, hitherto, been another 4 Group man to the core. He had begun his operational career as a Flying Officer flying Whitleys with 102 Squadron in June 1940, where, as already mentioned, he was a contemporary of the late 'Dinghy' Young. On the 12/13th of November he brought a massively damaged aircraft safely back from Germany, and received an immediate award of the DSO, thus giving an insight into the character, which would make him one of the most famous warriors in Bomber Command. With the advent of the Halifax, Cheshire was posted to 35 Squadron in January 1941, to join the likes of Tait and Holden, and was awarded the DFC in March. In early May, while the Halifaxes were grounded for essential modifications to be carried out, he landed a posting to the Atlantic Ferry Organisation and departed for Canada. A surplus of pilots caused him to kick his heels, and he took the opportunity to visit New York. Here he met the retired actress Constance Binney, whom he married in July. He returned alone to the UK soon afterwards to rejoin 35 Squadron, and set about persuading the Foreign Office to allow Constance to join him. This she did in October, and they set up home in a flat in Harrogate. Promotion to Flight Lieutenant had come in June, and at the conclusion of his second tour in February 1942 he was posted as an instructor to 1652HCU at Marston Moor. During this time he was writing his book, *Bomber Pilot*, which he had finished before he participated in all three of the Thousand Bomber Raids in May and June. He returned to a front line operational squadron in August 1942 as a Wing Commander, when given command of 76 Squadron, the unit in which his brother Christopher had served as a pilot until being shot down on his way to Berlin a year earlier. Christopher had survived, and was on extended leave in a PoW camp. Cheshire remained at 76 Squadron until April 1943, and at the conclusion of this, his third tour, he was promoted to Group Captain and posted as station commander to Marston Moor, a 4 Group training station. Here he had a converted railway carriage transported onto the site, where he lived with Constance. Although throwing himself into his new job, Cheshire was never really happy at being away from the operational scene, and when offered the post at 617 Squadron, he eagerly accepted it, even though it meant having to revert to the rank of Wing Commander.

Despite his own reputation and status within Bomber Command Cheshire's natural modesty left him somewhat in awe of Gibson, and he wondered how those at the squadron, who were survivors of the Gibson era, would receive him. He need not have been concerned. While Holden had been very much in the Gibson mould, Cheshire was entirely different. He was a friendly and approachable person, who took a genuine interest in those under his command. This attitude extended to the lowliest 'erk', whose name Cheshire would tend to remember, along with some details of his family or background. He enjoyed spending time with the ground crews, talking to them, sharing a cigarette, asking questions about technical matters or their personal concerns. This endeared him to his subordinates, and ensured their loyalty and willingness to go the extra mile on his behalf. Gibson, on the other hand, was inspirational to a section of his aircrew, but never wished or was able to bond with ground personnel. They would obey him to the letter and respect his rank and achievements, but do nothing extra for him out of personal affection and admiration.

Later, on the night that the 617 Squadron crews returned from North Africa, an all Lancaster force of over 400 aircraft went to Berlin, to resume the campaign against the Capital after the autumn break. Harris had stated in a memo to Churchill on the 3rd of November that he could 'wreck Berlin from end to end', if the Americans would join in. They, however, were committed to victory by invasion, and there was never a chance of securing their support. The attack on this night was scattered across the city, and achieved only modest success, although a diversion at Mannheim by over 300 Halifaxes, Stirlings and Lancasters produced better results, and helped to restrict losses from the main operation to nine aircraft. 617 Squadron would continue to be exempt from this bitter round of operations through the winter, as other tasks more suited to the particular skills of its crews awaited. A maximum effort force of over 700 aircraft returned to the Capital on the 22/23rd, and delivered the most destructive raid upon it of the war. At least 3,000 houses were destroyed, along with twenty-three industrial premises, while around 2,000 people lost their lives, and a further 175,000 were rendered homeless. A predominantly Lancaster force followed up this success twenty-four hours later, and guided by the glow of fires still burning beneath the clouds, it delivered another devastating blow. Lancasters again carried out a partially successful assault on the 26/27th, which fell mainly into industrial areas north-west of the city centre, and thirty-eight war industry factories were destroyed.

December began for 617 Squadron in frustrating fashion, with a planned operation being cancelled on each of the first three nights. Not so for the Lancaster crews of the main force, however, who found themselves heading back to the 'Big City' on the 2/3rd, only to lose forty of their number in return for relatively modest gain. On the following night, Leipzig underwent its most destructive raid of the war at the hands of 500 Lancasters and Halifaxes, and over 1,100 people were killed. On the 9th, four 617 Squadron aircraft and crews were lent to the secret 138 Squadron at Tempsford, for an operation over northern France on behalf of the Special Operations Executive. The crews were those of W/O Bull in ED886, F/O Weeden in ED825, F/L Clayton in ED906 and F/L McCarthy in EE131. As Lancasters were an unknown quantity at Tempsford, a station familiar only with Halifaxes at the time, a total of sixteen ground crew accompanied the detachment. Bad weather forced the arms drop to be cancelled, and a further attempt was made by three of them, W/O Bull, F/O Weeden and F/L Clayton, on the following night. None of the sorties was successfully completed, and two of the aircraft failed to return, ED886, which had taken Townsend to the dams, and ED825, which had been McCarthy's Chastise mount.

'Chuffy' Bull had crossed the French coast at 6,000 feet at 23.15, and then lost height to around 500 feet while trying to establish a pinpoint between Boulogne and St Pol. Light flak was encountered about five minutes later, and Bull made frequent course changes before they were hit, probably in the bomb bay, as the loss card makes reference to a flare igniting. The order to bale out was given immediately as Bull tried to gain some height, and the bomb-aimer was first away, followed closely by the navigator, flight engineer, front gunner and finally Bull himself. Why the wireless operator and rear gunner failed to survive is not clear, but it seems they went down with the aircraft, which crashed a few miles south-south-east of Doullens in the region of the Somme. Bull and three others were soon captured, while the front gunner, F/S McWilliams, managed to evade a similar fate, although their colleagues back home would not learn the happy news of their survival for some time. The occupants of the other Lancaster were less fortunate, though, and F/O Weeden and his crew all lost their lives when they too fell victim to flak while flying at low level in the same general area. Among them was F/S Walters, an American from Pennsylvania, who had enlisted in the RCAF. On the 12th Nicky Ross and crew flew down to Tempsford in JB139, and spent the next few days carrying out practice drops in preparation for another SOE sortie.

Only minor operations had been flown by the Command after Leipzig, and it was not until the 16/17th, that the main force Lancaster crews were recalled to arms. The target was again Berlin, and a late afternoon take-off had almost 500 aircraft winging their way to the target, timed to arrive overhead at around 20.00 hours. Less than an hour after these had departed for Germany, nine 617 Squadron Lancasters set off for France, their crews briefed to attack a flying bomb site at Flixecourt in the Pas-de-Calais. This would be the opening salvo of Bomber Command's night offensive against V-1 sites as part of the Crossbow campaign. It gave W/C Cheshire the opportunity to lead the squadron into battle for the first time, flying on this occasion in DV380. Accompanying him were the crews of S/L Martin in DV402, S/L Suggitt in DV382, F/L Kearns in ED912, F/L Shannon in DV394, F/L Wilson in ED932, P/O Willsher in DV393, F/L Munro in DV391 and F/L O'Shaughnessy in DV385. A similar operation was being conducted simultaneously by Stirlings of 3 Group at Tilley-le-Haut, and both forces were provided with Oboe Mosquitos to carry out the marking. Oboe had proved decisive at the Ruhr, and for city targets its accuracy was as good as pinpoint. For small targets, however, an error of just a few hundred yards could prove critical, and this was the case with both operations on this night. The markers for the Stirling raid missed the target by 450 yards, while the single Oboe Mosquito at Flixecourt failed to find the mark by a mere 350 yards. The 617 Squadron crews plastered the markers with their 12,000 pounders, and each one brought home an aiming point photograph, only to discover frustratingly, that the target had escaped damage. Post raid reconnaissance showed four craters in the target area, and five more within a reasonable distance, but no damage to the site itself. All arrived back safely, just as the main force crews were leaving the Berlin defence zone having carried out a moderately successful raid for the loss of twenty-five of their number. The real problems arose for these as they arrived home to find their stations blanketed in thick fog, many of them with insufficient fuel to reach a diversionary airfield. 1, 6 and 8 Groups were those most seriously affected, and twenty-nine Lancasters either crashed or were abandoned by their tired crews during the frantic search for somewhere to land. Around 150 airmen lost their lives in these most tragic of circumstances, when so close to home and safety.

From around 16.20 hours on the 20th, and for the following ninety minutes, 650 aircraft of the main force and Pathfinder squadrons began taking off and forming up for the long slog to Frankfurt. As this was going on at stations from County Durham to Cambridgeshire, eight 617 Squadron crews were preparing to use the main activity as cover for their operation to the Fabrique Nationale gun factory at Liége in Belgium. The FN Company had plants in both Belgium and France, and this site had been manufacturing a variety of weapons from pistols to shotguns and machine guns, including Brownings, for many years (the American, John Moses Browning, had actually died in Liége in 1926). The 617 Squadron aircraft took off either side of 18.00, with Cheshire again leading his men from the front in DV380, while the other crews were those of S/L Martin in DV385, S/L Suggitt in DV382, F/L Munro in DV391, F/L Kearns in ED912, F/L Wilson in ED932, F/L Rice in DV398 and P/O Willsher in DV393. Once over the target 8 Group Mosquitos provided Oboe marking, but the target indicators were not visible through the cloud cover, and after circling the target for twenty-five minutes, Cheshire ordered the crews to return home with their bombs. Willsher jettisoned his bomb for an undisclosed reason on the estimated position of the target. They adopted a return route slightly south of due west, which took them across the north-eastern corner of France to the English Channel. This was doubtless to give the defences in and around Brussels to their north a wide berth. Cheshire lost an engine over the Channel, but got back all right, while DV398 did not make it home with the crew of Geoff Rice. It was shot down during the return flight over Belgium, and Paul Brickhill writes that Martin saw a Lancaster going down in flames with one of the gunners still firing at his pursuer. Certainly there would have been night fighter activity in the area where Rice came down, between Charleroi and Mons, because of the Frankfurt raid. However, Rice, himself, on his return to the UK was unsure whether to ascribe the loss of his Lancaster to flak or to a night fighter, and could only report it to have been set on fire before falling into an uncontrollable dive. He gave the order to bale out at 14,000 feet, and recalls Dick MacFarlane handing him his parachute. The volume of wreckage of DV398 led the local people to believe it to be of a twin-engine type, and they reported that it had been blown up by its own bombs.

In fact, Rice was shot down by *Hauptmann* Kurt Fladrich, a *Staffel Kapitän* from 9/NJG/4 based at Juvincourt, near Reims in France. Misidentifying his victim as a Halifax, Fladrich recorded in his logbook that he delivered one attack from below and behind in his BF110G4, and set a fierce fire raging in the bomber's starboard-inner engine. The encounter took place at 20.29 at 4,200 metres, 500 metres north of Merbes-le-Château, south-west of Charleroi. Fladrich witnessed flames at what he believed was the point of impact on the ground, but it was probably the bomb load going up in the air. It was Fladrich's eighth kill, and he would survive the war with a tally of fifteen. It has been written that the Red Cross claimed F/S Gowrie was captured and later shot by the Gestapo. However, a report by the No. 2 M.R. & E. Unit refers to a German report describing the removal of six bodies from the crash site and they were interred in Gosselies cemetery in graves numbered 67 to 72. They were just six of more than 47,000 men of Bomber Command killed on operations, but they all had lives, hopes and dreams, and people to mourn their loss. Gunner Tom Maynard was the baby of the crew at just 20, while Ed Smith, the flight engineer, was 24 and had a wife in Berkshire waiting for him to return. John Thrasher and Chester Gowrie had come all the way from Canada to fight Nazism. Bomb-aimer and wireless operator respectively, they were 23 and 25 years of age. If Martin did, in fact, observe return fire, then it was probably Sandy Burns in the rear turret. He was just 22, and later that day the dreaded telegram would be on its way to his parents in Dudley. Along with navigator Dick MacFarlane, these were the men whose lives had been extinguished in a fraction of time as an explosion tore their aircraft apart and hurled their pilot out into space. The number of surviving Dams veterans was dwindling fast. We will return shortly to Geoff Rice.

The night's activity was not yet over for 617 Squadron. At 01.15 on the 21st, Joe McCarthy took off from Tempsford in EE131, and headed for France to carry out a drop on behalf of SOE. He was followed fifteen minutes later by 'Bunny' Clayton in ED906, at 02.24 by Nicky Ross in JB139 and finally by Ken Brown in EE146 at 02.37. For Ross, who was heading for the Rouen area to make his low-level drop, this was his first operation since joining 617 Squadron and his fiftieth in all. Unfortunately, not one of them was able to locate their assigned target in the conditions, and all were forced to abandon their sorties. It should be mentioned, that SOE sorties were highly exacting and dangerous, and required the most precise navigation in order to reach a tiny pinpoint at low-level at night. Even the experienced crews of 138 and 161 Squadrons were frequently forced to bring back their stores and agents, when either the conditions thwarted them or the reception party failed to show. Despite this, these remarkable men from the clandestine

Gibson's ED932 in the summer of 1943, showing additional cable cutters on wing leading edges.

ED886 in formation.

Trials type 464 Lancaster ED825 at Boscombe Down. Flown to Scampton on the afternoon of Operation *Chastise*, it became the last minute replacement for McCarthy and crew.

ED825 again. Note the ventral gun position. This was the only type 464 Lancaster so equipped.

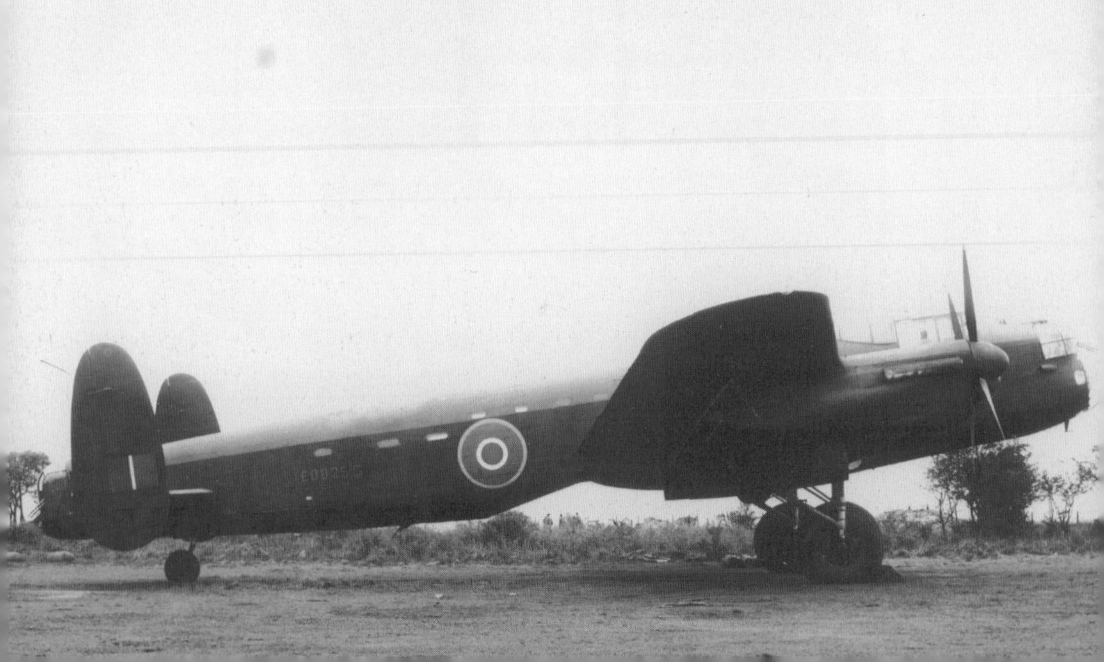

F/L David Shannon from Adelaide, Australia.

The remaining Canadian contingent after Operation *Chastise*.

The remaining Australian contingent after Operation *Chastise.*

F/L Horsley and crew at Woodhall Spa.

'Mac' Hamilton's Lancaster.

Joe McCarthy with air and ground crews at Woodhall Spa.

Chastise survivors, including pilots Martin, Rice, Maltby, Munro and Shannon. The WAAF is Faye Gillan.

Frank Garbas and Abram Garshowitz probably at Wigsley in late 1942.

Riding the monster. Ground personnel astride one of Wallis' giant bombs.

P/O George Divall, who, with his crew, was the last to arrive at 617 Squadron for training for Operation *Chastise*.

F/O Warwick, navigator to P/O Divall.

Sgt Williams, rear gunner to P/O Divall.

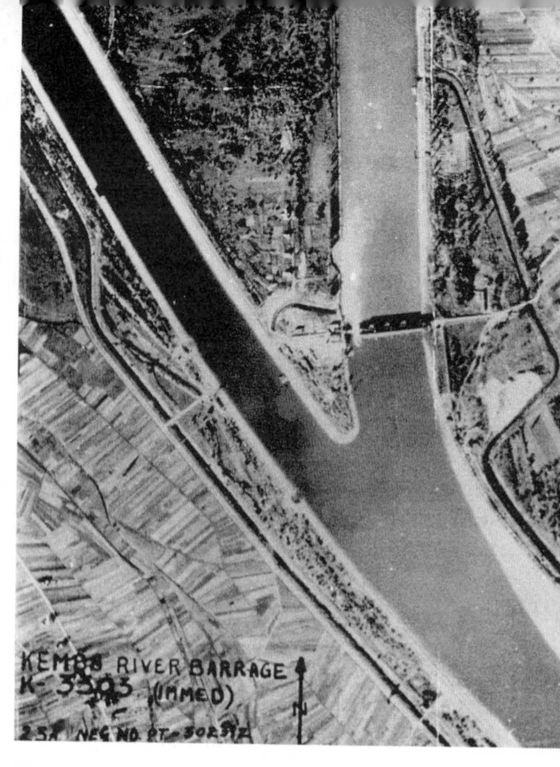

Reconnaissance photo of the Kembs Barrage at the joining of Germany, France and Switzerland.

W/C George Holden with the daughters of Scampton's intelligence officer.

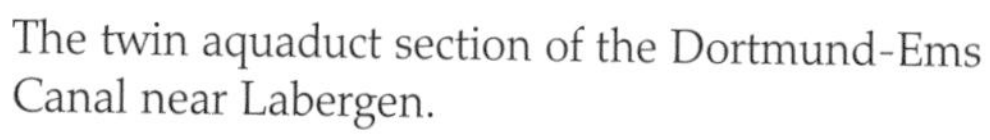

The twin aquaduct section of the Dortmund-Ems Canal near Labergen.

Four views of LAC Basil Pearson, who joined 617 Squadron in June 1943, and maintained the engines on Lancasters of some of the squadron's most notable crews.

Basil Pearson took this unofficial photo of W/C Cheshire's Lancaster at Woodhall Spa in 1944.

S/L Cockshott's Lancaster PD238 KC-H also at Woodhall Spa.

Basil's colleague, Godfrey, working on one of PD238's Merlin engines.

Ken Brown and crew at Woodhall Spa in 17.1.44 during period of the move from Coningsby.

Basil Feneron, Brown's flight engineer.

Ken Brown

From L to R: Steve Oancia, Grant MacDonald and Ken Brown.

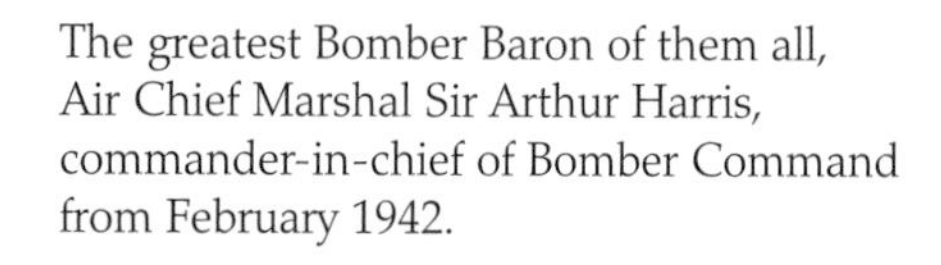

The greatest Bomber Baron of them all, Air Chief Marshal Sir Arthur Harris, commander-in-chief of Bomber Command from February 1942.

Air-Vice-Marshal Sir Ralph Cochrane.

W/C G.L Cheshire.

G/C Johnny Fauquier.

W/C Guy Gibson.

A posed picture of Gibson, the nation's hero.

Gibson speaking with Sir Archibald Sinclair, Minister for Air, in September 1944, a matter of days before Gibson went missing in action.

The well-known picture of Gibson and crew about to enter ED932 to head for the dams.

This often published photo purports to show a Lancaster taking off for Operation *Chastise*.

A trials Lancaster carries out a test drop of *Upkeep* at Reculver on Kent's north coast.

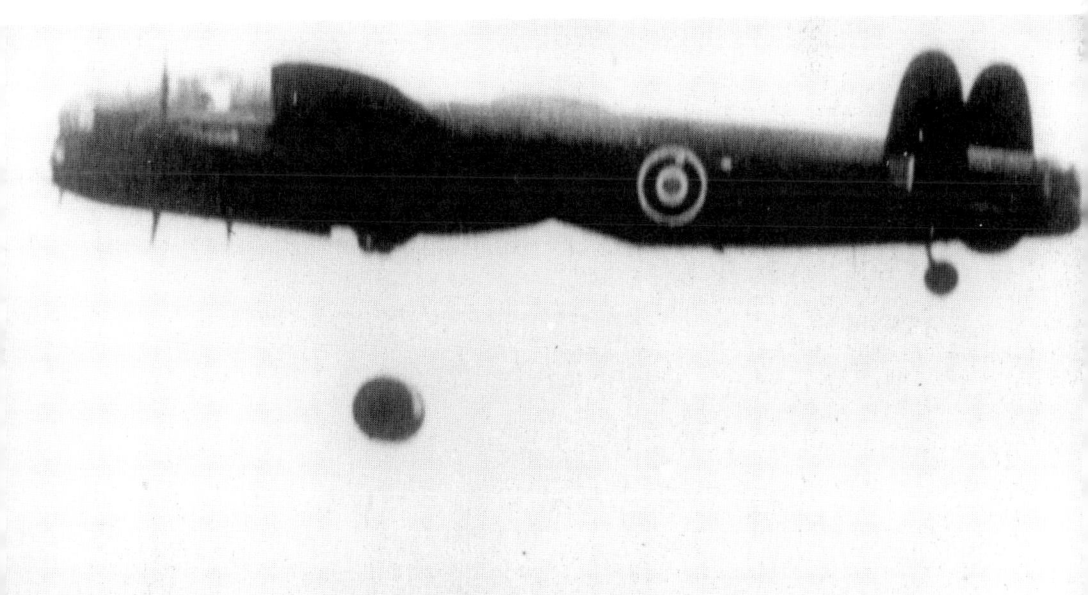

L - R. Bunny Clayton, David Maltby and "Mick" Martin in serious and formal pose.

His Majesty King George meeting ground crew at Scampton on 27.5 43.

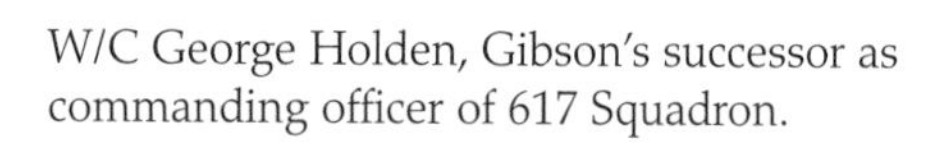

W/C George Holden, Gibson's successor as commanding officer of 617 Squadron.

'moon' squadrons displayed the most incredible fortitude and persistence to find their drop zones, and between them successfully completed many hundreds of operations during their wartime service.

Rice regained consciousness in a wood at around 08.30 on the following morning, the 21st, more than fourteen hours after taking off from Coningsby, and having 'lost' twelve hours since his last memory. His parachute was snagged upon a tree, and pieces of aircraft wreckage lay around him, although of more immediate concern were a broken wrist and a deep gash over his left eye. He deduced, that he had been thrown clear as the Lancaster disintegrated in the air, presumably through an explosion, and this harmonizes with local eyewitness accounts. Protected by an armoured seat, it was not unusual for a pilot to survive in this way, while the rest of the crew perished. Rice, of course, had no knowledge of his crew's fate at this point. Having hidden his parachute in the undergrowth he emerged from the wood into the small village of Binche, where he encountered three farm labourers, who took him to a farm. Here he was washed, fed and re-clothed, before being taken to another farmhouse, where he slept for six hours. He spent that night at yet another location, and moved on again on the following day to a house where he remained for five days over the Christmas period. While there he was taken to a doctor, who first x-rayed and then set his wrist in plaster. After Christmas he was taken by a gendarme to a kind of hospital run by sisters, and from there to a dentist at La Louviere, who claimed to be English, but was possibly a Belgian being used by the underground to weed out German infiltrators. Rice spent the next four or five days with a French Catholic priest, before returning to La Louviere, where he was given identity and work cards. Moved twice more, he was finally collected towards the end of January, and taken by train to Brussels via Charleroi, where he stayed for ten days with a blind lady. He spent the next seven weeks in the flat of a young married couple, but when one of their friends was arrested, it was decided to move Rice again, this time to the home of a local hospital manager, where he met up with an American bombardier. The latter was sent on to Antwerp, and Rice followed a week later, on the 28th of April, with two more Americans. They were handed over to another man outside the railway station, who was only able to accommodate two men, the Americans, and Rice was dropped off at a house nearby, where he was met by two other men of about his own age. One of them left to find a safe house for Rice, but returned with members of the secret police, and thus ended Rice's five months on the run. He spent the time from June 1944 to January 1945 at Stalag Luft III, before moving on to Stalag IIIA at Luckenwalde, from where he was liberated by Russian forces on the 21st of April. He finally arrived in the UK at RAF Cosford on the 26th of May.

Eleven 617 Squadron crews were briefed for an attack on a flying bomb site in the Abbeville–Amiens area on the 22/23rd, and they got away between 20.00 and 20.30 hours. Cheshire was last away in DV380, with ahead of him, Martin in DV402, Suggitt in DV382, Munro in DV391, McCarthy in ME559,

Kearns in ED912, Wilson in ED932, Clayton in ED906, Brown in DV394, Ross in JB139 and Willsher in DV393. The target could not be located in the conditions, however, and the operation was abandoned. It is believed, that the Oboe markers were delivered, but they could not be seen, and the most likely cause is their failure to burst. Surprisingly, a force of 3 Group Stirlings operating in the same area against a similar target experienced less difficulty, and carried out an accurate attack. A predominantly Lancaster force attacked Berlin again on the 23/24th, and this was one of the less convincing raids on the Capital, falling mainly into south-eastern suburbs, and destroying around 300 buildings for the loss of sixteen aircraft.

The fifth wartime Christmas came and went in relative peace, and it was on the 29/30th that the main force conducted its final operation of the year. This was also on Berlin, and was the first of three raids on the city in an unprecedented five nights spanning the turn of the year. Over 700 aircraft took off, and they delivered an attack that fell mainly into southern and south-eastern districts, where around 400 buildings were destroyed. On the following night 617 Squadron carried out its final operation of the year, with a return to the flying bomb site at Flixecourt by ten aircraft, this time led by the flight commanders, S/Ls Suggitt and Martin, in DV382 and DV402 respectively. They were accompanied by F/L Shannon in EE146, F/L McCarthy in ME559, F/L O'Shaughnessy in DV385, F/L Brown in DV394, F/L Clayton in ME555, F/L Munro in DV391, P/O Ross in ED932 and P/O Willsher in DV393, and all carried a single 12,000 pounder. Three Oboe Mosquitos plus a reserve provided the marking in clear conditions, but the target indicators were on average 300 yards from the site, and this was sufficient to render the attack ineffective. Munro's photoflash failed to release, and McCarthy's camera was inoperative, while Clayton had to take evasive action to avoid another Lancaster, and these were the only three to come home without a snapshot of the aiming point. Seven bombs actually fell within 120 yards of the markers, but they were not close enough. On the credit side, the frustration born out of these recent failures was to concentrate the minds of a number of squadron notables on overcoming the problem of marking a small target with precision. This brainstorming was to bear fruit in spectacular fashion in the coming year, but in the meantime, matters were not proceeding according to plan for this very special squadron. In May 1943, it had achieved outstanding success, and had passed into bomber folklore with its deeds splashed across the front pages of the world's press. The remainder of the year, though, had been characterized by gallant failure and bitter losses, and it had to be hoped and expected that better things awaited the squadron in 1944.

CHAPTER ELEVEN

A New Production, a New Role

In pursuit of precision while the winter campaign continues

New Year's Day brought the formation of 54 Base, which comprised the stations at Coningsby, Woodhall Spa and Metheringham. Changes in 5 Group's organisation during the first third of the year would make 54 Base home to perhaps the most experienced and elite collection of airmen in the entire Command. The year began for the main force with a disappointing all Lancaster raid on Berlin on New Year's Night. Very little damage resulted, and twenty-eight aircraft were lost. Among them was the one captained by W/C Abercromby, who had led the 617 Squadron remnant on the first Antheor Viaduct operation in September when commanding officer of 619 Squadron. He had replaced the missing W/C Hilton at 83 Squadron on the 4th of December, and taken his 5 Group attitudes with him to 8 Group. His view on the practice of weaving as a defensive measure against night fighters was to ruffle a few feathers at his new unit, most notably and appropriately those of F/O Chick, whose flying he described as cowardly. Chick refused to abandon his weaving policy, which had seen him through more than forty operations, and predicted that Abercromby would survive no more than three weeks if he flew straight and level. Chick completed his tour on forty-eight operations shortly afterwards, and lived to see his prophecy fulfilled.

Twenty-four hours later a similarly ineffective return to the Capital cost twenty-seven Lancasters. The Pathfinders in general and 156 Squadron in particular were taking a beating. There is little doubt though, that the beleaguered inhabitants of Berlin were also suffering, and shared the common hope with the hard-pressed crews of Bomber Command that their city would cease to be the main focus of Harris's attention. However, proud of their status as Berliners first and Germans second, they were a hardy breed, and just like their counterparts in London under the blitz of 1940, they bore their trials with fortitude and humour. During this, their 'winter of discontent', they taunted their tormentors by parading banners through the shattered streets, proclaiming, 'You may break our walls, but not our hearts'. They also sang along to the most popular song of the day, *Nach jedem Dezember kommt immer ein Mai*, (after every December comes always a May), the sentiments of which held promise of a change of fortunes with the onset of spring.

617 Squadron opened its 1944 account on the evening of the 4th of January with an operation by eleven aircraft to a flying bomb site in the Pas de Calais. Cheshire once more took the lead in DV380, taking with him as a passenger the not inconsiderable bulk of the Coningsby station commander, G/C 'Tiny' Evans-Evans. It was typical of Evans-Evans to want to mix it with the enemy, having been an 'operational type' earlier in the war. Since commanding 3 Group's 115 Squadron for the first six months of 1941 he had occupied a non-operational post, but his desire to remain 'one of the boys' and operate against the enemy had never left him. A life of relative inactivity and a healthy appetite had increased his girth substantially, and on those occasions when he managed to get into the pilot's seat of a Lancaster, he found it a tight fit. Sadly, his irrepressible spirit would unnecessarily cost him his life in action in 1945, when the end of the war was tantalisingly close. The other crews involved on this night were those of S/L Suggitt in DV382, S/L Martin in DV402, F/L Shannon in ME555, F/L Brown in DV394, F/L Clayton in ED906, F/L O'Shaughnessy in DV385, F/L Munro in DV391, F/L Kearns in ME559, F/L Wilson in ED932 and P/O Ross in DV393. The crews were airborne either side of 17.30 hours, each standard Lancaster carrying fourteen 1,000 pounders, while the two Type 464 variants contained a reduced load of eleven 1,000 pounders. They all returned less than four hours later, having, they believed, at last delivered an accurate and effective attack. Cheshire recorded that cloud made bombing difficult, and that the Oboe-laid red marker was not visible. However, two green target indicators with red candles could be seen intermittently, and he ordered the crews to aim for these. A stick of bombs fell across these target indicators, while others burst within them, but three other sticks were 150 yards wide of the mark. One of the latter may have been from Suggitt, who bombed from 10,300 feet at 19.23 with an unserviceable bombsight. Twelve of Martin's bombs went down at 19.15, but two hung up, and these were delivered in a second run five seconds after Suggitt's. Some crews seemed to find a fortuitous break in the clouds straight away, while O'Shaughnessy made five runs before he was sufficiently confident to let his bombs go. Nicky Ross heard Cheshire's order to bomb the green T.I.s, but someone else obliterated them before he could comply. He went round again, but by the time he arrived back over the target area, cloud obscured all ground reference, and he brought his bombs home. Subsequent reconnaissance revealed no new damage to this site.

In a welcome break from Berlin for the main force over 300 Lancasters and a handful of Halifaxes raided Stettin on the 5/6th. As always seemed to be the case at this target, the bombing was accurate, and caused the destruction of 500 houses. Severe damage was inflicted upon a further 1,100 houses, along with twenty-nine industrial premises, while eight ships were sunk in the harbour. The main force crews would now enjoy an eight-night rest, and during this period 617 Squadron undertook its final wartime change of address. An advance party left Coningsby for the short journey to Woodhall Spa on the 7th, and the main move took place over the 8th and 9th, while 619 Squadron travelled in the opposite direction. The officers were billeted in the elegant Petwood Hotel on the edge of the town, where it stands to this day resplendent in its extensive and beautiful grounds, while the NCOs were accommodated in Maycrete huts at nearby Tattershall Thorpe. Three more crews arrived on posting during week ending the 10th, including that of F/O Stout from 619 Squadron for their second spell with 617. The others were those of the American, Lt Knilans, also from 619 Squadron, while F/O Cooper came with his lot from 1660CU.

Hubert 'Nick' Knilans was to become one of 617 Squadron's characters, and unusually, he remained at Woodhall Spa for his entire operational career of two tours. Born in Wisconsin in 1917, Knilans joined the RCAF in October 1941, before America entered the war. After basic training as a pilot in Canada, Knilans arrived in the UK to continue his training, initially in Scotland, and then at 1660 CU at Swinderby. Here he gathered a crew around him, and was posted to 619 Squadron at Woodhall Spa in June 1943. His first two operations, against Cologne and Turin in July, were flown as 'second dickey' to experienced pilots. The Ruhr campaign had by this time almost run its course, and the Battle of Hamburg was about to begin. The first of the already described four major operations against Germany's second city became Knilans's first as crew captain on the night of the 24/25th. On return, a faulty or wrongly set altimeter almost ended the crew's career, but Knilans managed to fly his way out of trouble, and the Lancaster was soon repaired. They went to Essen on the following night and returned on three engines, and on the 27/28th they participated in the firestorm raid on Hamburg. In September Knilans was commissioned as a Pilot Officer, and in early October his rear gunner was killed by a night fighter during an operation to Kassel. Soon afterwards he was transferred to the USAAF, but was allowed to remain on attachment to the RAF, although sporting an American uniform in the rank of 1st Lieutenant. Knilan's first tour took him to Berlin on a number of occasions during November and December, and his final operation was the above-mentioned one against Stettin on the night of the 5/6th of January 1944. This coincided with the departure of 619 Squadron from Woodhall Spa to make way for 617 Squadron, and Knilans volunteered to remain in comfort at the Petwood to carry out a second tour with the Cheshire boys, rather than be posted to a training unit or the American 8th Air Force.

Ten crews were detailed for operations on the 10th, but this was cancelled, and the same thing occurred on the 14th. That night 496 Lancasters and two Halifaxes of the main force set out for Brunswick, to carry out the first major operation of the war against this historic town in north central Germany. No doubt there was relief among the crews at briefings that Berlin was not again the target. However, Brunswick lies a little to the east of Hanover, and the memory of trying to crack that difficult and expensive nut during the autumn was still fairly fresh. Brunswick was a target with some future significance for 617 Squadron, but on this night it escaped with fairly superficial damage, while the attackers paid for the failure with thirty-eight aircraft, eleven of them Pathfinders. The sorely afflicted 156 Squadron was well represented among the losses, and had now lost fourteen Lancasters and crews from three operations in just two weeks since the start of the year. A 617 Squadron operation planned for the 20th was cancelled, and six crews carried out low level bombing practice at dusk over the sea. During the course of this, ED918, the Lancaster flown to the Sorpe Dam by Ken Brown, bounced off the surface of the water before careering onto the beach at Snettisham and hitting a breakwater. F/L Tom O'Shaughnessy and his navigator, F/O Holding lost their lives, and two others sustained injuries, those of F/O Kendrick, the bomb-aimer, so serious that it would take him a year to recover and return to operations. As this tragedy was taking place, over 700 aircraft were arriving over Berlin to deliver an attack on the Capital through complete cloud cover, and this prevented the crews from making an immediate assessment of the results. It was later learned that the main weight of the attack had fallen into the hitherto less severely afflicted eastern districts, where moderate damage was caused. Thirty-five aircraft failed to return, and the Halifaxes sustained disproportionately high casualties.

Finally, on the 21st, two and a half weeks since the squadron's last operation, W/C Cheshire led a force of twelve aircraft back to the flying bomb site in the Pas de Calais, one of six similar targets for the night. He was again in DV380, and the other crews were those of S/L Martin in DV402, S/L Suggitt in DV382, F/L Munro in DV391, F/L Shannon in DV403, F/L Wilson in JB139, F/L McCarthy in ME559, F/L Kearns in ME557, F/L Clayton in ME560, F/L Brown in DV394, P/O Willsher in DV392 and P/O Ross in ME562. They took off shortly after 17.00 hours, with Cheshire carrying seven spot fires and six 30lb incendiaries along with his 1,000lb bombs, and Martin had some 500 pounders as well. After an initial reference was provided by two Oboe Mosquitos from 8 Group, Cheshire was able to obtain a clear site of the wood, wherein lay the target, but his bombing run at 7,000 feet was hampered by flares bursting directly ahead. They were in bomb-aimer Keith Astbury's line of sight at the critical moment, and he dropped a salvo rather than a stick, recognising that the markers were going to overshoot. Cheshire observed the salvo to burst in the north-eastern corner of the wood, before pulling away to circle and monitor the rest of the bombing. He saw six or seven night fighters to the south, but none came closer than five miles. F/L Wilson brought some of his bombs home after the spotfires burned out before he could complete a second run, and Brown and Willsher did likewise, but the others plastered the site, taking advantage of the clear visibility. Reconnaissance revealed considerable damage to the site, and this was in reality the first effective attack by the squadron against this type of target.

While the crews were on their way home, the main force was taking off for Magdeburg in eastern Germany, for the first major assault of the war on this city. The enemy night fighter force was fed into the bomber stream even before the German coast was crossed, and the two forces remained in contact all the way to the target. The operation was inconclusive, and a massive fifty-seven aircraft were lost, a new record, the Halifaxes again proving themselves to be markedly more vulnerable than the Lancasters. Fifty-six 3 Group Stirlings and twelve Lancasters from 617 Squadron returned to the Pas-de-Calais late on the 25th for another crack at the flying bomb sites. The Lancasters and crews were as per the last operation, except that F/L Brown was replaced by Lt Knilans, who was on his first operation with the squadron and flying in ME561, while Wilson was flying in DV385. This time it was a late take-off, between 22.10 and 22.31, and they were at the target in less than two hours. The first Oboe marker was right on the mark, but went out almost immediately, and red spotfires dropped probably by Martin were assessed as on or near the aiming point. Partial cloud cover was encountered, which made it impossible to mark from above, but difficult also from below because of the speed of the flares drifting across the target. Kearns bombed first at 23.53 from 12,000 feet, and Cheshire last at 00.39 after coming down to 5,300 feet. Some delivered all their bombs in one stick, while others made two runs, but the general impression was of an accurate attack, and all returned safely either side of 02.00 hours. Post raid reconnaissance revealed craters to the north-west of the target area and blocked approaches, but it was not possible to attribute specific damage arising from this operation. Canadian P/O Duffy was posted in towards the end of the month, but he would need to undergo conversion training at 5 LFS before being declared operational.

Although 617 Squadron had now completed its operations for the month, the main force still had a daunting schedule ahead of it. An unprecedented three Berlin operations in the space of four nights began on the 27/28th, when 500 Lancasters slogged their way to the Capital and delivered a scattered attack, which spread into dozens of outlying communities, something that had become a feature of the campaign. Twenty thousand Berliners were bombed out of their homes, and thirty-three Lancasters were missing. On the following night, the Halifax brigade joined in and contributed to a destructive raid, which hit mostly the western and southern districts, but many public and administrative buildings were damaged, and a further 180,000 people were rendered homeless. The cost, at forty-six aircraft, was high, but only one night's rest was allowed to lick the wounds before over 500 aircraft returned on the 30/31st. This was another destructive assault, which hit many parts of the city including the centre, creating large areas of fire and killing thousands of people. The heavy losses continued, however, and on this night they totalled thirty-three aircraft. Although the crews were not aware of the fact, this was the final concerted effort to destroy Berlin. Had the weather obliged, Harris might have mounted another major operation early in February, but in the event, it would be mid month before one could take place, and this would prove to be not only the penultimate raid on Berlin of the campaign, but the penultimate one of the war by RAF heavy bombers. There is no question that Berlin had been sorely afflicted during this series at the end of January, but it remained a functioning city and the seat of government, and nowhere were there the signs of the imminent collapse predicted by Harris. Earlier in the month, on the 13th, the squadron welcomed to its bosom F/L Bill Reid, who had been awarded a Victoria Cross for his courage during the raid on Düsseldorf on the 3/4th of November, while he was serving with 61 Squadron.

On the 2nd of February news came through from the Red Cross that 'Chuffy' Bull, his bomb-aimer, F/S Batey and his flight engineer, Sgt Wiltshire, were safe, and on extended leave in Germany. The news, that the navigator, Sgt Chamberlain, was also in captivity, would filter through later. Nine aircraft took part in a secret bombing practice on the 7th, and what they learned was put into effect on the night of the 8/9th, while the main force was still grounded by the weather. The operation gave Cheshire an opportunity to demonstrate just what 617 Squadron could achieve, and it proved to be a turning point. He and Martin had unofficially developed a system of delivering markers with pinpoint accuracy by diving a Lancaster towards an aiming point, and releasing the spot fires from low level before pulling out. This was a somewhat hairy exercise in a Lancaster, and the effort of pulling out almost tore the wings off. The idea was then presented to the ever-receptive AVM Cochrane, the 5 Group AOC, who cautiously gave the green light for a live trial to take place.

The target selected for the trial was the Gnome & Rhone aero engine factory at Limoges, and twelve crews were briefed accordingly. They were, W/C Cheshire in DV380, S/L Suggitt in ED763, S/L Martin in DV402, F/L Shannon in DV403, F/L Clayton in ME560, P/O Knights, recently arrived from 619 Squadron, in DV385, F/L Brown in DV394, Lt Knilans in ME561, F/L Wilson in ME559, P/O Ross in ME562, F/L Kearns in ME557, and F/O Willsher in DV393. Take-off took place between 21.07 and 21.25, and the target was reached shortly before midnight. On his fourth run across the target, having given the workers ample warning and time to vacate the factory, Cheshire dropped his incendiaries into the centre of the roof from under 100 feet, and Martin backed up with his spot fires and incendiaries some four minutes later. Five crews waiting above at 8,000 to 10,000 feet were carrying 12,000 pounders, Shannon, Clayton, Brown, Ross and Willsher, and four of these were direct hits, while Willsher's undershot by about 150 yards. The remaining five crews carried eleven 1,000 pounders each, and most of these fell across the target, although Wilson reported his bombs to have fallen at least 50 yards to the left after the plug on the control switch was found to be pulled out. The operation was an outstanding success, and the dramatic events were captured on cine-film. A photograph of Cheshire's markers cascading onto the factory was released to the press, and the actual footage has found its way into many documentary films since. Reconnaissance photographs showed immense damage to the target, with nine medium-bay sized workshops and a large multi-bay building all suffering heavily. Twenty-one out of forty-eight bays were destroyed, and a further twenty were badly damaged. Other buildings in the target area were also affected, and even the bays remaining intact had sustained internal damage from blast.

F/L Christopher 'Kit' Howard and his crew had been posted in from 17 OTU on the 7th, and five days later they joined Duffy and crew, who were already undergoing conversion training at 5 LFS at Syerston. On the 12/13th eleven aircraft took off for a reunion with their old friend, the Antheor Viaduct, with Cheshire, as always, leading from the front, this time in ME559, while his own DV380 was undergoing servicing. The other crews were those of S/L Martin as deputy leader in DV402, S/L Suggitt in DV382, F/L Munro in ME557, F/L Shannon in DV403, F/L Clayton in ME560, F/O Knights in DV385, F/L Brown in DV394, Lt Knilans in ME561, F/L Wilson in ED763 and P/O Ross in ME562. The crews were airborne for the target before 22.00 hours, having refuelled at Ford on the south coast on the way. A heavy flak defence greeted the force, and this and the searchlights hampered the efforts of Cheshire and Martin to mark at low level. Martin's aircraft was hit in the nose while in the act of marking, and his bomb aimer, F/L Bob Hay, was killed before he had time to release the spot fires. Hay had been with Martin since their days at 455 and 50 Squadrons, and had been the 617 Squadron bombing leader from the start, almost a year earlier. The flight engineer, F/L Ivan Whittaker, also sustained injuries to his legs, and the Lancaster was seriously damaged. Martin was forced to abort his sortie and make for Sardinia, jettisoning the 4,000 pounder en-route. Despite having no hydraulics, a safe landing was made on a small American airstrip with a very short runway terminating on a cliff top, and Whittaker was soon on his way to hospital.

Meanwhile, Cheshire had been unable to pick up the viaduct visually, and could only make out the line of the foreshore. Despite repeated attempts to approach the aiming point, he was beaten off by the fierce ground fire, and ultimately dropped his markers onto the beach. The following crews were instructed to adjust their aim accordingly, and one bomb fell within 15 yards of the target. That was not close enough, and as the Lancasters withdrew towards home, the viaduct was still standing. The operation was another gallant failure, and the crews were all back at Ford by 05.35. The weather closed in shortly afterwards, but Suggitt judged that he could make it back to Woodhall Spa, and took off sometime after 08.00 hours in poor weather. Ten minutes later, the Lancaster struck high ground ten miles north-east of Chichester, and seven of the eight men on board were killed instantly. Among them were the squadron intelligence officer, S/L Lloyd, and F/S Pulford DFM, who had been the flight engineer in Gibson's dams crew. His death, along with that of Hay the night before, reduced still further the number of dams survivors. Suggitt was found alive and delirious still strapped in his seat, but he never regained consciousness, and lost his fight for life at Chichester hospital at 16.00 hours on the 15th. He was replaced as B Flight commander by Les Munro. Reconnaissance photos of the viaduct taken later that day revealed new craters and a very near miss, but the structure remained intact.

This sad day also brought an influx of new crews to the squadron, ten of the Group's other units contributing one each. F/L Hadland arrived from 9 Squadron, F/L Edward from 50, F/L Fearn from 57, F/L Williams from 61, F/L Poore from 106, F/L Pryor from 207, F/O Kell and P/O Stanford from the RAAF's 463 and 467 Squadrons respectively, F/O Hamilton from 619, and P/O Cheney from 630. On the afternoon of S/L Suggitt's death, 891 crews were attending briefings for what would be a record-breaking operation that night. The Command was rested and replenished after two weeks on the ground, and this enabled Harris to assemble the largest non-one thousand force yet, and of course, the largest force ever sent against Berlin. It would be the first time that over 500 Lancasters and 300 Halifaxes had operated together, and they would deliver a new record 2,600 tons of bombs onto the Capital. Much of this was put to good use in central and south-western districts, where 1,000 houses were destroyed, along with over 500 temporary wooden barracks. Almost 1,200 fires were started, and many important war industry factories sustained damage, but forty-three aircraft failed to return from this last but one raid of the war by RAF heavy bombers on the 'Big City'.

The heavy brigade sat out the next three nights, before over 800 aircraft set out for Leipzig, and the greatest disaster to afflict the Command to date. Matters began to go awry as early as the Dutch coast outbound, when a proportion of the enemy night fighter force met the approaching bomber stream. The two factions maintained contact all the way to the target, which some main force aircraft reached ahead of the Pathfinders through wrongly forecast winds. They were forced to mill around in the target area, while they waited for the markers to go down, and collisions and the local flak batteries accounted for twenty-four of them. The operation itself was inconclusive in the face of complete cloud cover, and when all the returning aircraft had been accounted for, there was a massive shortfall of seventy-eight, a new record loss by a clear twenty-one aircraft. The Halifax percentage loss rate was the final straw for Harris, and the older Mk II and V variants were withdrawn from future operations over Germany, as had been the Stirlings towards the end of November. Despite the losses over the last two operations, almost 600 aircraft took off for Stuttgart on the 20/21st, and delivered a scattered but destructive raid, which hit central districts and suburbs in a quadrant from the north-west to the north-east. Only nine aircraft were lost, although a number of others crashed in England on return.

A new tactic was employed for the next two operations. The force was divided into two waves separated by two hours, in the hope of catching the night fighters on the ground refuelling and rearming as the second wave passed through. It was tried first at Schweinfurt on the 24/25th, and while the operation itself suffered from undershooting and was a failure, the second wave lost 50 per cent fewer aircraft than the first, in an overall loss of thirty-three. On the following night, Augsburg fell victim to one of those fairly rare occasions beyond the range of Oboe, when all facets of the plan came together in perfect harmony. Accurate Pathfinder marking was exploited by the main force, which produced concentrated bombing of the city centre. The heart of this beautiful and historic old city was torn out by fire, and centuries of culture were lost forever. Almost 3,000 houses were reduced to rubble, along with many public and architecturally important buildings, and around 700 people lost their lives. Twenty-one aircraft failed to return, suggesting that there was some merit in dividing the forces, and the tactic would continue to be used more or less until the end of the war.

At 617 Squadron the second half of February had been taken up with the funerals arising from Suggitt's crash, and intensive flying training for the new crews. One happy note was the arrival back from Sardinia of Martin on the 23rd, and he was sent straight off on leave. One interesting piece of 617 Squadron trivia concerned Joe McCarthy's original Dams Lancaster, ED915, Q-Queenie, which had become unserviceable on the very threshold of immortality. Joe's personal Lancasters always bore the code Q, and although he never actually carried out an operation in ED915, he regularly used it for testing and exercises right up to the end of February 1944, almost as if it were his own private taxi.

March was to bring unprecedented activity for 617 Squadron, and it should have opened its account on the night of the 1/2nd, but in the event, the operation was cancelled. There was no reprieve for the main force, however, which returned to Stuttgart and inflicted substantial damage on central, western and northern districts for the remarkably low loss of just four aircraft. 617 Squadron's opportunity came on the following night, when a BMW aero-engine factory and the adjacent G.S.P. machine tool works at Albert in France were selected for attention. Cheshire led the operation in DV380, carrying S/L Moyna to operate the cine camera. The other crews were those of the newly promoted S/L Munro in DV391, F/L Wilson in DV246, F/L Kearns in ME557, F/L McCarthy in ME559, F/L Cooper in DV394, F/L Poore in DV403, F/L Clayton in ME560, F/L Williams in EE131, F/O Stout in ED763, F/O Kell in ME555, F/O Knights in DV385, F/O Willsher in EE146, Lt Knilans in ME561 and F/O Ross in ME562. Cooper, Poore, Williams, Stout and Kell were all flying their first operations with the squadron, and for Poore it would be his twentieth in all. Cheshire, Munro and Wilson were carrying a mostly incendiary bomb load, while eleven others had a 12,000 pounder in the bomb bay, and Poore was the odd man out with fourteen 1,000 pounders. They got away either side of 19.00 hours, and reached the target some two hours later. Cheshire was unable to mark the target because of an unserviceable bomb site, but Munro dropped two spot fires right on the button from 6,000 feet, and the factory was plastered by most of the other crews, all under the watchful gaze of the station commander, G/C Philpott, who was flying with F/O Ross. An on the spot survey carried out in February 1945, when the factories were back in French hands, revealed such severe damage to the G.S.P. plant, that no attempt had been made to use it again, while the former BMW works was still capable of only 10 per cent of its former level of production.

A raid on the Ricamerie needle-bearing factory at St Etienne on the 4th was aborted when the crews encountered ten-tenths cloud over the target, and Cheshire was unable to make a positive identification. This would have been the first operation for the crews of F/L Hadland and F/O Duffy, but their turn would come at the same target next time round. This occurred on the 10th, when the full list of crews was; W/C Cheshire in DV380, S/L Munro in DV391, F/L Shannon in DV403, F/L Kearns in ME557, F/L McCarthy in ME559, F/L Wilson in JB139, F/L Clayton in ME560, F/L Cooper in DV394, F/L Hadland in EE146, F/O Duffy in ME555, F/O Knights in DV385, F/O Stout in DV246, Lt Knilans in ME561, F/O Willsher in DV393, F/O Ross in ME562 and F/O Stanford on his first operation with the squadron in EE131. Stanford, a genial South-Australian born in 1917, was working as a bank clerk when a RAAF recruiting train stopped at the Murray River town of Tailem Bend. He volunteered at once, but was rejected on medical grounds after it was discovered, that a severe blow to the head by a cricket ball some time earlier had left him concussed and potentially at risk at altitude. Four months later he presented himself at the recruiting centre at Adelaide, and by keeping mum about his injury, passed the physical with ease. After training in Australia and England he joined 467 Squadron RAAF just as the main phase of the Berlin campaign was getting into full swing. He flew eight times to the 'Big City' as captain and once as second pilot.

Unlike many trips to France, this one to St Etienne was to be a long one, for which take-off began with Cheshire at 19.27, and ended with Shannon at 20.05. The target was reached shortly after 23.00, and similar conditions were encountered to those thwarting the previous attempt. Cheshire went in at 1,700 feet, and managed to mark the western and eastern edges of this 170 × 90 yard target, setting it alight with incendiaries. Munro also went in low, before Cheshire ordered the main force to drop their 1,000 pounders on the glow of the fires visible through the cloud. Some crews were able to identify the target visually, while others bombed the fires as instructed, but it was not possible to assess the extent of the damage with any accuracy. Stanford's bombsight had become unserviceable during the outward flight, and Cheshire told him to hang about until the other crews had bombed. He was then called in downwind to avoid the smoke now emanating from the target, which was actually 1,200 feet above sea level, and he bombed visually from an indicated 3,000 feet. After his return at 03.48, Munro reported that one small factory building appeared to be wrecked, and he thought he could see four bomb holes in the roof of the main building. Any doubts about the effectiveness of the operation were vanquished by the reconnaissance photos, which revealed every building but one in this important plant to have been destroyed or extensively damaged. The main weight of the attack had fallen on the eastern part of the target area, and the multi-bay building had been destroyed by a combination of blast and fire. In addition, two long sheds had been almost totally destroyed, and others severely damaged.

An abortive operation to an aero-engine factory at Woippy by sixteen aircraft on the 15/16th gained some success, when night fighters repeatedly attacked Duffy's ME560. The rear gunner, F/S McLean, claimed two destroyed and two probables, and after the war it was confirmed that he, with assistance from the mid-upper gunner, W/O Red Evans, had indeed dispatched all four. F/L Edward flew with the squadron for the first time on this night, but like all the others, he was forced to bring his bombs home. The main force, meanwhile, returned to Stuttgart on this night, the first time it had operated in numbers since it had visited the same city two weeks earlier. This time the attack was less successful, and most of the bombing fell into open country. Night fighters arrived in the target area at the same time as the bomber stream, and thirty-seven aircraft were brought down.

The Michelin rubber works at Clermont Ferrand provided the target for sixteen 617 Squadron crews on the following night, and they were W/C Cheshire in DV380, S/L Munro in DV391, F/L Shannon in DV403, F/L McCarthy in ME559, F/L Kearns in ME557, F/L Wilson in JB139, F/L Cooper in ME562, F/L Hadland in ED763, F/L Edward in DV246, F/O Willsher in DV393, F/L Williams in ME555, Lt Knilans in ME561, F/O Kell in DV402, F/O Knights in DV385 and F/O Duffy in ME560. The crews became airborne either side of 19.30 hours, and on arrival at the target, Cheshire, Munro, Shannon and McCarthy all dropped spotfires or target indicators along with 30lb incendiaries from very low level in a four minute window to 22.50. One stick of incendiaries from Cheshire's aircraft undershot by up to a mile, but Munro's marking was spot on again, and with the target well alight the waiting crews were ordered to bomb on his spotfires. Ten 12,000 pounders were delivered with great accuracy between 23.03 and 23.17, and Edward's load of incendiaries went down with the last one. Cheshire reported a huge explosion in the target area at about 23.40, and the operation was declared to be another outstanding success, which was again captured on film by S/L Moyna, who was now a regular passenger in Cheshire's Lancaster. Cheshire and Shannon were the only two not to mention obtaining an aiming point photograph. Reconnaissance photos confirmed that all buildings had been damaged, except for the canteen. The largest building, measuring some 900 × 480 feet was hit by two 12,000 pounders, which demolished most of the structure and stripped the roof. Half of the inner-tube plant was destroyed and workshops and power stations damaged, mostly by blast rather than fire, as the low-level dropping of incendiaries tended to lead to concentration rather than a spreading throughout the target area.

On the 18th, thirteen crews were detailed for an attack on the Poudrerie Nationale powder factory at Bergerac. They were Cheshire in DV380, Munro in DV391, Shannon in DV403, McCarthy in ME559, Clayton in ME560, Wilson in JB139, Kearns, this time in ME562, F/L Pryor on his first operation with the squadron in ED763, Cooper in EE146, Knights in ME555, Willsher in DV393, Kell in Martin's beloved DV402 and Knilans in DV246. They all got away safely in a twenty minute slot from 19.28, with Cheshire carrying spotfires and 30lb incendiaries, and what could now be described as the 'Old Firm', that is Munro, Shannon and McCarthy, with similar loads plus a target indicator or two, to ensure that the target remained well marked. 12,000 pounders were borne aloft by Clayton, Wilson, Kearns, Knights, Willsher and Kell, while the remainder were to deliver incendiaries. Clayton's brief required him to conduct an experiment using a 1,000 pounder to detonate his 12,000 pounder as an airburst over the explosives storage area. Apparently it worked, because the entire dump went up, lighting the sky for ten seconds. Kearns was unable to release his bomb either mechanically or manually despite making four runs across the target. He pulled away, closed the bomb doors and the bomb-aimer plugged in the electrical circuit again. On reopening the bomb doors some ten miles east-south-east of the target the 12,000 pounder and flares fell out. Visibility was good, and the factory and storage buildings were clearly seen to be well ablaze after a number of large explosions. All participants landed safely back at Woodhall Spa between 02.02 and 02.30 from what was a completely successful operation. Again, the extent of the damage, particularly that caused by the blast, was confirmed by reconnaissance photos.

What must it have been like for the French people forced to work for the Germans in these factories selected for attack? Some of the buildings were well camouflaged, although by no means all, and the workers were assured by their German masters that they were unlikely to be bombed. Certainly, no air raid warnings were allowed to distract the workforce, so the workers organised their own spotters on the roof. They appreciated the apparent care taken by the RAF to attack after normal working hours, but before most people would have retired to bed. Whether the mid to late evening time-on-target of the 617 Squadron operations was planned for this reason is not known, but Churchill was very sensitive about French civilian casualties, and it was always a matter of concern to Cheshire.

This night also brought the first of two hugely destructive raids by the main force on Frankfurt. Over 800 aircraft destroyed or seriously damaged 6,000 buildings, most of them houses, and over 55,000 people were bombed out of their homes. The nitro-cellulose explosives works at Angouleme followed for 617 Squadron on the 20th, when fourteen crews were detailed to take part. On duty on this occasion were Cheshire in DV380, Munro in DV391, Shannon in DV403, McCarthy in ME559, Kearns in ME562, Wilson in JB139, Clayton in ME560, Williams in DV246, Cooper in DV385, Hadland in ED763, Edward in EE146, Willsher in DV393, Kell in DV402, and F/O 'Mac' Hamilton on his first operation with the squadron in ME555. Cheshire was first off at 19.18, and with the exception of Williams, the rest got away within twenty minutes. Williams's take-off was timed at 20.03, after he was forced to switch to the spare aircraft, when his own declared itself unserviceable. He also had a different bomb load from the others. With the exception of Cheshire and the 'Old Firm', who carried a single 8,000 pounder plus spotfires or TIs, all of the others were loaded with one 8,000 pounder and one 1,000 pounder, while Williams had eight 1,000 pounders in his bomb bay plus eight red spotfires. Munro dropped his store at 22.14 from 6,400 feet, and the others followed up over the next fifteen minutes or so from heights ranging from 6,000 to 10,700 feet. Most of the bombing was accurate, causing explosions and large fires, and Cheshire described the target as wrecked. He was right. Most of the plant's buildings were completely destroyed, and nearly all of those that weren't were damaged to some extent.

On the 21st, Martin, one of the founder members of the squadron, was posted to take up duties with 100 Group, which had been formed in the previous November to carry out a bomber support role in the area of Radio Counter Measures. The Group also used Mosquitos equipped with the Serrate radar device with which to hunt down and destroy enemy night fighters. It would not be long before Martin was flying one of these with 515 Squadron. The second main force raid on Frankfurt was carried out by almost 800 aircraft on the 22/23rd, and it was even more devastating than that of four nights earlier. All parts of the city were hit, but western districts suffered most grievously, and half of the city was left without electricity, gas and water for an extended period. Almost 1,400 people died over the two nights, and this major victory was achieved for the combined loss of fifty-five heavy bombers.

On the following night 617 Squadron sent fourteen aircraft to attack an aero engine factory at Lyons. The crews involved were Cheshire in DV380, McCarthy in ME559, Shannon in DV403, Kearns in ME557, Clayton in ME560, Cooper in DV394, Wilson in JB139, F/L Fearn on his twenty-second sortie in all and his first since joining 617, in DV385, Williams in EE131, Edward in EE146, Hadland in ED763, Willsher in DV393, Stanford in ME555 and Ross in ME562. Take-off time was as for the previous three operations, and they reached the target area some time after 23.00 hours. The non-marking element of the force were each carrying eleven 1,000 pounders, while Cheshire and Shannon were loaded with six each in addition to their spotfires, TIs and flares, and McCarthy had nine. Cheshire had been ordered not to mark from low level, and this should not have been a problem as a flare force provided by 106 Squadron was to illuminate the area for the 617 Squadron markers. Unfortunately, the flare force illuminated the wrong area, initially four miles too far north, then ten miles to the south and finally ten miles north again. 617 had to use its own flares, and the fact that they were too few added to the difficulties in identifying the target in the hazy conditions. Cheshire instructed the crews to overshoot the spotfires, but as the bombs had been fitted with delay fuses, they turned for home unable to determine the results of their efforts. Cheshire, though, remained behind in the target area to observe the outcome. Ross failed to pick up a divert signal on the way back, and he alone landed at Woodhall Spa, while the others all put down at Tangmere on the south coast. This was not the first occasion that difficulties had been encountered with flares, or that their performance had proved to be unsatisfactory. They were designed to burst at 4,000 feet, and drift slowly to earth, but some ignited at 8,000 feet, while others only did so on impact with the ground. This also happened if they were parachute flares and the parachute failed to open. Flares igniting at ground level created copious amounts of smoke as they burned out, and could easily obscure the aiming point.

The squadron would return to this target on the night of the 25/26th, but before that, the 24th was momentous for a number of reasons. Firstly, Shannon and McCarthy were made A and C Flight commanders respectively, and were recommended for the acting rank of Squadron Leader, Munro having already been installed as a flight commander some time earlier. Secondly, that night the main force conducted the nineteenth and final raid of the long-running campaign against Berlin, and the final raid of the war on the city by the RAF's heavy brigade. Over 800 aircraft took off, and they encountered unusually strong winds from the north at cruising altitude, which pushed them continually south of track, and broke the cohesion of the bomber stream. This led to scattered bombing at the Capital, and over a hundred outlying communities were afflicted. The south-western districts received most of the bombs, and housing was the chief victim. The jet stream wind continued to dog the crews on the way home, and many aircraft were driven over heavily defended areas of Germany, where they fell within range of predicted flak. A massive seventy-two aircraft failed to return, and over two thirds of them were brought down by ground fire. Also on the 24th a B17 arrived at Woodhall Spa with its American crew, who were to spend a few days with their 617 Squadron counterparts in an exchange arrangement.

On the following night sixteen 617 Squadron aircraft returned to Lyons for a second crack at the aero-engine factory. W/C Cheshire again took the lead in DV380, with S/L Shannon in DV403, S/L McCarthy in ME559, Kearns in ME557, Wilson in JB139, Clayton in DV394, Fearn in the now departed 'Mickey' Martin's DV402, Edward in EE146, Poore in DV391, Williams in EE131, Hadland in ED763, Pryor in DV385, Hamilton in ME555, Ross in ME561, Willsher in DV393 and Stanford in ME554. Cheshire carried F/S Pengelly as an additional gunner on this night to occupy the front turret, and a F/S Kimberley was also on board as the cine-camera operator. The usual take-off time had them arriving in the target area around 23.00 hours, and Cheshire, Shannon and McCarthy went in at low-level to deliver their spot fires and TIs. McCarthy is recorded in the ORB as dropping his from 50 feet. Unusually for 617 Squadron, there seemed to be some confusion concerning the accuracy of the markers, and Pryor aimed his twelve 500 pounders at the red spotfire to the east in accordance with instructions from Cheshire. Most of the others, he noticed, seemed to be bombing the wrong marker, and he described the raid as appearing to be very scattered. Certainly, Wilson admitted to misunderstanding the instructions and bombed the wrong spotfire. By the time that Hadland dropped the last bombs at 00.06, almost an hour after the raid began, smoke in the target area made it impossible to determine whether or not the factory buildings had been hit. Cheshire recorded fires covering approximately one square mile, and added that there was no attempt at photography. In fact, the bombing had been concentrated around the south-west of the factory. Stanford landed at Ford with an unserviceable wireless, and some kind of a leak from his starboard-inner engine. The American visitors had watched the squadron depart for the operation, and now they were invited to sit in on the debriefing.

Although the Berlin offensive was now over for the main force, the winter campaign still had a week to run, and two more major operations for the crews to negotiate. The first of these was delivered by almost 700 aircraft upon Essen on the 26/27th, when over 1,700 houses were destroyed, and forty-eight industrial buildings were seriously damaged. Thus was continued the remarkable run of successes against this once elusive target since the introduction of Oboe to main force operations a year earlier. On the 27th Cheshire went to Coleby Grange to receive instruction in a Mosquito, and two examples of the type were subsequently taken on squadron charge that day. The third attempt to nail the aero engine factory at Lyon was carried out by fifteen aircraft on the 29/30th. The crews were those of Cheshire in DV380, Kearns in ME557, Clayton in ME560, Ross in ME562, Knilans in ME561, Stout in ME559, Duffy in DV394, Stanford in ME554, Hamilton in DV403, Wilson in JB139, Poore in DV391, Pryor in DV402, Edward in EE131, Fearn in DV246 and Knights in DV385. They carried an unusual variety of bomb loads, Cheshire's consisting of spotfires, T.I.s and two 500 pounders, while Kearns had T.I.s and eight 500 pounders on board, Clayton spotfires, T.I.s and five 500 pounders, Ross, Knilans, Stout, Hamilton, Wilson, Poore, Pryor and Knights one 8,000 pounder and two 1,000 pounders, and Duffy, Stanford, Edward and Fearn fourteen 500 pounders. This time most of the hardware seemed to find the mark, and Clayton reported seeing the main factory building to be well alight with its roof gone. It was later assessed, that sixteen of twenty-two key buildings had been destroyed. Fearn's Lancaster was hit by heavy predicted flak, but no serious damage resulted. This proved to be the final operation of the month. On the following day Cheshire went solo for the first time in a Mosquito, and he would use his new skills to good effect in the coming months.

The month's activities were not quite over for the main force crews, who had just one more operation ahead of them before they would turn their attention to an entirely different campaign. The night of the 30/31st was to be devoted to a standard, deep penetration, maximum effort raid on the birthplace of Nazism, the southern city of Nuremberg. During the course of the day a conference had taken place between the Group commanders, at which a decision was taken to adopt a 5 Group inspired route, rather than go with one prepared by 8 Group planners as was usual practise. Whether the Pathfinder AOC, AVM Bennett, was party to the telephone discussion is unclear, but he threw a 'hissy-fit' when he learned that the route would take the bomber stream on a 250 mile-long straight leg from Belgium across Germany to a point about fifty miles north of the target, from where the final run-in was to commence. There were to be no feints, no diversions and no splitting of the force, and the first two elements at least represented a departure from standard routine. The Lancaster main force Group commanders seemed happy with the plan, but the Halifax operators were apparently less convinced. Under normal circumstances operational details were left in the hands of 8 Group planners, but Bennett was overruled and he predicted a disaster. Later on there were some doubts about the weather, when a 1409 Met Flight Mosquito crew reported finding no evidence of the forecast protective cloud at cruising altitude. As a result it was half expected that the operation would be scrubbed, but it was not to be.

795 aircraft took off either side of 22.00 hours and headed towards a catastrophe, and while climbing for height, the crews were struck by some unfamiliar features in the conditions. The moon, though fairly new, cast an unusually bright light, and the visibility possessed a crystal clarity, which had rarely before been encountered. The forecast cloud at cruising altitude did indeed fail to materialize, while a layer formed beneath the aircraft to silhouette them like flies on a tablecloth. To add insult to injury condensation trails formed to further advertise the aircrafts' presence, and the jet stream winds, which had so adversely affected the Berlin raid a week earlier, also put in an appearance, only this time blowing from the south. This again broke the cohesion of the bomber stream, and spread it out over a vast area. The combination of the route and the conditions handed the force on a plate to the night fighters, which were waiting at their control beacons almost in the path of the approaching bombers. The carnage began over Charleroi in Belgium, and the ground from there to Nuremberg was littered with the burning wreckage of RAF bombers. Over eighty aircraft fell before the target was reached, and those crews who either failed to notice the strength of the wind, or refused to believe the evidence, were blown up to fifty miles north of their intended track, and turned towards Nuremberg from a false position. Many of these were among the more than one hundred who bombed Schweinfurt in error, and the target city escaped with modest damage. Ninety-five aircraft failed to return home, and many more were written off in crashes, or with battle damage too extensive to repair.

Chapter Twelve

Supporting The Group

April and May; preparing for invasion

The Nuremberg disaster did nothing to relax the tensions between Cochrane and Bennett, both of whom were brilliant men with the finest tactical minds, but with diametrically opposed views on target marking. Bennett believed in high-level marking, for which complex techniques had evolved to deal with every contingency of condition. He believed low-level marking to be suicidal, and would not ask such risks of his crews. Cochrane would consider anything within reason to improve performance, and considered the risks to be acceptable. In fact, the degree of risk in a fast, low flying Mosquito was actually quite small. The only flaw in the system was, that thick, low cloud could prevent the marker crews from seeing the aiming point in time, and any markers delivered would be invisible to the heavy brigade flying above the cloud at medium to high level. Bennett's credibility lay in his unparalleled background and qualifications as a pilot and navigator. His operational experience was first-hand, and although it was two years since his last sortie, it was at least relevant to the current conflict. In contrast the much older Cochrane had no such operational credentials, but in dealings with Harris, there is little doubt that 5 Group held most of the trump cards. Harris had commanded the Group during the first year of the war, and Cochrane had served under him as a flight commander in Mesopotamia in the twenties. Having personally installed Cochrane as the 5 Group AOC early in 1943, he gave him the job of bursting the Ruhr Dams, and the success of this operation would have been as much a credit to Cochrane as to the crews who carried it out. Now the relationship between Cochrane and Bennett was about to plumb new depths as a result of the spectacular success of the 5 Group approach to target marking since the turn of the year.

As far as the main force was concerned, what now lay ahead of the crews was in marked contrast to that endured by them over the winter months. The new priority was the pre-invasion campaign, the main component of which was the Transportation Plan, the systematic dismantling by bombing of the French and Belgian railway networks. This would require attacks on all of the main railway centres with marshalling yards, along with the locomotive depots and repair and maintenance facilities. This had, in fact, already been put into practice by the Halifax and Stirling squadrons during March, with attacks on railway yards at Trappes, Le Mans, Amiens, Laon, Aulnoye, Courtrai and Vaires. Now that the entire main force had become available, the crews could look forward to shorter-range hops to France and Belgium in improving weather conditions, in place of the long slog to Germany on dark, often dirty nights. These operations would prove to be equally demanding in their way, however, and would require of the crews a greater commitment to accuracy to avoid unnecessary casualties among friendly civilians. The main fly in the ointment as far as the crews were concerned was a diktat from on high that decreed that most of such operations were worthy of counting as just one third of a sortie towards the completion of a tour, and until this flawed policy was rescinded, an air of discontent pervaded the bomber stations. Despite the prohibitive losses over the winter, the Command was in remarkably fine fettle to face its new challenge, and Harris was in the enviable position of being able to achieve what had eluded his predecessor. This was to hit multiple targets simultaneously with forces large enough to make an impact. He could now assign targets to individual Groups, to Groups in tandem or to the Command as a whole as dictated by operational requirements, and spread his Pathfinder crews around to provide a sprinkling for each raid. Also, while he was at the helm, his favoured policy of city busting would never be entirely shelved in favour of other considerations, and whenever an opportunity arose to strike against the cities, he would take it.

On the 2nd of April Cheshire was awarded a second Bar to his DSO, and celebrated the event on the 5/6th by going to war for the first time in a Mosquito. This would also be the first time that 617 Squadron marked for 5 Group, and it was to be a defining moment. A force of 144 Lancasters was made ready, seventeen of them provided by 617 Squadron, and the full squadron order of battle was; Cheshire in ML976, with F/O Kelly as navigator, Munro in LM482, McCarthy in LM492, Clayton in ME560, Cooper in DV394, Edward in EE146, Poore in DV391, Pryor in DV380, Fearn in LM485, Ross in ME562, Knights in DV385, Knilans in ME561, Stout in ED763, F/O Cheney on his first operation with the squadron, in DV393, Kell in DV402, Duffy in ME555, Stanford in ME554 and Hamilton in DV403. The main target was an aircraft repair factory at Toulouse, which Cheshire was to mark from low level in the Mosquito, while Munro and McCarthy were on hand to back up with spot fires from medium level, before joining the others in delivering 8,000 pounders. The other 617 Squadron aircraft were, in fact, carrying six 500 pounders in addition to their blockbuster. Part of the main force element was to attack three other targets on Toulouse airfield. After an outward flight for the Lancasters of almost four hours, Cheshire went in in the Mosquito at 00.17 at 800–1,000 feet, and lobbed two red spotfires onto the factory buildings with such accuracy, that it was not necessary for Munro and McCarthy to back up. Three minutes later Munro watched his 8,000 pounder fall into a large repair hangar from 10,000 feet, while McCarthy dropped his from 1,000 feet higher. The non-marker crews from 617 Squadron delivered their attacks from between 15,000 and 17,800 feet, while their 5 Group colleagues were assigned to lower flight levels, and all the attacks were completely successful, costing between them just one 207 Squadron Lancaster. S/L Moyna was on hand in Munro's aircraft to record the scene for posterity. All crews were diverted to Wescott on the way home, and when Pryor finally got back to Woodhall he ran off the perimeter track, damaging his rear turret, fuselage and tailplane. On learning of the success of the Toulouse operation, carried out as it was by ordinary crews from squadrons of the line without special training, Harris authorized 5 Group's independence from the rest of the main force.

Later on during the 6th, six H2s Lancasters arrived on temporary detachment from other 5 Group squadrons complete with air and ground crews. The aircrews were to remain permanently, but the ground crews would stay only while the aircraft were on charge. P/Os Castagnola and Ian Ross came with JB370 and ND472 respectively from 57 Squadron, P/O Carey brought ND339 from 106 Squadron, P/O Sanders came from 49 Squadron with ND683, P/O Watts and ND554 arrived from 630 Squadron, and P/O Levy and ND631 were posted in from 44 Squadron. Also posted in at the same time was F/L Fawke from 1660CU. Freddie Watts and his crew had begun their operational career with a trip to Berlin at the end of January. They didn't see the mighty city through the impenetrable cloud cover, but they made it home after a seven-hour trip to contemplate the fact that they now only had another twenty-nine operations to negotiate. The second and third came at Schweinfurt and Augsburg on consecutive nights at the end of February, while March brought two trips to Stuttgart, two to Frankfurt, and the disasters of the final Berlin raid and Nuremberg. With a number of other operations in the bag this brought the crew's time with 630 Squadron to an end on a total of eleven. During its time with 630 Squadron the crew's Lancaster ND554 was coded LE-C, 'Conquering Cleo', and bore a painting of a lion tearing up a swastika. Ian Ross had joined 57 Squadron from 1654CU, where his flight commander had been Drew Wyness. His first operation was a trip to Brunswick in mid January as 'second dickey' to Arthur Fearn, and six nights later he took his own crew to Berlin and returned on three engines. Berlin was the destination three more times in four nights at the end of the month, the second one again resulting in the loss of an engine, while the third one ended in an early return. The final raid of the winter campaign, the Nuremberg catastrophe, was the crew's fourteenth and last sortie with 630 Squadron.

P/O Levy had arrived at 44 Squadron with his crew as a Sergeant pilot on the 3rd of February, during the two-week stand-down in main force operations preceding the penultimate Berlin raid. The crew's first operation was the Leipzig disaster on the 19/20th, when technical problems forced them to return early and land at the emergency strip at Woodbridge on the Suffolk coast. Five nights later they completed the trip to Schweinfurt, before participating in the destruction of Augsburg twenty-four hours later. Levy was commissioned on the last day of the month, the 29th as it was a leap year, and celebrated with a raid on Stuttgart on the following night. During the final third of March Levy and his crew attacked Frankfurt on the 22/23rd, took part in the final attack on Berlin on the 24/25th, went to Essen two nights later and survived Nuremberg on the 30/31st. Bill Carey was a diminutive Australian who came to the squadron with eleven operations under his belt.

The new offensive got into full swing on the night of the 9/10th of April, when separate forces attacked railway targets at Lille and at Villeneuve-St-Georges on the outskirts of Paris. The former was directed at the Delivrance goods station by elements of 3, 4, 6 and 8 Groups, and it succeeded in destroying over 2,000 items of rolling stock, while also causing damage to buildings and track. Sadly, and almost inevitably, the collateral bombing of adjacent residential districts caused over 400 civilian deaths. The latter operation was aimed at the marshalling yards by a contingent from all of the Groups, and whilst this attack was believed to be moderately successful, almost 100 fatal casualties were inflicted on civilians here also. On the following night, five railway yards were attacked in France and Belgium, of which the marshalling yards at Tours were assigned to 5 Group. Only one of the night's targets escaped serious damage, but stray bombs at Ghent killed over 400 Belgian civilians.

On the same night 617 Squadron dispatched seventeen Lancasters and a Mosquito to a signals equipment depot at St Cyr. The crews were Cheshire in ML976, Munro in LM482, McCarthy in LM492, Clayton in ME560, Wilson in LM485, Poore in DV391, Fearn in DV393, Pryor in EE146, Cooper in DV394, Williams in EE131, Knilans in ME561, Duffy in ME555, Stanford in ME554, Stout in ME559, Cheney in JB139, Kell in ME557, Ross in ME562 and Knights in DV385. New pilots, Carey, Castagnola, Sanders and Levy, along with some other crew members, flew as passengers to observe the squadron's bombing techniques in operation, and S/L Moyna again set up his camera in Munro's Lancaster. They took off in a thirty-minute slot, Cheshire the last to depart at 23.59, and one hour and fifty-six minutes later he began his dive from 5,000 to 1,000 feet to deposit two red spotfires onto the western edge of the main target. He then called in Munro to place his markers more accurately on the centre of the target, but they fell some distance away. The Operations Record Book records Munro's spotfires falling at 02.02, and while this was going on the other 617 Squadron crews had to wait, finally coming in to bomb as the first markers had almost burned out. In his post raid report Cheshire described the first stick of bombs falling onto the north-west corner of the factory and starting fires. This was fortuitous, as it, in effect, remarked the aiming point. This first stick to fall was delivered from 9,300 feet at 02.06 by Lt Knilans, who himself witnessed the resultant immediate conflagration. Cheshire then ordered the other crews to aim for these fires. The spotfires carried by McCarthy were not required, but his single 8,000 pounder was, and this would soon join the 8,000 and 500 pounders carried by the remainder of the squadron. Munro mentions his own bomb falling into the centre of the fires already burning in the target area. Smoke rose to 8,000 feet, and hampered any further assessment of the results. All aircraft returned safely to Woodhall Spa, and with the exception of Clayton and Williams, whose cameras failed to function, each brought back an aiming point photo. Later in the day, Australian F/O 'Bunny' Lee and his crew arrived on posting from 106 Squadron, with which they had completed a tour of twenty-nine operations

Over 300 aircraft drawn from 1, 3, 5 and 8 Groups delivered Aachen's most serious raid of the war on the 11/12th, as a result of which, more than 1,500 people lost their lives, and this was followed by a period of minor operations. On the 14th, Bomber Command officially became subject to the dictates of SHAEF in preparation for the forthcoming invasion, and would remain thus shackled until the Allied armies were sweeping towards the German frontier at the end of the summer.

The end of an era came on the 15th, when most of the remaining original Type 464 Provisioning Lancasters were flown out to Metheringham for storage. The intention was to fly them occasionally and maintain them sufficiently to allow their return to operations should the need arise. On the following day S/L Shannon and F/Ls Kearns and Fawke were declared operational on Mosquitos, and their crews were unceremoniously put up for disposal, although Shannon retained the now F/O Sumpter as his navigator, while F/O Barclay performed that function for Kearns, and F/O Bennett for Fawke. On the 18th matters came to something of a head between Cochrane and Bennett, when 5 Group welcomed back into the fold two of its most prestigious former squadrons, 83 and 97. To add insult to injury it had already taken delivery of 627 Squadron with its Mosquitos three days earlier. All three squadrons were on permanent detachment from the Pathfinders, much to the chagrin of Bennett, who was infuriated at having three of his finest units taken from him, particularly so, as 5 Group was the recipient. The squadrons remained officially part of 8 Group, and the crews retained their ranks and coveted Pathfinder badge, but to all intents and purposes they were now 5 Group.

The transfer of these squadrons was not a reflection on Bennett, who had achieved remarkable success in bringing his Group to a peak of performance and efficiency. Rather, it was an indication of the success of the low level visual marking method pioneered by Cheshire and Martin. It was unfortunate, though, that the arrival of the two heavy squadrons at Coningsby was marred by the attitude of the base commander, Air Commodore Sharp. As the crews climbed out of the buses, already disgruntled at being removed from what they saw as an elite status at 8 Group, they were summoned to a lecture by Sharp, a man with no relevant operational experience. Instead of welcoming them as brothers-in-arms, he harangued them about their supposedly bad 8 Group habits, and told them to buckle down to learning 5 Group ways. This was an insult to battle-hardened airmen, for whom the new role of target illuminating would be a piece of cake compared with the complexities of their former job. It left a sour taste, and it would be a considerable time before a grudging loyalty developed to 5 Group. Whatever the circumstances leading to this situation, for the remainder of the war 5 Group had its own target marking force, with 83 and 97 Squadrons acting as the flare force and heavy markers, while 627 Squadron, after a bedding-in period, would take over the low-level visual marking role from 617 Squadron. From this moment also, 5 Group would be referred to in 8 Group circles somewhat disparagingly as the 'Independent Air Force', or the 'Lincolnshire Poachers', and the former appellation, at least, would prove to be an accurate description.

That night 617 Squadron operated four Mosquitos for the first time, accompanied by nineteen of its Lancasters to mark the marshalling yards at Juvisy for the Group. It is not possible to be certain which Mosquitos were in use from this point, as the ORB entries often differ from those in log-books, and the squadron kept changing its aircraft. Where there is major doubt, therefore, the Mosquito serials will be omitted from the narrative. The Mosquito pilots for this operation were W/C Cheshire, S/L Shannon, F/L Kearns and F/L Fawke, and they were guided to the target by three Oboe Mosquitos from 8 Group. The Lancaster crews were those of Munro in LM482, McCarthy in LM492, Wilson in LM485, Ross in ME562, Cooper in DV394, Knights in DV385, Willsher in DV393, Duffy in ME555, Stout in JB139, Poore in DV391, Pryor in EE146, Stanford in ME554, and seven crews on their first operation with the squadron. These were W/O Gingles in LM489, F/L Howard in ED763, F/L Reid in ME557, P/O Sanders in ND683, P/O Carey in ND339, P/O Ian Ross in JB370, and P/O Levy in ND631. 617 Squadron's heavy brigade got away between 20.25 and 20.46 carrying a mixture of 1,000 and 500 pounders and flares, while Munro, McCarthy, Wilson and Nicky Ross also had red spotfires on board. The Mosquitos left Woodhall Spa in a three-minute slot to 21.30, and they arrived in the target area shortly after 23.00 hours. The three 8 Group Oboe Mosquitos provided the initial reference for the 617 Squadron Lancaster element, and Stanford, Reid, Sanders and Levy all dropped their flares at 23.12, to be followed by the others over the ensuing five minutes. Despite the illumination Cheshire experienced difficulty in identifying the first aiming point, and called on which ever of the other Mosquito pilots who could see it to go in and mark. Fawke answered the call and dived down to 800 feet at around 23.20. Cheshire then ran in to mark the second aiming point at 23.21, diving from 5,000 to 2,000 feet to deliver four spotfires. Unfortunately, they all hung up and had to be brought home. Shannon and Kearns stood in reserve for the second batch of flares, but were not needed, and Cheshire ordered the other squadron Lancasters with spotfires to back up those delivered by Fawke. Apart from one or two wild sticks of bombs the attack by around 180

Lancasters of the Group seemed to be accurate and concentrated, and was witnessed by A/C Sharp from his vantage point in Duffy's ME555. Post raid reconnaissance confirmed the accuracy and concentration of the operation, which left track, rolling stock and engine and carriage repair sheds extensively damaged. The main lines were also severed at many points, but collateral damage was inflicted upon residential districts north-west of the target.

83, 97 and 627 Squadrons did not participate at Juvisy. No doubt incensed by their treatment at the hands of their new masters, the commanding officers refused to allow the crews to operate on the basis that they had not yet assimilated the techniques of the 5 Group method. In the event they did not have long to wait for their 5 Group baptism. A two-phase operation was planned against the marshalling yards at La Chapelle, north of Paris, to take place with an hour between the attacks. It would be mounted on the night of the 20/21st, and would be the first fully orchestrated performance by the newly independent Group. The plan called for 8 Group Mosquitos to drop cascading flares by Oboe to provide an initial reference, and for six Mosquitos of 627 Squadron to lay a screen of Window ahead of the approaching main force Lancasters. Once the target had been identified, the first members of the 83 and 97 Squadron Lancaster flare force were to provide illumination for the low-level marker Mosquitos of 617 Squadron. These would then mark the first aiming point with red spotfires for the main force Lancasters to aim at, and the whole process would be repeated an hour later at a second aiming point. The 617 Squadron element for the first phase consisted of Cheshire and Fawke in Mosquitos, Munro in LM482, with Air Commodore Satterly on board as an observer, McCarthy in LM492, Wilson in LM485, Duffy in ME555, Stout in ME559, Knilans in ME560 and Ian Ross in JB370. For the second phase Shannon and Kearns represented the Mosquito element, while the Lancasters were those of Howard in ED763, Reid in ME557, Stanford in ME554, Carey in ED817, Levy in ND631, Sanders in ND683, and P/O Watts, on his first operation with the squadron, in ND554. All of the squadron's Lancasters were loaded with twelve 1,000 pounders.

Zero hour was set for 00.05, and this required the first phase Lancaster brigade to depart Woodhall Spa either side of 22.00 hours, to be followed half an hour later by Cheshire and Fawke, while the second phase Lancasters became airborne around 23.15, with Shannon and Kearns bringing up the rear in their Mosquitos at 23.45 and 23.47 respectively. Two minutes before zero hour six 627 Squadron Mosquitos began dropping Window from high level, and continued to do so for seventeen minutes until the arrival of the main force. Drifting downwards in still air at the rate of 500 feet per minute, the Window would provide cover throughout the period of the main force's presence in the target area. The Pathfinder Mosquitos turned up on time, but their target indicators failed to cascade on impact on the first or southern aiming point. This eventuality had been anticipated, however, and it meant, that the first element of four flare-carrying Lancasters had to orbit, while plan B was put into action. A second batch of four aircraft arrived a minute or so later, and two of them dropped flares by Oboe, which allowed the remaining six flare carriers to deliver theirs. It was at this point, that the original Pathfinder target indicators began to burn on the ground. The only problem resulting from this hitch was the reduction in time for the low-level marking to take place. Rather than having an interval between the two elements of four flare-carrying aircraft, which would have allowed for an extended period of illumination, they all went down at once. In the event, this did not prove to be a problem for Cheshire, who released four spotfires from 1,200 feet at 00.16, and Fawke backed these up four minutes later. A VHF communication problem between Cheshire and the main force controller, W/C Dean of 83 Squadron, caused the opening of the attack to be delayed for a minute or so, but this was quickly sorted, and the initial bombing was accurate and concentrated. Smoke soon obscured the spotfires, however, and Dean found it necessary to remark the aiming point. At 01.11 Shannon marked the second or northern aiming point, and his spotfires were backed up by Kearns two minutes later. The second phase proceeded smoothly, and both halves of the railway yards were severely damaged. Reconnaissance photos taken on the following day again confirmed the remarkable concentration of the bombing, and the devastation around both aiming points. A bridge at the southern end of the yards was also severely damaged. While this raid was in progress, elements of 1, 3, 6 and 8 Groups were conducting a punishing assault on Cologne, which suffered the destruction of over 1,800 houses, and damage to hundreds of industrial and business premises.

Thus far the Group's low-level visual marking technique had not been tried out against a heavily defended target in Germany, and this would provide the real test. Brunswick had been attacked by the Command for the first time in numbers in mid January, and had escaped relatively lightly. As events were to prove, it would continue to be a difficult nut to crack until late in the year. This large town was selected as the proving ground for the 5 Group method just forty-eight hours after the La Chapelle operation, and a maximum 5 Group effort was called. As the target lay beyond the range of Oboe, there would be no Pathfinder involvement on this occasion, and 54 Base would have to provide all of the marking. The only non-5 Group participants were ten ABC Lancasters from 1 Group's 101 Squadron, which were to provide an RCM screen as well as carry a full bomb load. The Group carried out its own weather reconnaissance prior to the operation, and as the report from this was not encouraging, it was decided to send two 627 Squadron Mosquitos to the target area thirty minutes before zero hour. If they encountered cloud cover over the target, thus rendering the low-level marking method ineffective, they would inform the approaching flare force from 83 and 97 Squadrons to prepare skymarkers for the main force crews to aim at. The two Mosquitos were then to rejoin the main force and carry out a dive-bombing attack. Ten 627 Squadron Mosquitos were to begin dropping Window six minutes before they reached the target, arriving three minutes before zero hour, while the flare carrying Lancasters were to arrive five at a time at one minute intervals to provide seven minutes of illumination for the low-level element. This entire complex operational plan depended on good VHF communication, and sadly, this would prove to be the night's Achilles heel.

Munro was at the controls of the first 617 Squadron Lancaster to take off from Woodhall Spa at 23.15. He was in his usual aircraft, as was McCarthy, and the others were, Nick Ross in ME562, Duffy in LM489, Cooper in DV394, Stanford in ME554, Willsher in DV393, Poore in DV391, Stout in ME559, Fearn in DV246, Hamilton in DV403, Shannon's former chariot, Reid in ME557, Knights in DV385, Sanders in ND683, Ian Ross in JB370, Levy in ND472, Watts in ND554 and Carey in ED817, the second prototype Dams Lancaster. Watts was the last away at 23.35. Some of these were carrying six 1,000 pounders with spotfires to back up the marking if required, while others were loaded with nine 1,000 pounders and a 2,000 pounder, or a 2,000 pounder plus clusters of the new 'J' bomb incendiaries. The Mosquito element was as for the previous operation, and these faster-flying aircraft left just before midnight, arriving in the target area about ninety minutes later. Ian Ross was back at Woodhall Spa less than two hours after taking off. An astro comparison showed the DR and P4 compasses to be unreliable, and on the way home they dumped their 2,000 pounder in the sea. Communications difficulties had already manifested themselves by the time of Cheshire's arrival in the target area, interference on the VHF frequency preventing the weather Mosquito crews from contacting the flare force. The problem would eventually be traced to a single VHF set incorrectly fitted in a 617 Squadron Lancaster.

The initial flares were released over the town of Wolfenbüttel, five miles south of the intended location, and as Cheshire searched in their light at low level, he found only suburbs and open country. He withheld his spotfires and waited for the next batch of flares, which were a little to the north of Brunswick's centre, but close enough for Gerry Fawke to identify the aiming point and mark it with four red spotfires. Cheshire verified the accuracy of Fawke's work, and ordered Kearns to back up with a further four red spotfires, while Shannon held off and ultimately was not needed. This had now set the timing back by seven minutes. Cheshire called in the main force to bomb, and the initial salvos fell squarely into the town centre. However, the first spotfires began to burn out around four minutes after the opening of the attack, and Geoff Stout aimed his load at their estimated position. His incendiaries went down, but the 2,000 pounder hung up and was eventually jettisoned. Green target indicators were dropped to replace the extinguished red spotfires, in accordance with instructions at briefing, but unfortunately, they fell south-west of Brunswick, and inevitably began to attract later bomb loads. Cheshire was unable to communicate directly with the main force because of interference, but managed to get through to Munro, who could pass on his message by W/T. In the event, Munro apparently misheard Cheshire's message because of the interference, and he retransmitted instructions to bomb the green TIs. This was carried out by many of the remaining main force crews, and at least 50 per cent of the night's effort was directed away from the intended aiming point. Nevertheless, some useful damage was inflicted, and on the credit side, the losses were restricted to a very modest four aircraft. Meanwhile, the other Groups were busy over Düsseldorf, destroying or seriously damaging two thousand houses and dozens of industrial buildings, and while the Independent Air Force had got off lightly at Brunswick, twenty-nine aircraft failed to return from the Ruhr.

Having failed to prove conclusively the 5 Group method at Brunswick, it was decided to try again at the much bombed and consequently well-defended southern city of Munich. Just two nights after Brunswick 234 Lancasters and sixteen Mosquitos of 5 Group, accompanied by ten ABC Lancasters from 101 Squadron, set out for southern Germany. 617 Squadron dispatched the same four Mosquitos and crews, who departed Woodhall Spa around midnight, a remarkable three hours after the twelve Lancasters. The latter were led by Munro, unusually in LM485, and McCarthy in LM492, while the rest of the heavy element consisted of Cooper in DV394, Williams in EE131, Fearn in DV246, Reid in ME557, Hamilton in ME555, Stout in ME559, Stanford in ME554, Knights in DV385, Duffy in LM489, and Nick Ross in ME562. All the Lancasters were carrying 'J' clusters and standard 30lb incendiaries alone. Taking off at the same time were six other of the squadron's Lancasters, whose purpose was to provide a diversion for the main raid by dropping flares and target indicators over Milan. This contingent included four of the H2s equipped Lancasters, and the crews were Edward in ME560, Watts in ND554, Levy in ND631, Carey in ED817, Ian Ross in JB370 and Sanders in ND472.

As the 5 Group main force approached southern Germany via south-western France, feinting towards Italy, eleven 627 Squadron Mosquitos made for the target area by a more direct route to commence dropping Window two and a half minutes ahead of the flare force. Cheshire and Co also flew directly to the target, although skirting to the south of the well-defended city of Augsburg, and running the gauntlet of a continuous flak barrage. Munich boasted around 200 light flak guns and many searchlights, all of which seemed to greet Cheshire's arrival as the first flares were on their way down at 01.40. Cheshire dived through the murderous curtain of steel to release his markers from 1,500 feet squarely onto the aiming point, before screaming across the city at little more than rooftop height to make good his escape. The other three Mosquitos attempted to back up over the succeeding fifteen minutes, but Fawke's markers failed to release. Nevertheless, the 5 Group heavy brigade plastered the markers, and over 1,100 buildings were destroyed, mostly in the central districts of the city. It was on this trip that the squadron suffered the year's first operational loss of a crew, that of F/L Cooper, whose Lancaster, DV394, was shot down by a Ju88 R-2 night fighter of 1/NJG2 on the way home south-west of Ulm. The bomb-aimer, F/O Harden, was killed, while the remainder of the crew survived to fall into enemy hands. They had been undone by *Hauptmann* Gerhardt Raht, a twenty-three year-old ace operating out of Langensalza, for whom it was the thirty-first kill in a tally that would reach fifty-eight by war's end. Bill Reid arrived home with a hole in his starboard-inner nacelle courtesy of predicted flak, and a night fighter attacked Geoff Stout during the camera run without effect. The operation was declared an outstanding success, and it was probably this raid above all, which sealed the award of the Victoria Cross to Cheshire at the eventual end of his operational career of 100 sorties. The southern German city of Karlsruhe was the target for the other Groups on this night, but strong winds pushed the attack towards its northern half, and much of the bombing fell into open country.

617 Squadron had now closed its month's account, but the main force continued to pound its way across Germany and France, and three operations were laid on for the 26/27th. The main effort was directed at Essen, and returning crews claimed a successful outcome. The Independent Air Force went to Schweinfurt, where 627 Squadron carried out the low level marking for the first time as successors to 617 Squadron. Sadly, its maiden effort was not blessed with success under difficult circumstances and a spirited defence, and much of the bombing fell into open country. The other target was the railway yards at Villeneuve-St-Georges, part of which was accurately bombed by Halifaxes of 4 and 6 Groups. Aircraft from 1, 3, 6 and 8 Groups carried out a very successful raid on the highly industrialized town of Friedrichshafen on the 27/28th, where the night's principal targets were tank engine and gearbox factories. Over 60 per cent of the town's built-up area was estimated as destroyed, and tank production suffered a serious setback. The remainder of the month was devoted largely to railway targets, although small forces from 5 Group attacked a number of factories in France and Norway. F/L Hadland concluded his tour at the end of the month, and was posted to 5 LFS for instructional duties. April ended on a sad note for the squadron with news of the death of F/O Brian Jagger, who had been Shannon's front gunner on Operation Chastise and a regular in the mid-upper turret from then on until his posting to the Bombing Development Unit at Newmarket on the 6th of March. He had flown his last operation with Shannon on the 25/26th of January, and his commission had come through in February backdated to October. He had already advanced another rank since then, and at the time of his death he was still on the strength of the BDU at Newmarket. He was on board a BDU Lancaster on the afternoon of the 30th, when the dinghy somehow escaped from its stowage and fouled the tailplane, bringing the aircraft down with total loss of life.

Just one operation involved 617 Squadron during May, and even then it was only the Mosquito crews who were called upon. It was mounted on the 3rd, the day that saw 617 Squadron original F/L Ken Brown posted to 5 LFS as an instructor, having been preceded on the 1st by Foxlee and Simpson of Martin's Dams crew. The target for that night for 346 Lancasters of 1 and

5 Groups was the Panzer training camp and motor transport depot at Mailly-le-Camp in France. As home to the 21st Panzer division it was believed to hold many thousands of troops, and was one of the foremost tank training establishments outside of Germany. As such it was considered to be a threat to the forthcoming invasion, and a priority target, therefore, for elimination. It lay deep inside France, well to the east of Paris, around 130 miles from the nearest German frontier and 300 miles from the bomber stations in Lincolnshire. The plan was for 617 Squadron Mosquitos to mark two aiming points, one for each Group, before handing the target over to the master bomber, and although the site was expected to be well defended, it was not thought to be an unusually difficult operation. Cheshire was to act as marker leader, while W/C Deane of 83 Squadron was the overall controller. They attended separate briefings, and it seems that neither was fully aware of the complete picture, which included a separate aiming point for 1 Group's Special Duties Flight from Binbrook. Cheshire and Shannon got away from Woodhall Spa within a minute of each other shortly after 22.00 hours in, it is believed, ML976 and NS993 respectively, while Kearns and Fawke took off at 22.21 and 22.23 in Mosquitos DZ525 and DZ521, which had been borrowed from Woodhall Spa co-residents 627 Squadron.

Cheshire and Shannon were in position before midnight, and as the first flares from the 83 and 97 Squadron Lancasters illuminated the target below, Cheshire released his two red spotfires onto the first aiming point at 00.00½ from 1,500 feet. Shannon backed them up from 400 feet five and a half minutes later, and as far as Cheshire was concerned, the operation was bang on schedule at this stage. A 97 Squadron Lancaster also laid markers accurately to ensure a constant focal point, and Cheshire passed instructions to the main force controller to call the bombers in. It was at this stage of the operation that matters began to go awry. A communications problem arose, when a commercial radio station, believed to be an American forces network, jammed the VHF frequencies in use. A few crews from 9, 207 and 467 Squadrons heard the call to bomb, and did so, but for most the instructions were swamped by the interference. Deane then attempted to control the operation by W/T, but this also failed, and the wireless transmitter in his Lancaster was later found to be sufficiently off frequency to prevent the call to bomb from reaching the main force crews. Post raid reports are contradictory, and it is impossible to establish an accurate course of events, particularly when Deane and Cheshire's understanding of the exact time of zero hour differed by five minutes. Remarkably, it also seems, that Deane was unaware that there were two marking points, or three, if one includes 1 Group's Special Duties Flight. Cheshire, initially at least, appeared happy with the early stages of the attack, and describes the bombing as concentrated and accurate. It seems certain, however, that many minutes had passed between the dropping of Cheshire's markers and the first main force bombs falling, during which period Deane was coming to terms with the fact, that his instructions were not getting through. A plausible scenario is that, in the absence of instructions, and with red spotfires clearly visible in the target, some crews opted to bomb and others followed suit. These would have been predominantly from 5 Group, but as the 1 Group crews became increasingly agitated at having to wait in bright moonlight with evidence of enemy night fighters all around, some of them inevitably joined in.

Now a new problem was arising. Smoke from these first salvos was obliterating the entire camp, and Cheshire had to decide whether to send in Fawke and Kearns to mark the second aiming point. His feeling, and that of Deane, as it later transpired, was that it was unnecessary. The volume of bombs still to fall into the relatively compact area of the target would ensure destruction of the entire site. By 00.16, the first phase of bombing should have been completed, leaving a clear run for Fawke and Kearns across the target. In the event, the majority of 5 Group crews were still on their bombing run, a fact unknown to Cheshire, who asked Deane for a pause in the bombing while the two Mosquitos went in. As far as Cheshire was concerned, there was no response from Deane, who would, anyway, have been confused by mention of a second aiming point of which he was unaware. In the event, Deane's deputy, S/L Sparkes of 83 Squadron, eventually found a channel free of interference, and did, in fact, transmit an instruction to halt the bombing, both by W/T and R/T, and some crews reported hearing something. While utter chaos reigned, Kearns and Fawke dived in among the falling cookies at 00.23 and 00.25 respectively to mark the second aiming point on the western edge of the camp. At 2,000 feet, they were lucky to survive the turbulence created by the exploding 4,000 pounders, when 4,000 feet was considered to be a minimum safe height. They were not entirely happy with their work, but F/O Edwards of 97 Squadron dropped a stick of markers precisely on the mark, and S/L Sparks was then able to call the 1 Group main force in. Meanwhile, the night fighters continued to create havoc among the Lancasters as they milled around in the target area. As burning aircraft were seen to fall all around, some 1 Group crews succumbed to their anxiety and frustration, and in a rare breakdown of R/T discipline let fly with comments of an uncomplimentary nature, many of which were intended for and, indeed, heard by Deane. Despite the confusion the operation was a major success, which destroyed 80 per cent of the camp's buildings, and 102 vehicles, of which thirty-seven were tanks, while over 200 men were killed. Forty-two Lancasters failed to return, two thirds of them from 1 Group. The operation created a great deal of acrimony, and controversy abounds to this day. The fault lay with the inaccurate and contradictory information given at the various briefings, but much of the venom instigated by the heavy losses has unjustly been directed at Cheshire.

For the remainder of the month, the squadron was engaged in intensive training for a special operation in connection with the invasion. So secret was it that the Operations Record Book refers only to limited flying training. Some of the activity took place off the Scottish coast, where captured German radar installations had been set up at Tantallon Castle, and scientists were able to work out how best to create a ghost invasion fleet. Mostly, though, the squadron's tactics were worked out in trials against the Bempton radar at Flamborough Head on the Yorkshire coast near Bridlington, where a final trial was flown without informing the controllers. Their report of a large coastal convoy on their screens confirmed the effectiveness of the plan. As navigation was the critical aspect of the operation, however, the crews spent the bulk of their time concentrating on this using Gee sets. As far as the Command in general was concerned, railway yards and ammunition dumps occupied elements on the 6/7th, and airfields, coastal batteries and ammunition dumps were targeted on the 7/8th. Over 400 aircraft were sent against coastal batteries in the Pas-de-Calais on the 9/10th, to maintain the deception concerning the true location of the forthcoming invasion, and then it was back to railway installations at five sites on the 10/11th. 5 Group attacked a military camp at Bourg-Leopold in Belgium on the 11/12th, but haze forced the Master Bomber to halt proceedings part way through. Later on the 12th, Mosquito NT205 suffered an oleo leg collapse when it swung on take-off with Shannon at the controls.

On the 16th a party was held to celebrate the anniversary of Operation Chastise, and all ex-members of the squadron who took part in the famous operation were invited. Gibson was unable to attend, but he was there for a further celebration in the form of an all-ranks squadron dance on the 19th. Railways and coastal batteries continued to dominate main force activity for the remainder of the month, but Duisburg received its first major raid for a year on the 21/22nd, and Dortmund was similarly honoured twenty-four hours later. A 5 Group contingent participated in the former, but while the latter was in progress, the Independent Air Force returned to Brunswick, and again failed to deliver a telling blow. An attack by elements from all but 5 Group on two railway yards at Aachen on the 24/25th developed into an area raid, while small 5 Group forces were assigned to factories at Eindhoven and Antwerp, although neither of these operations was satisfactorily concluded. Other Dams veterans to depart during the course of the month of May were Johnson of McCarthy's crew, Clay of Munro's, Goodale of Shannon's and Whittaker of Martin's.

Chapter Thirteen

The Summer of '44

Taxable and Tallboy, Flying bombs, railways, oil and tactical support

June was to be another busy month for the Command, and the first four nights brought attacks on coastal batteries, signals and radar stations and communications ahead of D-Day. Over a thousand aircraft were aloft on the night of the 5/6th, D-Day eve, to target ten coastal batteries, while support and diversionary operations involved others. At briefings crews were not informed of the significance of the night's operations, but there was a strict ban on jettisoning bombs over the sea, and all were ordered to maintain briefed flight levels. 617 Squadron's contribution was perhaps the least spectacular of all its operations, although one of the most exacting and arduous, and certainly, one of the most important. Sixteen aircraft were detailed for Operation Taxable, the purpose behind all the secretive training in May. As already mentioned, this was a 'spoof', an exercise designed to simulate an invasion fleet on enemy radar screens. The intention was to divert the enemy's attention away from the actual landing grounds along the Normandy coast, by making them believe the invasion was destined for the Pas-de-Calais, thus reinforcing an already long-held German conviction. A similar operation conducted at a different location by 218 Squadron Stirlings under the code name, Operation Glimmer, would compound the deception. No details of this highly secret operation were made available for entry into the Operations Record Book.

Each 617 Squadron Lancaster carried two pilots, and up to twelve other crew members. Cheshire led the operation and the first of two sections in LM482 as second pilot to Munro, while the McCarthy/Shannon combination headed the second section in LM492. The other participating pilots and aircraft were; Reid/Kearns in ME557, Clayton/Carey in ME560, Wilson/Sanders in LM485, N. Ross/Fearn in ME562, Edward/I. Ross in EE131, Kell/Cheney in DV402, Stout/Watts in ME559, Willsher/Howard in DV393, Lee/Fawke in DV246, Knights/Poore in DV385, Williams/Stanford in ME554, Hamilton/Levy in DV403, Duffy/Gingles in ME555, and Knilans/Castagnola in ME561. In order to give the impression of a fleet of ships advancing at eight knots towards the French coast at Cap d'Antifer, sixty miles east of the Normandy beaches, eight 617 Squadron Lancasters had to fly line abreast two miles apart at 180 miles an hour dispensing Window at the rate of one bundle every five seconds. After heading for the French coast for two and a half minutes, all aircraft turned to port to complete a reciprocal course lasting two minutes and ten seconds. Each new circuit advanced the forward travel of the formation by one minute. The second section would take off later to be in place to relieve the first section after two hours. Any deviation from the detail of the plan, particularly with regard to timing, would be detected on the enemy radar screens, and would raise suspicions. The operation began with the departure of the first eight aircraft from Woodhall Spa shortly after 23.00 hours to take up their starting position off the Sussex coast at around midnight. Each aircraft remained airborne for four and a half hours, two of which were spent dropping Window and the crews flew their routines flawlessly, if unspectacularly. As dawn's early light began to break, all returned safely from their contribution to the landings on Fortress Europe. There was no reaction from the German side, but the operation had been just one of many designed to deceive and confuse, and in this, history shows it to have been successful.

Bomber Command aircraft were taking off throughout this momentous night, and some of those returning as daylight broke were rewarded with a glimpse through breaks in the cloud of the giant armada ploughing its furrow across the Channel below. It became a sad night for 5 Group, after W/C Jimmy Carter, 97 Squadron's commanding officer, failed to return from an operation against a coastal battery at St-Pierre-du-Mont. He and his highly experienced and decorated eight-man crew were lost without trace on a night of relatively few casualties.

A further 1,000 aircraft were employed against road and railway communications targets on D-Day night, and it was similar fare, although in smaller numbers, on the 7/8th and 8/9th. As part of this campaign to prevent the movement of enemy forces to the battle area, 617 Squadron was assigned to the destruction of the Saumur Tunnel between Tours and Angers, through which an important line linked south-western France with Normandy. It was an opportunity for the Squadron to renew the association with Barnes Wallis more than a year after its success with Upkeep. This time they would be carrying his 12,000lb Tallboy deep penetration bomb operationally for the first time. The Tallboy was a 21 foot long aerodynamic and ballistically perfect weapon, engineered to a very high standard. It was the next step in Wallis's use of shock wave technology to destroy otherwise impregnable structures. The shark-like projectile had to withstand an impact velocity, if dropped from its optimum height of 18,000 feet, of 750 mph, after falling for thirty-seven seconds. In order to achieve this without breaking up, it boasted a case thickness near its nose of more than four inches, and carried a charge weight of 5,200lb of Torpex. The depth of penetration into the earth depended upon the fuse delay time from 0.025 seconds upwards. At deepest penetration it was estimated to be capable of displacing one million cubic feet of earth, and creating a crater requiring 5,000 tons of earth to refill it. An instantaneous detonation, on the other hand, would produce a crater 25 feet in depth, and more than 80 yards across. In time, this revolutionary weapon would prove to have a number of unanticipated abilities.

The operation got under way with the departure of the Lancaster element, beginning with Kearns at 22.45. The crews involved in the main operation were those of Cheshire in NT202, Shannon and Fawke, it is believed in DZ418 and DZ421 respectively, although there is some dispute, Munro in LM482, McCarthy in LM492, Wilson in LM485, Kearns in DV246, Edward in EE131, Clayton in ME560, Poore in DV391, Reid in ME557, Duffy in ME555, Stanford in ME554, Stout in ME559, Cheney in JB139, Knights in DV385, Hamilton in DV403, Willsher in DV393, Nick Ross in ME562, Fearn in DV380, Kell in DV402 and Knilans in ME561, all of whom carried a Tallboy. A second element, consisting of Sanders in ED909, Martin's original Dams Lancaster, Levy in ND631, Watts in ED933, Castagnola in ND472, Ian Ross in JB370 and Carey in EE146, took off at the same time with a load of eight 1,000 pounders and six seven-inch clusters each to use against the nearby Saumur bridge. This operation would bring another milestone in the distinguished career of Nicky Ross, his seventieth sortie. In addition to the 617 Squadron effort, four 83 Squadron Lancasters were on hand to provide the illumination for this hurriedly prepared operation. Shannon's sortie was over almost as soon as it began, after an overspeeding port engine forced him to return some twenty minutes or so after take-off. The others arrived in the target area around 02.00 hours, and Cheshire delivered his spotfires at 02.06 after diving onto the southern aiming point from 3,000 to 500 feet. He complained that the flares were dropped too far to the south and the east, and only the last two or three were of any use. Some time later Fawke dropped three red spotfires onto the northern end of the tunnel, where the bridge was situated, and had time to witness the bombing of Cheshire's markers before his fuel situation demanded he turn for home.

Cheshire reported copious amounts of smoke as a result of the bombing, but considered that further backing up would not improve the situation. He observed 50 per cent of the bombs falling within 100 yards of the markers, with just one or two very wide of the mark. Munro recorded that the markers were in the cutting, and that most of the bombs fell around them, and he saw one direct hit. Bombing altitudes for those with Tallboys ranged from Hamilton's 8,200 feet to McCarthy's 10,500 feet, while those with 1,000 pounders attacked from between 3,000 and 6,500 feet. Sanders reported seeing a direct hit on the bridge five minutes before he bombed, and Watts thought the last three bombs of his stick fell directly onto it. One direct hit was scored on the tunnel, which blew a hole in the roof, and, it was hoped, that this might have brought tons of earth crashing down onto the track. Wilson made several runs across the southern aiming point, but found the marker extinguished before he was able to bomb. He finally released his Tallboy at the bridge, and saw it impact about 100 yards from the markers, observing many blue sparks near the bomb burst. Photographic reconnaissance showed an 85-foot diameter crater in the roof of the tunnel, and a total of seventeen others of varying dimensions within 220 yards of the southern entrance. The tracks were cut around 100 yards from this entrance, while a near miss on a road/rail intersection some distance away had cut all tracks and damaged the road. There was also a large crater blocking a road 180 yards east of the northern entrance. The evidence pointed to an entirely successful operation, and it seemed at least, that the tracks were still blocked up to two months after the operation. However, documentation surfaced after the war to suggest that the tunnel had been quickly returned to use by the Germans, but that the appearance of devastation was allowed to remain to give a false impression and discourage a further attack. This was a ploy later used at the Dortmund-Ems Canal. Whatever the truth, it was a very creditable performance by the crews, considering the absolute minimum of training allowed them. The entire month of May and first week of June had been taken up with the training for Operation Taxable, leaving just two days to prepare for Saumur. Once the crews became accustomed to the routine of delivering Tallboys, the margin of error would reduce to a matter of a few dozen yards.

On the 9/10th the emphasis for the main force was switched to four airfields south of the beachhead, Flers, Le Mans, Laval and Rennes, which were bombed by elements of 1, 4, 6 and 8 Groups to prevent them from being used by the enemy to bring up reinforcements. The six H2s equipped Lancasters returned to their former squadrons on the 10th, and with them went the ground crews, while the aircrews remained at 617 Squadron. Railway targets featured for the main force on the next three nights, and on the last of these, the 12/13th, a new oil campaign began at Gelsenkirchen. Elements of 1, 3 and 8 Groups carried out a highly accurate attack on the Nordstern refinery, and halted all production for several weeks at a cost to the enemy of 1,000 tons of aviation fuel per day. The 14th brought the Command's first daylight operations since the departure of 2 Group twelve months earlier. The raid took place in two waves against *S-Boots* and other fast, light marine craft moored in the harbour at Le Havre, which posed a threat to Allied shipping supplying the Normandy beachhead. The first phase was a predominantly 1 Group affair, which took place in the late evening, and included the participation of what amounted to a maximum effort by 617 Squadron. Its contribution involved three Mosquitos and twenty-two Lancasters, whose crews were to aim their Tallboys at either the *S-Boot* pens or at the *S-Boots* themselves moored in the harbour, and the whole operation was conducted under the umbrella of a fighter escort. The Mosquito element again consisted of Cheshire, Shannon and Fawke in NT202, DZ484 and DZ418 respectively, and the Lancaster crews assigned to the *S-Boot* pens were those of Munro in LM482, Poore in DV391, Clayton in ME560, Williams in EE131, Edward in EE146, Kearns in DV246, Nick Ross in ME562, Duffy in ME555, Hamilton in DV403, Kell in DV402, Stout in ME559, and Cheney in JB139. Those briefed to attack the *S-Boots* were McCarthy in LM492, Wilson in LM485, Fearn in DV380, Reid in ME557,

Howard in ED763, Knilans in ME561, Knights in DV385, Stanford in ME554, Willsher in DV393 and Gingles in LM489. A time on target of shortly after 22.30 had the Lancasters taking off between 20.10 and 20.25, while the Mosquito crews stayed at home for another hour. Cheshire records the squadron arriving at the target a little early, but going straight in to mark. He delivered his offset spotfires in between the two aiming points at 22.30½ after diving to 7,000 feet through fierce light flak, and within seconds the Tallboys were raining down onto the aiming points from 15,500 to 19,000 feet. Shannon and Fawke remained on standby to remark the aiming point if required, but this proved to be unnecessary. The offset method of marking allowed the spotfires to remain visible even though the aiming points themselves became obscured by smoke, part of which emanated from defensive smoke installations belonging to the occupiers. All the crews reported the bombing as accurate, with a number of direct hits on the pens and two enormous explosions at around 22.26, and McCarthy saw sticks of 1 Group bombs fall across the jetties. The raid was successfully concluded without loss to 617 Squadron, although Knights and Knilans returned with flak damage, and Sgt Crosby in Knilans's mid-upper turret collected a piece of shrapnel in his thigh and was admitted to station sick quarters. A predominantly 3 Group force followed up as darkness was falling, and few, if any of the enemy craft remained unscathed.

On the following evening an operation was mounted against a similar target at Boulogne by elements of 1, 4, 5, 6 and 8 Groups, but thick cloud over the target created problems, which were compounded by heavy and accurate flak. Cheshire was in NT202, the lone 617 Squadron Mosquito in action, and the Lancaster crews were those of Munro in LM482, McCarthy in LM492, Kearns in DV246, Clayton in ME560, Wilson in LM485, Howard in ED763, Poore in DV391, Fearn in DV380, Reid in ME557, Edward in EE146, Williams in EE131, Stout in ME559, Willsher in DV393, Knilans in ME561, Stanford in ME554, Knights in DV385, Nick Ross in ME562, Duffy in ME555, Hamilton in DV403, Cheney in JB139, Kell in DV402 and Gingles in LM489. Cheshire followed hard on the heels of the Oboe Mosquitos, and confirmed the accuracy of their target indicators for the 1 Group attack. However, recognising that the 617 Squadron Lancaster crews would not be able to make a visual identification of the aiming point because of the cloud, he retained his own red spotfires. Munro, meanwhile, had assessed the conditions as unfit for bombing, and ordered the squadron to return home, but Cheshire immediately called to say that it was clear below 8,000 feet. Munro descended, having rescinded his instruction, but on encountering poor visibility and enemy opposition at the lower altitude, he reinstated the order to go home. By this time Wilson, Howard, Poore, Stout, Willsher, Knilans, Stanford, Knights, Hamilton and Gingles had bombed from between 8,000 and 12,000 feet, but with one exception, the others brought their precious Tallboys home. McCarthy was thrown off course by the heavy flak during his bombing run, and having gone round for a second go, discovered that his Tallboy had already fallen off somewhere. On his way out of the target area at 22.45, Cheshire dropped two 500 pounders from 6,000 feet onto a flak position. The cloud also brought darkness earlier than on the previous night, and Stout made the point, that an earlier attack would have improved the bombing conditions. Despite the difficulties the raid was assessed as a great success. The pens were hit several times, and many of the dock facilities were severely damaged by the main force attack. There was also much loss of shipping, and rail facilities were disrupted. The port arsenal was almost entirely razed to the ground, and, inevitably, the town itself suffered severe damage. Hamilton's Lancaster was damaged by flak on this occasion, and he landed at West Malling, where his bomb-aimer, F/O Duck, was admitted to hospital with serious injuries.

The night of the 16/17th brought the start of another new campaign for the increasingly stretched resources of the Pathfinder and main force squadrons, this one against flying bomb launching and storage sites in France. The Command was to make a heavy commitment to eliminating this threat, and that of the other V-Weapons over the succeeding two and a half months, and 617 Squadron was to play a major role. The squadron was not involved on this first night, when elements of 1, 4, 5, 6 and 8 Groups accurately bombed four sites. Also on this night, 1, 4, 6 and 8 Group aircraft continued the assault on the enemy's oil industry with a scattered attack on the refinery at Sterkrade/Holten. The offensive against railways would also continue throughout the summer, and the bulk of the aircraft operating on the 17/18th were assigned to three such targets in France.

A concrete structure that was originally intended as a V-weapon storage and launching site at Watten became the objective for two 617 Squadron Mosquitos and nineteen Tallboy-carrying Lancasters in daylight on the 19th. Attacks on the site during 1943 had caused so much damage, that its purpose had been changed to the production of liquid oxygen for V-2s, which were to be launched from elsewhere. The construction was still in progress, and the site was not operational by this stage. Cheshire and Shannon led in NT202 and DZ421 respectively, while the Lancaster crews were those of McCarthy in LM482, Wilson in DV380, Poore in DV391, Clayton in ME560, Duffy in ME555, Cheney in JB139, Hamilton in DV403, Gingles in LM489, Edward in EE146, Reid in ME557, Williams in EE131, Howard in ED763, Knilans in ME561, Nick Ross in ME554, Knights in DV385, Stout in ME559, Willsher in DV393 and Kell in DV402. Nine Oboe Mosquitos provided the initial marking, before Cheshire delivered two red spotfires at 19.40 after diving to 3,000 feet. He was unable to see any result, though, and assumed that they had failed to ignite. Despite this, Shannon was not called in to back-up. The squadron was supposed to bomb in three waves, but the attack became a collection of single aircraft. As Knilans made his bombing run his bombsight became unserviceable, and all switches were put to 'safe'. Twenty seconds later the Tallboy fell off, and impacted about two and a half miles south of the target. This was observed by Jimmy Castagnola, who was not on the order of battle, but was flying with Knilans as a passenger, while some members of his and other crews did likewise in other aircraft. Kit Howard's Tallboy hung up, and he brought it home. The conditions thwarted the crews' best efforts, and no Tallboys fell closer to the concrete structure than 50 yards, although an immediate post raid report suggested an aiming point photo had identified one hit. A similar operation was attempted on the following day at a V-Weapon store at Wizernes, for which three Mosquitos and seventeen Lancasters were dispatched, but this had to be aborted because of excessive cloud. A second attempt launched on the 22nd was again frustrated by cloud, but it was only delaying the inevitable.

On the 24th Cheshire and Fawke led another operation against the target at Wizernes in NT202 and DZ415, and the sixteen Lancaster crews were those of Munro in LM482, McCarthy in ME559, Edward in DV403, Kell in DV402, Howard in ED763, Nick Ross in ME561, Reid in ME557, Williams in EE131, Wilson in DV380, Cheney in JB139, Willsher in DV393, Stanford in ME554, Gingles in LM489, Knights in DV385, Poore in DV391 and Clayton in ME560. The Lancasters took off in a ten-minute slot to 16.30, and both Mosquitos were in pursuit within twenty-five minutes. The Mosquitos were carrying four smoke bombs and two red spotfires, but Cheshire found he was unable to release either because of technical problems. Fawke delivered his at 17.50 after diving from 17,000 to 6,000 feet, and then watched the Tallboys winging down from either side of 17,000 feet. Bomb bursts were observed all around the target, on the railway line and near the mouth of the tunnel, and Bill Reid saw one Tallboy penetrate the roof, and appear to burst inside causing an eruption but no smoke. A number of very near misses were claimed, and, as Barnes Wallis was to assert, a near miss with an earthquake bomb was probably more effective than a direct hit, and would destroy a concrete structure by its shock wave effect. It was on this operation that the squadron suffered its first loss since April, when DV403 was shot down by flak over the target right in the middle of the attack. The Lancaster was seen by other crews to be hit in a wing, and to lose height slowly as fire took hold, before falling out of control and exploding above the ground. A number of parachutes were reported, and three of the crew, navigator F/O Pritchard, bomb-aimer F/S Brook and wireless operator F/S Hobbs, did survive. Sadly, F/L Edward DFC, his flight engineer and two gunners were killed, while the Canadian mid-upper gunner, P/O Johnston DFC, succumbed to his injuries shortly afterwards.

The main force had also been busy during this period, and 5 Group entered the oil campaign on the 21/22nd, when sending separate forces to attack the refineries at Wesseling near Cologne and Scholven-Buer in the Ruhr near Gelsenkirchen. Five ABC Lancasters from 1 Group were also involved at the former, while Oboe Mosquitos and a number of Pathfinder Lancasters were in attendance at the latter. The forecast clear weather conditions failed to materialize, and it proved impossible for the 627 Squadron Mosquitos to mark either target from low level. Bombing was conducted at Wesseling on

H2s alone, and at Scholven on skymarkers. A modest amount of damage was inflicted on both sites, but the Wesseling force was badly mauled by night fighters, and a massive thirty-seven aircraft were shot down. This amounted to almost 28 per cent of those despatched, and 44, 49, 57 and 619 Squadrons all lost six aircraft each. Earlier in the day a Mustang had arrived at Woodhall Spa as a gift from the American 8th Air Force, to act as the personal chariot of Cheshire, and it would not be long before he took it into battle for the first time. Railways and V-Weapon sites provided the targets for main force operations on the 22nd, 22/23rd, 23/24th, 24th and 24/25th.

On the morning of the 25th Cheshire climbed into his Mustang, HB837, for the very first time to prepare to lead a squadron contingent against a V-Weapon storage site at Siracourt, a target that had been attacked by a main force element a few days earlier. HB837 is believed to have been assigned an AJ-N code, but photographic evidence suggests that it actually bore no squadron markings, although it did have D-Day stripes. Also operating were two Mosquitos, NT205 and NT202, in the hands of Shannon and Fawke respectively, and seventeen Lancasters. These contained the crews of Munro in LM482, McCarthy in ME559, Clayton in ME560, Williams in EE131, Poore in DV380, Wilson in LM485, Howard in ED763, Reid in ME557, Nick Ross in ME561, Gingles in LM489, Kearns in ME554, Knights in DV385, Stanford in ME555, Carey in EE146, Kell in DV402, Willsher in DV393, and F/O Lee in JB139, on his first operation with the squadron. For the first time in his operational career Cheshire would have to navigate himself to the target, and this he managed to do, before diving from 7,000 to 500 feet to deliver his two spot fires at a few seconds after 09.00. The ORB suggests that Shannon put down smoke bombs and red target indicators, but Fawke's were not required. Shannon estimated three direct hits on the aiming point, and Fawke reported at least two, Williams claiming one of them, and Gingles suspecting that he scored another. Howard and Reid both suffered hang-ups on their first run, but released successfully on their second. The concentration of bombing around the aiming point was excellent, and the target was left wrecked. A number of accounts suggest that Cheshire's first landing in his new Mustang had to be undertaken in darkness. This is not so. The Command devoted the 25th to operations against flying bomb related targets, and all took place simultaneously in the morning, three other sites in the Pas-de-Calais coming under attack by around 300 aircraft from 1, 4, 6 and 8 Groups. The 617 Squadron ORB shows Cheshire landing at 10.18, in time for an early lunch, and even had the timings been transposed by twelve hours to the evening, with double summertime in force, 22.18 would still have been in daylight. Towards the end of the month, P/O Castagnola, a Maltese, was posted back to 57 Squadron, but it was a temporary move, and he would return in August. The remainder of the month was devoted to the same round of operations by the main force against railways and V-Weapon sites, while 617 Squadron, despite remaining on standby from the 27th to the 30th, stayed at home.

July opened as June had closed, with 617 Squadron crews standing by for operations on each of the first three days. It was similar fare also for the main force crews in terms of targets, flying bomb sites providing employment for over 300 aircraft on both the 1st and 2nd. It was the 4th before the Independent Air Force was next invited to re-enter the fray, when it was called upon to attack a V-Weapon storage site in caves at St-Leu-d'Esserent, some thirty miles north of Paris. The caves had originally been used for growing mushrooms, and they were protected by some 25 feet of clay and soft limestone, to say nothing of the anti-aircraft defences brought in by the Germans. There is some confusion concerning the timing of the operation, which involved not only seventeen Lancasters, a Mustang and a Mosquito from 617 Squadron, but also 231 Lancasters and fifteen Mosquitos from the Group, and a number of Pathfinder aircraft, which were probably Oboe Mosquitos to provide an initial reference point. Some accounts suggest that 617 Squadron attacked early in the evening, and was followed by the Group later on. However, the squadron's ORB shows the Lancaster element taking off either side of 23.30 hours on the 4th, and this coincides with the departure times for the rest of the Group. There were, in fact, two aiming points, the area dump for the main force, and the tunnel complex at Creil, a settlement three miles north-east of St Leu for 617 Squadron.

Cheshire got away in the Mustang at 00.15, four minutes after Fawke in NT205. The Lancaster crews were those of Munro in LM482, McCarthy in LM492, Wilson in LM485, Howard in ME557, Stout in ME559, Poore in DV391, Ian Ross in ME560, Knilans in ME561, Duffy in ME555, Sanders in DV385, Watts in ED763, Willsher in DV393, Williams in EE131, Lee in JB139, Kell in DV402, Pryor in ME562 and Gingles in LM489. At 01.30 Cheshire dived to 800 feet to deliver two red target indicators, but was unable to take any further part in the operation because of an unserviceable VHF set. Perhaps this accounts for Fawke not being invited to back up the markers, although he may not have been called in anyway. Twelve of the squadron's crews sent their Tallboys to earth from between 17,000 and 18,700 feet, but smoke began to obscure the aiming point, and five others, Poore, Ross, Sanders, Watts and Williams, brought their Tallboys home. There were no casualties among the 617 Squadron element, but the main force lost thirteen Lancasters, most of them to night fighters. The attack was a success on all counts, with a large section of earth measuring some 200 × 400 feet receiving a large number of hits and collapsing into underground workings. Railway tracks leading to the target were also cut by at least twenty-five craters, and a railway bridge over the River Oise was hit and partially destroyed.

On the 5th, having disposed of one enemy threat, the squadron took on the men of 627 Squadron in a cricket match, and disposed of them also! Meanwhile, on the same day over at 55 Base, East Kirkby, Guy Gibson was reacquainting himself with the Lancaster after his enforced long separation from the type. He spent half an hour stooging around Lincolnshire with Drew Wyness and his crew on an air-test, Wyness having been posted to 57

Squadron as a flight commander on his return to operations after a period of screening. Gibson had been posted to 55 Base in mid June as understudy to the base operations officer after completing a staff course.

On the 6th over 500 aircraft were engaged on operations against V-Weapon targets, and 617 Squadron was assigned to a V-3 super gun site at Mimoyecques. This massive underground site in the Pas de Calais was being constructed by thousands of slave labourers to house twenty-five enormous gun barrels aimed at London some ninety miles away. The guns, which, at 420 feet in length, were the largest in the world, were manufactured at the Krupp works in Essen, and used a multiple charge system to fire 150mm calibre shells with a muzzle velocity of 5,000 feet per second at the rate of five per minute. So deep were the tunnels built to house the weapon that very little of the site was visible from above ground.

Although Cheshire did not know, this was to be his final operation, not only with 617 Squadron, but also of the war in Europe. He took off in the Mustang at 14.23, and was followed a minute later by Fawke in Mosquito NT205. Seventeen Lancasters had already departed up to forty-five minutes earlier, and they were captained by Munro in LM482, Wilson in LM485, Stout in ME559, Ian Ross in ME560, Kell in DV402, Lee in JB139, Pryor in DV385, Fearn in DV380, Gingles in EE146, Poore in DV391, Willsher in DV393, Watts in ME557, Stanford in EE131, Howard in ED763, Nick Ross in ME562, Duffy in ME555 and Knilans in ME561. The target was difficult to identify because of all the craters from previous attacks, and even after Cheshire had opened the proceedings with a dive to 800 feet to deliver two red spotfires at 15.24, they did not show up well in daylight. Fawke was carrying two 500 pounders, and he dropped these onto a flak position in the target area. Arthur Kell lost an engine during his first run, so he went round again, while Lee was forced to jettison his bomb in the target area after being hit by flak. Paddy Gingles's bomb-aimer was unable to draw a bead on the target during the first run, and as they approached the aiming point for the second time he found it obscured by smoke and debris, so their Tallboy was dutifully returned to the bomb store. Freddie Watts and Nicky Knilans also brought their Tallboys back, the former after failing to identify the aiming point in time, while the latter had his bombsight fail. Again, a number of direct hits were scored, Duffy claiming one of them, and provisional reconnaissance revealed four deep craters in the immediate target area, one causing a large corner of the concrete slab to collapse. Seven other large craters were seen in the immediate vicinity of the target. Not only was this Cheshire's final operation, it also signalled the end for Nick Ross on a grand total of seventy-seven. He would be signed out on posting to 1661CU by 617's new commander, James Tait, on the 15th with the endorsement in his logbook, 'This officer has had an outstanding operational career. His courage and competency are worth the highest praise'. As confirmation of this he was awarded the DSO.

There would be no further operations for 617 Squadron until the 17th, but the Group returned to St-Leu-d'Esserent on the 7/8th. Although the operation was successful in blocking the entrance to the caves and the approach roads, enemy night fighters exacted a heavy toll of twenty-nine Lancasters and two Mosquitos. Earlier in the evening, elements of 1, 4, 6 and 8 Groups had begun yet another new campaign, to provide tactical support for British and Canadian ground forces as they attempted to spread out from the beach-head. More than 400 aircraft were involved in attacks on open ground between fortified villages north of Caen and the city itself. On the 10th Gibson teamed up with 'Mick' Martin for a local trip in a Mosquito, and this, without question, would have had him salivating at the prospect of returning to operations. The various campaigns would continue in the hands of the main force, while 617 Squadron stayed on the ground, and on the 12th, W/C Cheshire was posted from the squadron to 5 Group HQ, from where he proceeded to a Senior Commanders course at Cranwell. He had now completed one hundred operations in a glittering career spanning four operational tours, and this was to be capped by the award of the Victoria Cross two months later.

Cheshire was succeeded by the highly experienced W/C James Tait, who was apparently known to some as 'Willie'. In keeping with commanders since Gibson, Tait had 4 Group blood coursing through his veins, and had served previously with a number of its leading squadrons. It was no easy matter to find an officer of the appropriate stature to command such an elite body of men, who could step easily into the shoes of someone as unique as Cheshire. Tait was such a man. He had commanded 51 Squadron briefly between December 1940 and January 1941, before leading the Bomber Command contribution to the earlier-described ill-fated Operation Colossus from Malta, the airborne undertaking by the SAS in Italy in February 1941. He was posted to 35 Squadron shortly after its re-formation to introduce the Halifax to operations, and took command of 10 Squadron in April 1942, as stand-in for W/C Don Bennett, now AOC the Pathfinders, who was evading capture to return home from Norway after a failed assault on the *Tirpitz*. Tait then moved on to the command of 78 Squadron in July, and remained in post until November. Thereafter he completed a spell at 22 OTU, before joining 5 Group as Base Operations Officer at Waddington, where he apparently managed to notch up a number of further operations. He formally took command of 617 Squadron on the 12th of July. Also departing during the month were the three flight commanders and squadron founder members, Shannon, Munro and McCarthy. It was the end of an era. Munro went to 1690 BDTF on the 13th, McCarthy to 61 Base on the 20th, and Shannon to 27 OTU on the 24th.

On the 14th 'Mac' Hamilton flew to West Malling to collect his bomb-aimer, F/O Duck, who had spent the previous month in hospital, and was still a stretcher case. On board with him were the station medical officer and a WAAF nurse, who, along with the crew, survived unscathed the subsequent collapse of an oleo leg on landing at Woodhall Spa, which resulted in both port engines bursting into flames.

On the 17th W/C Tait led the squadron for the first time in a return to the V-Weapon store at Wizernes. He was in the Mustang, and according to the ORB, so was S/L Danny Walker as navigator. As the Mustang is a single-seater he must have been sitting either on the tail or on Tait's lap! Fawke took off first in NT202 at 11.28, a minute before his boss, but both had been preceded by the Lancaster element, which consisted of the crews of Knights in DV385, Pryor in LM485, Stanford in ME554, Lee in LM492, Fearn in DV380, Gingles in LM489, Kell in DV402, Willsher in DV393, Watts in DV246, Sanders in ME562, Knilans in ME561, Stout in ME559, Duffy in ME555, Hamilton in EE146, Cheney in LM482 and Levy in ED763. Fifty-nine minutes after take-off Tait dived to 500 feet to release two red spotfires onto the aiming point, and a minute and a half later Fawke did likewise from 3,000 feet. Over the next sixteen minutes the Tallboys rained down, and bomb bursts were seen all around the structure. One direct hit on the concrete dome was claimed by Bob Knights, but this proved to be an error, as photo reconnaissance revealed that no direct hits had been scored. There were, however, two large craters in an adjoining quarry, which caused a minor landslide, and evidence of other hits on the railway track and the tunnel entrance. It was a very successful operation, which sealed once and for all the fate of the site, although this was not at the time appreciated, and further operations against it would take place. Halifaxes and Stirlings were also in action on this day against two other flying-bomb related targets, and no losses were incurred during any of these operations.

Early on the following morning over 900 aircraft took off to lend support to Operation Goodwood, an armoured advance by the British Second Army in the Caen area. Five fortified villages to the east of the town were attacked in carefully controlled operations, which also involved elements from American units, and Bomber Command delivered 5,000 of the total of 6,800 tons of bombs dropped. This day also saw the arrival on posting to 617 Squadron of F/L Oram and his crew from 50 Squadron, and the appointment of Gerry Fawke as C Flight commander in place of Joe McCarthy. That night, 1, 6 and 8 Groups raided to great effect the oil refineries at Wesseling and Scholven-Buer, and halted production for a period at both plants. F/L Iveson, a future flight commander, came from 5 LFS on the 22nd, while F/L 'Bunny' Clayton went to 1663CU on the 23rd, at the conclusion of his tour. The following day brought daylight operations by elements of 5 and 8 Groups against two flying bomb sites. East Kirkby provided aircraft for the one at Thiverny, and piloting a 630 Squadron Lancaster with some of F/S Bowers's crew and a S/L Miller as navigator was Gibson. He returned triumphant with his first aiming point photograph for more than a year. On the 20/21st, W/C Tait led the squadron back to Wizernes, this time in Mosquito DZ484 with Danny Walker as navigator, with Fawke and Tom Bennett in DZ534, but adverse weather conditions prevented an attack from taking place, and the fifteen

Lancasters all returned with their Tallboys. Later on the 21st ED936, Rice's Chastise Lancaster, crashed at Woodhall Spa, presumably on landing after a training flight or an air-test, and it was subsequently struck off charge.

It had been two months since Harris had been able to launch a heavy attack against an urban target in Germany, and during this period it had been left to the Mosquito squadrons of 8 Group's Light Night Striking Force to disturb the sleep of the populace with nuisance raids. On the 23/24th more than 600 aircraft headed for Kiel, and emerged suddenly from behind an RCM screen provided by 100 Group, to catch the town's defences completely by surprise. All parts of the town were hit, in what was its most damaging raid of the war, and the *U-Boot* yards and naval installations were included in the extensive catalogue of destruction. The first of three raids on Stuttgart in five nights began on the 24/25th, and by the conclusion of the series on the 28/29th the city's central districts lay in ruins. On the morning of the 25th the Mustang and Mosquito NT205, with Tait and Fawke respectively at the controls, led sixteen Lancasters against the V-Weapon site at Watten. The Lancaster crews were those of Knilans in ME561, Poore in DV391, Hamilton in LM485, Sanders in ME562, Ian Ross in ME555, Williams in LM489, Reid in ME557, Howard in ED763, Stanford in ME554, Fearn in DV380, Levy in DV402, Watts in LM492, Knights in DV385, Stout in ME559, Cheney in DV393, and Carey in LM482. Even for the lumbering Lancasters this was an operation of less than three hours duration, and Tait would be back home in under two. The heavy element took off either side of 07.30, while Fawke got away at 08.10 and Tait eight minutes later. On arrival over the target Tait found marking to be unnecessary, and all but two of the Tallboys went scything down in a ninety second slot from 09.09½. 'Mac' Hamilton was the first to bomb, and he claimed a direct hit, while a second bull's eye was registered by Poore. Heavy and accurate flak was encountered, which damaged a number of aircraft, including Cheney's, and in the confusion caused by the loss of the intercom, his mid-upper gunner, Sgt McRostie, baled out and fell into enemy hands. The Tallboy was jettisoned a short distance south-south-east of the target, and the aircraft returned safely along with the rest of the squadron participants. There was much smoke and dust over the target area after the bombing, and the Tallboys had ½ hour delay fuses, preventing an immediate assessment of the outcome, but later reconnaissance showed at least two direct hits.

The 30th was devoted to operations in support of American ground forces in the Villers Bocage-Caumont area, for which almost 700 aircraft were dispatched, but cloud caused problems, and only a little over half of the force was able to deliver an attack. On the 31st 617 Squadron led a raid by ninety-seven Lancasters and six Mosquitos from 5 and 8 Groups on a V-weapon storage site in a railway tunnel at Rilly-la-Montagne. The 617 Squadron contingent consisted of Tait in Mosquito NT202 with Danny Walker in the right hand seat, Duffy in NT205 with F/O Don Bell beside him, and the crews of Sanders in ME562, Ian Ross in LM489, Knights in DV385, Reid in ME557,

Poore in DV391, Stanford in ME554, Hamilton in LM485, Stout in ME559, Willsher in LM492, Cheney in JB139, Howard in ED763, Fearn in DV380, Levy in DV402, Knilans in ME561, Williams in EE131 and Carey in DV246. Tait again decided, that the target was clearly visible after marking by Pathfinder Oboe Mosquitos, and the main force was called in without further marking being required. Two aiming points were employed, one at each end of the tunnel, and the 617 Squadron crews were divided between them. Ross, Knights, Williams and Carey were unable to pick up the aiming point in time, and brought their Tallboys home. The others went down within two minutes of each other from 20.18, while the 5 Group main force also peppered the site. A partially successful conclusion to the operation was marred by the loss of F/L Reid VC and his crew in ME557, which was struck by bombs from one of these 5 Group Lancasters flying well above. It happened only seconds after the Tallboy was released, and caused severe structural damage to the central fuselage, and tore out an engine on the port side. The gaggle was operating at between 16,000 and 17,000 feet at the time, and it took four minutes for the Lancaster to crash, after eventually breaking up in the air. Only Reid and his wireless operator, F/O Luker, survived, and they both fell into enemy hands. This was the day that brought another new arrival to the squadron in the form of F/L Cockshott from 1660CU, and he would be promoted to squadron leader to become a flight commander.

Chapter Fourteen

Life, and Sometimes Death, at Woodhall Spa

August's operations began for the squadron with an intended attack on a V-Weapon site at Siracourt in the late afternoon of the 1st. This was just one of numerous operations during the day against similar targets involving over 700 aircraft, most of which ended with a recall, presumably through unfavourable weather conditions. Tait led the flight out in Mosquito NT202 accompanied by fifteen Lancasters, but on arrival in the target area he found the target obscured by thick cloud and sent the squadron home. Attacks by daylight on flying bomb sites dominated the first six days of the month, but 617 Squadron's next target would be a bridge at Etaples on the morning of the 4th. In the meantime, though, on the 3rd, F/L Kearns was posted to 17 OTU at the conclusion of his tour. Tait was back in the Mustang for the Etaples Bridge, while Duffy flew NT205 as the lone Mosquito. The Lancaster crews were those of Howard in ED763, Poore in DV391, Fearn in DV380, Knilans in ME561, Oram on his first trip with the squadron in LM485, Stout in ME559, Willsher in LM492, Cheney in JB139, Kell in DV402, Levy in DV246, Williams in EE131, Ian Ross in ME554 and Gingles in LM489. Tait dived to 1,500 feet to deliver a smoke bomb as a marker, and Duffy attempted to do likewise at the southern end of the bridge, but nothing happened. Unusually, the Lancasters were each carrying twelve 1,000lb bombs, and these went down in a hail either side of 10.58. A number scored direct hits, while a few others straddled the structure, but the majority seemed to overshoot, possibly as a result of the cloudy conditions, and the bridge remained intact. Don Cheney remembers this operation.

> On Friday August the 4th, the squadron was in the air loaded with fourteen 500kg bombs, with which we attacked the railway bridge at Etaples. We bombed one after the other from a height of about 12,000 feet. There was an enormous amount of smoke and dust rising in the

target area after the first couple of salvos of bombs, so that the aiming point became almost obliterated. It had been marked by the squadron commander in his Mustang, but we could only see the flares from time to time through the growing accumulation of debris as the bombs fell. We bombed on a perfect summer's day at about noon, and did not encounter any enemy resistance, either flak or fighters. Our own fighter cover was very much in evidence above and below us. Later that day, after return to base, we all paid a visit to the intelligence office to see the bombing photographs taken by a Mosquito photo-reconnaissance aircraft. To our utter amazement and consternation the bridge still stood untouched with bomb craters all around it! We would have to come back another day.

This had been Cheney's thirty-eighth sortie in an operational career spanning twelve months and three squadrons. After completing basic training in his native Canada he arrived at 29 OTU at North Luffenham in England's smallest county of Rutland on the 16th of March 1943. His first operational flight was a 'Nickeling' trip to Paris in a Wellington on the 1st of July, and six weeks later he was posted to his first squadron. He arrived at 106 Squadron at Syerston on the 17th of August, a date now written in history as massively significant for the three main protagonists of the European war. During that momentous day the American 8th Air Force lost sixty B17s in raids against Schweinfurt and Regensburg, while that night, Bomber Command launched its epic attack on the rocket research establishment at Peenemünde. Cheney flew as second pilot to the experienced F/O Jan van Hoboken against Leverkusen on the 22/23rd in 'Admiral Prune II', ED593, a Lancaster immortalized in the background of an Imperial War Museum archive photo of Gibson and his flight commanders. Cheney captained a Lancaster operationally for the first time on the 27/28th, when Nuremberg was the target, and went to Mönchengladbach three nights later. The start of Cheney's tour coincided with the first phase of Harris's Berlin offensive, a three raid series spanning the end of August and start of September. Cheney's fifth operation was the final one of these, an all-Lancaster affair mounted on the night of the 3/4th of September. His Lancaster's port-inner engine cut during the bombing run, and he eventually bombed the capital from 12,000 feet on three engines, before returning safely. His twelfth operation took him and his crew to Düsseldorf on the 3/4th of November, when both port engines cut during the return flight, presumably as a result of battle damage. This robbed the Lancaster of hydraulic pressure, and a landing had to be made at Manston without flaps, after the undercarriage had been 'blown' down. The aircraft was severely damaged, but there were no injuries among the crew. It was on this night, that the recently missing Bill Reid had earned his Victoria Cross for his exploits in a 61 Squadron Lancaster.

This proved to be Cheney's final operation with 106 Squadron, and he was posted to East Kirkby on the 15th to join the newly formed 630 Squadron.

Three nights later Harris began the second and main phase of his Berlin campaign, and remarkably, ten of Cheney's eleven operations with 630 Squadron were to the 'Big City'. Not many crews lived long enough to make a similar boast. Consistently bringing back an aiming point photograph, and obtaining good results on the practice bombing range brought the crew to the attention of Group, and gained them an invitation to join 617 Squadron. This they agreed to do, and on the 15th of February 1944, the posting took place, thus probably sparing them from participation in the penultimate raid of the campaign on Berlin that very night. It was the 31st of March before Cheney got his hands on JB139 for the first time, the Lancaster which was to become his 'own', although at the time it was coded KC-X, rather than KC-V, to which it would be recoded on the 4th of April to become 'Dark Victor'. His first operation with 617 Squadron, and his twenty-third in all, was to Toulouse on the 5/6th of April in DV393. Cheney's continuing account provides an insight into life as a 617 Squadron officer in the second half of 1944.

> As our aircraft had received no damage during the Etaples operation and had performed perfectly, there were only one or two small points to mention to the ground crew chief. We made a short inspection together, examining tyres, undercarriage, ailerons and flaps, gun turrets and finally axles for any sign of oil leaks. I signed my short report on the Form 700, handed it to the flight sergeant, and flagged down the next crew bus bound for the flights. Our aircraft sat on a large round pad of concrete, which was big enough to turn the aircraft around on. This was known as the dispersal, and it was located about a half-mile or more from the flights. The other aircraft were parked on similar dispersals widely separated one from the other, so that a bombing or strafing attack or an explosion would not wipe out more than one aircraft. The bus stopped to pick up other air and ground crews who had finished their inspections and were heading back for a shower, a beer and a cigarette before tea. I was dropped at the C Flight shack, where quite a few of our mates were gathered around the crew roster board. It indicated, that there would be daylight operations again tomorrow, August the 5th, and the names of the crews and aircraft call letters chosen for the mission, ours included, had been posted. The weather was holding fine, sunny and warm, so we were not surprised, that we were 'on' again. In any case, the Etaples trip had been an easy one, and we were not overly tired. No target information was shown, but Group would inform the C.O. on the 'scrambler' tonight. I then jumped into one of the crew buses for the officers' mess, which was located in a beautiful rambling Spa hotel called Petwood about two miles from the aerodrome. After the Nissen huts we had lived in along with the snow, water and the mud on other squadrons, this was a very choice home indeed! All of the crews, having completed between ten and twenty ops or even more with other

squadrons, certainly appreciated, loved and respected their quarters. There was a fine large dining room, sitting room, separate bar, billiards room and a beautiful patio at the rear, where one could sit and bask in the sun on fine days. Out past the patio were winding paths and garden plots of varying shapes and sizes, and at the very rear of the large property was a picturesque lake complete with water lilies.

A few aircraft were taking off and landing, doing air-tests to make sure that certain repairs had been effective. Once in a while, one of the huge planes would thunder over the roof of the Petwood, giving rise to a roar of 'blimies' and 'mind my pint!' Tea and biscuits was available from about 4pm, and there was always a fierce rush for the magazine table to grab the two copies of the day's issue of the Daily Mirror. The Mirror featured the amorous adventures of a gorgeous blonde named Jane. Jane was invariably engaged in some slightly erotic or suggestive caper dressed in anything from nothing to her bra and brief panties. After tea and a chance finally to read Jane and view the scantily clothed pin-up girl in the centre of the Daily Mirror, we drifted outside for a smoke and a chat with some of the other crews, picked up a game of darts or cards, listened to the radio, or popped up to our rooms for a short nap. On the way upstairs I passed the bulletin board, which carries a CO's bulletin that ops are 'on' for tomorrow, and that briefing will be held for all designated crews at the flights tomorrow morning at 07.00 hours. This meant an early call in the morning, so all thoughts of a run over to the Red Lion pub in Stickford were put out of mind for tonight. At 18.00 I came downstairs and took a peek in the dining room, but everything was still quiet. Louder sounds were coming from the lounge and the bar, so I headed in that direction, where I picked up Roy Welch, Noel Wait and Ken Porter, who, by now, had also received their commissions as Pilot Officers. A few days previous we had had a rousing crew party for these three new 'sprog' officers, during which they got very well plastered, and the rest of us filled their brand new officer's dress hats with beer, then jumped on them a few times. Now they were 'operational'.

We had a couple of beers together in the bar, and treated some of our pals from other crews. The CO, Wing Commander Tait, was there, and quite enjoying himself with all the banter, a good deal of which was directed towards him and his navigator. Then we swung off to the dining room carrying a newly filled pint. Dinner consisted of horsemeat pie, boiled Brussels sprouts and mashed potatoes with some gravy. (Since the war, I have never been able to get a Brussels sprout near my mouth!) For dessert, there was the inevitable custard pudding with a sweet biscuit, tea or coffee. Back to the hall bulletin board to see if there was any more 'gen' since the last look. It appears, that the squadron will put up eighteen aircraft for ops tomorrow. After a couple more beers and a game or two of darts, I said goodnight to the lads, and wandered upstairs to bed about 21.30 hours.

At 04.30 hours, Don MacLean, my roommate, and I were awakened by a gentle tap on the door. A young WAAF entered with two steaming mugs of tea and a biscuit, said a cheery, 'Good morning, wakey, wakey', lifted the blind on the window, smiled and retired to repeat the same procedure with our buddies next door. Don MacLean was also a Canadian, and one of the 'originals', having been Joe McCarthy's navigator on the famous first operation against the Ruhr dams more than a year earlier. He was bright and cheerful, and was always somewhat concerned with my welfare, as I was a couple of years younger than he. He was also in love with one of the cute little WAAF officers on the base. We washed, shaved, and laid out our clothes for the day, being careful to empty our pockets of any items, which might provide useful information to the enemy in the event we were shot down and captured. These items included theatre ticket stubs, letters from friends, large denomination bank notes and the like. We donned battledress over a blue cotton shirt and underwear, black shoes and socks, stuck our officer's caps under our arms and headed downstairs for breakfast. Flight crews poured out of every door and flowed down the stairs to the dining room. There was the lovely scent of bacon in the air, which we knew would be accompanied by a couple of fried eggs each, as this was an 'ops' breakfast. The time was about 05.40. We were not disappointed with our bacon and eggs, fruit juice, toast and coffee. As we finished up we could hear the crew buses arriving in the courtyard ready to take us to the aerodrome and briefing. At 06.00 we piled into our transport, which, when full, precipitated a great stamping of feet and shouts of 'move off!'

The briefing room, or ops room, was a large hall containing rows of folding chairs, curtained windows and a raised podium at the end, on which stood a lectern with a microphone. Behind it was suspended a large map measuring some three metres by two, which could be rolled up and down like a window blind. It was now pulled fully down, but was covered by a double curtain, which could be parted by a draw cord. It partially obscured the long blackboard extending across the end wall. It was now 06.15, just time to have a last few puffs on a Woodbine before things started. Promptly at 06.30 the rear doors swung open. 'Humph', F/L Humphries, our great squadron adjutant, bellowed, 'Room ... attenn-shunn!' With a clatter of chairs and shoes we were on our feet, as the base commander, Air Commodore Sharp, strode in flanked by the station commander, Group Captain Philpott, and W/C Tait. Behind them trailed the meteorological officer, the intelligence officer and the Flight Commanders of A, B and C Flights. We were C Flight, which, until a month earlier, had been the command of S/L Joe McCarthy DSO DFC*. However, Joe had done nearly 100 ops, and word came down from the Group commander, AVM Sir Ralph Cochrane, that he was to stand down immediately, take leave, and await further orders. His successor was a very fine, experienced officer by the name of Gerry Fawke DFC*.

The Group Captain asked us all to please sit down, and the base commander opened the briefing. He welcomed new crews, and congratulated the squadron on its high rate of aircraft availability, information passed along to him from Group. The squadron commander then took over, and after a few preliminary remarks about certain developments being watched in enemy territory, e.g. movements of *Luftwaffe* fighter units, he began the briefing proper. It was a matter of great concern to the war cabinet and to the Admiralty, that the enemy was increasingly able to refit and turn around its *U-Boot* fleet in less and less time from its giant reinforced concrete pens at French ports such as Brest, Lorient and St Nazaire. This meant, that our Atlantic shipping lanes were under growing pressure from *U-Boot* attacks launched from these bases. It was our intention to put the bases out of action, and force the enemy to move his *U-Boots* further and further from their targets, where they would be even more vulnerable to air and sea attack. The CO then pulled the draw cord to open the curtain covering the map. A red ribbon, held in place by large map pins, stretched from base, south-west to the English coast, then across the wide part of the Channel to intersect with the northern coast of Brittany. At the French coast there was a slight change of course to the south-east, which carried the route across Brittany to a point almost midway between Brest and Lorient. At that point there was a very sharp change of course north-west towards Brest. The route home traced a path north to the Channel and on to the English coast, and so to base near the city of Lincoln. The purpose of the sharp change of course midway between Brest and Lorient was to keep the enemy guessing until the last minute as to what the target would be. This would give our attacking aircraft a certain element of surprise, and would also, we hoped, enable us to arrive over the target and bomb before the Germans could obscure it with their very efficient smokescreen. The longer we had to keep the target in view and make a good straight run-up to it, the better were our chances of high accuracy with our huge six ton Tallboy bombs, which, from high altitude, could slice through the six or more metres of reinforced concrete roofs of the pens and blow up inside, destroying the *U-Boots* and blocking the entrances with huge masses of broken concrete.

The CO described the route, take-off times, fuel loads, flight time to target, turning points, bombing altitudes, spacing of aircraft vertically and estimated time of attack. He advised that he and his navigator, Revie Walker, another of the originals and former navigator in David Shannon's crew, would be over the target at about 200 feet to lay long-burning bright red flares on the roof of the German installation. He would call in the bombers to make their attacks in the order in which they arrived over the target area, and as soon as he was satisfied that his flares were in exactly the right place. He would be flying his Mosquito, and there would be a second Mosquito flown by one of the Flight commanders ready to back him up. He informed us, that he would be circling the target between bombs to assess the accuracy and to call up any needed corrections. This was a technique developed by W/C Cheshire, the previous squadron commander, with devastating effect both by day and night. The bombing leader took over from the CO, and he repeated, that the bombing altitudes assigned to each aircraft were between 16,000 and 18,500 feet. The Tallboys were armed with time fuses with delays varying between eleven seconds and several hours. The intelligence officer made us feel very good, when he announced that Lockheed P-38 Lightnings from the USAAF fighter escort Group would provide air cover with a rendezvous at the French coast. They would be accompanied by a squadron of RAF Spitfires especially to look out for stragglers. His latest report on defences around the target showed that there were about seventy-three 88mm anti-aircraft guns, although only a small number were radar predicted. (I later ascertained from contacts in the Resistance, that the defences included 175 of the 88mm guns, almost all of which were radar predicted!)

The Met Officer predicted beautiful, clear summer weather over the entire route, including the target area. The Navigation Officer, Revie Walker, explained the various headings, noting his pleasure, that the wind speeds were expected to be light. He asked all navigators to report to his office following the briefing to collect their charts and any last minute instructions. The gunnery, signals and bombing leaders made similar requests. The pilots, myself included, always went from office to office in order to be as well informed as possible. The CO wound up the briefing with the advice, that start-up and take-off would be by Flights, and these times were posted in each Flight office. He wanted all aircraft in the air before 09.30, with the first one off promptly at 09.00. Start engines would be signalled by release of a green flare fired from the control tower. 'Humph' then called the room to attention, the rear doors swung open, and the 'big brass' filed out after wishing us all a good trip and safe return. The briefing room clock read 07.50.

At 08.20 aircrews picked up their parachutes, pulled on flying boots, and draped flying helmets with attached oxygen tubes and dangling intercom cords around their necks. Gunners wriggled into woollen turtleneck sweaters and electrically heated flying suits. The navigators wrestled with parachutes, briefcases full of maps and charts and 'computers', which they would use for quick calculation of wind changes and course alterations. Parachute harnesses were put on over the Mae West life jackets, and the parachute packs were carried by a cloth loop. They had strong steel U rings on their flat reverse side, into which the heavy snap fasteners on the harnesses would be buckled in the event of an order to abandon aircraft. During regular flight, each crewman had a specific

> position designated for stowing his parachute. My own was stowed behind the pilot's seat, and it was the duty of the flight engineer to retrieve it for me in case of emergency. Thus loaded down with our clothing and impedimenta, we flip-flopped our way out to the crew bus to be taken to the dispersal of 'Dark Victor'. I was fortunate, as were others who would be working in the heated cabin, in not having to wear the heavy electrically heated suit and bulky flying boots. The gunners, on the other hand, wore heavy, long woollen underwear next to their skin. On a warm August day, they could not wait to get into the air to cool off. Many also left the donning of heavy clothing until just before they boarded the aircraft. I wore only battledress and fleece-lined flying boots, the lower parts of which could be separated from the upper calf section to make them resemble ordinary black shoes.

This was the day on which F/L Wilson left the squadron on a posting to 1661CU, but probably not before he had waved his former colleagues off to Brest. Cheney continues:

> And so it was, that we fired up the engines and prepared to take off with the rest of the squadron in brilliant sunshine at about 09.30. With a mighty roar an aircraft sitting at the end of the runway lurched forward and quickly gathered speed. In seconds it was out of sight down the runway and we were moving up. My gunners were swinging their turrets back and forth, and raising and lowering their guns. Ken Porter barked into the intercom, 'That was Dick Willsher.' A second aircraft had already moved into position for take-off. Another great roar and it thundered off down the runway with Nick Knilans at the controls. Arthur Kell, my Australian friend, whose crew had joined mine for the special Operation Taxable on June the 6th, D-Day, was running up to full throttle against his brakes on the white hash marks at the take-off point. As Arthur let go the brakes, P-Popsie jumped forward and accelerated down the runway. I had already moved onto the hash marks, and eased the throttles forward, while holding the straining V-Victor against the brakes with my toes pressing hard on the tops of the rudder pedals. Ahead, P-Popsie rose into the air and banked slowly to port. Then it was our turn. Jim Rosher called out the airspeed as we hurtled down the white stripe with our 12,000lb Tallboy strapped securely beneath us, and I glued my eyes on the end of the runway coming up fast – ninety ... ninety-five ... hundred ... hundred and ten ... hundred and fifteen ... hundred and twenty. Victor was straining to lift off, but still felt a bit heavy. 'Give her a little more of a run', I whispered to myself. At a hundred and thirty I eased back on the yoke and she came off easily and smoothly. Roy Welch gave us the heading for our climb to bombing altitude at 17,500 feet, which we would not reach for another hour. Our course would take us over the south coast at Beachy Head, from where

we would alter course in order to clear Cherbourg. Another course alteration would bring us in over the north coast of Brittany, and we would then swing slightly north-east to bisect the line running between Brest and Lorient.

Tait took Mosquito NT202 for this operation, while Fawke was back in NT205. The fifteen Lancasters were carrying their more familiar Tallboys, and contained the crews of Howard in ED763, Poore in DV391, Fearn in DV380, Knilans in ME561, Oram in LM485, Knights in DV385, Sanders in ME562, Stout in ME559, Willsher in LM492, Cheney in JB139, Kell in DV402, Levy in DV246, Williams in EE131, Gingles in LM489, and Iveson in ME554, on his first operation since joining the squadron. The crews were on board their aircraft and at their positions by 08.50, and a green flare signalled engine start shortly afterwards. Take-off was without incident, and was followed by the long climb to bombing altitude, which, as Don Cheney stated, would occupy the next hour. 'Paddy' Gingles lost an engine while outbound near Bristol and was forced to abort his sortie, but the others pressed on in near perfect weather conditions, with visibility recorded by Tait as extreme. We return to Don Cheney's personal recollection of the day.

> At the rendezvous point on the north coast of Brittany we were comforted to catch the sun glinting off the P38s coming in high above us as they slid back and forth like friendly shepherds. As we approached our final turning point for the attack we had not seen enemy activity of any kind, flak or fighters, and this was going to be a 'piece of cake', we would lay our Tallboys right on the button.

It was a few minutes before noon when Tait dived towards the aiming point, releasing his smoke markers from 4,500 feet. Fawke's markers were not required, and he was able to sit on top and watch the show. He described the bombing as very concentrated, and observed the pens to be covered in bomb bursts and smoke. Two stray Tallboys were seen to fall into the water in front of the pens, but six direct hits were scored on the concrete roofs, two of them claimed by Knights and Stout. Don Cheney again takes up the story.

> Well before bomb release time Len Curtis had the aiming point clearly in view. At a distance of about eighteen miles I followed his calm emotionless directions over the intercom. I knew that he was intently watching the aiming point coming straight down the tracking line of his SABS. The target was still clearly visible – no smoke yet! Half way along our run to the target, I noticed that our aircraft was slightly in the lead of the others on either side. We were also tracking closer to the coastline on our starboard side than the others, though still over a large body of water. My eyes were glued to the instrument panel and felt as though they were being pulled out of their sockets. Time seemed to stand still,

and sweat trickled down my temples under the flying helmet. Shattering the intercom sequence between Len Curtis and me came the warning voice of Jim Rosher. "Flak straight ahead, port and starboard – our level!" The puffs of the exploding shells drift past in seconds, but I could hear the muffled boom and catch the angry red centres of the bursts dead ahead in my peripheral vision. They were close! Then whump, whump, whump under the nose and to each side. No question, we were flying straight into radar-predicted anti-aircraft fire! Then again suddenly – whump-clang, whump-clang, whump-clang four, five, six times. After one of the whumps there was a short cry over the intercom, and then another. This time we were not going to get off without some serious trouble! The aircraft filled with blue cordite smoke. The sky around us had erupted in angry black clouds with fiery red centres. The aircraft shuddered under the impact of a couple of direct hits. Another volley, another cry, then 'bomb gone!' from Curtis. Immediately, I banked to the left pushing forward on the control column to increase speed and lose altitude, the fastest way out of trouble.

Jim Rosher, like a big indestructible rock, had stood beside me spotting each Flak burst. I shouted to him to bring me a report on the condition of the crew. The intercom was working, and both mid-upper and rear gunners reported damage but turrets working, no fire and no wounds. Jim Rosher returned to my side looking grim. Len Curtis had come up from his nose position and was unpacking first-aid equipment. Rosher's report confirmed both gunners o.k. as well as himself and Curtis. However, navigator Roy Welch and wireless operator Reg Pool were badly wounded. Jim then began assisting Curtis in administering first-aid to the two wounded men. I looked back for the first time into the navigation and radio compartments. A near miss had sent shrapnel bursting up through the bomb bay, tearing a twelve inch splintered hole in the navigator's table. The rest of the compartment was a scene of chaos, but Roy was still seated at his table looking at his maps. There was no doubt, that we had taken two or more direct hits in the bomb bay just after releasing our Tallboy. Over the intercom I asked Roy if he were able to give me any kind of course to direct us to base. The Flak had stopped, and I had been able to level off on a heading out to sea. By this time the other aircraft had flown past us, dropped their bombs, and were turning inland to starboard. Reg Pool was slumped in his seat, his eyes wide and his skin very pale. Ken Porter had joined the others in tending the wounded. Roy Welch appeared beside me leaning unsteadily against the side of my seat. One hand held a large antiseptic pad, already stained with blood, which he pressed across his mouth and nose. Obviously, he was unable to speak. In his other hand Roy had a clipboard, which he held out in front of me. Across the paper attached to the board he had scrawled – 'heading 060 degrees'. I gave him the thumbs-up and a grateful nod, followed by a pat on the shoulder as he turned slowly to return to his seat. There were splatters of blood around his collar and the side of his head. Looking back again, I could see Reg Pool immobile in his seat, with two of the others tending him. Reg had been hit by the same bursts as Roy. It was now clear to see, that he had severe wounds to his chest, stomach and upper legs.

Jim Rosher had helped Roy back to his seat, while I continued my bank gently to port, intending to take Roy's course of 060 degrees. He then returned to my side, folded down his jump seat and stood to my right checking his instrument panel and keeping a lookout for trouble. He gave me a poke with his finger, and pointed to the starboard wing. There were a number of jagged holes of various sizes, and one between the starboard engines was large enough for a man to pass through! Flames were licking up from several of the holes, and a trail of black smoke and flame issued from the large one. I applied left rudder, causing the aircraft to sideslip to port to blow the fire away from the fuselage. At this point the starboard-outer engine failed, the propeller windmilling wildly as flames and black smoke belched from under the cowling. Rosher quickly and efficiently feathered the propeller and activated the Graviner fire extinguisher. The engine fire appeared to be under control as I continued to descend to a safer altitude, because the navigator and wireless operator were without an oxygen supply. A further damage report from the gunners and flight engineer indicated, that both wings were riddled with holes and the fuselage was badly torn in many places. The number 2 fuel tank was still burning, and the blue-orange flame was getting bigger. It was also spreading along the starboard wing. I ordered the crew to prepare to abandon aircraft. I can still hear the voice of rear gunner Noel Wait calling over the intercom, 'wait for me, wait for me!' My response was, 'don't worry, Noel, I'll give you time to get out.' As this was taking place I stared in horror at the flaming wing, and gritted my teeth in expectation of an almost certain explosion of the fuel tanks. I had seen several crews survive such an event, but the prospect was terrible to contemplate.

Heat was building up noticeably in the cockpit. I realised that there was absolutely no chance of putting out the fires, and gave the order to abandon the aircraft. As he came past me on his way to the forward escape hatch, Jim Rosher laid my parachute pack under my legs, having extracted it from under the back of my seat. He then proceeded into the nose with the navigator to join Len Curtis, who had already activated the release handle of the escape hatch. Unfortunately, either as the result of damage or a faulty mechanism, the jettison device caused the hatch to twist in the rectangular opening and jam, thus partially blocking it. Curtis and Rosher wrestled with the hatch cover, and finally forced it into a position, which allowed a man to squeeze through. The navigator left first, followed by the bomb-aimer and the flight engineer. Meanwhile, the mid-upper gunner, who had been helping to attend to his wounded comrades, went aft to secure his parachute, and left by the rear door, which had already been jettisoned by the rear gunner, when he baled out seconds before. The badly wounded wireless operator and I were now alone in the aircraft. Holding it as steadily as I could with one hand, I reached back to help Reg Pool to his feet. He kept shaking his head, but I persevered and he gradually crept towards me. As he slumped against the side of my seat, the plane began to wallow from side to side, and the nose began to drop, increasing the speed rapidly. I had to get back into the pilot's seat again in order to pull up the nose and apply some rudder control. I got out of the seat again, stood up, and clipped Reggie's parachute pack onto the snaps of his harness, placing his hand on the large steel ring of the ripcord activator. Each time I let go of the control column the aircraft would begin to nose downward, and I could feel the air speed build up quickly. It was necessary, therefore, that I move back and forth between the controls and the injured crewman. By this sequence of actions I was able to manoeuvre him to the escape hatch. I pointed to the ripcord, and asked him if he could pull it. He nodded. His legs were already dangling in space, and he was wriggling down through the partially restricted hatch. He waved at me to leave him and get out. I gave him a salute, and turned my attention to my own escape.

The aircraft had pitched into another dive as I turned to the controls. Looking to my right momentarily, I could see yellowish brown bubbles and blisters breaking out on the flight engineer's panel on the right side of the cockpit. I felt the heat increasing. I was certain that the machine would blow apart at any second. I was still standing in the passage beside the pilot's seat, my left hand on the controls. The noise was terrible. Air rushing through the nose and out through the rear door ten metres further down the fuselage howled like a tornado, and sucked any loose objects along with it. The roar of the three engines was thunderous. I pulled back on the control column, and the nose came slowly up . . . up . . . up. Now I could see the horizon, and realised that I was in a climb! The airspeed was falling off rapidly, so I pushed forward violently with both hands.. The machine levelled off, but I knew it would be momentary. I knew also, that there was no possibility of stabilizing the aircraft long enough to buckle on my parachute, get to the nose hatch and force myself through. Two alternatives remained, the rear door and the ditching hatch directly over the pilot's seat. I would never make it over the main spar, down the fuselage and past the flare chute to the rear door. I grabbed my chute pack from under the seat, and buckled it on to the big snap fasteners on the harness. With the chute pack now large on my chest, I climbed onto my seat on my knees, with my rump against the control column, grasped the handles of the hatch release and gave it a firm twist. The hatch cover flew off with a whoosh!

The noise and roaring of the wind increased. I tore off my sunglasses and helmet, and they went flying back into the cockpit. I got one foot up on the seat, then the other, crouching with my knees bent. Slowly I began to stand and stuck my head and shoulders out into the slipstream. But I was not far enough out to be able to jump clear of the aircraft. Putting one foot and then the other on the arm rests of the seat I could get somewhat further out, but then came to a stop. With the chute pack fastened to my chest, I was too fat to be able to pass through the hatch! I crouched back down inside the cockpit, by which time the nose had once again begun to dive more steeply and the airspeed was building up. I pulled on the controls to get the nose up again, and it came up a little. This time I have to make it! I flipped the chute pack upwards away from my body and stuffed it out of the hatch just before putting my chest out. It worked! I knew that I would be able to straighten up, but I also knew I then had to get my legs and feet up as high as possible, and push like hell with one great leap to have a chance of getting clear. Once more, with my feet on the arm rests of the pilot's seat I proceeded to get one knee on the outside edge of the escape hatch. Now I had to get the other foot higher. I felt around for the back of the pilot's seat, raised my foot until I could get a grip on the topmost part, then PUSHED with all my strength.

I shot out into the slipstream. The blurred lump of the mid-upper turret flashed past. The two big tail fins zipped by and I was tumbling in space, knees drawn up towards my chest. I can remember seeing blue sky with a few small white clouds, then some green and brown land, then some blue water, then sky again through my legs between my flying boots. The roar of the aircraft had disappeared and was replaced by the rushing of air in my ears. Tumbling over and over I waited a few seconds as I felt around for the large ring of the ripcord on the side of my chute pack. I found it, grasped it and pulled it straight out as hard as I could. It came away with incredible ease, and I was conscious of holding the ring in my hand with a two-foot length of fine steel wire attached to the end of it. Good Lord! I've pulled too hard, broken the cord and the chute isn't going to open! Whump!! With a sudden heavy jerk I flipped upright and the tumbling stopped, as did the rushing of air in my ears. I floated in silence with only the lazy flap-flap of the fully opened parachute pluming out in a beautiful white canopy above me. I heard the drone of the aircraft, and looking around me, I caught sight of our dear 'Dark Victor' about a half kilometre away. No other parachutes were visible. The plane had come out of a dive, and was climbing at a very steep angle. It got almost to the top of a loop, before stalling part way over on its back. Then the nose dropped suddenly, and with motors still revving, it fell in a classic spin towards the sea trailing flame and black smoke. For an instant I feared it would come around and hit me, but then, as it took its death dive, I felt a chill of horror. From my angle of view it appeared that it might crash in the town. This fear also passed, though, as it seemed to take an eternity for the plane to hit the water. Finally, there was a thunderous roar as it dived nose first into the sea. For a few seconds red flames mixed with black smoke towered fifty metres into the air, billowing and swirling. Then came a bubbling, boiling circle of churning, hissing seawater, a column of water vapour, a shower of splashes from pieces of flying debris, and then silence. The parachute flapped lightly in the breeze. A thousand metres below me and half a kilometre away nothing remained of my proud 'Dark Victor' but a small cloud of black smoke that spiralled upwards and then quickly dispersed in the sea breeze.

I sensed the droning of aircraft engines in the distance. Turning my head towards the sound, I could see the last several units of my squadron, who, having dropped their bombs, gradually disappeared, black specks against the distant blue sky. I could see no other parachutes in my vicinity. I tried to manoeuvre my parachute by pulling on the shrouds in an effort to make it drift towards land. It was very hard work, however, and I soon gave it up. I was alone in the sky. I had no sensation whatever of falling, it was more like being pinned to the sky like a toy doll. I had a sense of incredible relief at the thought of my miraculous escape from that burning machine. Was I dreaming, or could it really be true, that I was hanging here, my squadron gone, my comrades nowhere to be seen, and no telling what hostile reception awaited me in those green fields below. I doubt there was ever a greater feeling of loneliness! In that moment, out of nowhere, came the crackling roar of a Rolls-Royce Merlin engine to snap my silence and my dream. A Spitfire dived past me with a whistle twenty metres away to seaward. I could see the pilot's goggled face clearly as he had his canopy pushed back. He waved, and I waved back with enthusiasm giving the thumbs up sign. He wheeled round to seaward and made two or three more diving passes, following me down. I could see that I was still drifting over a large bay, and that I was almost certain to fall into the sea. This prospect did not cause me any particular anxiety, as I am a good swimmer, having spent much time around water and boats from the time I was very small. I gave no thought to the fact, that this would be my first dip in the salt water of the ocean! When I was fifty metres above the water, the Spitfire made a final pass, waggled his wings, climbed away and was gone. I was completely alone again.

Cheney was also now nearing the end of his journey to earth, and the sea was rushing up to meet him as he wrestled with his parachute to ensure the best possible attitude for entry. On impact he was submerged for the briefest moment as his Mae West inflated and thrust him back to the surface, where he bobbed like a cork until he got his bearings. The low-lying coastline 1,000 yards or so to his left offered the nearest landfall, and he initially made his way in that direction. As it came closer, though, he observed what looked like defensive obstacles. It occurred to him, that the beach may contain mines, and he began to consider other options. He decided to head back towards his right into the wider part of the bay, where he could make out a more steeply rising coastline with buildings of some sort. Although a strong swimmer, Cheney was beginning to feel the strain, particularly with his Mae West creating a drag effect to slow his forward progress. It was at this moment, that he thought he heard voices drifting across the water, and wondered if he might, perhaps, be hallucinating.

A small round nosed fishing boat materialized, bouncing its way towards him with around ten people on board shouting and gesticulating. Cheney assumed a German presence, and resigned himself to capture as strong arms lifted him bodily from the water. Then cheers, clapping and handshakes persuaded him that he was in friendly hands, and his mind grappled to comprehend the excited chatter in a French dialect. As the vessel turned towards land, Cheney enquired in schoolboy French where the Germans were, and he was told, 'Boches kaput', accompanied by a throat-slitting motion of the hand. And so began Don Cheney's month-long adventure in the hands of the French Resistance. He was landed at the fishing port of Douarnenez, in whose bay he had come down, some eighteen miles south of Brest. The town was in the grip of a confusing tussle with the German occupying forces, which had been about to surrender to the Resistance, but after a change of heart, reasserted themselves and retook the town. Although Cheney was unaware of the fact until after the war, negotiations were actually in progress between the occupying forces and the Resistance over a German surrender, while the 617 Squadron attack on Brest was in progress. By an incredible stroke of bad luck the local German commander had mistaken the anti-aircraft fire as artillery aimed at his forces, and broke off the negotiations. He threatened an armoured assault on the town and reprisals against the men folk if the Resistance did not capitulate, and in view of the superior enemy forces the locals decided to back down. Three days later, however, as American forces approached, the German garrison would withdraw from the town altogether, and take up positions in the surrounding countryside.

Once ashore, and with gunfire to be heard in the distance, Cheney and the other occupants of the boat ran the 200-yard length of the jetty to the point where it fanned out into paved streets on either side. The area was a beehive of activity with men, women and some children scrambling about, and many of the men were armed with rifles or revolvers. He was sat on a large rock or concrete block in the sun, and his wet battledress jacket and trousers removed. His top half was covered by a jacket someone had given to him, and it then dawned on him embarrassingly, that only his service underpants separated his nether region from the gaze of the world. An elderly man noticed his discomfiture, and quickly arranged for a blanket to be fetched from a nearby house. He was fussed over by the women folk before being questioned by a young English-speaking woman on behalf of her male companion, who was clearly someone of importance and was referred to as Le Compte. It was not until after the war that Cheney learned the identity of this man. He was the Vicompte de Jonquieres, and his female companion was Helène Damey, the niece of a prominent local doctor. Cheney was handed a tin of fish, but its smell and the seawater in his stomach made him heave. The locals were using a captured blond, teenaged German soldier as a 'gofer', and he eventually fetched some apple cider, which tasted wonderful to Cheney and he began to revive.

Cheney and the young couple were taken on a ten-minute journey by pickup truck, which wound its way up the steep narrow streets into the town to a safe house. Here he was left with a woman and her fifteen-year-old daughter, who fed and re-clothed him before showing him to a third-floor room where he soon fell asleep. He awoke four or five hours later as darkness was falling, and shortly afterwards the woman came to his room with her husband, a short, stocky, determined looking man, whom Cheney liked immediately. His name was Aristide Quebriac, a naval captain and the Administrator-in-Chief of the port authority, who was suspected by the commander of the German occupying forces to have much to do with the Resistance, and had, in fact, been one of the negotiating team at talks with the Germans as Cheney was being shot down. As a result of his associations with the Resistance he was frequently invited to the colonel's HQ for a chat, but was always allowed time by the soldiers sent to escort him to put on his impressive navy blue uniform with large gold stripes on the arm denoting his rank and his white cap. He explained to Cheney how the Germans respected his uniform and the status it represented. Cheney enjoyed an evening meal with the family, and was then taken to a long shed in the back yard, where a hiding place had been created behind a ceiling-high stack of wood. This was to be Cheney's 'bolt-hole' in the event of a search by the Germans, and he used it once over the course of the next day or so. With much gratitude Cheney enjoyed the hospitality and friendship of the local people, and he received regular visits from 'Le Compte' and Helène, who kept him up to date with news.

The news he was hoping for most was that all of his crewmates were safe, but the body of Reg Pool was recovered from the sea on the 7th, and Cheney was taken to identify him and attend his funeral. It was some time later, after Cheney had left Douarnenez, that the body of Roy Welch came ashore, and the fact that both men had been badly wounded, made their deaths easier to accept. The death of rear gunner Noel Wait, on the other hand, Cheney found harder to bear, because he had been uninjured on leaving the stricken Lancaster. He was, though, a non-swimmer, and was known to be fearful of baling out over the sea. His body was found entangled in his parachute shrouds, and it is believed, that he probably drowned while in a state of panic. Once the German forces had withdrawn from the town the tension was relaxed, and Cheney was able to move about more freely. On the 22nd of

August, after many tearful goodbyes, he and an American airman with whom he had become friends were taken the twenty kilometres to Quimper on the road to Lorient. Soon they would be passed on to the Americans, as would Cheney's flight engineer, F/S Rosher, and the mid-upper gunner, W/O Porter, and all would be back home by the first week of September. The lone captive from the crew, bomb-aimer F/S Curtis, was also released shortly afterwards, when American forces took the area.

CHAPTER FIFTEEN

Matters Maritime Continue

The Command revisits Germany

The squadron was back in action again on the evening after Brest, for an attack by two Mosquitos and twelve Lancasters on the *U-Boot* pens at Lorient. Tait and Fawke were in NT202 and NT205 respectively, and the Lancaster crews were those of Knights in LM492, Knilans in ME561, Fearn in DV402, Sanders in ME562, Oram in LM485, Iveson in ME554, Gingles in LM489, Carey in PD238, Howard in ED763, Stout in ME559, Willsher in LM492 and Kell in DV246. Tait released two red target indicators from 8,000 feet at 20.23½, and watched as the Tallboys fell in a rapid salvo at around 20.28 onto the easily identifiable target. Smoke prevented an accurate assessment of the bombing, but Tait saw none fall wide, while Fawke observed one direct hit and two very near misses. Bob Knights again claimed a bull's eye, as did Fearn, whose Tallboy was the first to go down. Howard thought his bomb struck the north-western corner of the pens, but this was where Fearns's impacted, and he may have been mistaken. What was not in doubt, however, was that it was another very impressive display of high-level precision bombing. Only three crews missed out, Ross and Hamilton failing to take off because their aircraft had not been made ready in time, and Carey, who jettisoned his Tallboy five miles from the target and two miles out to sea because of an electrical problem.

The squadron returned to the same location twenty-four hours later with Tait at the controls of a Mosquito accompanied by nine Lancasters, but they were recalled when in the target area, because American ground forces were believed to be in the vicinity. Earlier in the day F/O Duffy, having completed his tour and now awaiting a posting, took Mosquito NT202 for a spin over the Wainfleet bombing range accompanied by F/O Ingleby. Tragically, at around 11.00 hours, the aircraft crashed following structural failure, and both men were killed. Later that night over a thousand aircraft took off to lend support to Allied ground forces in the Normandy battle area, and two thirds of them delivered attacks under strictly controlled conditions. Besides such tactical operations during this period, the main force was continuing

The Kembs Barrage across the eastern branch of the Rhein at the point where Germany, France and Switzerland meet.

A Tallboy explodes close to the Kembs Barrage on 7.10.44.

The mighty battleship *Tirpitz* at her Norwegian mooring.

Tirpitz at her mooring off Haakoy Island in the Tromsö area.

Drew Wyness's Lancaster ME559 after its crash-landing near Yagodnik during Operation *Paravane*, the first of three attacks on *Tirpitz*.

W/C James Tait and crew posing in front of Tait's EE146 KC-D on return from the third and final operation against *Tirpitz* 12.11.44.

P/O Sanders and crew with ME562 KC-K as a backdrop.

Sir Archibald Sinclair, Minister for Air, congratulating W/C Tait at Woodhall Spa on 15.11.44 following the destruction of the *Tirpitz*.

The Bielefeld Viaduct viewed after 617 Squadron's final visit on 14.3.45.

F/O Phil Martin in PB996 YZ-C formating with G/C Fauquier in PD119 YZ-J, after delivering their Grand Slams onto the Arnsberg Viaduct 19.3.45.

The moment of impact of F/O Martin's Grand Slam at Arnsberg 19.3.45.

S/L Cockshott's PD114 over the Arbergen railway bridge near Bremen 21.3.45.

Tallboys awaiting transport to their 617 Squadron Lancasters.

The tail assembly of the Barnes Wallis conceived *Tallboy*.

F/L Sayers and crew in front of PD113 on 27.3.45., prior to the attack on the giant concrete construction at Farge on the banks of the Weser near Germany's north-western coast.

Johnny Fauquier's PD119 B1 Special YZ-J.

Another view of Fauquier's mount. The outward face of each fin was left black as a further identification mark to enable other aircraft more easily to formate on their leader.

A well-known squadron photo taken in June 1943 with Dams survivors and some replacement pilots.

Cheshire with air and ground crew in front of his 76 Squadron Halifax.

W/C Gibson reviewing ATC cadets on his way to give blood.

Gibson being comforted by a WAAF, a nurse and a cup of tea after giving blood.

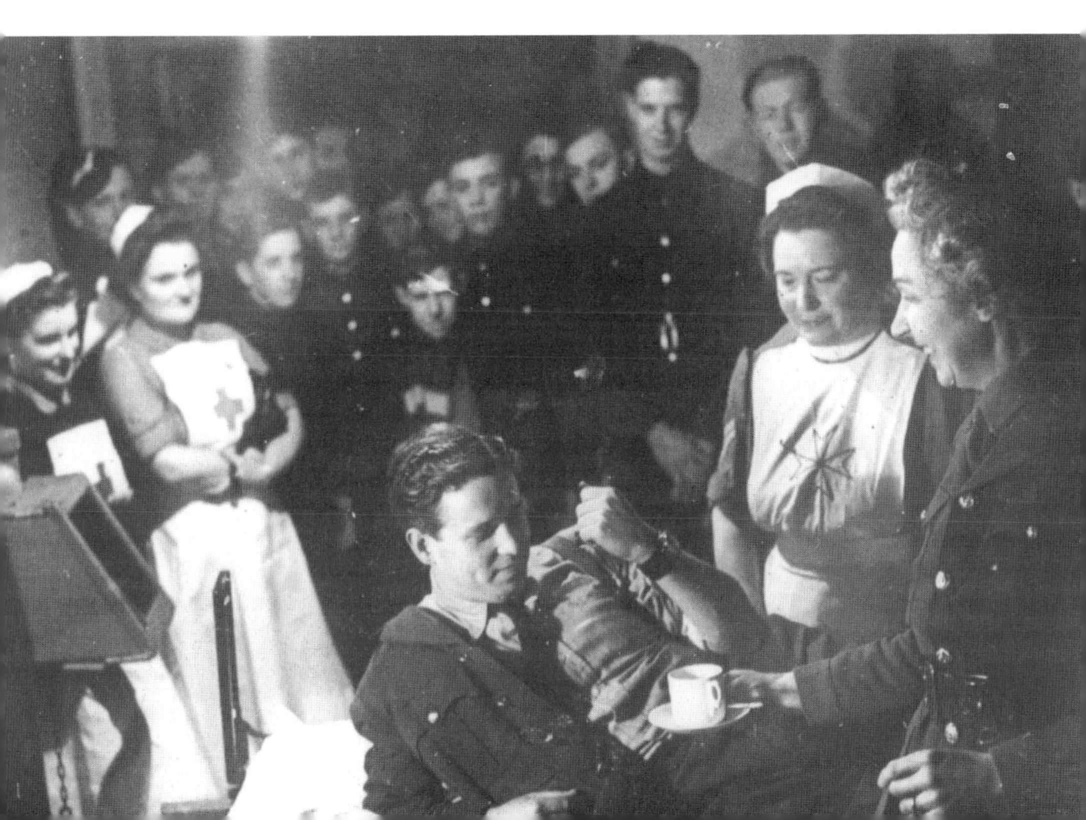

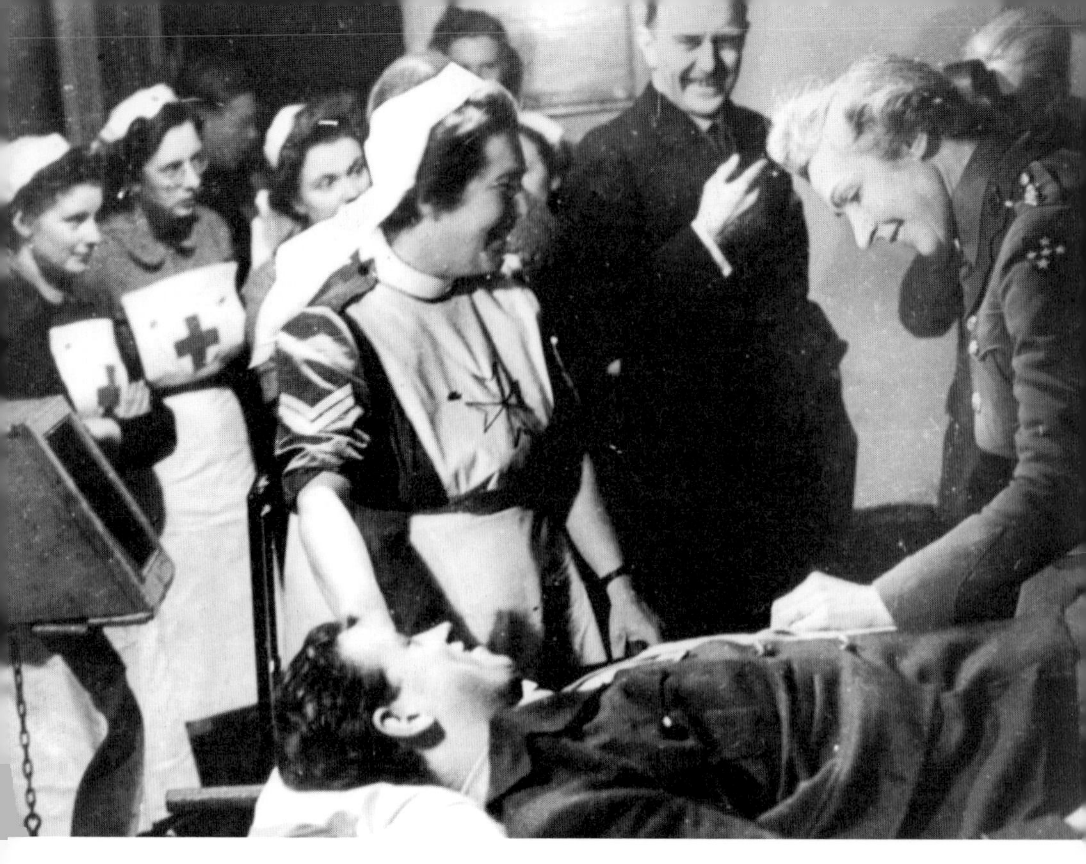

Removing blood from a national hero.

Gibson standing on the steps of Macclesfield town hall in early 1944, while he was considering standing as the conservative parliamentary candidate.

Trials drop of an *Upkeep* at Reculver in May 1943.

Upkeep, shadow and substance.

The consequences of releasing *Upkeep* from too low. Spray tears pieces from the Lancaster.

An *Upkeep* heaves itself out of the water.

ED932 banks low over the cameraman at Reculver.

to maintain the pressure on oil production and storage, flying bomb sites and railways. Three days after the tragic accident at Wainfleet, Ingleby was buried in Coningsby cemetery adjacent to the airfield.

The squadron's campaign against *U-Boots* and other targets nautical continued with a raid on La Pallice on the 9th. Tait was in NT205 on this occasion, with F/S Gosling in the right-hand seat. The latter was one of four new arrivals from 83 Squadron on the 10th of July, and they would eventually crew up with S/L Cockshott. The Lancaster crews were those of Howard in ED763, Pryor in ME561, Fearn in DV380, Oram in DV391, Iveson in ME554, Knights in LM482, Kell in LM492, Watts in DV246, Sanders in ME562, Hamilton in PD233, Gingles in PD238 and Ian Ross in ME555. These were to attack the *U-Boot* pens, while seventeen other Lancasters from the Group went for an oil depot. The target was a good deal further south than those recently attacked, and it took three hours to reach. Tait was carrying two 120lb smoke bombs, but decided not to use them. The first salvo of Tallboys headed towards the aiming point at 13.01 from an average of 17,000 feet, and the consensus was that the first one missed very narrowly, probably hitting the dock gates, while the second one, claimed by 'Mac' Hamilton, was a direct hit right in the centre of the roof. Kell also saw his bomb strike the aiming point, but then smoke and the generally poor weather conditions made it impossible to identify individual bomb bursts. In his post-raid report Tait referred to some loose bombing due to misidentification, but described the performance as good on the whole, and confirmed, that there appeared to be two direct hits. Reconnaissance confirmed a direct hit on the south-east corner of the pens, causing the collapse of a large section of roof, and three other direct hits with possible penetration.

On the 11th Duffy was laid to rest at the Stonefall Cemetery in Harrogate, in the beautiful section reserved for Canadian airmen, and the service was attended by members of his former crew as representatives of the squadron. The squadron returned to La Pallice that afternoon, with Tait in NT205 accompanied once more by Danny Walker. The heavy brigade consisted of S/L Cockshott in PD238 for his maiden operation with the squadron, Williams in EE131, Pryor in LM485, Oram in DV391, Fearn in DV380, Howard in ED763, Carey in ME554, Hamilton in PD233, Gingles in LM489, Sanders in ME562, Knights in LM492, Kell in ME561, Watts in DV246 and Willsher in LM482. Ian Ross was also supposed to be taking part, but his sortie was scrubbed when it proved impossible to bomb his Lancaster up in time. Possibly because of a shortage of Tallboys, the Lancasters were each carrying six 2,000lb armour-piercing bombs, and having become accustomed to loading just one Tallboy, this probably tested the armourers. The main force took off in a twenty-minute slot before noon, to be followed by Tait at 12.29. He arrived in the target area ahead of the Lancasters, which were delayed by ten minutes because of a change in the forecast winds. Fearn was not among them. He had lost his starboard-outer engine a little under two hours into the flight, and turned back after jettisoning his bombs over the sea. The others achieved an accurate and concentrated bombing performance with numerous direct hits, and although the operation was written up as a success, later photographic reconnaissance showed four hits but no penetration, and also demonstrated the futility of throwing conventional bombs at reinforced concrete.

The busy round of operations continued with an attack on the *U-Boot* pens at Brest on the 12th, this time with Tallboys in the bomb bays, and with W/C Tait flying a 617 Lancaster, DV380, for the first time. It should be remembered, that, as a former 4 Group man, all of his many previous operations in heavy bombers, other than those during his time on the Base staff at Waddington, had been flown in Whitleys and Halifaxes, so Fearn donated his own crew to look after the commanding officer. Fawke flew the lone Mosquito, NT205, to photograph the operation, and the other Lancaster crews were those of Cockshott in PD238, Pryor in LM485, Oram in DV391, Ian Ross in ME555, Hamilton in PD233, Gingles in LM489, Sanders in ME562, Watts in DV246 and Kell in ME561. Cockshott was last but one away at 07.01, but he was first back three hours and fifty minutes later with his Tallboy still attached after developing engine trouble. Hamilton's Tallboy was the first to go down onto the aiming point at 09.45, and was a direct hit followed immediately by two more. Fawke had a good view of the proceedings from 7,500 feet, and reported all but one of the bombs hitting the target, the errant one falling as a near miss into the water on the open side of the pens. Reconnaissance confirmed two direct hits with penetrations and another causing a crater on the roof.

The morning of the 13th brought a return to Brest, with Tait flying in EE146, which would become his personal transport. With him this time were four members of Kell's crew, one of Paddy Gingles's and F/L Larry Curtis, formerly of Mick Martin's crew. Fawke flew in NT205 as the camera Mosquito, taking off at 09.19, by which time Tait had been on his way for fifty minutes. The 617 Squadron element of thirteen Lancasters was joined by fourteen others from 9 Squadron, in the first of what would become a series of joint operations.

Five 617 Squadron crews were briefed to attack the U-Boot pens with Tallboys, and the others the derelict French cruiser *Gueydon* with twelve 1,000 pounders each. This was one of a number of ships, which, it was thought, the enemy might use to block the harbour entrance ahead of advancing American forces, and it was decided to sink them in safe positions. Assigned to the vessel were the crews of Cockshott in PD238, Willsher in ME561, Lee in LM482, Ian Ross in ME555, Oram in DV391, Pryor in LM485, Howard in ED763 and Sanders in ME562, while the crews of Williams in DV385, Hamilton in PD233, Knights in LM492, Watts in DV246 and Tait targeted the pens. From his vantage point, Fawke described the Tallboy bombing as good, and estimated three direct hits. Williams claimed one of them from 16,900 feet at 10.59, and Hamilton another, which struck the northern edge of the roof. The *Gueydon* was straddled by a number of sticks, but there were no confirmed hits, and she was still afloat as the force withdrew. The timing of this maiden joint operation was significant. Plans were afoot for an assault on the *Tirpitz* at its Norwegian moorings in Kaa Fjord employing Tallboys, and talks were in progress with the Soviets to allow the operation to be launched from Russian soil. Although the first Tallboys would not arrive at Bardney for 9 Squadron use until the 31st, this day's operation at Brest provided an opportunity for the two squadrons to operate in tandem and practise the tactics necessary for bombing a large stationary vessel under heavy fire.

The 14th was a day of high activity for the Command, which began at Woodhall Spa either side of 08.30 with the take-off of thirteen 617 Squadron Lancasters, and a single Mosquito, NT205, with Fawke at the controls. They were again accompanied by a contingent from 9 Squadron for another tilt at the *Gueydon* at Brest, and the payload for each aircraft on this occasion was six 2,000lb armour-piercing bombs. Tait reverted to DV380 for this trip, and retaining Gallagher and Curtis in his crew, he added four others, including bomb-aimer Keith Astbury, who had been flying with Munro, and wireless operator Arthur Ward, who was on his ninth operation since returning to the squadron in April after recovering from the injuries received in the crash in January as a member of O'Shaughnessy's crew. Cockshott was in PD238, Pryor in LM485, Oram in DV391, Fearn in ME561, Howard in ED763, Williams in DV385, Sanders in ME562, Watts in DV246, Lee in LM482, Willsher in DV402, Ian Ross in ME555 and Knights in PB415. Fawke took up his position at 8,000 feet to photograph the proceedings, and he spotted one bomb appearing to hit the stern of the ship. Only Lee among the others was able to confirm this and other hits, while a number of crews commented on near misses. The consensus, though, was that the bombing had generally overshot the mark. Kit Howard saw what he believed to be a hole in the ship's side, which caused air bubbles and a lightening of the water. Heavy flak was encountered over the target, and Williams and Willsher were too busy evading it to notice where their bombs fell. A number of aircraft were hit, among them Lee's and Pryor's. The former sustained an ankle injury as a result, but he brought the Lancaster home to a safe landing at Beaulieu. The latter's bomb-aimer, F/O Pesme, was killed instantly by a splinter of shrapnel when right over the aiming point, and the bombs were jettisoned. Reconnaissance showed both vessels to be still afloat.

That evening over a hundred 5 Group Lancasters carried out a second attack, and the *Gueydon* and another derelict warship, the *Clemenceau*, were both left sinking in safe positions. In between these two operations, over 800 aircraft were sent against seven enemy positions facing a Canadian advance in the Falaise area. Tragically, some of the bombing fell among Canadian troops in a quarry, and thirteen of them were killed, while fifty-three others were wounded. An enquiry revealed, that some crews had disregarded orders given at briefing to begin bombing only after a certain point on the ground had been reached, and a number of commanding officers found themselves on the carpet as a result.

F/O Castagnola returned from 57 Squadron on the 15th, and was joined by New Zealander F/O Joplin from 51 Base, whence also came F/L 'Benny' Goodman on the following day. The squadron was stood down on the 15th, but not so the rest of the Command. In preparation for his new night offensive against Germany Harris launched a 1,000 aircraft during the morning to attack successfully nine night-fighter airfields in Holland and Belgium. Gibson, now having moved to 54 Base at Coningsby from East Kirkby, flew to Deelen in a two seat Lockheed Lightning with S/L Ciano. This was one of two examples of the type under evaluation by 5 Group for use by their master bombers and deputies, and Gibson flew in one again a few days later with a S/L Howard, when following the bomber stream to Fecamp, although the dates in his log book appear to be inaccurate. 617 and 9 Squadrons joined forces again on the 16th for what became an abortive operation against the *U-Boot* pens at La Pallice. Tait was in EE146, and he continued to chop and change his crew, this time adding Terry Playford and Gerry Witherick as navigator and rear gunner respectively, who had formally flown with the now tour-expired Dickie Willsher. The Tallboy element consisted of Cockshott in PD238, Pryor in LM485, with F/O Woods as his replacement bomb-aimer, Sanders in DV402 and Knights in PB415. Those, like Tait, carrying six 2,000 pounders were Howard in ED763, Fearn in PD233, Oram in DV391, Carey in ME554, Ross in ME555 and Watts in PB416. A late afternoon take-off brought them to the target at 20.00 hours, and Tait identified what he thought was the *U-Boot* pens through a gap in the cloud. He released his six 2,000lb bombs, only to discover a few seconds later through a second gap, that he had been mistaken. Fawke was on hand in NT205, but photographs were impossible in the conditions, which also allowed no chance of a successful attack, and the remaining ten aircraft were sent home with their bombs.

That night the main force returned to Germany, with an outstandingly successful assault on Stettin by Lancasters, while a mixed force gained moderate results at Kiel. On the 17th F/O Pesme was interred at Stonefall cemetery, and the squadron was represented by Kearns and the founder members Len Sumpter and Dave Rodger, who were about to be posted on the 21st and 23rd respectively. 617 and 9 Squadrons returned to La Pallice on the 18th with Fawke in Mosquito NT205 to record the event, and Tait in EE146, Oram in EE131, Knights in PB415, Watts in DV402, Knilans in PD238 with Joplin as a passenger, and Pryor in LM485 each carrying a Tallboy. The others, Fearn in PD233, Howard in ED763, Levy in PB416, Ross in LM489 and Carey in ME555 had six 2,000 pounders in their bomb bays. Tait and Fearn were the first to release their bombs at 15.08, at which point Fearn's Lancaster was hit by flak. He immediately took violent evasive action, and as a result of the gyrations, he and his crew were unable to observe the fall and impact of their bombs. Tait saw a Tallboy burst on the south-west corner of the pens, and another slightly overshoot to the north. The others confirmed the accuracy of the bombing, and Pryor reported a second direct hit right in the centre of the aiming point, but smoke was beginning to obscure the target, and a final assessment was not possible. Fearn brought his extensively damaged Lancaster safely home along with the others. Reconnaissance pictures showed at least one and maybe two direct hits by Tallboys, but no penetrations. That night a devastating attack was delivered by around 250 Lancasters and Halifaxes on Bremen, in which over 8,600 houses and apartment blocks were destroyed by fire.

Unfavourable weather conditions helped to keep the squadron's crews on the ground for the next few days, and it was not until the early afternoon of the 24th that they were next called into action. At briefing they learned they were to attack the *S-Boot* pens in the Dutch port of Ijmuiden. There were actually two major structures in the port to house the *Schnellboote*, those referred to in British intelligence reports as the old one and the new one. The Germans knew the old one as *Schnellbootbunker* AY, and the new one as 2 or BY. The letters A and B represented 1 and 2, and Y was the code for Ijmuiden. The pens close to the mouth of the basin were the new ones, and were still under construction. However, in September construction would cease because of a shortage of materials, and the project would never be completed and the bunker never used. An entry in the naval commander's diary for the 6th of September tells the story.

> 6th September 1944. 10.00 hours. Have received an order to discontinue construction of the new *S-Bootbunker* at Ijmuiden (Bauwerk BY). The construction equipment is to be transferred to Germany. I emphasize that in the present situation no lorries can be made available for the transportation, and the evacuation of construction equipment will have to proceed via waterways.

The old pens occupied the northern end of the basin, and this was the structure selected as the squadron's target for today. Fawke was in NT205, the lone Mosquito, and in keeping with his role ever since Tait had reverted to a Lancaster, he was on hand for photographic reconnaissance, rather than to mark the target. Only eight 617 squadron Lancasters were involved in this joint operation with 9 Squadron, and they contained the crews of Tait in EE146, Howard in ED763, Iveson in PD238, Pryor in PD233, Carey in LM489, Ross in EE131, Watts in PB415 and Levy in PB416. All were armed with Tallboys as they took off between 12.14 and half past the hour, and they arrived at the target two hours later in good bombing conditions. Fawke took up a position at 4,000 feet, and recorded two hits in the water to the north, one near the south-east corner and another 50 yards to the south. He witnessed a very large explosion on the centre of the pens at 14.28, and the last three bombs fell into the smoke created by this. Ross and Watts were the first to bomb within seconds of each other, the former observing a direct hit in the centre of the roof, and his own bomb striking the north-western corner. Watts, on the other hand, saw the first four Tallboys go down, and thought the first hit the south-western corner, while the second and third fell into the docks about 100 yards from the mouth of the pens, and the fourth caused the large explosion in the centre of the roof. Whatever the individual impressions, the consensus was again that the operation had been concluded successfully. In fact, at least one direct hit had caused a large portion of the roof to collapse, and the rear of the pens was badly damaged. A later report determined that *S-Boot* pen A had received the 617 Squadron Tallboys, while 9 Squadron's efforts hit Ijmuiden West railway station, where six tracks and overhead lines were damaged and one man was killed. The office of a fishing company used by the Germans was also demolished, and various warehouses were either damaged or destroyed. Four German naval vessels were sunk, although one was later raised. In all eight *Kriegsmarine* personnel were killed and nineteen seriously wounded.

1, 3, 6 and 8 Groups carried out a partially effective attack on the Opel Motor factory at Rüsselsheim on the 25/26th, while the Independent Air Force raided Darmstadt, also in southern Germany. The latter was not a successful operation, but the failure would be rectified in horrifying fashion in a little over two weeks. 1, 3 and 8 Groups pounded Kiel on the following night, and 5 Group went to the limit of its range to attack the Baltic port of Königsberg, which was being used by the enemy to supply its eastern front. Most of the bombing fell into the eastern part of the town, and it would be necessary to return at a later date. 617 Squadron carried out its last operation of the month on the 27th, when shipping was attacked at Brest, again in concert with 9 Squadron. The ORB is not specific about the ships involved, but they were a freighter and a hulk. With Allied ground forces close by, one or both of the vessels were possibly intended for strategic sinking by the enemy to block access to the port and prevent its immediate use. Some accounts describe them as *Sperrbrecher*, the German word for blockade-runner, intending to portray the meaning of a blockage or artificial reef, but they are employing the wrong word. Twelve Lancasters were involved in the operation, crewed by Tait in EE146, Howard in NF923, Watts in DV246, Knights in PB415, Levy in PB416, Stout in LM482, Castagnola in DV402, Pryor in LM489, Hamilton in PD233, Iveson in PD238, Joplin in ME554 and Goodman in EE131, the last two mentioned operating with the squadron as crew captains for the first time. All carried twelve 1,000 pounders for this afternoon foray, and Fawke was again on hand in NT205 to photograph the results. Assessment was difficult, but one vessel seemed to be down by the bows as the force withdrew, and Fawke complimented 9 Squadron on the quality of its bombing. The hulk was not visible on reconnaissance photos, and it was believed, therefore, to have sunk, while the freighter appeared to be damaged.

By this time two more postings-in had taken place. The already mentioned S/L Wyness, a contemporary of Martin and Knight at 50 Squadron in 1942, arrived from 57 Squadron on the 25th to assume the role of flight commander, and F/O Huckerby came in from Cheshire's former command, 4 Group's 76 Squadron. The latter's posting is something of a mystery, as he was an experienced pilot, but carried out no operations with 617 Squadron before his posting out in February 1945. The final operations in the long-running flying bomb campaign took place on the 28th, and shortly afterwards the Pas-de-Calais fell once more into Allied hands after more than four years under occupation. 5 Group returned to Königsberg on the 29/30th, and dealt a severe blow to the town, despite having to sacrifice bombs for fuel, while 1, 3, 6 and 8 Groups destroyed over 1,500 houses and thirty-two industrial premises at Stettin, further west along the Baltic coast.

Chapter Sixteen

Tirpitz

The liberation of French ports

The Command would devote much of its effort during September to removing pockets of resistance from around the three major French ports still in enemy hands. Operations were mounted daily against Le Havre between the 5th and the 11th, although those on the 8th and 9th were severely restricted by the weather conditions. British ground forces followed up, and within hours of their attack the German garrison surrendered. At Woodhall Spa, meanwhile, the first ten days of the month brought more rumour than flying, as the crews were kept on standby for a special operation. Further crew movements took place during the period, which brought F/O Martin from 61 Squadron and F/L Sayers from 467 Squadron on the 1st, while the long-serving F/O Willsher departed for 5 LFS at the same time. 5 LFS retaliated by sending F/O Leavitt, an American, in the other direction on the 8th, but not to be outdone, the squadron dispatched F/L Poore there on the 13th at the conclusion of his tour. Phil Martin was another Australian who had joined 61 Squadron after a spell flying Wellingtons at 17 OTU, at Silverstone during December 1943 and January 1944, while the Berlin campaign was at its height. He was introduced to four engines via Stirlings at 1660CU at Swinderby, before spending twelve days learning to fly the Lancaster at 5 LFS Syerston. His first operation with 61 Squadron was as a second pilot on the 5 Group raid against Brunswick led by the 617 Squadron Mosquitos on the 22/23rd of April. With this one in the bag he completed another thirty sorties, finishing with a small-scale daylight attack by the Group on oil storage installations at La Pallice on the 19th of August.

Laid down in October 1936, the mighty battleship *Tirpitz*, sister ship of the *Bismarck*, represented a major leap forward in warship design, and was the means by which the *Kriegsmarine* intended to wrest control of the seas from the Royal Navy. She was launched in January 1939 in a blaze of publicity at a ceremony attended by Hitler himself and the entire Nazi hierarchy. An audience was transported to Wilhelmshaven from all over Germany to watch Frau von Hassel, the daughter of the man after whom the ship was named, perform the traditional act of breaking the champagne bottle over her bows. This she did with great reluctance and under pressure from the regime for which she had no sympathy. It was a further two years before *Tirpitz* was completed at a standard displacement of 41,700 tons, and with a main armament of eight × 15 inch guns. She had a design speed with a full load of thirty knots, and by 1944 a crew complement of more than 1,900 officers and men. At over 800 feet long *Tirpitz* was larger, faster, better armed and better protected than her British contemporaries, and these aspects alone would enable her to impact the war and British thinking without her ever engaging other surface vessels in combat at sea. The very fact that she existed, albeit for most of her career at her moorings in Norwegian fjords, was enough to keep Churchill and the Admiralty in a constant state of agitation. She had to be destroyed, and numerous attempts were made to penetrate her defences, some partially successful, others dismal failures. Bomber Command had last attacked the battleship in Norway at the end of April 1942, when a small force of Halifaxes and Lancasters from 4 and 5 Groups failed to inflict any damage, and the now AOC 8 Group, AVM Don Bennett, had been shot down and evaded capture. Other attempts were made by dive-bombers, manned torpedoes and X-craft (mini submarines), and while repairing the damage kept *Tirpitz* immobile, she was still a threat, an annoying itch that could not be ignored. As long as she remained afloat she would disproportionately occupy the minds of British war planners and tie up elements of the Royal Navy that were needed elsewhere.

On the 11th twenty crews departed Woodhall Spa, and set off for the gruelling flight to Yagodnik in the Archangel region of north-west Russia, from where Operation Paravane, the first of the squadron's three epic attacks on the *Tirpitz* was to be launched. This was to be another joint operation with 9 Squadron, which dispatched eighteen Lancasters. The 617 Squadron element consisted of Tait in EE146, Gingles in LM489, Ross in EE131, Carey in NF920, Iveson in ME554, Hamilton in PD233, Cockshott in PD238, Fawke in DV405, Sanders in ME562, Howard in NF923, Watts in LM485, Knights in DV391, Kell in LM482, Stout in ME561, Castagnola in PB415, Pryor in DV246, Levy in PB416, Knilans in LM492, Wyness in ME559 and Oram in ED763. Take-off began at 18.36 DBST, and Stout was last away at 19.37. Remarkably, and as a result of expert navigation, all the aircraft arrived in the general vicinity of Yagodnik, only to be thwarted by fog and the absence, through misinformation, of a guiding beacon. Carey's NF920 was damaged by flak over Finland en-route, and would not take part in the operation, and F/O Ross and S/L Wyness in EE131 and ME559 respectively, were compelled by fuel shortage to crash-land, and wrote off their aircraft. Four 9 Squadron aircraft also crash-landed and were damaged beyond repair. The remainder landed safely, although not all at Yagodnik. Lt Knilans's lobbed LM492 down in a field as his fuel was about to give out, and Iveson soon joined him. Tait arrived some time later as a passenger in an ancient Soviet biplane, and found his crews being entertained by Russian soldiers, male and female, in a wooden hut. Iveson had sufficient fuel to reach Yagodnik, and took off without incident. The Russians put some petrol into LM492, and Knilans flew it out, cutting a hundred yard long swathe through the treetops bordering the field in the process. A smashed perspex nose caused discomfort to the crew by allowing in a howling gale, and an engine overheated after foliage blocked the radiator. However, the weather was to delay the operation long enough to allow repairs to be completed successfully, and LM492 would take its place on the order of battle.

That night 5 Group returned to the southern city of Darmstadt, which had escaped the worst ravages of a Bomber Command assault just two weeks earlier. 226 Lancasters and fourteen Mosquitos took part, and the 5 Group marking method prepared the almost intact city perfectly for the kill. A firestorm erupted in the central districts, which destroyed everything it touched, and the final death toll was put at more than 12,000 people, with a further 70,000 rendered homeless. This was in a city with a population at the time of 120,000. On the following night 5 Group returned to southern Germany to wipe out the north and west central districts of Stuttgart, killing in the process more than 1,100 people. While this was going on, 1, 3 and 8 Groups were further north hitting Frankfurt for the final time in the war. Almost 400 aircraft were involved, and they inflicted massive damage on the city's western districts at a time when most of the emergency and rescue services were at nearby Darmstadt still fighting the fires from twenty-four hours earlier.

It was the 15th before the 617 and 9 Squadron operation could be launched from Russian soil against the pride of the German fleet, which lay at anchor in Kaa Fjord in Norway. Approaching from the land south-east of the target shortly before 13.00 hours double British summer time, the crews were able to observe the ship in the distance as it gradually became swallowed up by the smoke from smoke-pots, and it had become completely enveloped by the time that the first bombs went down. A gaggle of Tallboys was released at 12.56 DBST (13.56 local time) by Tait, Howard, Kell, Stout, Pryor and Oram from between 14,200 and 17,400 feet, and those of Fawke, Castagnola and Knilans followed during the next nine minutes. Hamilton suffered a hang up, and after three abortive runs, finally parted company with his Tallboy, either intentionally or involuntarily four miles south of the target at 13.15, while Gingles, Cockshott and Knights were unable to establish an aiming point, and took their bombs back to Yagodnik. Johnny Walker mines were delivered by Iveson, Sanders and Watts from between 11,000 and 12,000 feet, Iveson using those ferried to Russia by Carey, after being forced to jettison his own during the flight from England. (Johnny Walker mines were 400lb bombs with a 90lb Torpex charge. The bomb fell from the aircraft on a parachute that was released on impact with the water. A bouyancy chamber that was flooded and blown by means of a valve and gas allowed the bomb to sink to 60 feet and then rise to the surface. If it failed to hit a vessel it sank again, moved laterally 30 feet and rose again. It might do this several times. When the gas was expended it would explode.) One large explosion was witnessed by a number of crews, but it was impossible to assess the results. After the attack the crews returned to Yagodnik to prepare for the flight home. Nine crews arrived back on the 17th, but F/O Levy failed to return,

PB416 having crashed in mountains in Norway, killing all nine men on board, including two of S/L Wyness's crew. Another five crews returned to Woodhall Spa on the 18th, F/L Oram on the 19th, F/O Carey on the 20th, and F/L Knights was the last home on the 21st.

What was not at that time appreciated was the fact that *Tirpitz* had suffered damage from a direct hit right on the bows ahead of the anchor cable holders. The Tallboy, almost certainly the one delivered by Tait, passed through the ship and exploded about 35 feet from the stem below keel level, tearing a 32 × 48 foot hole in the starboard bow. This allowed the forward section of the ship to take on 1,500 tons of seawater, and such damage, along with that caused internally by a number of near misses, was sufficient to prevent her from returning to sea in the foreseeable future. German engineers reported that repairs would take nine months if there were no interruptions, but a committee chaired by Admiral Doenitz on the 23rd declared the vessel to be beyond repair. It was decided that she would be drafted into the new defensive line being prepared in the Lyngenfjord area, where her main armament could be put to good use. As a result, she would be towed to a new location at Tromsö in October for use as a floating fortress. To the Allies, however, she still appeared to offer a threat as a 'fleet in being'. Her new anchorage placed her 200 miles closer to the northerly British airfields, and just within range of the Lancaster force.

Six Lancasters were left behind in Russia, either because they were deemed to be beyond repair, or after having been cannibalised to keep the others airworthy. Russian Air Force personnel inspected them, and decided, that the two least damaged could be returned to flying condition. They were dismantled and transported to Kegostrov for repair and modification by the Air Force of the White Sea, which was to use them for unarmed marine patrols. The armament was removed, and the rear turret faired-over, while a Mk III Halifax style perspex nose was added, along with larger side windows for better observation. The RAF colour scheme was retained, but red stars outlined in black replaced the roundels. One of these Lancasters was Wyness's ME559, KC-Q, which now became 01, its new identification painted large in white. It was allocated to the 16th Transport Flight for convoy escort, submarine detection and general reconnaissance flights, and as a result of its handling qualities and long range, it proved to be popular with its new owners. It survived the war, and its last known role was as an educational aid at the Russian Aviation Technical College. The original identity of the other restored Lancaster is not known, but it was written off in a crash at the end of the war.

While 617 Squadron had been attending to *Tirpitz*, over 700 aircraft delivered 3,000 tons of bombs onto Boulogne and its environs on the 17th, and this, together with a ground assault, persuaded the enemy garrison to throw in the towel a week later. This left just Calais still under enemy occupation, and the first of six operations against enemy strong points around the port was mounted by over 600 aircraft on the 20th.

Two nights earlier, The 'Lincolnshire Poachers' had delivered a massively successful raid on Bremerhaven, and destroyed over 2,600 buildings. The following night, the 19/20th, was devoted to an attack by 1 and 5 Groups on the twin towns of Mönchengladbach and Rheydt, for which W/C Guy Gibson was to act in the role of Master Bomber. Gibson had been unhappy at being forcibly removed from his natural environment after the Dams success. He was a warrior, and the war had provided him with a purpose and an opportunity to develop characteristics, which might otherwise have remained dormant. The bomber station was his natural environment, where he revelled in his status as leader of the pack, and despite his inbred antipathy towards the rank and file, he was an inspirational squadron commander, who never failed to get the best from his crews. Like all the best of his kind, he led his men from the front, and chose to fly the most difficult, and often, groundbreaking operations. He had spent some of the first half of 1944 writing his book, *Enemy Coast Ahead*, while he was living in London, and had also been approached about becoming the conservative parliamentary candidate for Macclesfied. During August he resigned his nomination to stand, and languishing in a staff job as Senior Air Staff Officer (SASO) at 54 Base Coningsby, he was more desperate than ever to get back into the war before it ended. This desire was further fuelled by wangling a number of unofficial sorties with crews from East Kirkby. When the opportunity presented itself to fly as raid controller, he grabbed it with both hands.

His removal from the operational scene may have robbed him of his sense of direction, but not his arrogance, and this was much in evidence as the operation drew near. The role of Master Bomber was one for which he was not qualified, and the complex plan for this particular operation would have taxed even an experienced man. Gibson brushed aside the advice freely given by those who had performed the task many times, and at Coningsby, the home of the 5 Group Master Bomber fraternity, there was experience aplenty. He refused for some unexplained reason to accept the 627 Squadron Mosquito prepared for him by the ground crews, and insisted on another, which was duly provided in the form of KB267. Following some initial difficulties with the marking, the raid proceeded according to plan, although some crews bombed markers not assigned to them. Nevertheless, severe damage was inflicted on both towns, and Gibson was heard to order the crews home at the raid's conclusion. He never arrived back, and it was later learned that his Mosquito, a type with which he had only a fleeting acquaintance, had crashed and burned out on the outskirts of the southern Dutch town of Steenbergen, and he and his navigator, S/L Warwick, had been killed. Only Warwick could be identified by a letter found on his remains, and it was not until after the war that a second headstone in honour of Gibson was erected next to Warwick's in the local Catholic cemetery. No satisfactory explanation has been found for the loss of the aircraft. Eyewitnesses watched the Mosquito circle the town, and some claimed to have seen a bright light in the cockpit. The most likely cause of the crash was fuel starvation through a lack of familiarity by either occupant with the fuel transfer procedure.

On the evening of the 23rd 617 Squadron joined others of 5 Group to attack the River Glane underpass section of the Dortmund-Ems Canal near Ladbergen, the scene of the tragic events of twelve months earlier, when five out of eight crews had failed to return. Eleven of the 136 Lancasters were provided by 617 Squadron, and they contained the crews of Tait in LM485, Stout in NF923, Sanders in ME562, Martin in DV380 on his first operation with the squadron, Cockshott in LM489, Iveson in ME554, Hamilton in ME555, Wyness in DV402, Sayers in LM482, Castagnola in ME559, and Oram in DV393. All 617 Squadron aircraft were carrying Tallboys, and these were primed and ready to go as the target was approached in 7/10ths cloud at around 21.40 hours. Iveson reported being able to see the red TIs clearly from 16,000 feet at 21.42, but they disappeared frustratingly beneath the cloud just fifteen seconds before the release point was reached, and despite making two further runs, he could not pick up the aiming point again. He brought his Tallboy home, as did Sayers, who was over the target for thirty minutes, and seems to have had the TIs in sight throughout. His efforts were hampered by an unserviceable compass, however, and as he made his sixth run the TIs burned out. Wyness started his bombing run from 14,000 feet with the TIs in view, and had three good runs thwarted by cloud at the crucial moment. He was ordered to come down to 12,000 feet, and if unable to see the aiming point, to return to base with his bomb, and this is what he did. Sanders also brought his Tallboy home. Tait dropped his from 7,500 feet at 22.04, and Phil Martin followed suit from 8,000 feet eight minutes later during his sixth run. In between these, Cockshott, Hamilton and Castagnola delivered their bombs also from 8,000 feet, which was clearly the optimum altitude for the occasion, and Oram concluded the 617 Squadron effort from an even lower 7,000 feet at 22.16. He also commented on a good concentration of thousand pounders from the 5 Group main force, but no one was able to determine the effects of the bombing.

In fact, it had been a highly successful operation, which left both branches of the canal breached, and a six-mile stretch of this vital waterway drained, bringing a halt to all through-navigation until the 21st of October. On the debit side it had been an expensive operation, in which eleven Lancasters came to grief, and among them was one from 617 Squadron. Geoff Stout was on his way home with his Tallboy still attached, when a night fighter attacked NF923 over Holland. Three engines were knocked out, and a fire took hold in the bomb bay, forcing the crew to bale out. Five did so, F/Os Rupert and Petch and F/S Whitaker, bomb aimer, rear gunner and mid-upper gunner respectively, ultimately evading capture, but F/L Stout and his navigator, F/O Graham, died in the ensuing crash, and the flight engineer, P/O Benting, succumbed to his injuries while in captivity on the 25th. It had been their misfortune to stumble across the BF110 G-4 of *Hauptmann* Heinz-Wolfgang Schnaufer, operating at the time out of Dortmund, who would end the war as Germany's most successful night-fighter pilot with a total of 121 kills from 164 sorties. On this night alone Schnaufer claimed four RAF bombers over Holland in the space of thirty-two minutes in the Enschede, Winterswijk and Zutphen area, and it seems likely that Stout was the first. Schnaufer recorded his first victory at 22.53, and Stout's Lancaster crashed at 23.00, ten minutes before Schnaufer recorded his second kill. This remarkable young man would survive the war, only to lose his life in an automobile accident in France in 1950 at the still tender age of twenty-eight.

The series of main force operations against Calais continued daily from the 24th to the 28th, although poor weather conditions reduced the effectiveness of some of them. In the event Canadian forces took the port shortly thereafter. The game of musical chairs flared up again on the 26th, when F/O Flatman arrived at Woodhall Spa on posting from 5 LFS, to be followed three days later by F/L Gumbley. Also on that day, F/L Marshall was added to squadron strength from 1654CU.

The squadron parted company with its Mustang on the 2nd of October as it departed for 38 Maintenance Unit. The new month's operations began for 617 Squadron with a trip to the sea wall at Westkapelle on the island of Walcheren in the Scheldt Estuary on the 3rd, in company with elements of the main force. Heavy gun emplacements here were barring the approaches to the much-needed port of Antwerp, some forty miles down river, and operations to bomb them during September had failed to produce the desired results. As they were proving to be such difficult targets to bomb, it was decided to inundate them with seawater, and also thereby to create difficult terrain for the enemy to defend in the event of a land invasion. Eight waves of thirty bombers each attacked the target, and the fifth wave created a breach, which was widened by those following behind. The 617 Squadron element consisted of Tait and Fawke in Mosquitos NT205 and DZ415 respectively, and the crews of Cockshott in ME555, with the recent arrival Mark Flatman as a passenger, Goodman in LM489, Iveson in ME554, Wyness in NG180, a new Lancaster operating for the first time, Sayers in DV402, Joplin in DV393, Castagnola in DV385 and Martin in ME562. Tait arrived at the target at 14.55, while the main force assault was still in progress, and remained in the area for ten minutes to assess the situation. Fawke took photos from 3,500 feet at 15.05, by which time the sea wall had been breached over a length of 330 feet, and the floodwater had reached the town. It was clear to Tait that the job had already been accomplished, and he sent the squadron participants home with their valuable Tallboys.

A new Ruhr offensive began at Dortmund on the 6/7th at the hands of 3, 6 and 8 Groups, and further severe damage was inflicted on this much-bombed city. Meanwhile, 5 Group carried out a devastating raid on Bremen using its low-level visual marking method, and almost 5,000 buildings were destroyed or seriously damaged.

Chapter Seventeen

War Crime

On the 7th of October thirteen 617 Squadron crews were briefed for a daylight attack on the Kembs Barrage on the Rhine, deep in southern Germany and on the very outskirts of the Swiss city of Basle. Immediately north of the city the river divides into two branches in the shape of the letter Y running roughly north-west to south-east, and the dam-like objective, with its steelwork superstructure, stretched across the right-hand or eastern branch a matter of 200 metres north of the point of divide. This was also the spot where three countries joined, one neutral, one occupied and the other the occupier and aggressor. The western or left-hand bank of the right branch marked Germany's border with France, while Germany, France and Switzerland all met at the separation of the Rhine as it formed the Y shape. The plan of attack called for the force to be split into two elements, the first consisting of seven Lancasters, which were to bomb from above 6,000 feet with Tallboys fused to detonate on impact. The second section of six aircraft was to go in at 600 feet, with their Tallboys fused for a thirty-minute delay, and the whole force was to be escorted by three squadrons of Mustangs, which would be picked up at 4,000 feet over Manston.

The high Lancaster section consisted of Fawke in NG181, with the station commander, G/C Philpott, on board, Joplin in DV393, Iveson in ME554, Sayers in DV402, Gingles in LM489 with Mark Flatman as a passenger, Watts in LM485 and Castagnola probably in DV385, the last two also carrying an extra man. Tait was to lead the low section in EE146, with Cockshott in LM492, Sanders in ME562, Martin in DV391, Wyness in NG180 and Howard in LM482, the last mentioned carrying an extra gunner in the person of F/O Watkins, who had last flown with Oram. Wyness had not had an entirely settled crew since joining the squadron, and had flown with a succession of flight engineers and wireless operators. Those occupying these positions in his crew on the trip to Russia had died with Levy and crew on the way home. Wyness's wireless operator on this occasion, New Zealander F/O Bruce Hosie, was a veteran of seventy-two operations and still only twenty-one years of age. He had begun his first tour of operations in September 1942 as a member of 3 Group's 75(NZ) Squadron, which was equipped at the time with Wellingtons before converting to Stirlings. After completing thirty-one operations he was posted to 1665 Conversion Unit at Woolfox Lodge, from where he undertook five more sorties while instructing. He was posted to 617 Squadron in January 1944, and joined the crew of F/O Cooper. He flew operations with this crew until around the 22nd of April, when he presumably went on leave or fell sick, because he was not on board Cooper's Lancaster when it was shot down on the way home from Munich on the night of the 24/25th. Hosie then joined Bob Knights, and flew continually with him, up to and including the above-mentioned attack on the *Tirpitz*, which was his seventy-second operation. It is believed that Hosie acquired his seat in the Lancaster of Drew Wyness on the toss of a coin. As events were to prove, it was an unfortunate toss to win. Navigator F/L Williams DFC had been in 5 Group since beginning his operational career in October 1942 with 106 Squadron, commanded at the time by Gibson. Thereafter, he served with 61 Squadron before moving on to 57 Squadron, where he teamed up with 'Duke' Wyness, and he had fifty-two operations to his credit.

The two sections took off between 13.07 and 13.38, the latter time being that of Watts, who was temporarily delayed through technical problems. With Watts lagging behind, the rest flew out together in formation, and crossed into enemy territory without incident, remaining at a low enough level for Martin's navigator, F/S Jackson, to be able to spot the bells round the necks of cows crossing a bridge as the target was approached. The high force climbed to run across the target from the west, while the low force began a triangular dogleg circuit to bring them in from the east, before arcing round to the north to pick up the aiming point, with the city of Basle behind them.

Tait described the weather as 'touch and go' as they neared the target, but on arrival the area was found to be free of cloud and visibility was good. By the time that the low force was in position, some of the high force had already bombed. Watts was the first to do so, having caught up by cutting across the Swiss frontier. His Tallboy went down from 6,000 feet at 16.44½, and overshot by some 50 yards. Thirty seconds later, 'Slapsie' Sayers opened his bomb doors at 7,300 feet, whereupon his Tallboy fell out, buckling the doors as it went. Three minutes later and 600 feet higher Castagnola released his Tallboy, and watched it hit the barrage between the first and second piers. Within seconds Iveson bombed from 8,500 feet, but had to report his Tallboy falling onto the left riverbank some 400 yards south-east of the aiming point. A minute later Joplin bombed from 7,500 feet, and observed his Tallboy falling just beyond the barrage near the second pier from the left.

It was at this stage of the operation that the low section began to attack in staggered pairs, Tait first, with Wyness a few hundred yards behind. It is easy to imagine this attack as a daylight version of the run on the Möhne Dam, in which the Lancasters raced in low over the water and scraped over the parapet of the barrage to make their escape. This would be a false impression, however. At ultra low level it is possible to merge into the background for part of the approach, and to flash across the field of fire of gun positions on the beam faster than they can traverse. Not so at 500 to 600 feet, the minimum height considered necessary for the Tallboy to achieve the required trajectory for this operation. This was a kind of no-man's land altitude, at which the Lancasters would be in full view at all times, travelling relatively slowly across the sky, offering a large and inviting target for light flak. As had been tragically demonstrated at the Möhne, gunners learn quickly. After the first attack by Gibson had taken them by surprise, they knew exactly from where the next one was coming and where to aim, and that fact had cost the lives of Hopgood and four of his crew. Tait's run at the Kembs barrage also caught the gunners by surprise, and they were unable to fix their sights on him before he released his Tallboy accurately into the water ahead of the left hand sluice at 16.51. As he went in he noted that all trace of the detonations from the high-level bombs had disappeared, and that the barrage displayed no signs of damage. Having swung their barrels round belatedly to meet the oncoming Tait, the flak gunners, in particular those on the power station, were now ready to receive Wyness only seconds later. His Lancaster was raked unmercifully, and was apparently belching fire and smoke from both starboard engines before the release point was reached. Nevertheless, the Tallboy was discharged, and the flaming Lancaster roared over the steel superstructure of the barrage, weaving north along the right hand or eastern channel of the Rhine, its port wing brushing the French frontier

Now it was Howard's turn to run the gauntlet, with Martin about 400 yards behind and a little to his left. In the nose of DV391, bomb-aimer Don Day was finding it impossible to get a fix on the aiming point as the Lancaster bucked in Howard's slipstream and was rocked by exploding flak shells. The low-force aircraft had been fitted with bomb sights borrowed from Coastal Command, which had a sliding graticule, and had been designed for use against German *S-Boots* at low level. When the target appeared to keep pace with the graticule the bomb-aimer pressed the tit, but it wasn't happening for Don Day on this run, and he called for Martin to go round again. As he did so Howard also announced that he was pulling off for a second run after experiencing a hang-up. Martin called, "Hang on, we'll come round with you". As Howard and Martin banked in a tight turn to starboard, Cockshott and Sanders swept in to carry out their attacks. The turbulent air conspired with the flak shells to throw Cockshott's effort wide of the mark to the left and beyond the target at 16.54½, and Sanders's Tallboy also overshot a few seconds later, but at least both aircraft got through relatively unscathed.

By this time, Howard and Martin were back at their starting point about three miles from the target, and can have had no illusions about what awaited them. Before bending his head to his bombsight and the task ahead, Don Day watched Howard's Lancaster some 400 yards directly ahead and a little higher. When about two miles from the target he saw Howard's starboard tanks erupt, and great sheets of flame shoot out behind. From above, the other crews could only observe the unfolding drama as eight of their colleagues experienced their last few moments on earth. The scene was a kaleidoscope of exploding flak shells, flames and oily smoke, with Mustangs darting to and fro firing at the flak positions, the sun glinting off their canopies as the picturesque, sparkling Rhine became the backdrop to tragedy. LM482 banked to starboard engulfed in fire, and fell away to crash into a wood at Effringen-Kirchen within sight of the barrage. All of this had threatened to drag Don Day's eyes away from the moving graticule, but he resisted, shut his mind temporarily to the thought of an imminent violent death, noted that the shape of Howard's Lancaster was no longer in front, and sensed a Mustang, guns blazing, flash underneath at 45 degrees to his own line of approach. Another moment and he pressed the tit, feeling the floor of the Lancaster rise up to meet his prone body as the 12,000lb of dead weight was shed. It was an overshoot by 30 to 40 yards. In the rear turret Sgt Trebilcock had heard his pilot and bomb-aimer report that Howard had been hit, and was going down. It made him very angry. He opened up at the defences with his .303s, watching with satisfaction as his tracer scattered the gunners. He heard the call, 'Bomb gone', and this was followed by a violent jolt and an explosion. He knew that they too had been hit, but his skipper calmly called each crew-member in turn to check on their status, even as he struggled with the controls to keep the aircraft straight and level. They rocketed over the target, banking round to starboard, and almost found themselves caught in balloons on the Swiss side of the frontier. As they pulled away with damaged controls to begin the long flight home, Paddy Gingles dropped his Tallboy from 8,300 feet at 17.04, and listened as members of his crew described it overshooting and hitting a railway line. Gerry Fawke delivered the final bomb a minute later from 8,100 feet, having experienced difficulty in persuading it to release. It was Fawke's third run, and even then the Tallboy hung up for five seconds before falling away to hit the west bank of the river. A 627 Squadron Mosquito remained overhead until the delayed action bombs detonated, and the crew was able to report a successful conclusion to the operation, with a breach clearly evident at the left hand end, where Tait's Tallboy had landed. An unconfirmed report suggests that a Tallboy was recovered intact from the dyke at the side of the barrage, and that it may have been Howard's, jettisoned as he pulled away to crash, but released at too low an altitude to achieve the correct trajectory.

Martin, meanwhile, had negotiated the barrage balloons, and with tracer still flying indiscriminately around the sky, he raced across the red rooftops, Don Day noting the upturned faces of the startled Swiss subjects below. Once clear, Martin confided in his flight engineer, Jack Blagbrough, that he was getting no response from the rudder controls. Blagbrough went back to investigate, and found one severed end of the control wire. He wrapped it round the handle of the fire axe, plugged into the intercom, and stood by to receive instructions from his pilot. In this way the Martin crew eventually got back to Woodhall Spa, where they inspected the damage around the rear end, marvelling as they did so at how rear turret occupant Tommy Trebilcock had managed to come through with all his anatomical tackle intact. A total of 106 holes were counted in the Lancaster, but these were soon repaired by the ground crew. Martin was among those decorated for their exploits on this operation.

Wyness must have known that he and his crew would not be returning home. In a Lancaster threatening to blow itself apart at any moment, but too low for his crew to bale out, he had few options open to him. According to one unconfirmed report he headed north-west from the barrage following the course of the river, until he flew into the teeth of another flak position, which forced him to wheel back round to the south. A letter sent by the Air Ministry (New Zealand) to the parents of wireless operator Bruce Hosie in 1948 provides us with perhaps the most accurate sequence of events. It describes the Lancaster being hit by light flak and hitting a power line over or near the barrage, before coming down on the Rhine about 500 yards further on. The aircraft must have been close to becoming uncontrollable, and Wyness opted for a ditching with the hope and intention of gaining the sanctuary of the Swiss bank. The Lancaster came to rest intact in shallow water near the village of Rheinweiler. Two members of the crew ran along the starboard wing, jumped onto the French bank, and disappeared into woodland, while the remaining five inflated the dinghy and paddled away, presumably in the direction of Switzerland to gain the sanctuary of the neutral bank. The Germans dispatched a boat to intercept them, and this persuaded one crewmember to abandon the dinghy and swim to the French shore. The three men now on French soil were the gunners, F/O Cansell and F/S Horrocks, and the flight engineer, F/S Hurdiss. They were never seen alive again, and their bodies have never been recovered. It is believed, that they were captured, perhaps by French gendarmerie, and handed over to the Nazi authorities, or simply by the German occupying forces, and following their murder, were buried in unmarked graves.

Wyness, navigator, F/L Williams, bomb-aimer, F/O Honig and wireless operator, F/O Hosie, were captured by the *Wehrmacht*, and taken to Rheinweiler to be met by the local *Burgomeister*, along with officials from the *Gendarmarie* station at Schliengen, and the Kreisleiter of Mullheim, Hugo Grüner. They were put in pairs into two cars, one of them belonging to Grüner, and accompanied by a guard. One of the crewmen in Grüner's vehicle had an injured leg or foot. The car was driven in the direction of Schliengen, and at the village of Bellingen it turned off towards the river. It drew to a halt near the river bank at a place known as Steinplatz, and the guard, Rudolf Birlin, was ordered to take the prisoners to the water's edge, while a second guard, Hans Reimer, remained by the car. There is a strong suggestion, that Birlin was not a willing participant in what followed. Shots were fired, and the two airmen fell into the Rhine. Grüner, Birlin and Reimer returned to Rheinweiler to collect the two surviving airmen, and the bloody process was repeated. Grüner ordered the guards to remain silent about the incident, or at least to say that they had been ambushed, and that the prisoners had been taken from them. This kind of atrocity against RAF prisoners of war was a rarity, although there was a slight increase in 1945, as a desperate Germany's defeat loomed ever nearer. Even then, it was the civilian Nazi authorities, those individuals who owed everything to the party and knew their power was slipping from their grasp, that were most likely to commit war crimes.

The body of Wyness was recovered from the Rhine at Markolsheim, some 50 kilometres from where the ditching took place, and was initially buried there. The remains of F/L Williams were found nearby on the 24th of October, and interred at Salsbach, while F/Os Honig and Hosie were laid to rest at other locations. After the war all were re-interred in war cemeteries in Germany and France, and Wyness and Hosie now rest side-by-side in the French Cemetery at Choloy. After the war Rudolf Birlin was arrested and a trial convened by a French court in 1946. The case collapsed, however, because the crime had not taken place on French soil, and the victims were not French. The accused remained in custody at Neumunster pending a second trial by an American court. Hugo Grüner was arrested in May 1945, and indicted for the crime, remaining in custody until his trial in April 1946. In his defence he laid the blame on the Gestapo and Birlin, but escaped from custody at Recklinghausen in 1947, after being handed over to the Americans. He was never recaptured, but was tried in his absence at Hamburg in 1948, along with Birlin and Reimer. Reimer could not be found, and was assumed to be dead, and Birlin was found not guilty on the grounds that he had not actually committed the act, nor had he actively condoned or encouraged it. While he had not attempted to prevent the crime, it was accepted by the court, that any move on his part to do so would have resulted in his death also. Grüner was found guilty and was sentenced to death, but he remained at large to cheat the hangman. The writer of the poignant official letter mentioned above, sent to the parents of Bruce Hosie in a final confirmation of previous communications about his loss, spoke of the difficulty they would experience in learning of the manner of his death, but felt that they would, nevertheless, prefer to know the truth.

The failure of Operation Market Garden, the 'Bridge too far' disaster, had left the Allied right flank exposed, and earlier on the 7th, while the 617 Squadron crews were outbound for their appointment at the Kembs Barrage, the frontier towns of Cleves and Emmerich were heavily bombed by elements of 1, 3, 4 and 8 Groups to prevent the passage through them of enemy forces which might counter attack.

Chapter Eighteen

Tirpitz Rounds Two and Three

A hurricane devastates the Ruhr

The loss of two such experienced and popular crews as those of Wyness and Howard was a bitter blow to the squadron, but life and the war would go on, and Wyness was replaced as flight commander by F/L Iveson, who was promoted to Squadron Leader. Two more crews were posted in to 617 Squadron during week ending Friday the 14th, those of F/Ls Dobson and Anning, who both arrived from 44 Squadron. Dobson had been posted to 44 Squadron on the 21st of May, and he and his crew began their operational tour with a mining sortie on the 26/27th. Their tour reflected the diverse offensives in progress during the period, which saw them operating initially against gun batteries in the run-up to the invasion, before participating in the oil offensive at Wesseling, and the flying bomb and railway campaigns in France. There was little activity over Germany for the heavy brigade during this period, but the Dobson crew experienced city busting at Stuttgart twice during the three raid series towards the end of July. From mid August, however, the bulk of operations were directed against Germany, and the crew was involved in a number of these, completing their thirtieth and final operation at Kaiserslautern on the night of the 27/28th of September. Stuart Anning had been at 44 Squadron since the 1st of July, and between the 12th of that month and the 26/27th of September, he and his crew completed twenty-six operations, the last of them against Karlsruhe.

The day these crews arrived at Woodhall Spa was the day on which the Command launched its contribution to Operation Hurricane, a series of massive raids against Ruhr cities, as a demonstration to the enemy of the overwhelming superiority of the Allied air forces ranged against it. The much-bombed city of Duisburg was selected as the host for a raid by over 1,000 aircraft, which began departing their stations at first light, and arrived over the already shattered city shortly after breakfast time to deliver almost 4,500 tons of bombs under a fighter escort. Similar numbers returned that night to press home the point about superiority, and this massive figure of over 2,000 sorties in less than twenty-four hours was achieved without the assistance of the Independent Air Force. This took advantage of the night activity over the Ruhr to return to Brunswick, which, after four previous failures, at last succumbed to a heavy and accurate assault. All parts of the town were hit, but the old centre was completely destroyed, and large areas of fire were created. On the following day Lt 'Nick' Knilans was posted out of the RAF on completion of his magnificent service with both 619 and 617 Squadrons. The citation for his DFC approved on the 9th of March 1945 reads:

> This officer has been operating with a special duties squadron and has participated in many sorties against small and precise targets, vital to the enemy's war effort. These attacks have been made in daylight and from low altitude in the face of intense enemy opposition from the ground. Lieutenant Knilans has participated in sorties against flying bomb and rocket installations and submarine pens at Brest, Lorient and Le Havre and by his imperturbability, courage and efficiency he has contributed largely to successes achieved.

Although volunteering for operational duties with the USAAF in the war against Japan, Knilans would fly no further operations before the end of hostilities.

Wilhelmshaven was pounded by almost 500 aircraft on the 15/16th, the final raid of the war on this port, and Stuttgart sustained further serious damage at the hands of 1, 3, 6 and 8 Groups on the 19/20th. 5 Group went to Nuremberg on this night, and although missing the city centre aiming point, destroyed 400 houses and forty industrial buildings, mostly in southern districts. The Hurricane force moved on to Essen on the evening of the 23rd, and this raid was followed by another on the 25th, by which time the city had ceased to be a major cog in the munitions production machine. Cologne's turn came initially on the 28th in a two phase attack, which left over 2,200 apartment blocks in ruins, and also inflicted heavy damage on industrial premises, power stations, railway communications and harbour installations. This was, in fact, a busy day for the Command generally, involving further operations against gun emplacements on Walcheren, and a 5 Group raid on the *U-Boot* pens at Bergen in Norway. As far as 617 Squadron was concerned, poor weather had curtailed activity for much of the month after the Kembs operation, but postings continued with F/L Fearn going to 1661CU, F/L Williams to 1660CU, and F/L Gavin arriving from 51 Base, all during the last week. However, the squadron was also stirred into action on the 28th, when twenty aircraft flew to Lossiemouth and Milltown to join 9 Squadron for Operation Obviate, the second assault on *Tirpitz*, which, having been moved to Tromsö, was now close enough to reach from Scotland. The crews were those of Tait in PD371, Fawke in DV405, Iveson in ME554, Knights in PB415, Hamilton in PD233, Pryor in LM492, Sayers in DV402, Oram in ED763, Marshall in DV391, Gumbley in DV380, Goodman in

EE131, Gingles in LM489, Castagnola in DV385, Martin in PD238, Sanders in ME562, Joplin in ME561, Watts in LM695, Leavitt in NG181, Carey in NF920, and Dobson as a reserve.

Take-off from the advanced bases began shortly after 01.00 hours on the 29th, and it was not completed until an hour later. The route to the target took the aircraft from their forward bases to North Uist (position A), then A to 63.00N 02.00E (position B), B to 65.00N 06.47E (position C), C to 65.34N 15.00E (position D), D to 69.00N 19.50E (position E), E to 69.39N 18.50E (target). The return route was target to 69.20N 14.30E (position F), F to B, B to A, A to Lossiemouth. Although the weather was reported as fine in the target area, by the time the force of thirty-seven aircraft began final approach at between 12,000 and 16,000 feet, a layer of cloud was sliding across the aiming point, and completely concealing the ship from most crews just before the Tallboys went down. Oram was the first to bomb at 07.49 from 15,500 feet, closely followed by Iveson. After delivering his Tallboy at 07.51½ Sayers observed a big flash from the ship, believed to be a bomb burst, and Marshall actually saw a bomb enter the water just off the beam on the starboard side. Knights confirmed this, adding, that the ship rocked considerably, and thick brown smoke billowed from the midships area, while black smoke followed an explosion in the starboard bow. Castagnola watched a bomb fall towards the *Tirpitz*, and shortly afterwards there was a flash and a column of smoke. Joplin was another witness to a bomb burst on the forward end of the ship, and Martin thought he saw one at the stern, but for the others it proved impossible to assess the results. Some crews made repeated runs to try to catch a glimpse of their quarry through the bombsight, but Pryor, Leavitt and Gumbley retained their bombs in the absence of a firm aiming point. Carey's NF920 was severely damaged by fire from *Tirpitz* immediately after bombing, after five previous runs across the target. Hits in a fuel tank caused excessive fuel loss, and this necessitated a forced landing in Sweden, which was safely accomplished, although Carey's knee struck the P4 compass as the Lancaster came to a sudden halt, and he sustained an extremely painful dislocated knee-cap. He and his crew were, of course, interned, and enjoyed the legendary hospitality of their hosts for a number of weeks while Carey's injury was being tended. The remaining crews returned safely to their advanced bases, after more than twelve hours in the air, although Joplin initially was forced to put down at Scatsta on the Shetlands because of fuel shortage, before continuing on to Milltown, and thence to Woodhall Spa on the following day. This proved to be 'Mac' Hamilton's final operation with the squadron, but he would remain at Woodhall Spa until being posted out in December. Though *Tirpitz* was still on an even keel and above water, she had indeed received a mortal blow during this attack. A Tallboy had exploded less than 20 yards from the rudders on the port side, opening plating and allowing the sea in, and the port propeller shaft was bent. The latter could only be repaired in a dockyard, and henceforth German authorities referred to the *Tirpitz* as the 'floating battery'. However, as this was still not apparent to British authorities from photographic reconnaissance, a third operation was deemed necessary.

In the meantime, the Hurricane force returned to Cologne on the evenings of the 30th and 31st, and inflicted further massive damage, before moving on to Düsseldorf on the 2/3rd of November, where 5,000 houses were either destroyed or seriously damaged. On the 4th nineteen 617 Squadron crews, including a reserve, returned to Lossiemouth and Milltown to join 9 Squadron in preparation for the next assault on *Tirpitz*, but bad weather intervened, and with no immediate prospect of an improvement they returned to Woodhall Spa and Bardney respectively on the following day. While the squadron was away for the night, the Hurricane force pounded Bochum, and 5 Group returned to the Dortmund-Ems Canal at the Ladbergen section north of Münster, which had enjoyed two weeks of trouble-free navigation after being repaired following the September attack. The repairs were undone, and the waterway was left once more drained and unnavigable. As the unofficial canal-busters, the Group attempted to breach the Mittelland waterway near its junction with the Dortmund-Ems at Gravenhorst on the 6/7th, but the marker fell into the water and was extinguished before most of the force had bombed, causing the operation to be aborted. S/L Hamilton was posted in from 1 Group's 625 Squadron on the 9th, not to be confused with F/L 'Mac' Hamilton, who was shortly to be posted away from the squadron. The weather continued to be uncooperative to 617 Squadron until the 11th, when eighteen crews, plus F/L Gavin as the reserve, flew back to Lossiemouth, to prepare for an early start next day. That night 5 Group attacked the Rhenania-Ossag oil refinery at Harburg, south of Hamburg, but it seems that most of the bombs hit the town instead.

The decisive blow against the *Tirpitz*, Operation Catechism, was launched on the 12th, with F/O Kell first away, at 02.59 in NG181, and Jimmy Castagnola bringing up the rear twenty-six minutes later. The other aircraft and pilots on this momentous occasion were: Tait in EE146, Iveson in ME554, Sayers in LM492, Marshall in DV391, Dobson in PD371, Anning in ED763, Knights in PB415, Gumbley in DV405, Gingles in LM489, Flatmanin PD233, Ross in ME555, Joplin in ME561, Castagnola in DV385, Watts in LM485, Sanders in ME562, Leavitt in DV393 and Lee in DV380. The operation proceeded as before, again in company with 9 Squadron, but on this occasion, there was no impediment to visibility, and the ship was presented to the approaching bomb aimers, in the opening stages at least, as a naked target. Tait could see steam issuing from Tirpitz's funnel as he arrived, and his Tallboy was the first to go down at 08.41 from 13,000 feet. He was unable to pick out its burst, but he did note, that ensuing bombing was concentrated around the target. Over the next minute Tallboys went down from Iveson, Knights, Gingles, Joplin, Castagnola, Watts, Sanders and Lee. Knights watched the first four Tallboys fall and called their point of impact in order as: on or near the starboard quarter, starboard bow, port bow and near the funnel, and his own as 10 yards off the port quarter. He remained over the target until the end of the attack, and saw a large explosion at 08.51, the timing of which was confirmed by Stuart Anning. A smaller explosion followed two minutes later. By the time Knights left the scene he was able to report the *Tirpitz* listing heavily to port. He confirmed the accuracy and concentration of the 617 Squadron bombing, while noting bombs from 9 Squadron, who were using the Mk XIV bomb sight, falling 200 yards, 500 yards, a quarter of a mile and one mile away from the target. Gingles thought he scored a direct hit, but flak damage persuaded him not to hang around and he turned away. Castagnola reported his Tallboy falling towards the centre of the superstructure, and witnessed a direct hit followed by a cloud of smoke, which enveloped the ship. Joplin confirmed one direct hit and two near misses, while Watts saw a possible bullseye, one overshoot, one undershoot and two wides. Sanders watched his bomb fall with someone else's, and both appeared to hit the edge of the ship near the centre. Lee's Tallboy disappeared into the smoke, by which time the *Tirpitz* seemed to have ceased firing. Kell made his approach along the length of the ship, turning to starboard and running in on the bows. His effort was a direct hit or very near miss, which was swallowed up by the reddish-brown smoke issuing forth from in front of the superstructure. A number of crews also reported a dull red glow from near the forward end. The squadron's last bomb, that of F/L Sayers, fell at 08.45. In all four direct hits were later confirmed by photographic reconnaissance, which showed the mighty ship to have turned turtle at her moorings.

Tirpitz had been brought to 'action stations' at 09.00 German time, and the first visual rather than radar sighting of the approaching Lancasters took place at 09.27 when they were still twenty-five miles away to the south-east. There were no smoke generators operating on the ship itself, and those on the shore were ineffective. *Tirpitz* opened up with her main armament, her fifteen-inch A and B turrets, at 09.38 at a range of thirteen and a half miles, and the secondary armament of six and four-inch guns joined in when the attacking force had closed to nine and a half miles. The leading section of Lancasters led by Tait scored two direct hits, one Tallboy striking to the port of B turret and the other on the port side amidships, entering the ship through the catapult track and exploding as it passed through the armoured deck over the port boiler room. A gaping hole some 45 feet in length was torn in the vessel's side from the bilge keel to the upper deck exposing its innards to the sea. This area flooded immediately, causing a list to port of between 15 and 20 degrees, a situation made worse by a near miss. Within the next two or three minutes a third direct hit on the port side and another near miss exposed the interior of the ship amidships along a length of more than 200 feet. By 09.45 the *Tirpitz* had heeled over to forty degrees to port, and *Kapitän zur See* Junge ordered the lower decks to be evacuated. The starboard armament had managed to maintain a gallant defence during this period of carnage above and below decks, but at 09.50, by which time the roll to port had reached seventy degrees, a fire reached the C turret magazine, and the ensuing explosion blew the turret out of its barbette. Just two minutes later mighty *Tirpitz* capsized having rolled through 135 degrees. The attack on the 29th of October had altered the profile of the seabed, which was in the process of being built up to provide a stable platform for *Tirpitz* to rest on. Those near misses increased the draught and allowed the battleship to turn turtle, when it would otherwise have been prevented from doing so by its superstructure. One can only imagine the horror of being on board *Tirpitz* during the engagement described above. In all 971 men lost their lives, many trapped inside the monster as it capsized, although eighty-five were pulled from this tomb when rescuers cut through the steel plates of the hull. Neither 617 nor 9 Squadrons incurred losses, and the crews landed back at Lossiemouth between 14.47 and 16.59. Ten of the triumphant crews returned to Woodhall Spa on the following day, and the remainder on the 14th, and W/C Tait went to London that day to take part in a radio broadcast about the raid.

CHAPTER NINETEEN

On The Other Side of The Hill

What, though, of the German response to the threat against the *Tirpitz*, one of the Reich's major national treasures, and one in which was invested so much national pride? Aside from a spirited defence from her own main armament, she appeared to be bereft of the principal component of protection, namely air cover. Whenever Germany's naval units in the past had been vulnerable to enemy attack, and were within range of protection from the air, it was provided. Why had *Tirpitz* been denied a fighter umbrella at such a critical moment? There is no question, that had fighters of the *Tagjagd* entered the fray from the nearby fighter base at Bardufoss, they would have mauled the slow-moving and heavily laden Lancasters during their bombing run. Two months hence over Bergen a number of 9 and 617 Squadron crews would be able to testify to the effectiveness of Fw190s against a bomber. Some of the answers to this perplexing question can be found in the transcript of a court martial held over the 17th, 18th and 20th of December, just five weeks after the loss of *Tirpitz*, which was convened to identify those who should carry the blame. The tenor of the proceedings was almost certainly coloured by the need to find a scapegoat. Even so, I believe the events are essentially as those testified to by the accused and the witnesses, and it is only the interpretation that has been contrived to enable guilty verdicts to be handed down.

Perhaps the principal scapegoat among the *Luftwaffe* ranks was Major Heinrich Ehrler. Major Ehrler was no ordinary officer, and it is worth considering his career in some detail to understand the extent to which the court was prepared to go to apportion blame. He was born on the 14th of September 1917 near Mosbach in southern Germany as the son of a carpenter. On leaving state school in 1932 he learned the butchery trade, and then became a representative. He enlisted in the armed forces in 1935, and served in the artillery, seeing action as an *Unteroffizier* in the Flak service during the Spanish Civil War. In 1940 he began his training as a pilot, and was posted to 4/JG77 (later 4/JG5) on the 1st of February 1941. He gained his first kill, a British bomber, over the Norwegian coast in the autumn of

1941, before being posted to the Eismeer front (Arctic Sea) to operate against the Russians. Here he was able to demonstrate his skills as a fighter pilot, and in mid May 1942, with eleven kills to his credit, he was posted to 6/JG5, which he led as a *Staffelkapitän* from the 22nd of August 1942. Between the months of January and September of that year he achieved a total of fifty-four kills, numbers 2 to 55, and after around sixty-four kills he was decorated with the Knight's Cross. On the 1st of June 1943 he was promoted to the command of II/JG5, and celebrated in style five days later by shooting down four Hurricanes (kills 96 to 99). His 100th followed within days, and after 112 he was awarded the Oak Leaves. On the 26th of November 1943 he gained kills number 117 to 120, and on the 17th of March 1944 he shot down numbers 124 to 131. On the evening of 25th of May he defeated four opponents, and in the early morning of the following day five more (147 to 155). He became commander of JG5 on the 1st of August 1944, and by the time of his arrival at Bardufoss on the 9th of November his tally of kills stood at 199.

The court martial assessment of Ehrler described him as having a strong personality and an assured, confident bearing, and of being of respectable character with much initiative. His negative attributes included impulsiveness, which led him to be sometimes rash and inconsiderate in his judgement and attitude, and excessive ambition, which made him poorly disposed to reprimands and advice. He was, though, a convinced National Socialist. He was further described as a battle-hardened and prominent fighter pilot, skilled in single combat, and an inspirational leader and example to his subordinates. It was thought that his rapid rise to his present position had left him with too little experience in military matters generally, and in the training of his subordinates in particular, and that he, therefore, did not fit the requirements of a squadron commander in the western theatre of operations. It seems rather strange, that Ehrler would have been allowed to progress as he did, if he did not possess all the necessary qualities, and one suspects, that the assessment had been contrived to satisfy the circumstances of the 12th of November. It is true that the *Luftwaffe*'s highest scoring aces operated against the Russians, suggesting that in the air, at least, the eastern and Eismeer fronts were less demanding than the western. That said, 199 kills speaks for itself, and one again senses, that the court's assessment has been driven by the need to drag into the spotlight an officer of sufficiently high status to atone for the collective sins of all involved in the *Tirpitz* affair. The loss of the *Tirpitz* required a sacrificial lamb of some prominence to absolve all the inadequacies of the German military, and who better than a national hero who happened to be in the wrong place at the right time.

Essentially, the facts, as established by the military court are these. Bardufoss was the nearest airfield to the *Tirpitz*, lying only a matter of ten minutes flying time away, and Tromsö could actually be seen from an aircraft flying at an altitude of 5,000 feet over the airfield. Until the 10th of November, Bardufoss accommodated the 4th Squadron of *Jagdgeschwader* 5 (JG5). Its brief was to defend the areas of Bardufoss, Tromsö and Narvik, and also to guard against landings from the sea and from the east. On the 4th of November High Command ordered JG5 to begin withdrawing to Stavanger, leaving behind 9 *Staffel*, which was combined with *Nachtjagdgeschwader* 8 (NJG8) to form a battle group. On the 9th of November the squadron commander, Major Heinrich Ehrler, arrived at Bardufoss from his command post at Banak to oversee the reorganisation and the re-equipping of 9 *Staffel* with Focke-Wulf Fw190s, a process that was expected to allow Ehrler to return to his main duties and depart for Alta on the 11th.

The court now considered the operational situation facing Major Ehrler during his fateful few days at Bardufoss. Firstly, a total of twenty-two Fw190s were taken on charge to replace the existing Bf109s, but they were of two series with different radio equipment, and this meant that air-to-air communication was possible only between aircraft of the same series. Secondly, he discovered that almost all of his pilots were unfamiliar with the Fw190, and in particular, his squadron and flight leaders had never flown them. Thirdly, among the pilots available to him were some young ones without battle experience, who had been held back to act as replacements after JG5 withdrew to Stavanger a few days earlier. Ehrler convinced himself, that they lacked knowledge of the area, the weather conditions and the special flying requirements of the region, and discovered also, that they had no experience of flying in formation. To overcome this weakness he brought the tyros together into a special flight, which, for the purpose of this chapter, will be referred to as a training flight, and had them practice local flying, while he schooled them in formation. Accordingly, he decided to extend his stay at Bardufoss until the morning of the 12th, to give his young charges as much time as possible under his tutelage. Fourthly, Bardufoss was not an ideal airfield in the event of a scramble. The runway was bordered at one end by a ridge, which prevented a take-off in the general direction of Tromsö. It was only possible to take off towards Sweden, and this, together with the unfavourable location of the command post and dispersals, substantially increased taxi time and consequently the time it took to get into the air. Squadrons at other airfields were able to get airborne within three minutes, while at Bardufoss it took nine. Finally, those supposedly tasked with protecting the *Tirpitz*, and who within weeks would be facing charges of disobedience and dereliction of duty for failing to do so, had not been informed that this heavy responsibility was theirs, and did not even know where the mighty battleship was lying at anchor. They understood she was somewhere near Tromsö, but as this was a restricted area, her precise location was secret.

A further consideration for the court was the command structure at Bardufoss during those few days when Major Ehrler was present. It is difficult to compare an RAF unit with its *Luftwaffe* counterpart, but in general terms the *Luftwaffe Geschwader* or squadron is best seen as a Wing or even a Group, which had *Gruppen* or RAF squadron-sized units under it. The individual *Gruppen* had their own commanders and flight commanders, while the *Geschwader Kommodore* was in overall command of the entire unit. When Major Ehrler, as *Geschwader Kommodore*, arrived at Bardufoss, therefore, he immediately assumed seniority over the squadron and flight commanders already there, something which would prove crucial at his trial. On the basis of an order from *Reichsmarschall* Goering himself in February 1944, which was confirmed by *Luftflotte* 5 on the 24th of March, a fighter readiness command post was to be set up on the airfield at Bardufoss close to the dispersals, and linked to the fighter command post. The fighter command post was to be occupied at all times by an officer, and this had been adhered to until the departure of JG5, but not thereafter. As overall commander of the fighter units at Bardufoss during his few days in residence, Major Ehrler was ultimately responsible for ensuring the latter, and for leading his units from the ground from the command post.

Next the court looked at the structure of the information services, whose brief it was to provide early warning of enemy aircraft, and accurate details of their position, altitude and heading. The Divisional *Funkmeldungzentral* or signals centre (Div-FMZ) was located at Bardufoss, from where it controlled the main warning centres at Bardufoss, Narvik and Tromsö. They were served by a number of *Freya* and *Wasserman* radar installations, which were directed primarily towards the sea. Others were in the process of being set up on the Swedish frontier, but they were not yet in service. A twin telephone line existed between the Div-FMZ at Bardufoss and the Bardufoss main warning centre, so that they could report independently of each other. The *Tirpitz*, lying at anchor at Tromsö, was not linked in the normal way to the main warning centre, but could receive all incoming reports through a special telephone line. Controlling the whole situation was the Korps-FMZ of the Commanding General of the German Air Forces in Finland. This was based at Moen, and had the air units in the Bardufoss area under its control. The events of the 12th of November would bring the leaders of all these establishments before a military court, either as accused or as witnesses.

Now to the events themselves, which culminated in the battleship *Tirpitz* lying keel uppermost at her moorings in Tromsö Fjord. It should be remembered, that the German timings quoted here are one hour ahead of those in RAF records. Twenty minutes before 08.00 hours on the 12th of November 1944 a report was received by the Div-FMZ in Bardufoss, that three Lancasters had entered the Mosjoen area at medium level from the east. Immediately thereafter, came a report of the approach of another Lancaster somewhat further north on a north-easterly course. The arrival of these reports had been delayed to some extent because they were routed via Bodö and Fauske, before being passed on to Div-FMZ. Once in the hands of the senior officer at the Div-FMZ, *Leutnant* Leo Beniers, the two reports were withheld by him until 08.18. Only then did he notify the fighter command post and put the reports on the general network, and it was at this time that confusion began to creep into the proceedings. There then followed the reports, 'air warning for Bodö', and 'all clear for Bodö', the latter coming through at 08.56. The Div-FMZ assigned a specific grid reference, 16N, to the initial report of the three Lancasters at 07.39. On duty at the fighter command post at this time was *Stabsgefreiter* Boehk, whose job was to enter the position of enemy aircraft on the situation map. Unfortunately, a second map, an overview, hung near the situation map, and somehow, Boehk confused the two. This resulted in his entering the incursion in Grid 27S rather than in Grid 16N. This gave the impression, that the three Lancasters were withdrawing to the east in an area to the north-west of Hammerfest. The command post clerk, *Unteroffizier* Ullrich, assumed, therefore, that the reports were of no interest to the Bardufoss fighter units, as the area into which the enemy aircraft were heading was the operating zone of units from Alta and Banak, and he felt it unnecessary to pass on the information to Major Ehrler. As Div-FMZ did not mention Grid 16N again, Boehk did not notice his error, and neither Major Ehrler nor any of his senior officers was aware of the approach of RAF bombers towards Swedish airspace. At 08.34 it was reported that four further Lancasters had been tracked at medium level between 07.54 and 08.26 on a coded heading. The *Korps*-FMZ also received the news of the enemy incursions in the general signals traffic, but it never reached the right people. Head of the *Korps*-FMZ was *Leutnant* Helmut Wissenbach, who had just received permission from his superior, Major Egeler, to make an official visit to Bardufoss. Only minutes later he became aware of the incursions, but neglected to pass this information up the line of command before departing for Bardufoss as planned.

Three or four days earlier, *Kapitänleutnant* Fassbender, the head of the Flak defence unit on the *Tirpitz* itself, had spoken on the telephone to *Oberleutnant* Härer at the main warning centre at Tromsö. He asked whether the means were in place to transmit information to the head of fighter operations. Härer assured Fassbender, that the passing of information about enemy incursions to Bardufoss, where the fighter signals officer, *Leutnant* Beniers, was stationed, was one of his most important responsibilities. At around 08.00 hours on the 12th, Fassbender received a report from the duty officer at the air-warning centre on the *Tirpitz* about the approach of four-engine aircraft in the Bodö area. When the report of the approach of three further Lancasters was received on the Tirpitz, Fassbender telephoned *Leutnant* Hamschmidt, the head of the main warning centre at Tromsö, and advised him, that the weather conditions were favourable for an attack, and indeed, that the same preconditions existed as for the attack on the ship on the 29th of October. He asked Hamschmidt to contact Div-FMZ at Bardufoss, so that fighter cover would be guaranteed at all costs. When the report of four further Lancasters in the Mosjoen-Bodö area was received on the *Tirpitz* a little later, Fassbender called *Oberleutnant* Härer, and advised him also of the similarities to the situation on the 29th, and the likelihood that an attack on the *Tirpitz* was imminent. He asked him to make available the data on the enemy activity to stations as far as Drontheim, and under all circumstances to guarantee fighter protection. In the event, neither Hamschmidt nor Härer made contact with the fighter command post at Bardufoss.

At around 08.40 a precautionary Flak alarm was sounded on the *Tirpitz*, and about ten minutes later an air raid alarm. Tromsö then received two reports about a Boston, which was outside of the region flying a southerly course, and was not, therefore, involved in the expected attack on the *Tirpitz*. At around 09.14 the *Tirpitz* sighted the enemy formation on radar at a distance of about 120km or 75 miles to the south. The intention to attack the *Tirpitz* now seemed clear, and Fassbender had a 'visual' warning transmitted to the main warning centre at Tromsö, who relayed it immediately to Bardufoss. After receipt of this report the main warning centre had the *Tirpitz* check the situation, because of more recent information on the enemy formation's position and altitude. In the meantime, however, the *Tirpitz* had detected a second wave, and transmitted the following message to the main warning centre at Tromsö: 'Second wave approaching from the south; height 3,500m, range around 100km'. This message was received by telephone at the main warning centre at Tromsö at 09.16, and was rebroadcast immediately in identical wording. At Div-FMZ in Bardufoss *Obergefreiter* Müller, who was employed as a receiver, was occupying the Tromsö desk. He took the incoming message from Tromsö, and entered it in a receipt book kept by him. He then had it drawn on the situation map, and called it on the message speaker to *Unteroffizier* Hirrich, whose job was to coordinate by telephone with all relevant agencies. Müller called, 'another wave from the south', but, crucially, did not pass on the details of range and altitude. He would later tell the court martial, that he did not receive this vital information, indeed, that at that precise moment, interference on his telephone line blocked out any further communication, and he was not even aware that he had not received the entire message. In the absence of this data, Hirrich spoke into his telephone the fateful words, 'position unknown'.

Throughout this time, *Kapitänleutnant* Fassbender was repeatedly in contact with the main warning centre at Tromsö, asking whether the fighters had been cleared for take-off. Hamschmidt passed the enquiries on to Div-FMZ at Bardufoss, where Müller was again the receiver, and he called on the speaker, "Question from Tromsö, have the fighters taken off?" Inexplicably, these enquiries never got through to the fighter command post itself. Towards 09.25 the *Tirpitz* transmitted the following urgent message to Bardufoss: 'Order from the commander of the *Tirpitz*. Get the fighters off immediately!' Tromsö also passed on this message verbally to Bardufoss.

At the business end of Bardufoss airfield 9 *Staffel* was standing at three minutes readiness on the orders of Major Ehrler, to protect both the airfield and the training flight against surprise attack. The training flight was at fifteen minutes readiness, again on the orders of Ehrler, who was as yet unaware of the situation brewing up around the *Tirpitz*. Ehrler's thoughts were, in fact, on his imminent return to Alta, and he took himself off to the command post at around 08.50 to make preparations for his departure.

The preparations completed, and still unaware of the reported incursions in the Mosjoen area, he began to make his way to his aircraft, a Bf109. He then realised he had forgotten something, and returned to the command post. Just as he was about to leave it again, a report came through from the *Tirpitz* via the Div-FMZ about an enemy bomber formation. According to Ehrler's testimony at the court martial, the message was vague, mentioning only, 'the sound of aircraft, position and altitude unknown'. The time was 09.18, and Ehrler immediately ordered 9 *Staffel* to cockpit readiness and the training flight to three minutes readiness. Ehrler tried unsuccessfully to acquire more information from Div-FMZ, and kept his pilots on the ground in the meantime. A second message came through minutes later, again referring to the sound of aircraft, this time located in Grid 16N. On receipt of this second report at 09.23 Ehrler ordered 9 *Staffel* to scramble, and he himself was first away. According to the testimony of *Hauptmann* Franz Dörr, a squadron commander in JG5, and who had arrived at Bardufoss the day after Ehrler, he was in his quarters when he received news of the approaching enemy bomber formation. He drove immediately to the command post to assume command of the training flight, and arrived at 09.25, just in time to watch Ehrler take off. As 9 *Staffel* was about to follow him into the air under the leadership of its flight commander, *Leutnant* Gayko, a Junkers aircraft landed and blocked the runway for about five minutes.

When Ehrler reached an altitude of around 2,000 metres he looked down, and saw all the other aircraft still on the ground with their engines running. At the same time he established, that his radio was unserviceable, and that he could not make contact with either the fighter control centre or the other aircraft. He decided, therefore, to fly on alone, in the hope of locating the enemy formation and achieving his 200th kill. Assuming that the *Tirpitz* was the target he at first flew to Balsfjord, which he reached between Storesteinnes and Vollan. He did not know the precise location of the *Tirpitz*'s anchorage, only that it was somewhere near Tromsö. From Balsfjord he flew due north at an altitude of 6,000 metres to an island north-east of Tromsö, then along the outer coastline to the west, before turning south-east and flying back to Balsfjord over Malangen at an increased speed at between 5,000 and 6,000 metres. During this flight he saw nothing of the enemy, but neither did he see the *Tirpitz*. Ultimately he decided to fly on to Alta, and as he turned towards the north-east over Storesteinnes he saw in the distance over to his left a 100 metre high column of white smoke, and above it at around 4,000 metres black smoke from flak bursts. Indeed, at this very moment, at 09.42, the *Tirpitz* was under attack from the bomber formation, which had apparently sneaked in behind Ehrler from the south and south-east. Ehrler flew towards the flak bursts reducing altitude on the way in the hope of cutting off the enemy's avenue of retreat, which he believed would be at low level to the west. Despite searching the coastal area from north-east to south-west he failed to encounter British bombers, and consequently resumed his course for Alta.

9 *Staffel* eventually got away five minutes after Ehrler. Leutnant Gayko had to take off last, after assisting one of his pilots with a recalcitrant engine. *Oberfeldwebel* Bössenecker took temporary command, until engine trouble forced him to return early. He handed over the leadership to *Oberfähnrich* Höhn, while *Leutnant* Gayko flew on independently. The 9 *Staffel* pilots also saw the flak in the Tromsö area, but no enemy aircraft. Gayko reported attacking a Liberator a number of times, but without result. Before leading the training flight off the ground, *Hauptmann* Dörr received a report from Div-FMZ about twenty Lancasters heading towards Bardufoss at 09.25. As this message suggested a threat to the airfield, the protection of which, according to standing orders, was the prime responsibility of the Bardufoss fighter units, he believed he should not leave it exposed. Consequently, Dörr decided to delay the take-off until the next clear-cut report came through. This one had the Lancasters heading for Tromsö, leaving Dörr in no doubt, that the *Tirpitz* was, indeed, the target. He ordered the training flight into the air, and was himself first away at 09.36. As he and the others flew towards Tromsö they could see the clouds from Flak bursts at 4,000 metres. Dörr saw nothing of the *Tirpitz*, but there was a twin-engine enemy aircraft flying towards the north-west, which he was unable to pursue. During the return flight, though, shortly before reaching the airfield, ground control advised him of an enemy aircraft, which he shot down about twenty kilometres north-east of Bardufoss. The identity of the victim is not known, but it was not an RAF bomber.

Among the superb books written by the late Werner Girbig, a highly respected historian and authority on the *Luftwaffe Tagjagd*, was one entitled *Jagdgeschwader 5. 'Eismeerjäger'*. In it he provides eyewitness accounts from participants, which generally support the enquiry's version of events, while arriving at a different conclusion as to responsibility for failures in procedures. Firstly, he establishes that the Lancaster formation was first registered on that morning of the 12th on the radar on the island of Doenna, north-west of Mosjoen. The formation was tracked moving towards Sweden, but it was more than an hour later, when other radar stations picked up the return of four-engine aircraft north of the Torneträsk Sea heading on a northerly course for Norway. It was then that JG5 was ordered into the air by the radar centre at Bardufoss, and to proceed to the Swedish/Norwegian frontier and Tromsö, where an attack on the *Tirpitz* was expected. In the book, *Leutnant* Gayko confirms that the unit's brief during Major Ehrler's presence was simply to re-equip and protect the airfield, and that nothing had been said about taking over defence of the *Tirpitz*. Gayko himself saw a number of four-engine aircraft at a height of 1,000 to 2,000 metres in loose formation over the airfield, and after helping with the troublesome engine already mentioned, he took off at 09.30, about ten minutes after the rest of the squadron had climbed away. During his ascent Gayko saw flak on the horizon and flew towards it, but it stopped before he reached it. Down below in front of Tromsö he could see a ship lying with its keel uppermost, but he saw nothing of the enemy or, indeed, of his own colleagues. Shortly before landing he encountered a four-engine aircraft, which had flown over the airfield at 3,000 to 4,000 metres. He attacked twice from head-on, but on each occasion his guns jammed after firing off a few shells. A recent incident involving the shooting down of a Swedish fighter over Finland had caused diplomatic repercussions, and made violating Swedish airspace a sensitive matter. As the Swedish frontier loomed up he was forced to break off his attack. A Messerschmitt suddenly appeared nearby, the one containing Major Ehrler, as it happened, but he too had to give up the chase for the same reason.

One of Gayko's pilots on that morning was *Unteroffizier* Heinz Orlowski. The following letter is reproduced with his kind permission and that of 9 Squadron archivist, Roger Audis, to whom the letter belongs.

> After having belonged to 13/JG/5 I did not arrived at Bardufoss until the 10th of November and joined *Oblt* Gayko's 9/JG/5. I landed there with my Fw190-A3, No. 17, at 12.15 hours from Banak, where I had taken off with two other colleagues at 10.45 hours. Few of my former squadron comrades were there, and I found many new faces and comrades who were raw and without any battle experience, or had just converted from the Messerschmitt 109 to the Fw190.
>
> I felt very lost when the scramble was ordered by signal rockets on the 12th of November. My aircraft was parked near the command post, and here I received the only instructions for this operation from our technical officer Drolshagen, who said something like, 'Enemy aircraft ... course east ... follow the commander'.
>
> I rolled to the runway and waited for some minutes for a leader to take off whom I could follow. However, none of the assembled aircraft did take off. I had no radio contact with the other pilots, and clearly, no one understood my questions made with hand gestures. Therefore I took off heading inland at 09.25. Apparently, I was considered a leader of the group, because the others formated on my right side as I slowed down in the climb. Since there seemed to be nobody else to take command I increased speed and altitude and assumed the course I had been told.
>
> We didn't see any enemy aircraft, but instead, anti-aircraft fire in the direction of Tromsö. Therefore, I flew with the formation towards it, and met two 109s coming back in our direction. I remembered the second part of the order, so I turned and followed them, in the assumption, that this was the leading officer. The two 109s flew to Bardufoss and landed. We also returned to Bardufoss. I arrived there at 10.30 hours, without having made contact with the enemy. Only when I was back on the ground did I learn from my mechanic Hiller what had happened, because he welcomed me with an excited stammer, 'Did you get them?', and when I enquired, 'Whom?', he said, 'Four-engine aircraft, very low over the airfield.'

Soon I learned what the target had been for the four-engine aircraft, the *Tirpitz*, whose existence at Tromsö had been unknown to me.

At 11.50 I took off once more because of a Mosquito, but without success. This flight took only twenty-five minutes. So much for the 12th of November 1944.

Oberleutnant Kurt Schulze was a pilot and the adjutant of III/JG5. He recalls that fateful Sunday morning clearly. He had arrived at the command post at the same time as *Hauptmann* Dörr, having been alerted by the sounding of the air raid siren at about 09.10. It initially seemed from the situation map, that the enemy bombers were to the south near Alta, rather than near Bodö, and this explains why there was no urgency in informing the Bardufoss fighter units. Once this error had been rectified, and a further report had come in, the plotters were shocked to realise, that the enemy was south-east of Bodö and only about five minutes away from Bardufoss. The alarm went off accompanied by the order to scramble, and as soon as they had the enemy's course, Dörr and Schulze took off. This would have been about eleven minutes after the alarm, and as they climbed away they heard a report over the radio, 'Flak fire over Tromsö', which effectively confirmed that the attack on *Tirpitz* was already in progress. With no enemy aircraft in sight, and no further reports on their whereabouts, Schulze headed back to Bardufoss and was among the first to land. As Ehrler never came back without a kill, Schulze began to make preparations to celebrate his commander's 200th victory on his return.

These then were the events surrounding the loss of the battleship *Tirpitz* according to the court of enquiry and some of the participants. Clearly, something had gone wrong on the German side in the area of communications, and now the search was on to find someone to blame. Turning again to the court proceedings, the gist of the charges against those mentioned in the above accounts was;

Major Ehrler; (a) That between the 10th and 12th of November 1944 at Bardufoss he contravened the orders of the *Reichsmarschall* concerning the handling of information between the radar stations and the fighter command post, thereby enormously compromising the battle readiness of the unit.

(b) That during the same period he failed to ensure the permanent presence in the command post of an officer.

(c) That on the 12th of November he delayed the take-off of the Bardufoss fighter units from the first report at 09.18 until 09.23.

(d) That he wilfully left his unit, for which he was obliged to provide leadership, and flew alone.

(e) That he falsely claimed his radio equipment failed after take-off, and was unable to lead his unit as a consequence.

***Hauptmann* Dörr**; that on the 12th of November at Bardufoss, despite the express orders of Major Ehrler, he delayed the take-off of his unit from 09.33 until 09.40, thereby preventing it from making contact with the enemy.

***Leutnant* Beniers**; that on the 12th of November; (a) at the Div-FMZ at Bardufoss for no good reason he failed to pass on the 08.00 report of an enemy approach in the Mosjoen area until 08.18.

(b) During the attack on the *Tirpitz* he took it upon himself to address the enquiries concerning the state of readiness of the fighter units at Bardufoss, without making reference to the fighter command post, and thereby prevented the seriousness of the situation from being recognised.

(c) On receipt of the garbled message concerning a second wave approaching the *Tirpitz* he failed to check back to obtain precise details of its position and altitude, under which circumstances an earlier take-off would have been possible.

***Oberleutnant* Härer**; that on the 12th of November at Tromsö, following a telephone conversation with *Kapitänleutnant* Fassbender, he failed to immediately make contact with the Div-FMZ and the fighter command post to ask for fighter protection, even though Fassbender had advised him to do so.

***Leutnant* Hamschmidt**; that on the 12th of November, after receipt of the first report of enemy aircraft in the Mosjoen area, he failed to follow up the demand of Fassbender to contact Div-FMZ and the fighter command post to ensure immediate fighter protection.

***Leutnant* Wissenbach**; that on the 12th of November he failed to pass on the initial reports of enemy activity in the Mosjoen area to the relevant parties, and is thereby to blame for the fact, that action was not taken in good time.

***Stabsgefreiter* Boehk**; that on the 12th of November in the fighter command post he entered the data from the initial reports of enemy activity in the Mosjoen area by mistake in the Hammerfest area on the situation map, which had the effect of masking the true significance of these incursions from the fighter units.

The accused all put forward a defence against the charges and the outcome was as follows; Major Ehrler was sentenced to a three-year term of imprisonment and to loss of rank for disobedience. *Leutnant* Beniers received a one-year term of imprisonment for three counts of reckless dereliction of duty in the field. *Oberleutnant* Härer and *Leutnant* Hamschmidt were likewise handed a one-year term for reckless dereliction of duty in the field. *Hauptmann* Dörr, *Leutnant* Wissenbach and *Stabsgefreiter* Boehk were cleared. The sentences had to be confirmed by the Commander-in-Chief, Adolf Hitler. In a memorandum from the Führer HQ dated the 1st of March 1945 he wrote;

I

> The sentence against Major Ehrler I confirm, but commute to the effect that a three-month confinement in a fortress will stand in place of imprisonment. The loss of rank is cancelled. The completion of the sentence I suspend, in order to give the subject the opportunity to prove himself at the front.

II

> The sentences against *Oberleutnant* Härer, *Leutnant* Hamschmidt and *Leutnant* Beniers I confirm. The completion of the sentence I suspend to allow the subjects opportunity to prove themselves at the front.

III

> The sentences against *Hauptmann* Dörr, *Leutnant* Wissenbach and *Stabsgefreiter* Boehk I confirm.
>
> Signed, Adolf Hitler, and countersigned by Keitel, the Chief of the High Command of the *Wehrmacht*.

At the age of 28 Major Ehrler was a broken man, and he flew his final sorties without much will to fight. He achieved his 200th kill on the 20th of November, and possibly four more before he became engulfed in the furore following the loss of the *Tirpitz*. His friend Theo Weissenberger took him onto the squadron staff at JG7 on the 27th of February 1945, so that he could take advantage of Hitler's leniency to 'prove himself at the front'. It seems inconceivable, that a fighter ace with more than 200 kills to his credit from over 400 sorties should be put in such a position. Despite his loss of enthusiasm for the fight, he returned to the fray in the western theatre of operations, and flying the Me262 jet fighter he claimed four more kills over the ensuing weeks. Two of these were American B17s on the 4th of April, kills number 207 and 208, and one version of this encounter has Ehrler ramming his final victim after running out of ammunition. This cannot be confirmed, and the precise details of his fatal crash at Stendal near Berlin are unknown.

It is clear from the above, that the failure to provide the *Tirpitz* with air cover came as the result of a catalogue of failures in communication. In defence of the fighter units at Bardufoss, however, a number of indisputable facts come to light. Firstly, the prime directive under which they were operating was the protection of Bardufoss itself. Secondly, they had not been told specifically, that they were responsible for providing air cover for the

Tirpitz. Thirdly, the location of the *Tirpitz* was a closely kept secret, and its precise mooring was not known to the relevant authorities within the fighter units based at Bardufoss. Fourthly, the ongoing conversion from the Bf109 to the Fw190 during those fateful few days, combined with the lack of a unified communication system between Fw190s of different series and the relative inexperience of a proportion of the pilots, fatally reduced the battle effectiveness of the Bardufoss units. In the final analysis the Bomber Command attack on the *Tirpitz* occurred during a window of extreme good fortune. Had it been launched a day or two earlier or later, the outcome might well have been other than that recorded by history.

CHAPTER TWENTY

The Final Winter

There were no further operations to occupy the crews for the remainder of the month of November, but postings during this period involved S/L Calder arriving from 1652CU on the 9th, S/L Brookes from 22 OTU on the 21st, and F/Ls Horsley and Lancey from 5 LFS on the 25th. Calder was another graduate of the 4 Group academy of excellence, and had commanded the home echelon of 76 Squadron between July and August 1942, before handing over the reins to Cheshire.

Horsley's path to 617 Squadron was, perhaps, less exalted, but was an example of determination. A 5 Group man through and through, he had completed his first tour as a wireless operator/gunner with 50 Squadron on Hampdens and Manchesters in 1941/42. His final operation was the first 1,000-bomber raid against Cologne on the night of the 30/31st of May 1942 as a member of P/O Manser's crew. They were in a clapped-out Manchester borrowed for the occasion from 106 Squadron, which was hit by flak over the target and badly damaged. As the crippled aircraft lost height over the German/Belgian frontier, Manser ordered the crew to bale out, while he remained at the controls to give them a chance to do so. He was unable to save himself, however, and died in the ensuing crash. P/O Horsley and four others evaded capture, and their testimony was instrumental in sealing the posthumous award to Manser of the Victoria Cross. It took Horsley twelve weeks to get home via France, Spain and Gibraltar, and he was then sent to Canada as an instructor. While there he managed to get himself on a pilot's course, and was posted to 617 Squadron on his return home. Quite how this happened is unclear, in view of his inexperience as a bomber captain, and the fact that evaders were rarely returned to bomber operations in case they came down again in enemy territory, were captured, and revealed information about their helpers. Such men would normally continue their flying careers as instructors, or might transfer instead to another Command.

Although 617 Squadron had time on its hands, there was still plenty to occupy the main force during the month, and almost 1,200 aircraft were committed to attacks on three small German towns on the 16th in support of a planned American advance. Düren, Jülich and Heinsberg are situated in an arc respectively from north to east of Aachen, and 1 and 5 Groups were assigned to the first mentioned, which they all but erased from the map, killing over 3,000 people in the process. Oil targets dominated the remainder of the period, although 5 Group returned to both the Dortmund-Ems and Mittelland Canals on the 21/22nd, and left both of them extensively drained. This must have been particularly galling for the Germans, who had only just completed repairs to the former, and were about to resume navigation. Following these attacks repairs to the Mittelland were completed quickly, and through traffic resumed on the 10th of December, two weeks before it was possible at the Dortmund-Ems. Munich was the Group's target on the 26/27th, and returning crews claimed this as an accurate attack, which caused particular damage to railway installations.

December was another busy month for personnel movements at 617 Squadron, beginning on the 1st, with the departure of F/L Knights and F/O Gingles to RAF Hurn. S/L Powell arrived from 20 OTU on the 5th, F/L McLoughlin from 5 LFS on the 8th, and F/L Price also from there on the 9th. The first major operation of the month involved 1, 4, 6 and 8 Groups in a raid on Hagen in the Ruhr on the 2/3rd, and the town was left a shambles. With the Americans now in the Eifel region of western Germany, the town of Heimbach was attacked by a predominantly 1 Group force on the 3rd, and this was followed up on the 4th by a small scale 8 Group assault on the nearby Urft Dam, which failed to cause a breach. The Urft was built over a five-year period from 1900, and was a prototype for all future gravity dams in Germany, including the Möhne. At the time of its construction it was the largest dam in Europe. It stands fifty-five metres above the valley floor, is 226 metres in length and six metres wide at the top, holding back something like 45 million cubic metres of water. Karlsruhe wilted under a heavy raid by 1, 6 and 8 Groups that night, while 5 Group delivered the sole major attack of the war on Heilbronn. The town's only significance was as a link in the north-south railway network, and in a few horrifying minutes of precision bombing over 80 per cent of its built-up area was reduced to rubble, and 7,000 people lost their lives. The town of Soest, just to the north of the now famous Möhne Dam, suffered the destruction of 1,000 houses at the hands of 1, 4, 6 and 8 Groups on the 5/6th, and on the following night, while an oil refinery at Leuna and railway yards at Osnabrück were being raided by other Groups, 5 Group targeted Giessen to good effect.

On the 8th a second attempt was made on the Urft Dam, this time by over 200 Lancasters of 5 Group, a force which included nineteen aircraft from 617 Squadron led by Tait in EE146. The others were Calder in NG181, Cockshott in PD238, Iveson in ME554, Brooks in DV385, Hamilton in DV380, Oram in ED763, Pryor in LM485, Sayers in DV402, Marshall in DV391, Goodman in NF992, Gavin in LM489, Dobson in PD371, Gumbley in DV405, Sanders in PB415, Leavitt in LM695, Martin in DV393, Flatman in ME555 and Joplin in ME561. Ten-tenths cloud greeted the force, and Tait assessed that there was no chance of the conditions changing. In the absence of any serious anti-aircraft fire the force remained in the target area for some time, orbiting and approaching from various directions, and the dam was glimpsed and identified from time to time. However, there was no chance of the 617 Squadron crews establishing a bombing run, and at 11.40 Tait recalled them, terminating their part in the operation for this occasion. 128 aircraft of the main force did bomb, however, but the effort was scattered, and no breach occurred. Oram, it seems, was able to deliver his Tallboy, which was seen to overshoot, and Joplin's Lancaster was hit by the single flak battery operating to the north of the target. He landed safely at Manston, as did most of the other squadron aircraft, and returned to Woodhall Spa in veteran DV405 on the following day, while his Lancaster underwent repair. Hamilton and Brookes also sustained flak damage, and the latter put down at the American base at Sudbury.

On the afternoon of the 11th seventeen of the squadron's aircraft again found themselves over the beautiful countryside of the Urftsee, which now lies within the Eifel National Park. The 617 Squadron element was in the company of over 200 others from the Group to try again to hit the dam. The crews involved were those of Tait in EE146, Brookes in ME555, Iveson in ME554, Calder in NG181, Cockshott in PD238, Oram in ED763, Marshall in DV391, Pryor in LM485, Goodman in NF992, Dobson in PD371, Gavin in LM489, Martin in DV393, Joplin in DV402, Leavitt in LM695, Gumbley in DV405, Sanders in PB415 and Flatman in PD233. The crews' determination not to waste their Tallboys was made manifest by the spread of time elapsing between the first and last bombs to go down. Oram bombed first at 15.19 and Marshall last at 16.05, and a variety of altitudes was chosen between 6,000 and 10,000 feet. Tait found it difficult to assess the results, but saw his own bomb hit the apron, and another overshoot to the right. Iveson reported the first explosion to be on the dam itself, while his own bomb fell just to the left of the overflow. He saw two others fall into the water, one exploding, the other not, and as he pulled away from the target he witnessed a direct hit. Cockshott made five runs over a thirty-five minute period, each one hampered by cloud, and then his bombsight packed up and he brought his bomb back. Gavin completed eight runs, and eventually carried out a manual release after a partial hang-up, but his bomb overshot. Sanders was thwarted by smoke from the main force bombing, and in the end Tait ordered him to take his bomb home. It was later assessed that about 13 feet had been blasted off the top of the dam. In fact, the overflow, which forms the right-hand third of the structure and is designed as a stepped cascade, was totally destroyed, and a giant V-shaped fissure was left in the main dam wall. However, the wall was not breached, and the Germans were able to release water whenever the mood took them to hamper the advance of American ground forces.

December's operations continued for 617 Squadron on the 15th, when seventeen aircraft were dispatched to the older *S-Boot* pens at Ijmuiden, those designated AY by the Germans. This was in response to a SHAEF meeting on the 5th of December, in which the senior commanders recommended that the RAF's special squadrons should attack the giant installation. The crews were those of Tait in EE146, Brookes in DV391, Cockshott in PD238, Iveson in ME554, Calder in PB415, Goodman in NF992, Gumbley in DV380, Pryor in LM485, Oram in ED763, Marshall in DV402, Castagnola in PD371, Flatman in PD233, Ross in ME555, Joplin in LM489, Martin in DV393, Kell in NG181 and Watts in LM695. The force encountered heavy flak, which damaged a number of the Lancasters including PB415 of S/L Calder, who subsequently made an emergency landing at Woodbridge. Flatman had a hang up on his first two runs, and while opening his bomb doors in preparation for a third, the Tallboy fell out over the sea. A similar occurrence afflicted S/L Brookes, whose gyro toppled, requiring him to circle for fifteen minutes south-west of the target while he waited for it to settle down. This it refused to do, and while the bomb-aimer was attempting to re-cock the bomb, it fell out about four miles west of Ijmuiden. Tait claimed a direct hit on the southern end of the pens from a modest 9,300 feet at 15.11, some minutes after Goodman and Gumbley had delivered their Tallboys within fifteen seconds of each other. Both claimed a direct hit on the north-western corner of the roof, although Gumbley assessed the other bomb as a near miss. In actual fact, ten bombs went down within seconds of each other between 15.03 and 15.04. In addition to those of Goodman and Gumbley mentioned above, they were those dropped by Cockshott, Iveson, Oram, Castagnola, Ross, Joplin, Martin and Kell. Inevitably, smoke began to obscure the aiming point very quickly, and it became increasingly difficult to interpret the scene below. Oram estimated six direct hits, but was unable to plot the fall of his own bomb. All of the crews returned safely, but the Lancasters of Watts and Marshall were hit by flak, and they brought their bombs home. The former sustained damage to the front turret, which reduced visibility, probably as the result of leaking hydraulic fluid, and the latter lost his starboard-inner engine, as well as having numbers 1 and 2 tanks holed on the port side. Photo-reconnaissance revealed two Tallboys to have penetrated the shelter destroying one *S-Boot* and damaging six others. Six pens were rendered unusable, and another boat was trapped inside by debris. Despite this, the scale of renewed *S-Boot* operations on the 22/23rd and 24/25th of December caused a top secret priority dispatch to be rushed to the Admiralty on Christmas Day calling for further operations against both Ijmuiden and Waalhaven (Rotterdam).

The operations against the *Schnellboot* were a backhanded compliment to *Kommodore* Rudolf Petersen, the *Führer der Schnellboote*, (motorboat commander-in-chief), who, with the recapture of the French ports by the Allies, had only Waalhaven and Ijmuiden at his disposal to protect the *Schnellboot* fleet. Petersen, who was born in Denmark in 1905, joined the *Kriegsmarine* in 1925, and had been involved with *Schnellboote* since 1934. In April 1942 he became *Führer der Schnellboote*, and remained in command until war's end, rising through the ranks to *Kommodore* in September 1944. His status was recognised by the award of the Knight's Cross with Oak Leaves in June 1944. The series of operations against Rotterdam and Ijmuiden convinced him that the massive structures themselves were attracting the attention, and as such they no longer afforded protection for his craft. In effect, they could no longer fulfil their function, and he decided to disperse the vessels around the harbour. This, as Petersen feared, exposed their thin skins to attacks by Coastal Command and the Fleet Air Arm, to say nothing of the effects of bad weather, but it was the least evil option available to him. From the dawn of the New Year he implemented the policy, sometimes employing the pens for a proportion of his force according to circumstances. Petersen's worst fears would be realized on the 6th of February, when Coastal Command fighter-bombers attacked the unprotected vessels, while those inside the pens remained unharmed. Nevertheless, there were no *S-Boots* inside the pens when 617 Squadron turned up two days later for an operation dealt with in this book at the appropriate juncture. Petersen survived the war and died in 1983.

A successful raid was mounted against I G Farben chemicals factories in Ludwigshafen and nearby Oppau by 1, 6 and 8 Groups that night. This highly important company with plants in various parts of Germany, was engaged in the production of synthetic oil, and, as was discovered after the war, was guilty of using slave labour. 4, 6 and 8 Groups delivered a heavy raid on Duisburg on the 17/18th, the night on which 1 Group devastated Ulm, while 5 Group took another swipe at Munich and claimed a positive outcome.

On the 21st sixteen 617 Squadron aircraft took off in the late afternoon for the distant destination of Pölitz, near Stettin, to attack a synthetic oil plant as part of a 5 Group effort involving over 200 aircraft. The various Bergius synthetic oil refineries dotted around Germany were producing the bulk of the country's aviation fuel, and like the others, this one at Pölitz had been attacked earlier in the year by the American 8th Air Force. This night's effort was to be the first of a number of attacks on this target by Bomber Command over the ensuing weeks, until it was certain that no further production was possible. The operation came as something of a surprise to the 617 Squadron crews, who, in the face of generally unpleasant weather conditions, had been stood down after lunch. The information provided at briefing was not received with enthusiasm by the crews, who learned, that they were to carry Tallboys, but would be reliant on the accuracy of 83 and 97 Squadron marking. It was not, necessarily, that they lacked faith in the ability of the marker crews, but rather, that the system employed by them was insufficiently pinpoint for the accurate delivery of Tallboys. An additional bind was the expectation of a diversion to Scottish airfields on return, because of forecast foggy conditions in Lincolnshire throughout the night.

Engines were run up and the pre-take-off checks were about complete when a delay was called and engines were shut down. At the restart Jimmy Castagnola was first away at 16.44, and Brooks and Flatman brought up the rear, both timing their take-offs at 17.02. The squadron was ultimately led by S/L Cockshott in PD238, in the absence of S/L Calder, who was forced to abandon his sortie about ninety-five miles out from Bridlington, when

EE146 suffered a port-inner engine failure. He would eventually put down at Milltown, his briefed Scottish diversionary airfield, some three hours later, having jettisoned his Tallboy. The other crews were those of Iveson in ME554, Brookes in LM489, Marshall in PD371, Pryor in DV380, Oram in ED763, Goodman in NF992, Gumbley in DV405, Kell in NG181, Watts in LM695, Flatman in PD233, Ross in ME555, Castagnola in LM492, Martin in DV393 and Joplin in ME561. The outward flight was relatively uneventful, but Watts discovered he had an unserviceable bombsight, and was within half an hour of Pölitz when efforts to repair it were finally abandoned. Nevertheless, he continued on to make a pass over the oil refinery with the rest of the squadron.

Once in the target area the force encountered poor visibility, and this difficulty was compounded by heavy defensive fire. The anticipated confusion over the accuracy of the markers also materialized, but a Master Bomber was on hand to recommend a group of markers as the correct aiming point, and the 617 Squadron crews began their bombing runs across the target. They were not accustomed to dropping Tallboys in the 'approximate' area of a target, and made repeated runs in the pursuit of accuracy. Both Cockshott and Iveson had their bombsight gyro topple, but the former released his bomb on his fourth run. The latter was unable to identify the target after three runs, and decided to bring his Tallboy home, Marshall doing likewise. Brooks dropped his Tallboy at 22.08, but didn't see it burst, and was then hit by flak. Pryor was happy with his run and did see his bomb impact, but was not able to assess its accuracy. Oram plotted his bomb to have fallen 100 yards north of the aiming point, which, under the circumstances, was a good effort. Perhaps Kell summed up the general situation best, when he described his experience as follows:

> 1 × Tallboy. 22.04. 16,350 feet. Impossible to assess bombing. TIs were very scattered. Target area very smokey from flares. We made two runs. The flares were too far east. We could not pick out the actual target. The yellow TIs were on the edge of the forest to the south, and the reds and greens to the north. So we chose a point in between the two. We bombed on the third run.

Later photographic reconnaissance did show some damage to the installation, including the collapse of a power station chimney, which broke a section of pipeline.

There was now a long return journey to negotiate, which would take the crews over Denmark, and this was undertaken by most without incident. During the course of the homeward leg, conditions at the Lincolnshire airfields proved to be better than forecast, and the diversion to Scottish airfields was subsequently cancelled. However, the conditions took a turn for the worse at the last minute, and instructions were received from 54 Base for aircraft to land at the first available airfield. The murky conditions greeting the returning crews over Lincolnshire precluded landings at airfields not equipped with FIDO, and this meant that the circuits at Metheringham and Ludford Magna would soon become crowded. The Joplin crew could see the diffused glow from the FIDO installation at Ludford Magna, and began to circle it, while attempting to obtain landing instructions and keeping a sharp eye out for other aircraft. Joplin tried a number of channels, but heard nothing from the ground, while the dwindling fuel state reduced his options in terms of diverting elsewhere. He knew the minimum safety height for the area, and remained above it according to his altimeter, but suddenly, there was an impact, and the outer section of the port wing folded upwards.

Joplin called for full power in an attempt to keep the damaged Lancaster airborne, but it continued to sink with engines roaring. In the few seconds remaining the crew scrambled to crash positions and braced themselves for the inevitable. There was an initial bounce, and then the main impact, and by the time that all forward motion had ceased, the front section had become detached and was some distance ahead of the main fuselage. A fierce fire took hold, but those crewmembers who were able, took control of the situation, and all the survivors, including a badly injured Joplin, were removed from immediate danger. In the face of fire and exploding ammunition this required great courage, particularly on the part of navigator Basil Fish, who had initially been knocked unconscious, and was now the only member of the crew sufficiently mobile to seek help. He tried to get into the burning section of fuselage to rescue his two unaccounted-for crew mates, F/O Yates, the mid-upper gunner, and F/O Walker, the bomb-aimer, but was driven back by the searing heat after gaining an impression of one or perhaps two charred bodies.

Having settled his surviving comrades and ensured that Joplin was as comfortable as possible with his shattered legs, Fish set off into the bitter cold conditions to find help. His nightmare trek across fields and through hedges eventually brought him to a farmhouse without a telephone, but the kindly farmer escorted him to a public phone in the next village. Finally, almost three hours after the crash, help arrived at the scene. The death of F/O Walker was particularly tragic. He had initially joined the squadron with Williams's crew, and completed twenty-eight operations before Williams was screened in August. He had then become Bob Knights's bomb-aimer for three more trips, leaving him on thirty-one when Knights was screened in December. Tait arranged for Walker to be declared tour expired, but Walker reckoned that his conscience would not be satisfied with anything less than the requisite number expected of everyone else. When Joplin's Bomb-aimer became unavailable for the Pölitz raid through sickness, Walker had fatefully jumped at the chance to fill in. Joplin believed at first, that all had survived the crash, and was devastated to learn of the two fatalities. He took the blame upon himself, and became seriously depressed. His injuries were such, that he would take no further part in squadron operations, but one further blow awaited him at the hands of senior officers, who spent their winter nights in conditions of comfort and safety. An enquiry into the crash concluded, that Joplin had been disobedient in not adhering to standard approach regulations. These regulations were generally ignored by all even in decent weather conditions. His logbook was endorsed accordingly, as was that of Basil Fish.

The final wartime Christmas Day passed uneventfully for 617 Squadron and the 'Independent Air Force', but Boxing Day was interrupted for some crews from the latter and from each of the other Groups. They were called into action against enemy positions around St Vith in the Ardennes, as the German breakout began to falter in what became known as the Battle of the Bulge. On the 28th W/C Tait bade farewell to 617 Squadron, as did G/C Philpott, the station commander, to Woodhall Spa, and a joint party was held in their honour, at which was announced the award of a record third Bar to Tait's DSO. His replacement, the grizzled, tough and highly experienced Canadian, Group Captain Johnny Fauquier, was also introduced to the squadron during this occasion. Fauquier was a legend in 4, 6 and 8 Groups, and would end the war as Canada's most decorated airman. He was born in Ottawa in 1909 as the son of a construction tycoon who built the Ontario leg of the transcontinental railway. He excelled at all forms of sport, and academically he was particularly accomplished in mathematics. His family connections opened up a whole world of opportunity to him, and he initially became a stockbroker. This, however, was anathema to a man with a taste for fast cars, motorcycles and brawling. He learned to fly, proving to be a natural pilot, and started a bush-pilot operation during the mining boom in Quebec. He joined the RCAF at the outbreak of war, and was frustratingly put to basic instructing duties for the first eighteen months. By the time he got into the war with 405 (Vancouver) Squadron RCAF in 4 Group Bomber Command in 1942 he was already 32 years of age, and 10–12 years older than most of his contemporaries. He eventually gained command of 405 Squadron while it was a 4 Group unit in 1942, and returned again in 1943, when it became the only RCAF squadron to become a member of the Pathfinder Force. He acted as Master Bomber or deputy on a number of major operations, and like his predecessors at 617 Squadron, he was accustomed to leading from the front. G/C Philpott's successor as 'station master' at Woodhall Spa was the newly promoted Air Commodore 'Mouse' Fielden, who had distinguished himself back in 1942 as the first commanding officer of 161 Squadron, one of 3 Group's two clandestine units operating on behalf of SOE and SIS.

On the following afternoon, Calder led a force of sixteen aircraft to bomb the Waalhaven *S-Boot* pens at Rotterdam. He and his crew were in ME554, and the other crews involved were those of Brookes in NG228, Cockshott in PD238, Hamilton in DV380, Pryor in LM485, Gumbley in DV405, Dobson in PD371, Gavin in LM489, Goodman in NF992, Oram in ED763, Flatman in PD233, Ross in ME555, Kell in NG181, Leavitt in DV393, Watts in LM695 and Castagnola in LM492. They arrived at the target shortly before 15.00 hours, and Gavin and Flatman sent their Tallboys hurtling earthwards at 14.56. Within two minutes all but Dobson's had been delivered, and his was the last at 15.05. Brookes claimed a direct hit on the northern end of the pens from 18,000 feet, and the consensus was, that three Tallboys found the mark, with many others falling as near misses. Cockshott reported a hole in the centre of the structure as he made a second run right over the target. Reconnaissance revealed a great deal of damage to the shelters, but the Germans had learned from their past experience, and dispersed the vessels around the port, thus sparing them from destruction. On the following early evening, Calder again took the lead in ME554, for an operation by thirteen aircraft to a similar target at Ijmuiden. When they arrived, they encountered low cloud, and Calder went beneath it to 4,000 feet to assess the situation. As the cloud was moving in rather than out, he decided there was no point in hanging around, and sent the force home with their bombs.

On the 31st, Fauquier took the squadron into battle for the first time, when flying in Tait's favourite EE146. He was at the head of a twelve-strong force briefed to attack shipping in Oslo Fjord, where the principal targets were the German warships *Köln* and *Emden*. Each Lancaster carried a Tallboy fused to explode 100 feet below the water. The accompanying crews were those of Calder in ME554, Brookes in NG228, Cockshott in PD238, Pryor in DV391, Gumbley in DV405, Goodman in NF992, Flatman in PD233, Oram in ED763, Ross in ME555, Leavitt in DV393 and Kell in LM695. Flying in Cockshott's front turret was the previously mentioned F/L Horsley, who although now a pilot, was reverting to his former trade to gain experience of the squadron's unique operating techniques. They arrived in the target area a fraction before midnight, and observed both vessels making for open water. The bombing began shortly afterwards, Fauquier's Tallboy falling around 100 yards to port of one of them. He ordered the force to orbit to the north dropping flares, and activity continued in the target area for the next fifty minutes, as some crews made repeated runs in an attempt to draw a bead on the elusive quarry, but no hits were scored. A near miss off the port side of the Emden swung her to starboard and brought her to a standstill, but this was scant reward for the effort expended. The year's final personnel movements involved F/O Lee departing for 26 OTU and S/L Fawke going to Merryfield, while F/O Speirs arrived from 467 Squadron RAAF.

It had been a year of spectacular successes for the squadron, and extremely low losses after the disappointments and high casualty rate following the Dams operation in the previous year. Some of the Lancasters entering the new year had been on squadron charge since 1943, and this would have been almost unheard-of in a main force squadron. A succession of outstanding commanding officers had maintained the squadron at the absolute peak of efficiency and performance, and this was to be continued to the end of the bombing war. The Command, for its part, had emerged from the ashes of the winter campaign, and helped magnificently to ensure the success of the invasion. Bomber Command was now a juggernaut, capable of dispensing annihilation wherever it went, and some of the heaviest raids at its hands still lay in the future. The unmistakeable scent of victory was wafting across from the Continent, but much still remained to be done before the proud, resourceful and tenacious enemy finally laid down his arms.

CHAPTER TWENTY-ONE

Earthquake

1945; the end in sight, new leadership, Grand Slam. Germany is pounded to destruction

The new year began with a flourish as the *Luftwaffe* launched its ill-conceived and ultimately ill-fated Operation *Bodenplatte* (Baseplate) at first light on the 1st of January. The intention to destroy elements of the Allied air forces on the ground at the recently liberated airfields in France, Holland and Belgium was only modestly realised, and cost the *Luftwaffe* around three hundred of its frontline day fighters, at a loss rate of 30 per cent. More critical, though, were the 250 pilots, who were killed, wounded or captured, and this was a blow from which the *Luftwaffe Tagjagd* would never recover. 5 Group opened its 1945 account by canal-busting at the Dortmund-Ems near Ladbergen on New Year's Morning, and having caused a breach there, did the same at the Mittelland Canal at Gravenhorst that night. The Dortmund-Ems would now be out of commission until the 6th of February, but it was the end of the line for the Mittelland, which, although repaired, would be hit again before it could be reopened to traffic. The Group rested on the 2/3rd while Nuremberg suffered the destruction of over 4,600 houses and apartment blocks and 2,000 medieval houses at the hands of 1, 3, 6 and 8 Groups. Two plants belonging to the I G Farben chemicals company were pounded at Ludwigshafen on the same night by elements of 4, 6 and 8 Groups. In the early hours of the 5th, the Group joined forces with 1 Group to provide the main force element for what would become a controversial raid on the French town of Royan. This was in response to a request from Free French forces, which were laying siege on their way to the port of Bordeaux. The German garrison commander had offered to evacuate the civilian population, but most declined, and many of them paid the ultimate price as their town was reduced to rubble. Hanover was raided on the 5/6th for the first time since the series in the autumn of 1943, while a 5 Group element bombed a supply line at Houffalize in the Ardennes. Attacks on Hanau and Neuss followed on the 6/7th, operations which 5 Group sat out, but it provided a contingent for Munich on the 7/8th.

Although the main force was finding itself fully occupied, the weather at the beginning of 1945 was too inhospitable to accommodate the exacting operational flying requirements of 617 Squadron. Operations planned for the

5th, 6th and 7th were cancelled, and the runways were cleared of snow for another on the 11th, which too was called off because of the weather conditions. Matters had improved sufficiently by the 12th for the operation to go ahead, however, and it was to be a long trip to Norway to bomb the *U-Boot* pens and floating dock at Bergen, and shipping in the harbour. Fauquier was in Mosquito NT205, with Canadian S/L Glen Ellwood in the right hand seat, the latter not to be confused with the F/O M Ellwood flying as wireless operator to Ian Ross, whose career will be considered later. Glen Ellwood had served with Fauquier at 405 Squadron, the only Canadian Pathfinder unit, and was at the 6 Group station at Skipton-on-Swale at the end of December, when the call came through from his former boss to join him at Woodhall Spa. The sixteen Lancaster crews were assigned to one of the specific objectives as follows: the *U-Boot* pens, Brookes in NG228, Powell in LM695, Leavitt in DV380, Iveson in NG181, Hamilton in Tait's old EE146, Dobson in LM485, Marshall in DV391, Goodman in DV402, Price in PD238 and Gavin in ME562; the floating dock, Martin in DV393, Sanders in LM489 and Pryor in PD233; shipping, Ross in NF992, Watts in DV405, and Castagnola in LM492. 9 Squadron also contributed sixteen Tallboy carrying Lancasters, and take-off took place between 08.25 and 09.15.

The target area was reached shortly before 13.00 hours, by which time the Mustang fighter support had been observed to sweep in from higher up. It was immediately clear that visibility was going to be compromised by ground haze, and the gaggle began to break up as the crews assigned to the floating dock and shipping searched for an approach offering a clearer view. The visibility problem was soon to be exacerbated by the smoke from the exploding Tallboys, the first of which, according to the ORB, was delivered onto the southern corner of the pens from 16,000 feet by S/L Brookes at 12.58. Goodman followed up two minutes later, only to find the bombsight unserviceable, and frustratingly, this would be the only time the target was clearly visible to his bomb-aimer. They made five more runs across the target over the ensuing thirty-eight minutes, as the bomb-aimer, F/L Hayward, tried to use his SABS as a fixed sight, but he never again obtained a fix through the smoke, and they turned for home with the Tallboy still aboard. Dobson, Price and Gavin also made up to five runs each with a functioning SABS but were forced to give up and likewise bring their Tallboys home. Leavitt dropped his bomb into the smoke at 13.04½, but was unable to pinpoint its burst, and Marshall's went down some three minutes later. The members of Marshall's crew were unable to determine the fall of their bomb, but did see what they thought was the first one to go down, possibly that dropped by Brookes, overshooting to the left by 150 yards. Hamilton's bomb-aimer identified the pens on the first run, but called for a second one, at the end of which the Tallboy hung up. By the time a third circuit was completed, the aiming point was obscured by smoke, and theirs became yet another Tallboy to be returned to store.

Powell gave up trying to find the aiming point at 13.41, but during the course of his runs across the target, he or his crew observed two detonations, one around 300 yards to the south of the target, and the other on a hillside six miles due west. One of the former may have belonged to Tony Iveson, whose Lancaster found itself in heavy flak, and was attacked by an enemy fighter. The port-inner engine caught fire, and the tail plane and rudder on that side sustained damage. Iveson ordered the Tallboy to be jettisoned fused over an uninhabited area, and warned his crew to prepare to abandon the aircraft, which was wallowing along in a nose up attitude and losing height. Rear gunner, Ted Wass, plugged into the intercom to report that he and two others were now ready to bale out, and on hearing the confirmation, 'OK', assumed this was the order to go. He, the wireless operator, F/O Tittle, and mid-upper gunner, Sgt Smith, departed the aircraft by parachute, and the fighter broke off the engagement. The Lancaster was hit again by flak as it turned away from the target area, and it looked as if a safe return across the sea was going to be out of the question. Directional control was proving difficult because of the damage to cables, and Iveson was forced to maintain pressure on the port rudder pedal to prevent the aircraft from turning to starboard. Determined not to spend the last few months of the war in captivity, though, Iveson and the remaining crewmembers set about the task of getting home. Bomb-aimer Frank Chance lashed a rope around the port rudder pedal and secured it to the camera mount to enable Iveson to relieve the pressure on his leg. Flight engineer 'Taff' Phillips went aft and found the severed cables, and through a process of trial and error he and his pilot worked out a system to get them back to Sumburgh in the Shetlands. They arrived in one piece, justly proud of their achievement, but devastated by the loss of three of their number, whom, they hoped had landed safely. In fact, wireless operator Les Smith had damaged a leg on landing, and came to on a stretcher being borne by four German soldiers. Both gunners were also ultimately taken into captivity. Arthur Kell flew up to Sumburgh on the following day to collect Iveson and the others, but they would fly no further operations with the squadron, and it would be July before the Lancaster came home.

The three crews assigned to the floating dock were experiencing great difficulty in picking out their target. Runs were made from various directions, but it was only visible from directly above, and with smoke drifting towards this aiming point from the pens, the prospects were poor. After ten runs Don Day spotted a merchantman heading for the town, and Martin, his pilot, called up Fauquier for permission to attack it. Fauquier, realising the floating dock was a lost cause, gave the go-ahead, and Day had the target smack in his sight just seconds from release, when a flak shell exploded beneath the Lancaster and peppered the underside with shrapnel. The Tallboy took most of it, and fell away minus part of its tail assembly. The arming wire had been cut, and this meant, that the bomb fell harmlessly into the sea without detonating. The bomb doors were riddled with holes, but, luckily, no vital parts of the aircraft had been hit. Sanders was also unable to identify the floating dock after making five runs, and followed Fauquier's orders to attack shipping instead. His bomb was dropped from 15,000 feet at 13.32, and was described as a near miss. The third member of the floating dock trio was Pryor, whose PD233 became another victim of fighters. They had already made six runs across their target, and were in the process of a seventh, when a fighter appeared on the starboard beam. Pryor turned towards the enemy in the standard evasive manoeuvre, and as he did so, a second fighter closed the trap by attacking from the port side. The port-outer engine was damaged and had to be feathered, and at least one other engine lost power. Pryor threw the Lancaster around the sky like a fighter, and the Tallboy was jettisoned. This was most likely the explosion on the hillside witnessed by Powell. The damage was sufficiently serious to persuade Pryor that there was almost no chance of negotiating the sea crossing to Scotland. He considered a crash-landing, but the hilly terrain precluded that option, and when an Fw190 drew alongside, its pilot gesticulating to the crew to get out, the game was effectively up. Pryor dragged the crippled aircraft up to around 1,500 feet over an island, and was the last to leave, having pointed the nose of his Lancaster out to sea. All but one of the crew landed safely, the exception being F/O Kendrick, who, it will be recalled, had been severely injured almost exactly a year earlier, when O'Shaughnessy crashed on Snettisham beach during training. He was the first to leave the aircraft through the front hatch, and was observed from the ground to fail to deploy his parachute. Only recently returned to operations, it seems he hit his chin on his way through the hatch, and was knocked unconscious. He was found in deep snow with severe head and back injuries, and despite being tended by local people, he succumbed three days later without regaining consciousness.

Witnesses on the ground also reported the empty Lancaster being chased out to sea by the Fw190s, which belonged to either the 9th or 12th *Staffel* of III/JG5 operating out of Herdla. These were units from the same JG5 commanded by Major Ehrler until his court martial resulting from the *Tirpitz* affair. One of the fighters appears to have collided with the Lancaster, and following an explosion, both aircraft went into the sea. The German pilot, *Unteroffizier* Kirchner, was killed. It was later reported, that the second Fw190 ran out of fuel on the way back to its base, and although *Feldwebel* Lieber was observed to carry out a ditching, he also failed to survive.

Castagnola was able to watch the opening of the raid as he stalked a ship, upon which he intended to drop his Tallboy, and he confirmed Marshall's observation, that the first bomb to go down on the submarine pens was an overshoot. He unloaded his 12,000 pound monster weapon at 13.09 from 14,850 feet, and his bomb-aimer, P/O Hoyland, watched it all the way down to the stern of the vessel, a minesweeper, which it penetrated like a hot knife through butter. The effect was immediate, and the ship could be seen to settle in the water. After about three minutes it was rent by an explosion, possibly from its boiler, and then rolled over onto its side and sank with twenty of its crew killed or missing. As it disappeared beneath the waves Watts was aiming his Tallboy at another vessel, a tramp steamer, which turned out to be the *Olga Siemens*, but he missed by around 75 yards. Nevertheless, the explosion caused a serious leak in the hull of the 3,300 ton vessel, and it had to be beached. As he pulled away Watts's attention was attracted by the sight of Ross's Lancaster trailing smoke, and being chased out to sea by two Fw190 fighters. He was clearly losing the fight with gravity, and his crippled Lancaster sank lower and lower over the cold ocean. Watts instinctively dived in pursuit of the pursuers, at the same time seeking and obtaining permission from Fauquier to do so. Both of Ross's port engines were by now feathered, but at least they had stopped smoking. The front turret of Watts's Lancaster opened up at around 250 yards, and the two fighters broke away and disappeared. Ross was seen to ditch off the Norwegian coast, and he and his crew were then observed to climb out onto the wing and inflate their Mae Wests. The Lancaster showed no signs of sinking, but, worryingly, there was no evidence of a dinghy. Watts climbed up to 5,000 feet to get off an air sea rescue call, and saw the rest of the squadron heading homewards high above. Remarkably, Castagnola had also raced to help Ross, and was circling the area, but neither crew was aware of the other's presence until they compared notes back home.

Watts remained at the scene until his fuel situation forced him to leave, by which time he knew, that an Air Sea Rescue Warwick was on its way from Sumburgh. The Warwick took off at 14.43, and arrived a little over an hour later to find the Lancaster still afloat, but only just. By the time it had circled and dropped a lifeboat at 16.05, the Lancaster had disappeared beneath the waves, and the crew was in the water. In the fading light, one man was seen to be swimming towards the lifeboat, but the approach of an enemy fighter forced the Warwick crew to turn for home. Watts, meanwhile, had landed at Sumburgh, having completed the final approach on fumes, and as he taxied off the runway, the engines cut. Throughout the night Coastal Command Catalinas searched the sea right up to the Norwegian coast, one of them with a Leigh Light, but no trace was found of the Ross crew or the lifeboat. Three Warwicks and three Ansons continued the search on the following day with a fighter escort, but they also found nothing, and the search was called off as darkness fell. It is believed by some, that the enemy fighter seen earlier by the Warwick crew strafed and killed the unfortunate crewmembers.

The wireless operator in Ross's crew was F/O Ellwood, for whom this fateful operation had been his sixty-third in a remarkable wartime career. He had originally attended gunnery school, passing out on the 9th of August 1940 to go to 16 OTU. He joined 106 Squadron in mid October, but remained non-operational, and moved on to 44 Squadron at Waddington at the start of November. Here he joined the crew of P/O Sandford, with whom he flew his first operational sortie on the 12th of November against Dortmund. In January 1941, after completing eight more sorties as a wireless operator/ gunner with P/O Sandford, he joined the squadron's D Flight, which was evaluating the Douglas Boston DB7 'Havoc'. His pilot now was F/O Romans, who would be selected that May as one of the elite airmen to join 2 Group's 90 Squadron for high-level daylight operations in the ill-fated B17C, or Fortress I as it was known in the RAF. Sadly, Romans was to lose his life when fighters shot down his B17 over Norway that September. Towards the end of February Ellwood was posted to 25 OTU at Finningley, where he flew with a number of notable pilots, including three future participants in the epic Augsburg raid in the following year, Penman, Garwell and Hallows. He also teamed up with W/C Taafe, who had commanded 50 Squadron the previous year, and the already mentioned S/L Russell, who commanded the same squadron in the following year and later 138 Squadron. S/L Burnett was another future squadron commander with whom Ellwood flew, he eventually taking over at 9 Squadron.

Ellwood remained at 25 OTU until early December 1941, when he joined 97 Squadron at Coningsby as a member of the crew of the already mentioned F/L Penman DFC. His first operation was flown in a Manchester against Wilhelmshaven on the 10/11th of January 1942, and this was his tenth sortie in all. 97 Squadron was in the process of converting to Lancasters as the second squadron in the Command to do so, following in the footsteps of 44 Squadron, and working up to operational status in a new type required a lengthy process. Consequently, Ellwood had to wait until the 10/11th of April for his next sortie, and his first in a Lancaster, by which time the squadron had moved from Coningsby to nearby Woodhall Spa. The target was Cologne, from where the aircraft returned with flak damage. Over the ensuing days a number of long distance flights were undertaken in formation by crews from both 44 and 97 Squadrons independently of each other, one of which culminated in a simulated attack on the town of Inverness. On the morning of the 17th six crews from each squadron plus two reserve crews assembled in the briefing rooms at Waddington and Woodhall Spa to learn of the operation to be launched that afternoon. The men were incredulous at the prospect of flying to Augsburg, deep inside southern Germany, at low level in daylight, and few thought they would return home. Indeed, only one aircraft from the 44 Squadron contingent made it back, that flown by W/C Nettleton, who was subsequently awarded the Victoria Cross. Ellwood's former pilot, F/L 'Nick' Sandford, was killed with his crew, one of four victims of Bf109s over France on the outward flight. Garwell, with whom Ellwood had flown at 25 OTU, force-landed his Lancaster beyond the target, and survived with all but one of his crew as a PoW. 97 Squadron's six, in contrast, slipped unnoticed into Germany, but lost two aircraft during the attack on the MAN diesel works. Penman's Lancaster was hit by light flak, but no serious damage resulted, and they got home under the cover of darkness without further incident. Penman was awarded the DSO, and there was a DFM for one of his crew, but Ellwood and the others received nothing other than a 'well done'! The previously mentioned 'Darky' Hallows, with whom Ellwood had also flown at 25 OTU, was among those returning safely to Woodhall Spa, and as events came full circle now in January 1945, he was about to come back to that very station as the newly appointed commanding officer of 627 Squadron.

After completing further sorties Ellwood became attached to the squadron's Conversion Flight, but returned to operations with a W/O Cullinane in July, and in October he was declared tour expired with a total of thirty-three sorties to his credit. He spent 1943 at 14 OTU Cottesmore, before joining 617 Squadron in January 1944, having officially remustered as a wireless operator. He carried out the first operation of his second tour with F/L 'Bunny' Clayton on the 2nd of March, flew with Shannon on the 10th, Cheshire on the 23rd, and over the succeeding weeks operated with Pryor, Willsher, Cooper and Knights, before settling with Kearns for seven operations. Thereafter, he joined F/L Williams for three operations, F/O Ross for two, F/L Iveson for one, and finished his second tour with the first attack on the *Tirpitz* as a member of S/L Fawke's crew. With fifty-three sorties to his name Ellwood threw himself immediately into a third tour, beginning with the second operation against the *Tirpitz* at the end of October, which he also flew with Fawke. In December he teamed up again with F/O Ian Ross for operations against the pens at Ijmuiden and the oil refinery at Pölitz among others, before this last and fateful Bergen operation. On the 13th of March, Norwegian fishermen recovered Ellwood's body from the sea, and he is the only member of Ross's crew to have a known grave. This account of Ellwood's career is part of the Bomber Command story, which too frequently focuses on the pilots, and thereby fails to give sufficient attention to the heroic contribution to victory of other crewmen. As a postscript to the operation, three Tallboys apparently penetrated the roof of the *U-Boot* pen, and there was much internal destruction, although only two *U-Boots* were slightly damaged.

Although 617 Squadron had now concluded its operational activity for the month, the rest of 5 Group was kept busy, focusing particularly on the enemy's oil industry. A return was made to the refinery at Pölitz on the 13/14th, when better than forecast conditions allowed low level marking to take place, and the operation was claimed as a success. Two nights later the synthetic oil refinery at Leuna near Merseburg was attacked in two phases three hours apart, by 1, 5, 6 and 8 Groups, who left it severely damaged. Forty-eight hours later it was the turn of the oil plant at Brüx in Czechoslovakia to suffer a complete breakdown in production after a visit from 5 Group, and this was the last major outing of the month for the Independent Air Force. The month saw four aircrew officer pilot arrivals on posting to 617 Squadron, those of F/L Beaumont from 5 LFS, F/L Hill from 61 Squadron, Lt Adams, an American, from 630 Squadron and F/L Warburton from 57 Squadron.

February began with three major main force operations on the 1/2nd, against Ludwigshafen, Mainz and Siegen, the last mentioned by 5 Group. This was one of a number of raids during the first week of the month to be spoiled by cloudy conditions over the target, and most of the bombing on this occasion fell into open country. It was a similar story for the Group at Karlsruhe on the 2/3rd, and this operation was a complete failure. It was the 3rd before 617 Squadron operated again, this time with a visit to the midget submarine pens at Poortershaven, from where 'Biber' operations were launched. The Biber was an ill-conceived and desperate attempt by Germany to interfere with Allied naval supply and support operations at a time when the war was essentially lost. The one-man craft was hastily developed and put into service. It carried a torpedo on each side, was powered on the surface by a petrol engine and when submerged by batteries. Once its power was exhausted it was at the mercy of the current, and many drifted into oblivion with their pilots. Other unfortunate pilots died of carbon monoxide poisoning as exhaust fumes infiltrated the tiny cockpit compartment. Sadly, life in Germany was cheap at this stage of the war, and few Biber pilots survived to tell their sorry tale.

Fauquier led the squadron into battle in NG445, and the others involved in this operation were Cockshott in PD238, Goodman in PB415, Horsley in ME554, Flatman in EE146, Gavin in LM489, Gumbley in DV405, Price in DV380, Watts in LM695, Martin in DV393, Brookes in NG228, Powell in PD371, Oram in ED763, Marshall in DV391, Lancey in LM485, Castagnola in DV385, Calder in NG489 and Sanders in ME562. Fauquier was first away at 14.00 hours, and it was an hour and fifty-one minutes later that the Tallboys began to fall. Fauquier reported a good gaggle formation, and all of the Tallboys went down on the first run with good concentration. As always, smoke made it difficult to assess the outcome accurately, but Flatman reported three bombs in the water close to and outside of the breakwater, three to four more close to the entrance to the pens, one on a nearby railway and another about 200 yards north of the aiming point. Price and Powell claimed direct hits, and others watched their bombs fall into the smoke directly over the aiming point. All aircraft returned safely to Woodhall Spa either side of 17.00 hours, after barely three hours in the air. Post-raid photographs of craters revealed that five to six Tallboys had inflicted heavy damage on the pens and quays. The entrance to the southern dam of the basin had been cut, military installations south-east and north-west of the pens were seriously afflicted, the floating crane used for lifting the vessels in and out of the water had been hit, and the railway line north of the target area serving the pens had been cut in three places. None of the submarines themselves appeared to be damaged, but they were unable to carry out any operations for a month, and this allowed vital Allied supply convoys unmolested access to the River Scheldt.

This successful operation was followed by an intended assault by seventeen aircraft on the important viaduct at Bielefeld on the 6th. Fauquier led the squadron away in NG445 at 08.14, but by the time the target was reached some two hours or so later bad weather had intervened, and the attack was abandoned. All the Tallboys were brought home. This day's failure became the start of what was effectively a campaign against the viaduct until its eventual destruction some weeks later, while the structure's stubborn refusal to fall was almost a symbolic reflection of Germany's dogged commitment to continuing the fight despite the war having already been lost. What we know as the Bielefeld Viaduct actually stands on the outskirts of the small town of Schildesche, one of a number of similar communities making up the Bielefeld urban area, and it is known in Germany as the Schildesche rather than the Bielefeld Viaduct. Construction of the impressive twenty-eight arch edifice began in 1845, and was completed two years later. It was built to carry the new Cöln-Minden railway line across the Johannisbach Valley, and would eventually become a vital link in the east-west communications network. Between 1914 and 1917 a second viaduct was built alongside as a mirror image to cope with the increasing amount of traffic, and it was this imposing twin structure that now faced 617 Squadron. As ground forces moved towards the German frontier during the autumn of 1944, American bombers began to target the Bielefeld area, pitting the landscape around the viaduct with bomb craters, and inflicting casualties upon the local populations.

1, 4, 6 and 8 Groups heavily bombed the frontier towns of Goch and Cleves on the 7/8th, while 5 Group took another crack at the Ladbergen section of the Dortmund-Ems Canal, which had now been repaired yet again. The Germans had pushed a large volume of traffic through the waterway on the 6th and the 7th, and had plans to deceive aerial reconnaissance in the future. Delayed action bombs were employed on this night, but photo-reconnaissance later showed that most of the weaponry had fallen into neighbouring fields, and that there was only minor damage at dispersed locations, which was rapidly repaired. The canal was reopened for a day to let traffic through, and then it was drained to give the appearance of still being out of commission. An accumulation of traffic would now be allowed to build up, and this would be pushed through the refilled canal on the 25th, before it was drained again.

While 617 Squadron had been attending to the submarine pens at Poortershaven on the 3rd, 9 Squadron had visited the new and, as it turned out, abandoned *S-Boot* pens at Ijmuiden. Now 617 Squadron returned alone to the latter on the 8th to finish the job. Fauquier was again in NG445, and the others were Calder in NG489, Castagnola in DV385, Sanders in ME562, Martin in PB415, Watts in LM695, Flatman in NG339, Lancey in LM485, Gumbley in DV405, Oram in LM492, Cockshott in PD238, Brookes in NG228, Goodman in NG340, Dobson in ED763 and Price in DV380. Taking off either side of 08.00 the squadron reached the target area at 09.30, and ran in at heights ranging from 14,200 to 16,000 feet. Twelve Tallboys went down at 09.33, a minute after Castagnola's, and two minutes before the remaining two, and at least two direct hits were observed by Fauquier and one near miss. The Germans had again dispersed the vessels around the port, however, and none of them was damaged. A vertical reconnaissance photograph taken by a 542 Squadron pilot and an oblique one provided by 541 Squadron produced an interpretation report describing a hit at the north end of the pens where the final concrete roof had not yet been laid. This portion of the roof was declared to be destroyed over three pens with additional damage to the north wall. It further described a near miss and five other craters, one of which was within 100 feet of the west side of the shelter. In fact, no hits were scored, but a very near miss had knocked a section of wall out of alignment. This was the only operation by 617 Squadron against the new bunker, but the Americans made a number of attacks employing Disney bombs.

That night a two-phase attack on the refinery at Pölitz was opened by 5 Group, and concluded by 1 and 8 Groups to end production finally at the plant for good. The Churchill inspired series of attacks on Germany's eastern cities under Operation Thunderclap began at Dresden in another standard two-phase operation on the 13/14th. 5 Group opened proceedings with over 240 Lancasters bombing on markers delivered from low level by 627 Squadron Mosquitos. Over 800 tons of bombs were unloaded into the beautiful and historic city in a partially effective assault, which was hampered by layers of thin cloud. By the time that the 529-strong 'Platerack' force of 1, 3, 6 and 8 Group Lancasters arrived on the scene some three hours later, guided unerringly to the mark by the fires now burning fiercely in the city, the cloud had drifted away. A further 1,800 tons of bombs rained down onto the hapless city and its population, which had been massively swelled by an influx of refugees fleeing from the eastern front. The bombing triggered a similar chain of events to those devastating parts of Hamburg in July 1943, and around 35,000 people died in the ensuing firestorm. (This figure has been settled upon in recent years as a realistic estimate, although some commentators claim a death toll of 135,000 to be more accurate). The Thunderclap force moved on to Chemnitz on the following night, but the presence of thick cloud led to a scattered and relatively disappointing raid. 5 Group did not take part, but was also active over eastern Germany at the time delivering a partially successful attack on an oil refinery at Rositz.

Earlier on that morning of the 14th, 617 Squadron had sent nineteen Lancasters back to Bielefeld, but cloud prevented the attack from taking place, and all the Tallboys were returned to the dump. 1, 3, 6 and 8 Groups undertook the penultimate heavy raid of the war on Dortmund on the 20/21st, the night on which a 5 Group attack on the now repaired and about-to-be-returned-to-use Mittelland Canal at Gravenhorst was aborted because of cloud. On the following night forces of over 300 aircraft each plastered Duisburg and Worms, while 5 Group tried again at the Mittelland Canal, and this time left it drained and unnavigable. One of the nine missing Lancasters from this operation was an 83 Squadron aircraft piloted by the 43-year-old G/C 'Tiny' Evans-Evans, the station commander at Coningsby. While his flying skills in a Lancaster were not universally admired, and one wonders how he managed to persuade others to fly with him, his courage was never in question. His already mentioned desire to remain 'one of the boys' cost him his life along with all but one of those on board, who, it seems, were mostly from 97 Squadron.

On the afternoon of the 22nd, while 9 Squadron took a dogleg southerly route to another architecturally impressive viaduct at Altenbeken, 617 Squadron adopted an almost due easterly track from Cromer straight across the Ijsselmeer and Holland and into Germany to return to Bielefeld with eighteen Lancasters armed with Tallboys. Fauquier led in NG445, and he was accompanied by Carey, fresh from his sojourn in Sweden, in NG494, Castagnola in DV385, Gavin in LM489, Powell in NG228, Anning in LM492, Sayers in DV402, Dobson in PD371, Sanders in ME562, Goodman in ME554, Gumbley in DV405, Marshall in DV391, Calder in NG489, Watts in LM695, Leavitt in PB415, Price in PD238, Martin in NG340 and Hill in NG339. The first Tallboys went down shortly before 16.00 hours during the initial run, but some crews went round for a second or third run. Fauquier bombed on his second run, and saw his bomb overshoot by 50 yards. Carey undershot by around 40 yards, but noted a possible direct hit on the northern end. Castagnola thought his bomb may have been a direct hit on the northern end, but it was at least a near miss, while Calder claimed a direct hit. The structure was peppered with near misses of around 40 to 50 yards, and although some crews believed it had been damaged, photo-reconnaissance revealed it to be still intact.

The Krupp works was one of the main victims of a 4, 6 and 8 Group raid on Essen on the 23rd, and Pforzheim suffered a catastrophic raid at the hands of 1, 6 and 8 Groups that night. In a twenty-two minute orgy of destruction a massive area of the town became engulfed in flames, and over 17,000 people lost their lives. On the 24th cloud prevented 617 Squadron from delivering an attack on the Dortmund-Ems Canal at Ladbergen, for which eighteen aircraft had taken off, led again by Fauquier. Marshall suffered a coolant leak in his starboard outer immediately after take-off, and did not proceed beyond local airspace. Among his crew were original 'Dambusters' Len Sumpter, formerly Shannon's bomb-aimer, and Doug Webb, Townsend's rear gunner. This abortive trip proved to be the squadron's last operational activity of the month. Pilot postings during the month were as follows; F/Ls Quinton and Rawes came in from 5 LFS, S/L Gordon from 189 Squadron, and F/L Trent from 1 Group's 625 Squadron, while P/O Huckerby went to 1660CU and S/L Iveson to 6 LFS.

The final major raid of the war on Mannheim took place on the 1st of March, and the 2nd brought a similar milestone for the once magnificent city of Cologne. The first of two bombing phases heaped more misery on the Rhineland Capital, but the 3 Group second phase was abandoned early on, after the failure of a G-H station in England. Four days later American forces captured the city. 5 Group returned to the Dortmund-Ems Canal for the final time on the 3/4th, while it was still drained, and just before the next major push of traffic was planned. The embankments and underpass were damaged so severely, that repairs were still in progress when the approach of

Allied ground forces brought work to a halt on the 30th. Operation Thunderclap made good the recent inconclusive raid on Chemnitz on the 5/6th, and left much of it in flames, while 5 Group took advantage of the activity there to slip over to Böhlen and inflict some modest damage on its oil refinery. On the following night the Group attacked the small port of Sassnitz on the island of Rügen near Peenemünde on the Baltic coast, causing extensive damage to the northern half of the town, and sinking three ships in the harbour. The oil refinery at Harburg was the target for the 7/8th, and this proved to be another successful operation for the 'Independent Air Force'.

A further attempt to take out the Bielefeld viaduct was launched on the 9th with Fauquier this time in Mosquito NT205, accompanied in the right-hand seat by F/L Bayne. Nineteen Lancasters were also involved, take-off beginning with Castagnola at 14.25 and ending with the squadron commander at 14.56. Some three and a half hours later they were back with their bombs still attached, having been thwarted by cloud. The 11th brought an all-time record for the Command, when 1,079 aircraft, the largest force ever dispatched to a single target, took off in the late morning to raid Essen for the last time. The record lasted for a little over twenty-four hours, and was surpassed on the following afternoon, when 1,108 aircraft departed their stations for Dortmund. This was a record, which would stand to the end of hostilities.

Like the scent of a fox to a pack of hounds the lure of the Bielefeld viaduct drew 617 Squadron on yet again on the 13th, when Fauquier reverted to a Lancaster, this time PB119. A further nineteen Lancasters were involved in the early afternoon departure from Woodhall Spa, captained by Cockshott, Calder, Brookes, Powell, McLoughlin, Goodman, Hill, Gumbley, Warburton, Sayers, Lancey, Anning, Rawes, Adams, Flatman, Martin, Speirs, Castagnola and Carey. Once again the weather intervened, however, and around four hours later they came home to return their valuable stores to the dump. Although the ORB describes the bombs carried by Fauquier and Calder as Tallboys, they were both flying in Lancaster BI Specials. PD119 and PD112 respectively were among a batch of aircraft belonging to C Flight, which had front and dorsal turrets removed, no bomb doors, a modified bomb bay faired fore and aft, strengthened undercarriage, uprated engines, and two less crew members, specifically to carry Wallis's scaled up Tallboy, the 22,000lb Grand Slam. They also bore a YZ code, while A and B Flights retained KC. The Grand Slam earthquake bombs had been going to war for the first time, but Fauquier and Calder were now forced to make a landing with the war's heaviest bomb still on board. For extra insurance they put down on the very long emergency strip at Carnaby.

The operation was rescheduled for the following afternoon, and the target's charmed life was soon to be brought to an abrupt end. Sixteen Lancasters were prepared on this occasion, but Fauquier's PD119 became unserviceable immediately before take-off. Calder, not wishing to be the victim of a hijack by his commanding officer, turned a Nelsonian blind eye to the gesticulations of his superior, gunned the engines, and took off to become the first to drop a

Grand Slam in anger. Anger was the emotion felt by Fauquier as he watched the graceful upward arc of PD112's wings bearing the ten-ton monster weapon aloft. The other crew captains and Lancasters were: Brookes in NG228, Powell in PD371, Goodman in NG494, Hill in LM489, Gumbley in DV405, Warburton in DV380, Sayers in DV402, Lancey in LM485, Anning in LM492, Rawes in DV391, Flatman in NG339, Martin in PB415, Speirs in LM695 and Carey in NG489. There was no cloud on this occasion to protect the viaduct, and Calder's Grand Slam went down from 11,965 feet at 16.28¼ on the squadron's second pass over the target, and at precisely the same moment that Martin released his Tallboy. Other Tallboys dropped within seconds came from the Lancasters of Gumbley, Brookes, Hill, Lancey and Flatman. Sayers's Tallboy had actually been the first to go, but this fell out as the bomb doors were opened during the initial approach at 16.12. The bomb seemed to be undamaged as it fell away, and was seen to rotate in the prescribed manner, but whether or not it detonated is not recorded. Rawes was unable to pick up the aiming point along with the others, so went round again, trying to follow the road from Bielefeld to the south of the viaduct. The Tallboy was released at 16.37, and only then did the crew realise, that they were off track. The bomb fell onto a crossroads some 750 yards south-west of the target.

On the ground the residents of Schildesche, Brake, Theesen and the other communities were becoming accustomed to the air raid alarms and the routine of going to the municipal shelters. Some, though, knowing the viaduct to be the objective, felt able to stay above ground and watch the proceedings. As the Grand Slam left Calder's Lancaster it was described variously as looking like a telegraph pole and a beer bottle, but was certainly larger than anything ever previously seen to fall from an Allied bomber. As it detonated and threw a column of whitish smoke and earth into the air, the ground shook in Schildesche. Three kilometres away in Theesen, onlookers felt their clothes move as the blast sent out an airborne shockwave. When the smoke had cleared, the result of the bombing could be seen in the form of five collapsed arches on both viaducts covering a distance of 130 yards. The general feeling among the local populace was one of relief. Now that the viaduct had gone, there would be no more trains and no further need to bomb. As medical services reached the scene they encountered a dozen or so young flak helpers lying dead with others injured, and these brought the total number of fatalities in Schildesche as a result of air raids from the autumn onwards to around fifty. No further bombs fell in the Schildesche area, and two and a half weeks later American troops marched into Bielefeld.

On return to Woodhall Spa Calder reported a 30-yard undershoot of his Grand Slam on the southern end of the viaduct on the Schildesche side, and this was confirmed by photographic reconnaissance. He also saw a direct hit, which was one of a number claimed by other crews, among them Hill and Gumbley, and Brookes thought his might have been. Goodman saw his Tallboy explode on the railway line by a road crossing, while Flatman believed his impacted on the road running beneath the viaduct. The result was the collapse of 100 yards of this formerly illusive structure, and all aircraft had returned safely to base. That night 5 Group attacked the Wintershall oil refinery at Lützkendorf, and left moderate damage in its wake.

On the 15th Calder and Cockshott, in company with fourteen Lancasters of 9 Squadron, took Grand Slams to the Arnsberg viaduct in PB996 and PD114 respectively. Cockshott bombed on his fourth run from 13,600 feet, but haze obscured its point of impact, and Calder brought his bomb home from what was an unsuccessful operation. While Nuremberg was being pounded by a predominantly 1 Group force on the 16/17th, 5 Group attacked the old cathedral city of Würzburg and destroyed almost 90 per cent of its built-up area in seventeen minutes of precision bombing. On the 19th the operation to the Arnsberg viaduct was repeated by nineteen aircraft, and this provided Fauquier with the opportunity to deliver his first Grand Slam. The crews involved were those of Fauquier in PD119, Cockshott in PD238, Powell in PD121, Calder in NG445, Gumbley in PD117, Warburton in LM489, Sayers in PB997, Anning in PB998, Rawes in PD113, Dobson in PD116, Trent in LM485, Gavin in PD131, Goodman in PD130, Hill in PD118, Flatman in PD129, Carey in PD132, Martin in PB996, Speirs in PB415 and Adams in ME562. Fauquier, Gumbley, Gavin, Goodman, Flatman and Martin were all armed with Grand Slams, and the commanding officer released his at 10.54 from 13,000 feet, noticing that the bombing generally was tending to overshoot the mark. Nevertheless, Dobson claimed a direct hit with his Tallboy, and Hill reported seeing this and a second one, and when the smoke had cleared sufficiently, at least two arches of the viaduct were seen to be down. The second direct hit observed by Hill may have come from either Cockshott or Speirs, the former claiming to have nailed the aiming point, while the latter saw his effort hit near the right hand or tunnel end. Sayers experienced a hang-up on his first run and went round again with the same result. 5 Group continued its assault on the enemy's oil industry on the 20/21st with an attack on the refinery at Böhlen. Accurate marking and bombing halted all production at the plant, and it was still out of action when the war ended.

The Arbergen railway bridge in the south-eastern suburbs of Bremen in northern Germany was the target for an attack by twenty 617 Squadron aircraft on the 21st. The crews were those of Fauquier in PD119, Calder in PB996, both carrying a Grand Slam, Gordon in PD115, Cockshott in PD114, Gavin in PD116, Goodman in PD130, Hill in NG494, Gumbley in PD117, Price in PD118, Warburton in PD128, Powell in PD133, Dobson in PD130, Rawes in PD113, Sayers in NG445, Anning in LM695, Trent in PD238, Lancey in NG489, Flatman in NG339, Carey in PB997 and Speirs in PD129. Calder released his Grand Slam from 13,690 feet at 10.05½, but was unable to determine its point of impact. Fauquier's fell away ten seconds later from 14,000 feet, and he plotted its impact as 200 yards north of the target. The Price crew was the only one to report seeing a direct hit, but the structure succumbed anyway under the weight of numerous near misses. PD117 was hit by heavy flak, and was seen to fall in flames a dozen or so miles south of the centre of Bremen, before exploding on impact. As a BI Special it contained a five-man crew, and sadly, Barney Gumbley and his colleagues were all killed. No remains were recovered, and the names of the crew are perpetuated on the Runnymede Memorial. Five other aircraft also sustained damage, but all returned safely. That night 150 Lancasters of 5 Group targeted the Deutsche Erdölwerke oil refinery at Hamburg, destroying twenty storage tanks, and the plant was still inoperative at the cessation of hostilities.

A bridge over the River Weser at Nienburg, north-west of Hanover, was the target for twenty 617 Squadron aircraft on the afternoon of the 22nd, six of them carrying Grand Slams. These were Gordon in PB996, Cockshott in PD114, Powell in PD121, Gavin in PD134, Rawes in PB997 and Anning in PD133. Those with Tallboys were Fauquier in NG445, Calder in PD115 or PD113, Price in PD135, Goodman in PB415, Hill in NG494, Warburton in PD128, Sayers in PD132, Trent in LM485, Lancey in NG489, Horsley in PD238, Flatman in LM695, Carey in PD131, Speirs in PD112 and Brookes in NG228. Fauquier observed three direct hits, one of which was Cockshott's Grand Slam, and Rawes also believed his to have found the mark. In order not to waste the precious bombs the 4th and 8th rows of the gaggle had been instructed not to bomb on the first two runs, and in the event, the bridge was destroyed without them. This enabled Powell to bring his Grand Slam home, along with the Tallboys carried by Brookes and Speirs.

On the following day a similar number of aircraft returned to the Bremen area to attack another railway bridge. Fauquier led the operation in PD119, with Powell in PB996, Calder in PD112, Cockshott in PD114, Gavin in PD134 and Flatman in PB997, all armed with Grand Slams, and Brookes in PD133, Gordon in PB998, Price in PD113, Goodman in PB415, Hill in NG494, Warburton in LM695, Sayers in PD132, Anning in PD118, Trent in PD115, Lancey in NG489, Horsley in PD238, Carey in PD131, Speirs in PD130 and Leavitt in LM492, each with a Tallboy. Powell was forced to abort his sortie while still over the airfield twenty minutes after take-off. A problem with his starboard outer would have prevented him from maintaining gaggle speed, and it seems he jettisoned his Grand Slam over a designated area. Sayers managed to gain a little more distance before he too suffered a starboard-outer engine failure, and he returned his Tallboy to store. A few minutes after Sayers landed, Trent came back with a complete failure of the oxygen system, and his Tallboy was also saved for a future occasion. It was a rare occasion indeed, if not a unique one, for three 617 Squadron aircraft to return early from the same operation with technical failures. A little over three hours after take-off, at 10.04, Fauquier released his Grand Slam from 16,500 feet. According to Brookes, the first three bombs to fall were direct hits, but in the space of a minute from 10.03.47 Warburton, Gordon, Gavin, Anning and Carey all claimed hits, as did Cockshott and Horsley shortly

Joe McCarthy in his 'office'.

Ralph Allsebrook and crew while serving with 49 Squadron.

Astell's navigator, Floyd Wile, pictured in the glasshouse of their 617 Squadron Lancaster during training for Operation *Chastise*.

Geoff Rice and crew.

The remains of F/L Harold Wilson's Lancaster JA898 KC-X lies adjacent to the Dortmund-Ems Canal on the morning of 16.9.43.

A fine view of ED817, one of the prototype Dams Lancasters.

'Mac' Hamilton and crew.

Bob Horsley and some of his crew.

Guy Gibson as a lowly Pilot Officer with his Hampden at Scampton during his 83 Squadron days.

Gibson in Rugby attending his brother's wedding. The bandaged arm was the result of a dog bite.

Alick and Guy Gibson outside the register office at Rugby after the former's wedding.

Gibson at Syerston flanked by John Searby, left of picture, and Peter Ward-Hunt.

Drew 'Duke' Wyness while at 50 Squadron.

The morning after the night before. The Möhne Dam viewed from the reservoir side on the morning of 17.5.43.

The German military recovering the wreckage of EE130 AJ-A from the Wet Triangle at Bergeshövede on the morning of 16.9.43. S/L Wyness and crew lost their lives.

Another view of AJ-A's recovery. A group of people visible extreme left centre of the photograph includes Frau Erika Kaiser, who lives to this day on the quayside within yards of Allsebrook's crash.

A flak position close to the Mittelland canal.

The crane knocked into the basin after being struck by AJ-A as it crashed.

Don Cheney and crew.

Veterans of the successful *Tirpitz* operation pose at Woodhall Spa on the day after.

'Mac' Hamilton.

The wreckage of Les Knight's JB144 KC-N near Den Ham in Holland on the morning of 16.9.43.

Unofficial photo of 9 and 617 Squadron Lancasters at Yagodnik during the first attempt on the *Tirpitz*. 9 Squadron aircraft are to the left. The pictures were taken from Mac Hamilton's PD233. Top right is Kit Howard's KC-M.

Another view. The Lancaster next to Hamilton's is Nicky Knilans KC-W. Its nose is clearly damaged as the result of a hairy take-off from a field where Knilans had put down while lost.

S/L Cockshott's Lancaster at Woodhall Spa.

The paddleboat accommodation for 9 and 617 Squadron officers at Yagodnik.

Townsend and crew at the investiture 22.6.43.

Mick Martin's damaged Lancaster DV402 KC-P on a Sardinian airfield on 13.2.44. The Squadron bombing leader, F/L Bob Hay, was killed by flak during the attack on the Antheor Viaduct on France's Riviera coast.

'Bunny' Clayton.

afterwards. Opposition in the form of flak and jet fighters was fierce, and a number of aircraft sustained damage. Lancey's was hit by flak just ten seconds before bomb release, and the air pressure to the bombsight was cut. The bomb was dropped as soon as the bomb-aimer regained composure, but it would have undershot the aiming point. Goodman's, on the other hand, overshot after hanging up for fifteen seconds. Calder's Grand Slam was released as planned, but his bomb-aimer was unable to observe its fall through a shattered clear vision panel. By the time Hill came in to bomb, the aiming point was obscured by smoke, and it was decided to abort. For the same reason an immediate assessment of the damage to the bridge was impossible, but the number of direct hits suggested a successful outcome.

The month's final operation took place on the 27th, when twenty aircraft were sent to the *U-Boot* pens at Farge, a small port on the eastern bank of the Weser north-west of Bremen. In his classic book, *The Dambusters*, Paul Brickhill describes the target as the largest concrete structure in the world, measuring some 1,450 by 300 yards, with a reinforced concrete roof 23 feet thick. At the time of the attack it was still under construction and was not operational. This time fourteen 617 Squadron aircraft carried Grand Slams, and they were Fauquier in PD119, Calder in PD118, Brookes in PD131, Cockshott in PD114, Powell in PD121, Price in PD128, Sayers in PD113, Anning in PD139, Trent in PD116, Leavitt in PD129, Marshall in PD115, Flatman in PB996, Carey in PB997 and Lancey in PD130, while Tallboys were transported by Goodman in NG228, Hill in LM485, Warburton in LM695, McLoughlin in PD371, Beaumont in PD238 and Speirs in NG339. Goodman aborted his sortie almost immediately after take-off when an engine failed, and he landed back twenty minutes later. Lancey was, likewise, still over the airfield gaining altitude when he too was forced to call a halt, but he remained airborne for a little over two hours, probably to burn off fuel before landing with his monster bomb. The seventeen remaining aircraft pressed on, arriving in the target area shortly before 13.00 hours, and Warburton's Tallboy was the first to go down, just thirty-three seconds after the hour. Eleven seconds later Fauquier's Grand Slam arrowed towards the aiming point, followed by those of Leavitt and Flatman almost simultaneously six seconds later. Fauquier recorded his effort as an overshoot by 10 yards, and he observed a second bomb undershoot by a similar margin, but was unable to confirm anything beyond this. Calder saw one direct hit on the roof about 100 yards east of the aiming point, and Brookes claimed a direct hit right on it. Other direct hits were claimed by Warburton, Anning, Marshall and Speirs, while Beaumont had to abort when another aircraft slid in directly beneath his just as the point of release approached. It was another masterly display of precision bombing, though, and photo reconnaissance confirmed two direct hits by Grand Slams, which had penetrated the partially completed roof and caused a great deal of it to collapse. The structure was still incomplete at the end of hostilities. Crew postings during the month brought F/L Wilson from 227 Squadron, F/O West from 463 Squadron, and

S/L Ward from 57 Squadron, while out went F/O Stanford to 11 PDRC, and F/O Sanders and F/L Oram to 54 Base, all at the conclusion of their tours.

April would see the final operations by 617 Squadron before the end of hostilities, but the month's first effort by fourteen aircraft on the 6th, to attack shipping at Ijmuiden, fell foul of the weather conditions. 617 Squadron joined forces with 463 and 467 Squadrons RAAF for this operation, the two latter carrying 1,000 pounders. The process of attaining operational altitude with a full bomb load was a protracted affair, and it took almost an hour and three quarters to reach the Dutch coast. On arrival nine-tenths cloud was visible to the north, while over the target itself there were no breaks. Calder, who was in temporary command of the squadron while Fauquier took three days leave, assessed the situation as hopeless, and the operation was aborted. The time was 09.43, and Calder touched down at Woodhall Spa sixty-three minutes later. The operation was rescheduled for 617 Squadron alone on the early evening of the following day, and was led this time by Cockshott in PD114. He had been detailed to act as controller for the previous day's effort, but had been forced to pull out with intercom trouble. Also operating were Calder in PD132, Powell in PD131, Goodman in PB998, McLoughlin in PB996, Horsley in PB997, Price in PD133, Leavitt in PD129, Marshall in PD134, Lancey in PD130, Anning in PD135, Castagnola in PD113, Adams in PD128, Gordon in LM485 and Beaumont in PD238. All were carrying Tallboys, and Leavitt, Beaumont and Gordon claimed direct hits on the target ship, the 4,500 ton *Van Riemsdijk*, a merchantman, which had been built in Amsterdam and launched in April 1941, but never completed. She was seized by the Germans in October 1941, and was eventually towed to Ijmuiden in September 1944 to be sunk between the two jetties to block the harbour entrance. Probably because of the effectiveness of German *S-Boot* operations from Ijmuiden, which required the port to remain accessible, the sinking was not carried out. The rest of 617's hardware fell onto the quayside or close by into the water, and as the force withdrew the ship seemed to be down by the stern, and was later reported to have sunk. The interpretation report confirmed this, stating:

> The block ship is down by the stern and listing to starboard with the after well-deck awash on the starboard side. The vessel is probably resting on the bottom. Six large craters are to be seen around the Berghafen, five on the southern side and one on the northern.

In fact, the *Van Riemsdijk* had not been hit, but a number of very near misses had opened up her bottom and allowed the water in. Remarkably, she was raised in October 1946, completed and put to work, remaining in service with Dutch operators until 1967, when she became Panamanian registered until being sold for scrap in 1979. That night 5 Group attacked a benzol plant at Molbis near Leipzig, and put an end to all further production. On the following night the oil refinery at Lützkendorf was dealt a similarly fatal blow, and it would not be necessary for the Command to return.

On the 9th heavy flak greeted the squadron's seventeen aircraft over the *U-Boot* pens at Hamburg, and six aircraft were hit. The force, which took off around 14.30, consisted of Fauquier in PD119, Calder in PD112, Gordon in PD115, Powell in PD131, Goodman in PB998, Beaumont in NG339, McLoughlin in PB996, Horsley in PB997, Price in PD133, Leavitt in LM695, Warburton in PD127, Marshall in PD134, Anning in PD135, Sayers in PD130, Speirs in PD118, Castagnola in PD113 and Adams in PD139. Fauquier and Calder carried Grand Slams, which were released from 17,000 feet within seconds of each other at 17.36. The former struck the north-eastern corner of the roof and the latter the west side, while Beaumont, McLoughlin, Horsley, Price, Leavitt, Anning and Castagnola all claimed direct hits with their Tallboys. Some of the others were unable to assess the accuracy of their delivery because of smoke, but members of Anning's crew reported all but two bombs falling on the target. A heavy escort of Spitfires and Mustangs engaged the enemy fighters, and the operation was a complete success.

An attempt to take out the warships *Prinz Eugen* and *Lützow* at Swinemünde on the Baltic coast on the 13th was frustrated by cloud and was abandoned. It was a long round-trip of six and a half to seven hours, made even longer by the fact, that there was nothing to show for it. The *Lützow* had actually begun life as the *Deutschland*, and was completed on the 1st of April 1939 as one of three 'pocket' battleships. The others were the *Admiral Scheer* and the *Admiral Graf Spee* of Battle of the River Plate fame. Not wishing to risk the loss in battle of a ship bearing the name of the fatherland, Hitler ordered the renaming in February 1940, after the sale of the original *Lützow* to the Russians. The 15th brought a similar disappointment, when cloud was encountered during the outward flight and persisted all the way. The force continued on to within eighteen miles of the target, but the operation was then abandoned and the Lancasters landed back at Woodhall Spa within four hours. Relaunched on the 16th in excellent weather conditions, eighteen Lancasters converged on the aiming point shortly before 18.00 hours. The crews were those of Fauquier in PD119, Gordon in PD115, Brookes in PD130, Powell in NG228, Gavin in PD116, Hill in PB997, Horsley in PB998, Quinton in NG494, Price in PD133, Leavitt in PD114, Warburton in PD128, Anning in PD132, Rawes in PD371, Trent in NG340, Flatman in PB996, Speirs in PD118, Castagnola in PD113 and Adams in PD139. Most had Tallboys in their bomb bays, but Powell, Quinton, Rawes and Trent were each carrying twelve 1,000lb bombs. Fauquier misidentified the target, and his bomb was aimed at a vessel on a canal closer to the town of Swinemünde, missing it by 10 yards. The force encountered murderous flak, and the Lancasters captained by Gordon and Gavin sustained damage. Gordon was forced to abandon his first run after flak severed his throttle controls, causing a loss of power in his port-outer engine. A second run was found to be inaccurate and was scrubbed, and as the squadron made its second run, Gordon found himself about ten miles behind and unable to catch up. He tried again to go it alone, but found the target enveloped in smoke, and bombed a village instead on the way home. Gavin jettisoned his live Tallboy short of the target after being hit, and he estimated it undershot by a quarter of a mile. S/L Powell's NG228 was another victim, and was seen to go down in flames having lost a wing, before ultimately crashing into woods. One parachute was observed at around 2,000 feet, but there were no survivors, and this was the last operational casualty to be suffered by the squadron. A number of crews reported seeing a possible direct hit on the stern of the *Lützow*, and there were many near misses. Hill thought his Tallboy may have found the mark, and the *Lützow* had, in fact, been mortally wounded, although it seems did not sink. In the context of the war, though, it was scant consolation for the loss of the Powell crew so close to the end. In the event, *Lützow* was blown up and scuttled by her own people on the 4th of May. As for *Prinz Eugen*, it is uncertain whether she was at Swinemünde at the time, but she was one of only two major German surface vessels to survive the war and was surrendered on the 8th of May eventually to be commissioned into the US Navy. Later on the 16th 5 Group embarked on the first of three long-range operations against railway targets. Two hundred Lancasters subjected the yards at Pilsen in Czechoslovakia to an accurate attack, and twenty-four hours later it was the turn of similar installations at Cham, a town close to Germany's border with that country.

On the 18th over 900 aircraft bombed the town and naval base on the island of Heligoland, leaving it with the appearance of a cratered moonscape, and this was followed up on the late afternoon of the 19th by twenty Lancasters of 617 Squadron and a contingent from 9 Squadron. The purpose of the operation was to knock out the heavy gun emplacements, which barred Allied access to the north-western German ports. The 617 Squadron crews were those of Fauquier in NG445, Calder, now shown in the ORB as a Wing Commander, in PD118, Gordon in PD115, Brookes in PD121, Gavin in PD116, Horsley in PB998, Quinton in PD238, Beaumont in NG339, Hill in NG494, Leavitt in PD129, Adams in PD139, Warburton in PD128, Trent in PD132, Lancey in NG340 or PD130, Anning in PD135, Rawes in PD130, Marshall in PD133, Flatman in PD114, Speirs in LM695 and Castagnola in PD134. Calder, Gordon, Brookes, Anning, Flatman and Castagnola each carried a Grand Slam on its final employment, while the others dropped Tallboys. Under the umbrella of a strong fighter escort the force came in from the north at an average height of 10,000 feet, and according to the spread of bombing times in the ORB, the crews took their time to ensure as far as possible an accurate delivery. Brookes appears to have bombed on the first run at 16.39, but as this is more than twenty minutes before the next bomb went down, it is possibly a typographical error, and should perhaps read 17.39. In the event he reported his Grand Slam undershooting by about 30 yards and hitting the base of the cliffs, but observed another bomb hit the centre of the battery. This could have been Gavin's, which was the next to fall at 17.01, and he did claim a direct hit. Fauquier bombed on his second run at 17.08, and his Tallboy struck ground about 20 yards east of the aiming point. Nine bombs went down more or less together at 17.32, and Calder's Grand Slam accompanied Marshall's Tallboy at 17.33 to bring the raid to an end. Rawes was the only one not to bomb, having been unable to achieve a correct heading in time to set up the SABS, and he brought his Tallboy home. Any lingering threat from the batteries on Heligoland was now removed. Later that evening a force of over a hundred 5 Group Lancasters returned to Czechoslovakia, and dealt effectively with the railway yards at Komotau.

On the 25th, 359 Lancasters and sixteen Mosquitos of 1, 5 and 8 Groups, including sixteen from 617 Squadron, carried out, what was for most squadrons the final bombing operation of the war, an attack on the SS barracks at Hitler's 'Eaglesnest' retreat at Berchtesgaden in the Bavarian mountains. Taking off between 04.15 and 04.40 the 617 Squadron aircraft and crews for this fitting and almost symbolic operation were: PD131 S/L Brookes, PD121 S/L Ward, PD116 F/L Gavin, PB998 F/L Goodman, PB997 F/L Hill, PD127 F/L Horsley, NG494 F/L Quinton, NG339 F/L Beaumont, PB129 F/L Leavitt, PD139 Lt Adams, PD134 F/L Marshall, PD130 F/L Lancey, PD135 F/L Trent, PD114 F/O Flatman, PD132 F/O Speirs, and NG340 F/O Frost, a new arrival, and operating with the squadron for the first time. Brookes, Ward and Gavin were unable to identify the aiming point in time, and did not bomb. Leavitt was dissatisfied with his first run and asked permission to carry out a second. He was unable to raise S/L Brookes, however, because of confusion over the radio frequency, and by this time was alone in the target area. This was not a healthy position to be in, so he turned for home, and to give himself a chance to catch up with the others, the bomb-aimer, F/S Oldman, aimed the Tallboy at a viaduct over a road on the track home. It missed. Marshall was unable to identify the aiming point, and he dropped his bomb on a railway and road junction. New boy Frost picked up the aiming point only when directly over it, and bombed the town of Berchtesgaden as an alternative. Trent and Speirs, meanwhile, had suffered the frustration of hang-ups. At 12.59 that afternoon, F/O Mark Flatman landed PD114 at Woodhall Spa, and in so doing brought to a conclusion the operational wartime career of a squadron, which, in two short years, had become an indelible part of RAF folklore and a byword for excellence. During the afternoon almost 500 Halifaxes and Lancasters of 4, 6 and 8 Groups attacked heavy gun positions on the German Frisian island of Wangerooge, which stood between the Allies and the north German ports. That night, 5 Group bombed an oil refinery at Tonsberg in Norway, and then, except for the Mosquitos of 8 Group and elements of 100 Group, it was all over.

On the 28th G/C Fauquier relinquished command of the squadron on a posting to the Air Ministry. He had completed three tours and almost a hundred operations, and was the proud bearer of the DSO and two Bars and a DFC. He died in April 1981. He was replaced at 617 Squadron by W/C John Grindon, who had been in command of 630 Squadron at East Kirkby since October. Grindon was a native of Newquay in Cornwall, where he was born in 1917, just a few weeks before his father was killed at Ypres. He was educated at Dulwich College and the RAF's University of the Air at Cranwell. After passing out in 1937 he joined 98 Squadron, before moving on to 150 Squadron in 1939. Equipped with the Fairey Battle 150 Squadron became part of the Advanced Air Striking Force, which moved to France as the Second World War began. Grindon was absent from the squadron on a navigation course during May 1940, when 150 Squadron and the others equipped with Battles suffered massive casualties during the German advance across the Low Countries and France. He spent the next four years as an instructor in Canada and as a staff officer at Bomber Command, before re-entering the operational scene as a flight commander with 106 Squadron at Metheringham in July 1944. He completed sixteen sorties with 106 Squadron, beginning at Kiel on the night of the 23/24th of July, and ending at Bremen on the 6/7th of October. The posting of Grindon to 617 Squadron was testimony to his calibre as 630 Squadron's commanding officer, and later in the year he would be awarded the DSO in recognition of his wartime service. His citation read:

> In the course of numerous operational sorties, W/C Grindon has established an excellent reputation for leadership, energy and courage. The worst weather or the heaviest opposition have never deterred him from the accurate completion of his allotted tasks. Over such heavily defended targets as Königsberg, Bremen and Bergen he has braved intense anti-aircraft fire, and despite damage to his aircraft on more than one occasion, has always fulfilled his mission. On one occasion, during a daylight attack on Homberg, severe damage was sustained and his aircraft became difficult to control, but, in spite of the danger, W/C Grindon continued to lead his formation with skill and determination. He has at all times set an outstanding example.

W/C Grindon died on Remembrance Day 2001 at the age of 84.

On VE Day five aircraft took part in Operation Exodus, the repatriation of Allied prisoners of war. Crew postings had continued through the month, as some of those who had helped drive the final nails into the Nazi coffin completed their tours. F/Os Watts and Carey went to 54 Base on the 9th and 20th respectively, and F/L Dobson to 6 LFS on the 23rd. In their place came F/Ls Bullock and Sheridan from 467 Squadron, F/L Langley, F/O Adams and the already mentioned F/O Frost from 5 LFS, F/L Brian from 189 Squadron, and finally, F/L Barker from 630 Squadron.

It is perhaps true to say, that 617 Squadron was among the most effective of the small forces employed by the Allies in any theatre of operations, but it is unfair to use the squadron as a yardstick by which to judge the performance of others. 617 Squadron was never part of the nightly grind of operations during the area offensives, and always enjoyed the very best in equipment, personnel and leadership. From the start it was a special unit, entrusted with special tasks, which it rarely failed to accomplish, and although it occasionally operated as part of a larger force, or in concert with 9 Squadron, it usually assumed the leading role. 617 Squadron lives on, and those currently serving as members of it are justly proud of its traditions. They are, though, a different breed, because the world in general and the RAF in particular have changed beyond recognition. Since those early days in 1943 more than sixty-five years have passed, during which advancing technology has added immeasurably to man's ability to destroy. Even so, the advent of smart and laser guided bombs has not improved dramatically on the accuracy achieved by 617 Squadron so long ago, although technology has certainly improved consistency.

The above is a true account of the lives of some extraordinary and very gallant young men from Britain, the Empire and Commonwealth and the United States. Their like will not be seen again, because the world that created them and which they graced, like them, has passed into history. New generations of their families live on, and I'm sure, take pride in the fact that their forebears were part of the most famous squadron in RAF history. All those of us involved in the writing of this book and in the uncovering of the history contained herein humbly share that pride.

Appendix A

Roll of Honour

Those who lost their lives while serving with 617 Squadron

(C) R.C.A.F. (A) R.A.A.F. (NZ) RNZAF. * BAR

Operation Chastise 16/17th May 1943

	Lancaster ED934 AJ-K	Lancaster ED864 AJ-B
Pilot	P/O V.W. Byers (C)	F/L W. Astell DFC
Flight engineer	Sgt A.J. Taylor	Sgt J. Kinnear
Navigator	P/O J.H. Warner	P/O F.A. Wile (C)
Wireless operator	Sgt J. Wilkinson	Sgt A. Garshowitz (C)
Bomb-aimer	Sgt A.N. Whitaker	F/O D. Hopkinson
Front gunner	Sgt J.McA. Jarvie	Sgt F.A. Garbas (C)
Rear gunner	Sgt J. McDowell (C)	Sgt R. Bolitho

	Lancaster ED927 AJ-E	Lancaster ED925 AJ-M
Pilot	F/L R.N.G. Barlow DFC (A)	F/L J.V. Hopgood DFC*
Flight engineer	Sgt S.L.Whillis	Sgt C. Brennan
Navigator	F/O P.S. Burgess	F/O K. Earnshaw (C)
Wireless operator	F/O C.R. Williams DFC (A)	Sgt J.W. Minchin
Bomb-aimer	Sgt A. Gillespie DFM	
Front gunner	F/O H.S. Glinz (C)	P/O G.H.F.G. Gregory DFM
Rear gunner	Sgt J.R.G. Liddell	

	Lancaster ED865 AJ-S	Lancaster ED910 AJ-C
Pilot	P/O L.J. Burpee DFM (C)	P/O W. Ottley DFC
Flight engineer	Sgt G. Pegler	Sgt R. Marsden
Navigator	Sgt T. Jaye	F/O J.K. Barrett DFC
Wireless operator	P/O L.G. Weller	Sgt J. Guterman DFM
Bomb-aimer	Sgt J.L. Arthur (C)	F/S T.B. Johnston
Front gunner	Sgt W.C.A. Long	Sgt H.J. Strange
Rear gunner	F/S J.G. Brady (C)	

	Lancaster ED937 AJ-Z	Lancaster ED887 AJ-A
Pilot	S/L H.E. Maudslay DFC	S/L H.M. Young DFC*
Flight engineer	Sgt J. Marriott DFM	Sgt D.T. Horsfall
Navigator	F/O R.A. Urquhart DFC (C)	Sgt C.W. Roberts
Wireless operator	Sgt A.P. Cottam (C)	Sgt L.W. Nichols
Bomb-aimer	P/O M.J.D. Fuller	F/O V.S. MacCausland (C)
Front gunner	F/O W.J. Tytherleigh DFC	Sgt G.A. Yeo
Rear gunner	Sgt N.R. Burrows	Sgt W. Ibbotson

Dortmund-Ems Canal 14/15th September 1943

(Aborted)

	Lancaster JA981 KC-J
Pilot	S/L D.J.H. Maltby DSO DFC
Flight engineer	Sgt W. Hatton
Navigator	F/S V. Nicholson DFM
Wireless operator	F/S A.J. Stone
Bomb-aimer	P/O J. Fort DFC
Gunner	Sgt V. Hill
Gunner	W/O J.L. Welch DFM
Gunner	H.T. Simmonds

Dortmund-Ems Canal 15/16th September 1943

	Lancaster EE144 AJ-S	**Lancaster EE130 AJ-A**
Pilot	W/C G.W. Holden DSO DFC* MID	F/L R.A.P. Allsebrook DSO DFC
Flight engineer	Sgt D.J.D. Powell MID	F/S P. Moore
Navigator	F/L T.H. Taerum DFC (C)	P/O N.A. Botting
Wireless operator	F/L R.E.G. Hutchinson DFC*	F/O J.M. Grant DFC
Bomb-aimer	F/O F.M. Spafford DFC DFM (A)	F/S R.B.S. Lulham
Gunner	P/O G.A. Deering DFC (C)	Sgt I.G. Jones
Gunner	F/O H.J. Pringle DFC	F/S W. Walker
Gunner	P/O T.A. Meikle DFM	F/S S. Hitchen

	LancasterJA874 KC-E	**Lancaster JA898 KC-X**
Pilot	P/O W.G. Divall	F/L H.S. Wilson
Flight engineer	Sgt E.C.A. Blake	P/O T.W. Johnson
Navigator	F/O D.W. Warwick (C)	F/O J.A. Rodger
Wireless operator	F/S J.S. Simpson	W/O L. Mieyette (C)
Bomb-aimer	F/S R.C. McArthur	F/O G.H. Coles (C)
Gunner	Sgt A.A. Williams	F/S T.H. Payne
Gunner	Sgt G.S. Miles	Sgt G.M. Knox
Gunner	Sgt D. Allatson	F/S E. Hornby

	Lancaster JB144 KC-N
Pilot	F/L L.G. Knight DSO MID (A)

Transit from Rabat 17/18th November 1943

	Lancaster ED735 KC-R
Pilot	F/L E.E.G. Youseman DFC
Flight engineer	P/O S.J. Whittingham DFM
Navigator	P/O L. Plishka (C)
Wireless operator	F/O W.C. Grimes DFM
Bomb-aimer	F/S R. Florence DFM (NZ)
Gunner	P/O A.M. Laughland DFM (C)
Gunner	W/O J.B. De C. O'Grady (C)

SOE Operation to France 10/11th December 1943

	Lancaster ED825 AJ-E	Lancaster ED886 AJ-O
Pilot	F/O G.H. Weeden (C)	
Flight engineer	Sgt A.W. Richardson	
Navigator	P/O R.N. Jones	
Wireless operator	F/S R.G. Howell	
Bomb-aimer	F/S E.J. Walters (C)	Sgt J.McL. Stewart
Gunner	Sgt B. Robinson	
Gunner	W/O R. Cummings (C)	F/S D.M. Thorpe (C)

Liege 20/21st December 1943

(Abandoned)

	Lancaster DV398 KC-Z
Flight engineer	F/S E.C. Smith
Navigator	F/O R. MacFarlane
Wireless operator	W/O C.B. Gowrie (C)
Bomb-aimer	W/O J.W. Thrasher (C)
Gunner	F/S T.W. Maynard
Gunner	F/S S. Burns

Training 20th January 1944

	Lancaster ED918 AJ-F
Pilot	F/L T.V. O'Shaughnessy
Navigator	F/O A.D. Holding

Antheor Viaduct 12/13th February 1944

	Lancaster DV402 KC-P
Bomb-aimer	F/L R.C. Hay DFC* (A)

Transit 13th February 1944

	Lancaster DV382 KC-J
Flight engineer	F/S J. Pulford DFM
Navigator	P/O J.I. Gordon DFC (A)
Wireless operator	P/O S.G. Hall (A)
Bomb-aimer	F/O N.J. Davidson (C)
Gunner	F/S J.P. Riches
Gunner	F/O J.McB. Dempster DFM (C)
Intelligence officer	S/L T.W. Lloyd DSO

15th February from above

Pilot	S/L W.R. Suggitt DFC (C)

Munich 24/25th April 1944

	Lancaster DV394 KC-M
Bomb-aimer	F/O G.J. Harden DFC

Wizernes 24th June 1944

	Lancaster DV403 KC-G
Pilot	F/L J.A. Edward DFC
Flight engineer	F/O L.W.J. King DFC
Gunner	P/O J.I. Johnston DFC
Gunner	W/O T.W.P. Price (C)
Gunner	F/S S. Isherwood

Rilly-la-Montagne 31st July 1944

	Lancaster ME557 KC-S
Flight engineer	F/S D.G.W. Stewart
Navigator	F/O J.O. Peltier (C)
Bomb-aimer	P/O L.G. Rolton DFC
Gunner	F/S A.A. Holt
Gunner	W/O J.W. Hutton

Brest 5th August 1944

	Lancaster JB139 KC-V
Navigator	P/O R. Welch
Wireless operator	F/S R.H. Pool
Gunner	P/O W.N. Wait

Training 7th August 1944

	Mosquito NT202 AJ-N
Pilot	F/O W.A. Duffy DFC (C)
Navigator	F/O P. Ingleby

Cruiser *Gueydon*, Brest 14th August 1944

	Lancaster LM485 KC-N
Bomb-aimer	F/O C.P. Pesme (C)

Transit from Russia 17th September 1944

	Lancaster PB416 KC-V
Pilot	F/O F. Levy
Flight engineer	Sgt P.W. Groom
Navigator	F/O C.L. Fox
Wireless operator	F/S G.M. McGuire
Bomb-aimer	F/S E.E.S. Peck
Gunner	P/O A.F. McNally (C)
Gunner	F/S D.G. Thomas
Passenger	F/O J.F. Naylor
Passenger	F/O D.C. Shea DFC

Dortmund-Ems Canal 23/24th September 1944

	Lancaster NF923 KC-M
Pilot	F/L G.S. Stout DFC
Flight engineer	P/O A.W. Benting
Navigator	F/O C.E.M. Graham MID

P/O Benting died of his injuries on the 25th.

Kembs Barrage 7th October 1944

	Lancaster NG180 KC-S	Lancaster LM482 KC-Q
Pilot	S/L D.R.C. Wyness DFC	F/L C.J.G. Howard
Flight engineer	F/S T.J. Hurdiss	P/O F.C. Hawkins
Navigator	F/L R.H. Williams DFC	F/L T.J. Tate
Wireless operator	F/O B.J. Hosie (NZ)	P/O R.D. Lucan DFM
Bomb-aimer	F/O H.W. Honig	P/O E.A. Hartley
Gunner	F/S T. Horrocks	W/O P.E. Woods
Gunner	F/O G.E. Cansell	F/S H.G. Clarke MID
Gunner		F/O D.T. Watkins DFC

Pölitz 21/22nd December 1944

	Lancaster ME561 KC-T
Bomb-aimer	F/O A.J. Walker DFC
Gunner	F/O R.B. Yates

Bergen 12th January 1945

	Lancaster NF992 KC-B	Lancaster PD233 KC-G
Pilot	F/O I.S. Ross (A)	
Flight engineer	F/S W. Walter	
Navigator	W/O S.R. Anderson DFM	
Wireless operator	F/O M. Ellwood DFM MID	
Bomb-aimer	P/O E.G. Tilby	F/L G.A. Kendrick
Gunner	F/S L.D. Griffiths	
Gunner	F/S A.F. McKellar	

(F/L Kendrick died of his injuries on the 15th)

Arbergen Bridge 21st March 1945

	Lancaster PD117 YZ-L
Pilot	F/L B.A. Gumbley (NZ) DFM
Flight engineer	F/O E.A. Barnett
Navigator	F/O K. Gill DFC CdeG
Bomb-aimer	F/L J.C. Randon
Gunner	F/O G. Bell

Battleship *Lützow*, Swinemünde 16th April 1945

	Lancaster NG228 KC-V
Pilot	S/L J.L. Powell DFC MID
Flight engineer	F/S H.W. Felton DFM
Navigator	F/L M.T. Clarke DFC
Wireless operator	P/O K.A.J. Hewitt
Bomb-aimer	F/O A.L. Heath
Gunner	F/S W. Knight
Gunner	F/O J. Watson

Those formerly of 617 Squadron who also lost their lives

Mannheim 23/24th September 1943

	49 Squadron Lancaster ED702
Pilot	P/O C.T. Anderson
Flight engineer	Sgt R.C. Paterson
Navigator	Sgt J.P. Nugent
Wireless operator	Sgt W.D. Bickle
Bomb-aimer	Sgt G.J. Green
Gunner	Sgt A.W. Buck
Gunner	Sgt E. Ewan

Nuremberg 30/31st March 1944

	Lancaster ND390 of 97 Squadron
Gunner	F/L R. A. D. Trevor-Roper

Training 30th April 1944

	Lancaster ND553 serving with the bombing development unit Newmarket
Gunner	F/O B. Jagger DFM

Mönchengladbach/Rheydt 19/20th September 1944

	627 Squadron Mosquito KB267 AZ-E
Pilot	W/C G.P. Gibson VC DSO DFC

Mittelland Canal 21st November 1944

	49 Squadron Lancaster PB300 EA-K
Navigator	S/L P. Kelly DFC*

APPENDIX B

Stations, Commanding Officers, Aircraft and Aircrew Killed

STATIONS

Scampton	21.03.43. to 30.08.43.
Coningsby	30.08.43. to 10.01.44.
Woodhall Spa	10.01.44. to 17.06.45.

COMMANDING OFFICERS

Wing Commander G.P. Gibson	21.03.43. to 03.08.43.
Wing Commander G.W. Holden	03.08.43. to 16.09.43.
Squadron Leader H.B. Martin (Temp)	16.09.43. to 10.11.43.
Wing Commander G.L. Cheshire	10.11.43. to 12.07.44.
Wing Commander J.B. Tait	12.07.44. to 29.12.44.
Group Captain J.E. Fauquier	29.12.44. to 28.04.45.
Wing Commander J.E. Grindon	28.04.45. to 09.08.45.

AIRCRAFT

Lancaster 1/111	03.43. to 06.45.
Mosquito	03.44. to 05.45.
Mustang	06.44. to 05.45.

AIRCREW KILLED

190

(includes some on detachment for specific operations)

Appendix C

Operational Records

Operations	Sorties	Aircraft Losses	% Losses
101	1,599	32	2.1

Category of Operations

Bombing	Leaflet	Other
99	1	1 (D-Day spoof)

Lancaster

Operations	Sorties	Aircraft FTR	% Losses
101	1,478	32	2.2

Mosquito

Operations	Sorties	Aircraft Losses	% Losses
36 (included in above)	75	0	0.0

Mustang

Operations	Sorties	Aircraft Losses	% Losses
6 (included in above)	6	0	0.0

Appendix D

Table of Statistics

Out of 59 Lancaster squadrons

42nd highest number of Lancaster overall operations in Bomber Command.
41st highest number of Lancaster sorties in Bomber Command.
36th highest number of Lancaster operational losses in Bomber Command.

Out of 19 Mosquito squadrons

Lowest number of Mosquito overall operations, sorties and operational losses in Bomber Command.
The only squadron to operate a Mustang in Bomber Command.

Out of 22 Squadrons in 5 Group

18th highest number of overall operations in 5 Group.
16th highest number of sorties in 5 Group.
17th highest number of aircraft operational losses in 5 Group.

Out of 17 Lancaster squadrons in 5 Group

3rd lowest number of Lancaster overall operations in 5 Group.
3rd lowest number of Lancaster sorties in 5 Group.
3rd lowest number of Lancaster operational losses in 5 Group.

Out of 2 Mosquito squadrons in 5 Group

Lowest number of Mosquito overall operations, sorties and aircraft operational losses in 5 Group.

Appendix E

Aircraft Histories

Lancaster	From March 1943.
W4358 DX-L	From 57Sqn on loan. Returned to 57Sqn.
W4822 DX-P	From 57Sqn on loan. Returned to 57Sqn.
W4921 AJ-C	From 106Sqn. No operations. To 619Sqn.
W4926 AJ-Z	From 97Sqn. No operations. To 1654CU.
W4929 AJ-J	From 61Sqn. No operations. To 619Sqn.
W4940 AJ-B	From 57Sqn. No operations. To 1660CU.
W5008 DX-B	From 57Sqn on loan. Returned to 57Sqn.
DV155	To 44Sqn.
DV156	To 50Sqn.
DV178 EA-N	From 49Sqn on loan. Returned to 49Sqn.
DV246 KC-U	To 1661CU.
DV380 KC-N/X/P	To EAAS.
DV382 KC-J	Crashed in the South Downs while in transit to Woodhall Spa after the Antheor Viaduct raid 13.2.44. S/L Suggitt.
DV385 KC-A/V/T	Flew on two *Tirpitz* operations. To 46MU.
DV391 KC-W/O/Y	Flew on all three *Tirpitz* operations. To 46MU.
DV393 KC-T/R/E	To 9Sqn.
DV394 KC-M	FTR Munich 24/25.4.44. F/L Cooper.
DV398 KC-Z	FTR Liege 20/21.12.43. F/L Rice.
DV402 KC-P/X	Landed in Sardinia following operation to the Antheor Viaduct 12.2.44. F/L Martin.
DV403 KC-L/G/X	FTR Wizernes 24.6.44. F/L Edward.
DV405 KC-J	Flew on all three *Tirpitz* operations. To 44MU.
ED305 KM-S	From 44Sqn on loan. Returned to 44Sqn.
ED329 AJ-T	From 207Sqn. Training only. To 57Sqn.
ED437 AJ-N/V	From 50Sqn. Training only. To 622Sqn via 1661CU
ED631 KC-E-	From 622Sqn. To 115Sqn.
ED735 AJ-R	From 44Sqn. Lost without trace in the Bay of Biscay area during transit from Rabat 17/18.11.43. F/L Youseman.
ED756 AJ-H	From 49Sqn. Training only. To 619Sqn.
ED763 AJ-D/KC-Z	From 467Sqn. Flew on all three *Tirpitz* operations.

ED765/G AJ-M	Type 464 1st prototype. Crashed on Ashley Walk Range while training 5.8.43. F/L Kellaway.
ED817/G AJ-C/X-	Type 464 2nd prototype. To 46MU.
ED825/G AJ-T/E	Type 464 3rd prototype. McCarthy, Operation Chastise. FTR from SOE sortie on behalf of 138Sqn, F/O Weeden 9/10.12.43.
ED864/G AJ-B	Type 464. Astell. FTR Operation Chastise 16/17.5.43.
ED865/G AJ-S	Type 464. Burpee. FTR Operation Chastise 16/17.5.43.
ED886/G AJ-O	Type 464. Townsend, Operation Chastise. FTR from SOE sortie on behalf of 138Sqn, W/O Bull 10.12.43.
ED887/G AJ-A	Type 464. Young. FTR Operation Chastise 16/17.5.43.
ED906/G AJ-J	Type 464. Maltby, Operation Chastise.
ED909/G AJ-P/P-	Type 464. Martin, Operation Chastise.
ED910/G AJ-C	Type 464. Ottley. FTR Operation Chastise 16/17.5.43.
ED912/G AJ-N/S	Type 464. Knight, Operation Chastise. To 46MU.
ED915/G AJ-Q	Type 464. To 46MU.
ED918/G AJ-F	Type 464. Brown, Operation Chastise. Crashed on Snettisham beach during training 20.1.44. F/L O'Shaughnessy.
ED921/G AJ-W	Type 464. Munro, Operation Chastise. To 46MU.
ED924/G AJ-Y	Type 464. Anderson, Operation Chastise. To 44MU.
ED925/G AJ-M	Type 464. Hopgood. FTR Operation Chastise 16/17.5.43.
ED927/G AJ-E	Type 464. Barlow. FTR Operation Chastise 16/17.5.43.
ED929/G AJ-L	Type 464. Shannon, Operation Chastise. To 46MU
ED931 DX-C	From 57Sqn on loan. Returned to 57Sqn.
ED932/G AJ-G/V	Type 464. Gibson, Operation Chastise. Scrapped 1947.
ED933/G KC-X/N/N-	Type 464. To 46MU 2.45.
ED934/G AJ-K	Type 464. Byers. FTR Operation Chastise 16/17.5.43.
ED936/G AJ-H	Type 464. Rice, Operation Chastise. SOC 28.7.44.
ED937/G AJ-Z	Type 464. Maudslay. FTR Operation Chastise 16/17.5.43.
ED999 EA-A	From 49Sqn on loan. Returned to 49Sqn.
EE130 AJ-A	FTR Dortmund-Ems Canal 15/16.9.43. F/L Allsebrook.
EE131 KC-B/L	Crash-landed in Russia during the first *Tirpitz* operation 12.9.44. F/O Ross.

EE144 AJ-S	FTR Dortmund-Ems Canal 15/16.9.43. W/C Holden.
EE145 AJ-T	Crashed on landing at Scampton while training 6.6.43. F/L Munro.
EE146 AJ-K/KC-D	Flew on two Tirpitz operations (W/C Tait). SOC 24.4.45.
EE147 AJ-L	To 619Sqn.
EE148 AJ-U	To 626Sqn.
EE149	To 619Sqn.
EE150 AJ-Z	To 619Sqn.
EE170	Training only. To 619Sqn.
EE185 KM-K	From 44Sqn on loan. Returned to 44Sqn.
EE197 DX-Y	From 57Sqn on loan. Returned to 57Sqn.
JA703 KM-W	From 44Sqn on loan. Returned to 44Sqn.
JA705 OL-M	From 83Sqn. Training only.
JA874 KC-E	From 61Sqn. FTR Dortmund-Ems Canal 15/16.9.43. P/O Divall.
JA894 KC-T	From 49Sqn. To A&AEE.
JA898 KC-X	From 619Sqn. FTR Dortmund-Ems Canal 15/16.9.43. F/L Wilson.
JA981 KC-J	Crashed in North Sea after recall from the Dortmund-Ems Canal operation of 14/15.9.43. S/L Maltby.
JB139 KC-X/V	From 49Sqn. FTR Brest 5.8.44. F/O Cheney.
JB144 KC-N	FTR Dortmund-Ems Canal 15/16.9.43. F/L Knight.
JB370 DX-U-	From 57Sqn. Returned to 57Sqn.
LM309 AJ-X	From 9Sqn. Training only. To 619Sqn.
LM482 KC-W/Q	FTR Kembs Barrage 7.10.44. F/L Howard.
LM485 KC-N/U/H	Flew on first and last *Tirpitz* operations.
LM489 KC-L/A/N	Flew on all three *Tirpitz* operations.
LM492 KC-Q/W	Flew on all three *Tirpitz* operations.
LM695 KC-N	From 463Sqn.
ME554 KC-F	Flew on all three *Tirpitz* operations.
ME555 KC-C	To 9Sqn.
ME557 KC-O/S	FTR Rilly-La-Montagne 31.7.44. F/L Reid.
ME559 KC-Q/Y	Crash-landed on arrival in Russia for the first *Tirpitz* operation 11/12.9.44. S/L Wyness.
ME560 KC-H	Crashed while landing at Woodhall Spa after a ferry flight 14.7.44. F/O Hamilton.
ME561 KC-R/T	Flew on all three *Tirpitz* operations. Crashed in Lincolnshire on return from Politz 22.12.44. F/O Joplin.
ME562 KC-Z/K	Flew on all three *Tirpitz* operations.
ND339 ZN-Z-	On detachment from 106Sqn. Returned to 106Sqn.
ND472 DX-O-	On detachment from 57Sqn. Returned to 57Sqn.

ND554 LE-N-	On detachment from 630Sqn. Returned to 630Sqn.
ND631 KM-B-/Z-	On detachment from 44Sqn. Returned to 44Sqn.
ND683 EA-P-	On detachment from 49Sqn. Returned to 49Sqn.
NF920 KC-E	FTR *Tirpitz* (force-landed in Sweden) 29.10.44. F/O Carey.
NF923 KC-M	FTR Dortmund-Ems Canal 23/24.9.44. F/O Stout.
NF992 KC-B	FTR Bergen 12.1.45. F/O Ross.
NG180 KC-S	FTR Kembs Barrage 7.10.44. S/L Wyness.
NG181 KC-M	To 195Sqn and back. Flew on two *Tirpitz* operations.
NG228 KC-V	FTR Swinemünde 16.4.45. S/L Powell.
NG339 KC-G	
NG340 KC-L/U	
NG445 KC-E	
NG489 KC-M	
NG494 KC-B	
NN702	From 630Sqn.
PB342	From 61Sqn. To 1653CU.
PB415 KC-S/O	Flew on all three *Tirpitz* operations. SOC 4.45.
PB416 KC-V	Crashed in Norway on return from Russia (First *Tirpitz* operation) 17.9.44. F/O Levy.
PB996 YZ-C	B1 Special.
PB997 YZ-E	B1 Special.
PB998 YZ-D	B1 Special.
PD112 YZ-S	B1 Special.
PD113 YZ-T	B1 Special.
PD114 YZ-B	B1 Special.
PD115 YZ-K	B1 Special.
PD116 YZ-A	B1 Special.
PD117 YZ-L	B1 Special. FTR Arbergen Railway Bridge 21.3.45. F/L Gumbley.
PD118 YZ-M	B1 Special.
PD119 YZ-J	B1 Special.
PD121 YZ-S	B1 Special.
PD127 YZ-F	B1 Special.
PD128 YZ-R	B1 Special.
PD129 YZ-O	B1 Special.
PD130 YZ-D/W/U	B1 Special.
PD131 YZ-V	B1 Special.
PD132 YZ-X	B1 Special.
PD133 YZ-P	B1 Special.
PD134 YZ-Y	B1 Special.
PD135 YZ-W	B1 Special.
PD136 YZ-N	B1 Special.
PD139 YZ-W/L	B1 Special.

PD233 KC-G	FTR Bergen 12.1.45. F/L Pryor.
PD238 KC-B/H	
PD371 KC-S/W	
PD418	To 467Sqn.
Mosquito	From March 1944.
DZ415 AZ-Q/A	From 627Sqn on loan as required.
DZ418 AZ-L	From 627Sqn on loan as required.
DZ421 AZ-C	From 627Sqn on loan as required.
DZ484 AZ-G	From 627Sqn on loan as required.
DZ521 AZ-M	From 627Sqn on loan as required.
DZ525 AZ-S	From 627Sqn on loan as required.
DZ534 AZ-H	From 627 Sqn on loan as required
DZ547 AZ-E	From 627Sqn on loan as required.
DZ637 AZ-O	From 627Sqn on loan as required.
KB215 AZ-H	From 627Sqn on loan as required.
ML975 HS-M	From 109Sqn on loan as required.
ML976 HS-N/L	From 109Sqn on loan as required.
NS992 AJ-N/S	To 515Sqn.
NS993 AJ-N/L	To 515Sqn.
NT202 AJ-N	To 417Sqn and back. Crashed at Wainfleet Sands while training 7.8.44. F/O Duffy.
NT205 AJ-L	
Mustang	From 22.06.44 to 2.10.44.
HB837 AJ-N	To 541Sqn via 38MU.

Heaviest single loss. 16/17.05.43. Operation Chastise. 8 Lancasters FTR.

Key to Abbreviations

A&AEE	Aeroplane and Armaments Experimental Establishment.
AA	Anti-Aircraft fire.
AACU	Anti-Aircraft Cooperation Unit.
AAS	Air Armament School.
AASF	Advance Air Striking Force.
AAU	Aircraft Assembly Unit.
A/C	Air Commodore
ACM	Air Chief Marshal.
ACSEA	Air Command South-East Asia.
AFDU	Air Fighting Development Unit.
AFEU	Airborne Forces Experimental Unit.
AFTDU	Airborne Forces Tactical Development Unit.
AGS	Air Gunners School.
AMDP	Air Members for Development and Production.
AOC	Air Officer Commanding.
AOS	Air Observers School.
ASRTU	Air-Sea Rescue Training Unit.
ATTDU	Air Transport Tactical Development Unit.
AVM	Air Vice-Marshal.
BAT	Beam Approach Training.
BCBS	Bomber Command Bombing School.
BCDU	Bomber Command Development Unit.
BCFU	Bomber Command Film Unit.
BCIS	Bomber Command Instructors School.
BDU	Bombing Development Unit.
BSTU	Bomber Support Training Unit.
CF	Conversion Flight.
CFS	Central Flying School.
CGS	Central Gunnery School.
C-in-C	Commander in Chief.
CNS	Central Navigation School.
CO	Commanding Officer.
CRD	Controller of Research and Development.
CU	Conversion Unit.
DGRD	Director General for Research and Development.

EAAS	Empire Air Armament School.
EANS	Empire Air Navigation School.
ECDU	Electronic Countermeasures Development Unit.
ECFS	Empire Central Flying School.
ETPS	Empire Test Pilots School.
FIU	Fighter Interception Unit
F/L	Flight Lieutenant.
Flt	Flight.
F/O	Flying Officer.
FPP	Ferry Pilots School.
F/S	Flight Sergeant.
FTR	Failed to Return.
FTS	Flying Training School.
FTU	Ferry Training Unit.
G/C	Group Captain.
Gp	Group.
HCU	Heavy Conversion Unit.
HGCU	Heavy Glider Conversion Unit.
ITW	Initial Training Wing.
LFS	Lancaster Finishing School.
MAC	Mediterranean Air Command.
MTU	Mosquito Training Unit.
MU	Maintenance Unit.
NTU	Navigation Training Unit.
OADU	Overseas Aircraft Delivery Unit.
OAPU	Overseas Aircraft Preparation Unit.
OTU	Operational Training Unit.
P/O	Pilot Officer.
PTS	Parachute Training School.
RAE	Royal Aircraft Establishment.
SGR	School of General Reconnaissance.
Sgt	Sergeant.
SHAEF	Supreme Headquarters Allied Expeditionary Force.
SIU	Signals Intelligence Unit.
S/L	Squadron Leader.
SOC	Struck off Charge.
SOE	Special Operations Executive.
Sqn	Squadron.
TF	Training Flight.
TFU	Telecommunications Flying Unit.
W/C	Wing Commander.
Wg	Wing.
WIDU	Wireless Intelligence Development Unit.
W/O	Warrant Officer.

Bibliography

Air War over France. Robert Jackson. Ian Allan.
Als Deutschlands Dämme Brachen Verlag. Helmut Euler. Motor Buch.
At First Sight. Alan B. Webb.
Avenging in the shadows. Ron James. Abington Books.
Avro Lancaster. The definitive record. Harry Holmes. Airlife.
Avro Manchester. Robert Kirby. Midland Counties Publications.
Battle-Axe Blenheims. Stuart R. Scott. Budding Books.
Battle Under the Moon. Jack Currie. Air Data.
Beam Bombers. Michael Cumming. Sutton Publishing.
Beware of the Dog at War. John Ward.
Black Swan. Sid Finn. Newton.
Bomber Command. Max Hastings. Pan.
Bomber Command War Diaries. Martin Middlebrook/Chris Everett. Viking.
Bomber Group at War. Chaz Bowyer. Book Club Associates.
Bomber Harris. Dudley Saward. Cassel.
Bomber Harris. Charles Messenger. Arms and Armour Press.
Bomber Intelligence. W.E. Jones. Midland Counties Publications.
Bomber Squadron at War. Andrew Brookes. Ian Allan.
Bomber Squadrons at War. Geoff D. Copeman. Sutton Publishing.
Bombers over Berlin. Alan W. Cooper. Patrick Stephens Ltd.
Bombing Colours 1937–1973. Michael J.F. Bowyer. Patrick Stephens Ltd.
Confounding the Reich. Martin W. Bowman/Tom Cushing. Patrick Stephens Ltd.
De Havilland Mosquito Crash Log. David J. Smith. Midland Counties Publications.
Despite the Elements. 115 Squadron History. Private.
Diary of RAF Pocklington. M. Usherwood. Compaid Graphics.
Each Tenacious. A.G. Edgerley. Square One Publications.
Feuersturm über Hamburg. Hans Brunswig. Motor Buch Verlag.
Forever Strong. Norman Franks. Random Century.
From Hull, Hell and Halifax. Chris Blanchett. Midland Counties Publications.
Gordon's Tour with Shiney 10. J. Gordon Shirt. Compaid Graphics.
Great Raids. Vols 1 and 2. Air Commodore John Searby DSO DFC. Nutshell Press.
Halifax at War. Brian J. Rapier. Ian Allan.

Hamish. The story of a Pathfinder. Group Captain T.G. Mahaddie. Ian Allan.
Heavenly Days. Group Captain James Pelly-Fry DSO. Crecy Books.
In Brave Company. W.R. Chorley. P.A. Chorley.
Joe. The autobiography of a Trenchard Brat. Wing Commander J. Northrop DSO DFC AFC. Square One Publications.
Lancaster at War. Vols 1, 2, 3. Mike Garbett/Brian Goulding. Ian Allan.
Lancaster. The Story of a Famous Bomber. Bruce Robertson. Harleyford Publications Ltd.
Lancaster to Berlin. Walter Thompson DFC*. Goodall Publications.
Low Attack. John de L. Wooldridge. Crecy.
Massacre over the Marne. Oliver Clutton-Brock. Patrick Stephens Ltd.
Master Airman. Alan Bramson. Airlife.
Melbourne Ten. Brian J. Rapier. Air Museum Publications (York) Ltd.
Mission Completed. Sir Basil Embry. Four Square Books.
Mosquito. C. Martin Sharp & Michael J.F. Bowyer. Crecy.
Night Fighter. C.F. Rawnsley/Robert Wright. Collins.
Night Flyer. Squadron Leader Lewis Brandon DSO DFC. Goodall Publications.
Night Intruder. Jeremy Howard-Williams. Purnell Book Services.
No Moon Tonight. Don Charlwood. Goodall Publications.
On The Wings Of The Morning. RAF Bottesford 1941–45. Vincent Holyoak.
On Wings of War. A history of 166 Squadron. Jim Wright.
Only Owls And Bloody Fools Fly At Night. Group Captain Tom Sawyer DFC. Goodall Publications.
Pathfinder. AVM D.C.T. Bennett. Goodall Publications.
Pathfinder Force. Gordon Musgrove. MacDonald and Janes.
Reap the Whirlwind. Dunmore and Carter. Crecy.
Royal Air Force Aircraft Serial Numbers. All Volumes. Air–Britain.
Royal Air Force Bomber Command Losses. Vols 1, 2, 3, 4, 5, 6. W.R. Chorley. Midland Counties Publications.
Silksheen. Geoff D. Copeman. Midland Counties Publications.
Snaith Days. K.S. Ford. Compaid Graphics.
Start im Morgengrauen. Werner Girbig. Motor Buch Verlag.
Stirling Wings. Jonathon Falconer. Alan Sutton Publications.
Strike Hard. A bomber airfield at war. John B. Hilling. Alan Sutton Publishing.
Sweeping the Skies. David Gunby. Pentland Press.
The Avro Lancaster. Francis K. Mason. Aston Publications.
The Berlin Raids. Martin Middlebrook. Viking Press.
The Dambusters Raid. John Sweetman. Arms and Armour Press.
The Halifax File. Air-Britain.
The Hampden File. Harry Moyle. Air-Britain.
The Handley Page Halifax. K.A. Merrick. Aston Press.
The Hornets' Nest. History of 100 Squadron RAF 1917–1994. Arthur White. Square One Publications.
The Lancaster File. J.J. Halley. Air-Britain.

The Other Battle. Peter Hinchliffe. Airlife.
The Pendulum and the Scythe. Ken Marshall. Air Research Publications.
The Starkey Sacrifice. Michael Cumming. Sutton Publishing Ltd.
The Stirling Bomber. Michael J.F. Bowyer. Faber.
The Stirling File. Bryce Gomersall. Air-Britain.
The Wellington Bomber. Chaz Bowyer. William Kimber.
The Whitley File. R.N. Roberts. Air-Britain.
The Squadrons of the Royal Air Force. James J. Halley. Air-Britain.
They Led the Way. Michael P. Wadsworth. Highgate.
To See The Dawn Breaking. W.R. Chorley.
Valiant Wings. Norman Franks. Crecy.
Wellington. The Geodetic Giant. Martin Bowman. Airlife.
White Rose Base. Brian J. Rapier. Aero Litho Company (Lincoln) Ltd.
Wings of Night. Alexander Hamilton. Crecy.
2 Group RAF. A Complete History. Michael J.F. Bowyer. Crecy.
101 Squadron. Special Operations. Richard Alexander.
207 Squadron RAF Langar 1942–43. Barry Goodwin/Raymond Glynne-Owen. Quacks Books.
408 Squadron History. The Hangar Bookshelf. Canada.